REASSE
RESOUR

REASSESSING HUMAN RESOURCE MANAGEMENT

Edited by

Paul Blyton and Peter Turnbull

SAGE Publications
London · Newbury Park · New Delhi

First published 1992   **Reprinted 1993**

SAGE Publications Ltd
6 Bonhill Street
London EC2A 4PU

SAGE Publications Inc
2455 Teller Road
Newbury Park, California 91320

SAGE Publications India Pvt Ltd
32, M-Block Market
Greater Kailash – I
New Delhi 110 048

British Library Cataloguing in Publication Data

A catalogue record for this book
is available from the British Library

ISBN 0 8039 8697 1
ISBN 0 8039 8698 X (pbk)

Library of Congress catalog card number 92–056724

Typeset by The Word Shop, Bury, Lancs.
Printed in Great Britain by The Cromwell Press Ltd,
Broughton Gifford, Melksham,
Wiltshire.

CONTENTS

PREFACE

The past decade has witnessed a number of significant developments in the world of work. New organizational structures have emerged and important changes taken place in the socio-economic, political and legal contexts in which organizations operate. There have also been notable changes in the extent, form and content of management education, reflected in the expansion of the business school sector and a refashioning of postgraduate qualifications centred on the MBA. In parallel with this has been the emergence of a business vocabulary quite distinct from that in use before the 1980s. A prime example of this has been in the area of employee relations where 'Human Resource Management' (or 'HRM') has gained increasing acceptance in preference to 'personnel management'. For some observers this represents no more than a re-labelling, a quest perhaps for a more fashionable packaging or a desire to avoid the echoes of earlier adversarial relations. For others, however, HRM represents a qualitatively different approach to the management of employees, based on premises quite distinct from those underpinning personnel management. For this latter group, HRM represents neither the latest management whim, nor simply the preference for a new label, but rather constitutes a key issue within contemporary work organizations.

Yet, in reviewing the various arguments about its nature, content and consequences, it is immediately apparent that the vocabulary of HRM has surpassed both its conceptual and empirical foundations – the rhetoric has outstripped the reality. As the contributors to this volume demonstrate, conceptually it is possible to identify a number of tensions and contradictions between the various elements or policy goals of HRM, while empirically it is difficult to find examples of organizations that operate what might even loosely be termed HRM. The one impacts upon the other: when firms attempt to implement HRM they run up against its inherent contradictions and inconsistencies. This collection is an attempt to restore greater balance to the debate on HRM, to cast a critical eye over the concept and to illustrate the problems that different types of organization face when they attempt to 'transform' personnel management into human resource management.

The debate on HRM now cuts across a number of academic disciplines and subject areas, including economics, sociology, politics, business administration, industrial relations, and organizational behaviour. For student and academic readers in those areas, our purpose is to identify, explore and evaluate the conceptual and empirical limitations of HRM. These limitations manifest themselves in two ways. First, rather than a general theory of employee management, HRM is more appropriately viewed as an umbrella term for a series of practices that have come to prominence during the past decade. As such it must be considered alongside – rather than a superior replacement for – other practices and approaches associated with the management of employees, with due account taken of the macro and micro-level factors acting to support HRM practices over others. Second, and relatedly, as simply a set of practices, HRM does not represent a conceptual 'tool kit' for the analysis of the more fundamental issues of management–worker relations: issues of, *inter alia*, power, control, conflict, compliance, consent and dependence. HRM is the latest management *response* to these issues, not an *explanation* of them. If anything, the rhetoric associated with HRM has served to obscure rather than illuminate these fundamental questions.

For practitioners, the book identifies the myriad problems that emerge when attempting to select from the menu of HRM initiatives. Arguably this is of much greater value than any 'how to do it' checklists of HRM – in any case, there is no shortage of such texts on the market. In fact, since it is often argued that HRM is no more than 'good' personnel management – and as a number of personnel management books have been simply re-labelled to reflect this – practitioners already know 'what to do'. Therefore, the emphasis of this volume is on 'what might be the consequences of trying to do it', rather than 'how to do it'. Given the dearth of empirical evidence on HRM, the present volume will therefore provide a valuable reference for personnel and other managers interested in gaining a more comprehensive understanding of the changes in approach which are occurring in the way people at work are managed.

At the time of the book's conception all the contributors were members of a single institution. Early discussions with our colleagues at the Cardiff Business School indicated that several of the projects then being undertaken could shed important light on many of the key dimensions of the HRM debate, and provide a range of empirical evidence on its implementation and effects in industry. Of course, basing such a collection on the activities and thoughts of members of just one institution is bound to bring with it certain limitations. But by utilizing the people and projects we knew best, and by encouraging the contributors to explore the rhetoric and reality of HRM, the tensions and the contradictions, we have sought to achieve a degree of cohesion and common focus across the chapters and, more generally, a greater critical awareness of the meanings and implications of HRM.

In acknowledging the many sources of help we have had in bringing this collection together we would like to thank first and foremost our colleagues at the Cardiff Business School. Those who contributed to the book have had to endure our many requests and cajolings. Those who have not written chapters have also contributed valuably through their continuing discussions on HRM and related issues. Finally, we would like to thank Sue Jones at Sage, both for her initial enthusiasm and continued encouragement for the project.

Paul Blyton
Peter Turnbull
March 1992

CONTRIBUTORS

At the time the collection was conceived all the contributors were members of the Cardiff Business School, University of Wales. Since that time, Graham Sewell has joined the School of Management, UMIST, and Caroline Lloyd the Centre for Industrial Relations, University of Keele.

INTRODUCTION

1 HRM: DEBATES, DILEMMAS AND CONTRADICTIONS

Paul Blyton and Peter Turnbull

The latter half of the 1980s and the opening years of this decade have seen the construction of a significant Human Resource Management (HRM) 'infrastructure'. In the UK texts and journals have appeared with HRM in the title, professorial chairs and Business School divisions in HRM established, undergraduate, postgraduate and post-experience courses begun. Such developments have acted to reinforce consideration of HRM within work organizations themselves. The building of this infrastructure has also meant that the vocabulary of HRM (indeed several vocabularies) has become increasingly commonplace. Not only in academic circles, but as Storey and Sisson (1990: 62) point out, in a wide variety of work contexts:

> It seems that even the most unsophisticated organisation has issued its statement of 'Mission'; has declared commitment to direct communication with its 'most valued asset' – its employees; has experimented with quality circles; looked to performance related pay; brushed down its appraisal system; re-considered its selection procedures and declared its commitment to training.

Yet how much substance lies behind this terminology? In the absence of extensive empirical data – and more fundamentally a lack of agreement of what HRM is – opinions vary on the extent and pace of adoption of HRM. In the USA, Skinner (1981: 107) observed that, in the early 1980s, 'Human resources management seems to be mostly good intentions and whistling in the dark or averting unionization.' Despite the massive growth of a new literature on HRM (for example, Beer et al., 1984; Fombrun et al., 1984), the inclusion of HRM on MBA programmes, and the widespread use of the term in the US business community, by the end of the decade it was still evident that, 'Its impact as a means of utilizing human resources more efficiently will have been minimal in all but a small handful of cases' (Guest, 1990: 389). Similarly in the UK, there is widespread agreement that, in one way or another, the adoption of HRM has so far been limited: limited to a small number of (largely foreign-owned) 'exemplar' companies; limited in the sense of organizations adopting HRM in a very partial and piecemeal way; and limited in many cases to a mere re-labelling of existing activity and positions (see, for example, Storey, 1989; Storey and Sisson, 1990).

Consideration of whether these albeit limited developments nevertheless represent the first stages in a more thoroughgoing transformation to HRM is hindered by a number of critical problems, many stemming from the central question of what exactly is HRM? The ways in which the term is used by academics and practitioners indicates both variations in meaning and significantly different emphases on what constitute its core components. From this central uncertainty, many other questions and problems flow. Is HRM significantly different from personnel management? Why did it only surface in Britain in the later 1980s, while in the USA the term has been in widespread usage for a much longer period? Does HRM represent a coherent, integrated and, above all, effective method of managing employees? Does it improve company performance? Can it be effectively integrated with wider business strategy? Does HRM embody the solution to ever-changing and more competitive product markets? Is HRM equally applicable in all types of organizations? Can it be applied equally well in different national contexts? What is its relationship to questions of power and control within the organization?

Several of these questions inform the present book. An important starting point for the analysis of HRM is the more recent work by American scholars (for example, Beer et al., 1984; Fombrun et al., 1984) which has crossed the Atlantic to influence the subsequent development of the HRM debate in Britain. Within this debate several writers, notably a number of contributors to John Storey's (1989) edited volume, have provided an initial UK perspective on HRM. The particular contribution made here by the Cardiff group relates to: the competitive context within which (and partly as a response to which) the developments in HRM are occurring; empirical evidence on many of the substantive dimensions of HRM; and fresh conceptual critique. What emerges is that the surface neatness, indeed the *sine qua non* of HRM – the consistency and coherency of its constituent elements, which in turn cohere directly with broader organizational objectives – belies an organizational reality in which the achievement of required coherence, conformity and employee commitment is far more problematic, if not untenable. The source of this discrepancy is itself debatable: possible explanations range all the way from inconsistencies between the various elements of HRM itself to basic conflicts stemming from the commodity status of labour and the primacy of profit within capitalist work relations. Before we can examine the evidence which the different contributors bring to bear on these issues, however, it is necessary first to address briefly the questions of how different observers view HRM.

What is Human Resource Management?

The nature of human resource management is, according to Torrington (1989: 60) 'not yet clear. Like most innovations it tends to be whatever the person speaking at the time wants it to be.' This would seem to apply almost equally to practitioners and academics alike. A large-scale survey of corporate managers, for example, found that while 80 per cent of corporate personnel chiefs claimed to have an overall human resources policy very few, when asked, could describe it (Marginson et al., 1988). Among academics the opacity surrounding HRM stems partly from the breadth of definitions adopted. Such broad definitions are evident, for example, in the two journals of HRM launched in 1990, the *Human Resource Management Journal* and the *International Journal of Human Resource Management*. Keith Sisson, editor of *HRMJ* applies the term HRM 'in the most general of senses to refer to the policies, procedures and processes involved in the management of people in work organizations' (1990: 1). As such, the term is able to embrace more traditional subject areas such as industrial relations, personnel management, organizational behaviour and industrial sociology. Similarly, Michael Poole, editor of *IJHRM*, argues that beyond the central aspect of HRM being the link with business policy and strategic management, 'the subject is perhaps best viewed as involving a synthesis of elements from international business, organizational behaviour, personnel management and industrial relations' (1990: 1–2). Of course, both editors are concerned to establish HRM as a field of study rather than a theory of management. Indeed, Poole (1990: 1) expresses the hope that the *IJHRM* 'will establish the field as a social science discipline'. In addition, however, both editors attempt to distinguish the key features of HRM.

Sisson (1990: 5) suggests that there are four main features increasingly associated with HRM:

1 a stress on the integration of personnel policies both with one another and with business planning more generally;
2 the locus of responsibility for personnel management no longer resides with (or is 'relegated to') specialist managers, but is now assumed by senior line management;
3 the focus shifts from management–trade union relations to management–employee relations, from collectivism to individualism;
4 there is a stress on commitment and the exercise of initiative, with managers now donning the role of 'enabler', 'empowerer' and 'facilitator'.

The first point suggests that HRM is not only a strategic activity in itself, but one which is now central to the achievement of business objectives: the human resource is now recognized, and utilized, as the most valuable of all organizational assets. The second point identifies the need for personnel managers to 'give away' responsibility for the management of human assets to senior (line) management. The third point indicates a general move away from 'industrial relations' to 'employee relations', while the fourth point suggests that the creation and management of organizational culture are as important as the organization's work itself, with individuals offered the opportunity to realize their full potential, ably assisted by line management. Similar points emerge from the Harvard model (Beer et al., 1984) which Poole (1990: 3) endorses as the most influential and familiar approach to HRM in both academic and business circles. Thus:

> human resource management is viewed as strategic; it involves all managerial personnel (and especially general managers); it regards people as the most important single asset of the organization; it is proactive in its relationship with people; and it seeks to enhance company performance, employee 'needs' and societal well-being. (Poole, 1990: 3)

The Harvard model is widely recognized as drawing its academic lineage from the human relations school, with a consequent emphasis on communications, teamwork and the utilization of individual talents. In contrast to the Harvard model's 'developmental humanism' and the recognition it gives to multiple stakeholders, the more strategic approach emphasized by the Michigan School (Fombrun et al., 1984) is avowedly unitarist in outlook: a form of 'utilitarian-instrumentalism' which provides a singular endorsement of managerialist views (see Hendry and Pettigrew, 1990). Similarly, in Britain a contrast has been drawn between 'soft' and 'hard' versions of HRM, the former emphasizing the 'HR' and the latter the 'M' of Human Resource Management (Guest, 1989b; Storey, 1989: 8). Thus the 'soft' version is seen as a method of releasing untapped reserves of 'human resourcefulness' by increasing employee commitment, participation and involvement. The central thrust of the 'hard' version of HRM, on the other hand, is as a method of maximizing the economic return from the labour resource by integrating HRM into business strategy (Keenoy, 1990a: 3).

Extensive and detailed consideration of the definition and meaning of HRM has been made by David Guest. In a series of articles (1987, 1989a, b, 1990, 1991), Guest defines HRM essentially in terms of four key policy goals: high commitment, high quality, flexibility and strategic integration. He argues that only when a coherent strategy, directed towards these four policy goals, fully integrated into business strategy and fully sponsored by line management at all levels is applied, will the high productivity and related outcomes sought by management be achieved. Such a strategy is only likely in the presence of a supportive leadership from the top, reflected in the organization's culture and backed by an explicit strategy to utilize human resources (1990: 378). Drawing on the Harvard model, Guest also seeks to give HRM the status of a 'theory', thereby taking us full circle from an everyday term to denote any or all of the policies, procedures and processes involved in the management of people at work via a 'field of study', to a full-blown theory of management. The ensuing confusion is the central issue addressed by Mike Noon (Chapter 2) who considers whether HRM is a 'map', a 'model' or a 'theory'. The significance of the different terms is that, in Noon's words, 'as a model or a theory, HRM is elevated to a position of scholarly and practical importance in terms of its analytical and predictive powers, whilst as a map it only lays claim to being a diagnostic tool aimed mainly at practicing managers'. Drawing on the work of Dubin (1978), among others, Noon suggests that 'we should bring HRM down from the lofty heights of a theory to, at best, a style of management'.

As well as its conceptual status, a crucial dimension of HRM, as noted by Legge (1989: 40) and others (for example Keenoy, 1990a, b), lies in its ideological and philosophical underpinning, which aligns with (and may be interpreted as a response to) the rise of Thatcherism and the 'New Right' in the 1980s. As HRM has become 'the conceptual euphemism to describe *all* the apparently transformative changes in the management of employment relations in the 1980s' (Keenoy, 1990b: 370), this signals the importance of also examining the deeper meaning and morality of HRM. As Tom Keenoy and Peter Anthony (Chapter 14) argue, 'HRM reflects an attempt to redefine both the meaning of work and the way individual employees relate to their employers. As such, it is both a reflection and a constitutive element of the historical project known as the "enterprise culture".' The 'brilliant ambiguity' of the term HRM (Keenoy, 1990b: 371) is, according to this line of argument, by no means accidental. As Keenoy and Anthony demonstrate, 'the litany of innovative HRM social practices . . . should be regarded as cultural constructions fabricated through government policy and corporate administrative *fiat*. They are self-conscious attempts not merely to change social behaviour but to transform the norms and values guiding social behaviour.' According to Keenoy and Anthony then, the agenda (hidden or otherwise) underpinning HRM is significantly distinct from that typically informing earlier periods of personnel management. The question still remains, however, whether the components of HRM themselves constitute a marked departure from the policies and practices comprising personnel management.

HRM and Personnel Management – Is There a Difference?

By imposing particular conditions on HRM, it is possible to argue that it is significantly different from personnel management. Moreover, the contentions that HRM is proactive rather than reactive, system-wide rather than piecemeal, treats labour as social capital rather than as a variable cost, is goal-oriented rather than relationship-oriented, and ultimately is based on commitment rather than compliance (Beer and Spector, 1985; Guest, 1991; Walton, 1985), suggest that it is 'better' than personnel management. If HRM were the latest washing powder, no doubt the advertisers would tell us that it will wash our whites whiter and our colours brighter, is environmentally friendly and will even remove those stale odours that personnel management left behind. In this up-beat, proactive, goal-oriented characterization, the significance of HRM is also signalled in its 'discovery' by chief executives (Fowler, 1987: 3): that is, a recognition of the importance of human resource issues to overall business objectives. Yet in contrast, many observers clearly believe that HRM is simply a re-labelling and re-packing of personnel management, promoted by personnel managers (and their educators) 'in search of enhanced status and power' (Torrington, 1989: 64).

From an historical and evolutionary viewpoint, Torrington (1989: 65–6) has argued that 'personnel management has grown through assimilating a number of additional emphases to produce an ever-richer combination of expertise . . . HRM is no revolution but a further dimension to a multi-faceted role'. This point is echoed by Guest (1991: 169) who notes that, 'Chameleon-like, personnel managers will innovate if others decide that innovations are required.' But while suggesting that HRM is simply the latest elaboration of personnel management, Torrington also acknowledges that while personnel management is supply-driven, HRM is demand driven:

> Personnel management is directed mainly at the employees of the organization, finding and training them, arranging their pay and contracts of employment, explaining what is expected of them, justifying what the management is doing and trying to modify any management action that could produce an unwelcome response from the employees. In contrast, the human resource manager starts not from the organization's employees, but from the organization's need for human resources: with the demand rather than the supply. (1989: 60)

In short, HRM emphasizes strategy and planning rather than mediation and problem-solving (1989: 61). Torrington further asserts that the chameleon has already changed colour, that HRM 'has now been assimilated as personnel management has adapted to the decline of collectivism and the increase of opportunity' (1989: 61). This claim is made despite the fact that Torrington's own research in 1984–5 (MacKay and Torrington, 1986) had revealed that most personnel managers did not like HRM and regretted the need to be more 'hard-nosed' or 'tough' (this apparent contradiction between HRM being based on employee commitment, while at the same time requiring personnel managers to be 'tough' and 'hard nosed', is one we return to below).

One of the distinctions between the ways in which personnel management and HRM are typically conceived is that while personnel management is something that managers 'do' to employees, HRM is applied to management and workforce alike. This distinction is elaborated by Legge (1989) who compares personnel management and HRM as normative models and actual practices. Though there are no 'single' models of either personnel management or HRM, Legge concludes that at a normative level there is relatively little which differentiates the two. Only three significant differences are identified: that HRM is applied to managers as well as employees; that HRM concerns the management of people *and all other resources* in a business unit, and always in pursuit of the bottom line; and that HRM emphasizes the management of organizational culture as the central activity of senior management (Legge, 1989: 27–8).

If, as Legge suggests, HRM is essentially a more strategic management task than personnel management in that it is experienced by managers as the most valued company resource to be managed, then it seems essential to determine empirically whether management actually endorse HRM. This is the central focus of the chapter by Michael Poole and Roger Mansfield (Chapter 12), who provide empirical verification for Torrington's contention that, in more recent years, HRM has been assimilated by British managers (at least along several key dimensions). Moreover, Poole and Mansfield's survey includes all types of manager. Thus, their findings indicate that attitudes consistent with HRM have been embraced by managers in a range of functions, not just by the personnel specialists.

The management of organizational culture, the third difference referred to by Legge, is more contentious. Throughout the past decade, the 'excellence' literature has laid great stress on the importance of culture, of creating a culture which is consistent with the organization's goals, and of managing the creation and maintenance of this culture effectively. In adopting this general argument, writers of HRM texts have tended therefore to assume that culture can be 'managed'. Yet in reality, the ability to do this is far from self-evident. Indeed, there remains considerable disagreement as to what organizational culture is, how it can be measured, whether all organizations possess a culture, what the relationship is between culture and other organizational characteristics (such as 'climate') and whether cultures are open to managerial intervention (Dastmalchian et al., 1991: 33–4). In Chapter 5, Emmanuel Ogbonna argues that managing culture is 'an ideal which falls short of reality'. From his review of existing studies, and particularly his own work in the UK retailing sector, Ogbonna holds that most attempts to 'manage' culture result in behavioural compliance rather than more deep-seated belief and attitude changes. If, as Ogbonna suggests, culture cannot be easily 'managed' or 'created', then what is the purpose of the rhetoric attached to HRM? In the last decade we have been presented with images of managers as 'change masters' (Kanter, 1984) pursuing 'excellence' (Peters and Waterman, 1982) and the HRM policy goals of quality, flexibility, harmony, commitment, integration and involvement. As Keenoy (1990b: 374) asks, why has making money become associated with 'a fundamentalist evangelical crusade'? The answer, for Keenoy and many others, is that:

> far from indicating a new era of *humane* people-oriented employment management, the primary purpose of the rhetoric of HRM might be to provide a legitimatory managerial ideology to facilitate an intensification of work and an increase in the commodification of labour – both of which can be regarded as part of the 'solution' to the crisis. (Keenoy, 1990b: 374–5)

In other words, to understand what HRM is, and what its significance is, we need to look at the context in which it has emerged and the ideological purpose it serves.

Competition, Crisis and HRM

In an historical context, the emergence of HRM in Britain *in the 1980s*, as opposed to its more established use in the USA (notwithstanding the work of Beer et al., 1984 and Fombrun et al., 1984), can probably only be understood in relation to the severity of economic recession in early 1980s and the subsequent intensification of (international) competition. As Richard Whipp (Chapter 3) argues, interest in the management of people is long standing, with successive 'innovative' approaches reflecting the social and economic conditions in which they emerged. This not only helps to explain the timing of the appearance of HRM in the UK, it also places its development in perspective. According to Whipp, rather than HRM being seen as 'somehow the ultimate or most highly developed form of managing the workforce, such innovations are attempts to meet particular historical circumstances'. But while those circumstances 'compel' managements to look for 'alternatives' such as HRM, those same circumstances make the introduction of new approaches more difficult. Pressures of competition and a lack of stability in markets in turn subject innovations such as training to pressures of both cost and uncertainty. Thus, intensified competition may 'necessitate' a new approach to the management of employees, but at the same time provides a context unconducive to the fostering of new, long-term initiatives. Moreover, as Whipp points out, there is no simple connection between HRM and competitive performance.

While competition may represent a general imperative for managers to adopt HRM, the influence of Japanese companies has been more direct, both in the competitive process itself and as 'role models' for new management initiatives such as HRM. Contrary to the association of such practices with 'developmental humanism', however, Rick Delbridge and Peter Turnbull (Chapter 4) demonstrate that Japanese-style HRM is more closely aligned with the 'hard' versions of HRM, and invariably involves an intensification of the work process and a diminution of worker autonomy and employee influence. Consequently, the attempted emulation of such practices can provoke a hostile response from the workforce. Nevertheless, given the commercial success of Japanese corporations in world markets, this has given a specific imperative for change in work systems and personnel policies: for managing in competitive markets, there would indeed appear to be 'no alternative'. HRM in whatever form is thus widely heralded as essential to meet the challenge of competition, in particular that from Japan.

Greater competition may provide the context in which HRM is gaining prominence, but it is insufficient in itself to explain the remarkable level of interest in the idea. This, according to Storey (1989: 8), is also attributable to the marked departure from the prevailing employee management orthodoxy which HRM represents: 'it promises an alternative (or more accurately and significantly) a *set* of alternatives to what might be described as the "Donovan" model'. In short, HRM not only represents a challenge to personnel management but also the traditional pattern of industrial relations, built around trade unionism and the formalization of collective bargaining procedures and joint regulation. But can HRM be effectively implemented in 'brownfield' sites? Several structural constraints have already been identified, most notably the weakness of management education and training in Britain, aspects of (diversified) organizational structures, the nature and standing of different occupational specialisms and professions (notably the dominant position of financial accountancy) and the pattern of ownership (Storey, 1989; Storey and Sisson, 1990). More importantly, if HRM is an alternative to Donovan, it must be capable of transforming the traditional pattern of industrial relations. Surveys of British industrial relations in the 1980s have attested to the durability of many structural aspects of these relations (Batstone, 1984; Daniel and Millward, 1983; Millward and Stevens, 1986). Of course, *form* may remain while *content* evaporates, and this is reflected in the gradual erosion of joint regulation (Millward and Stevens, 1986: 248). Yet for the economy as a whole, union density remains at around 40 per cent, and collective bargaining remains the principal mechanism for pay determination: the pattern is indeed one of both continuity as well as change (Kelly, 1990).

Such continuity is evident in the case studies discussed by Miguel Martinez Lucio and Syd Weston (Chapter 13), as part of their broader examination of the implications of HRM for (British) trade unions. In one case they discuss, where HRM-type initiatives have been introduced into a well-established, multi-union plant with a history of effective shop steward organization and, at times, militant workforce, the new initiatives have often developed alongside, rather than in place of, established patterns of communication, negotiation and so on. Thus, while HRM represents a direct challenge to these traditional structures and procedures, cutting right across established areas of trade union influence, they are nonetheless subject to negotiation as the frontier of control is redefined. HRM is *not* just a matter of management will, as some texts appear to suggest, but is subject to the countervailing power of organized labour.

Given these constraints stemming from the existing industrial relations context, it is not surprising that Guest (1987, 1989a) identifies four 'preconditions' for the achievement of his four HRM policy goals, namely a greenfield site with a carefully selected ('green') labour force untainted by any exposure to an 'undesirable' industrial sub-culture; a highly professional management team, preferably Japanese or American; intrinsically rewarding work; and security of employment. In practice, however, high levels of competition can make the last of these difficult to achieve, if not impossible (Whipp, Chapter 3), while Japanese style work and employment practices, usually found operating on greenfield sites, rarely appear to offer intrinsically rewarding work for other than a minority of the workforce (Delbridge and Turnbull, Chapter 4). All in all, therefore, it is unsurprising that, as several previous studies have confirmed, very few British firms have actually adopted HRM, or at best display only one or two component features of HRM (Storey, 1989; Storey and Sisson 1990). But it is not simply these external structural and contextual constraints which have brought about this limited adoption of HRM; important internal inconsistencies within HRM can also be identified which under-mine its coherency as a form of employee management.

Contradictions in HRM

Legge (1989: 29) identifies HRM to be problematic at two levels, the level of integration and a deeper level where HRM confronts the contradiction inherent in the commodity status of labour under capitalist employment relations and the conflict of interest this engenders between purchasers and suppliers of labour. This latter issue, which is also confronted by personnel management, is one we return to in our final chapter. In terms of the problem of integration, however, this is itself evident at two levels: the *external* 'fit' of HRM with the organization's broader business strategy; and the *internal* consistency of the policy goals of HRM itself. On the former, Legge notes the difficulty of matching HRM policy to business strategy *per se*, especially in a diversified organization. This is particularly problematic in highly competitive or recessionary conditions where the 'needs of the business' are likely to undermine any internal 'fit' with core ('soft') HRM values: shedding labour for example will severely challenge, if not destroy, an organization's HRM image of caring for the needs and security of its employees. Attempts to resolve this contradiction, argues Legge, emerge either by reference to some version of 'tough love' (being 'cruel to be kind', to secure the long-term interests of the (remaining) workforce), or more explicit reference to the 'needs' of the market and the need for HRM to reinforce values such as quality, customer service and so on. This applies in mass production and service industries alike, as several chapters in this volume illustrate (notably Chapters 4, 5, 6 and 11). It can also give rise to 'hard' and 'soft' forms of HRM being espoused simultaneously. In relation to flexibility, for example, firms facing competitive product and skill markets may on the one hand apply 'soft' forms of HRM to key workers, developing those employees through multi-skilling, while at the same time responding to competitive pressures and market fluctuations through policies of numerical flexibility and precarious employment among those groups less central to the production process and/or more easily replace-able from the external labour market (Blyton and Morris explore the issue of flexibility in Chapter 7). Similarly, the nature of production technology, a factor often overlooked in the study of HRM, plays a major role in delineating 'key' from 'other' employees. The implication, as Caroline Lloyd and Mike Rawlinson point out (Chapter 11), is that management's ability and/or willingness to implement an HRM-type strategy, and more specifically the nature of that strategy, will depend partly on the position of employees *vis-à-vis* that production process.

In terms of aligning HRM and business strategy, the fundamental problem is that in most cases HRM issues are both subordinate and secondary to business strategy. It is not simply that the search for profit overrides the policy goals of HRM, but arguably that HRM is pursued *only* in the belief that by raising employees' commitment, flexibility, the quality of their work, *inter alia* the bottom line will be improved. If pressures for securing a return on investment are strong enough, short-term considerations and perspectives will tend to predominate over long-term ones. In general, short-term financial criteria operate against longer-term strategic HRM developments such as investment in training. These pressures can be acutely felt in decentralized organizations as Ian Kirkpatrick, Annette Davies and Nick Oliver demonstrate (Chapter 8). As more organizations decentralize, establishing strategic business units with responsibility for cost and profit levels, the short-term perspective of those units pulls in the opposite direction from the longer-term, developmental orientation of HRM. The irony is that responsibility for personnel management/HRM is increasingly integrated into the line management of decentralized operations, which proponents of HRM advocate. Guest (1987: 51) for example, suggests that 'if HRM is to be taken seriously, personnel managers must give it away'. But when those personnel managers give it away in the decentralized organization, they may also give it up. And even if the policy goals of HRM are retained, the ability of line managers actually to manage the human resource is questionable. As Jim Lowe demonstrates (Chapter 9), the implementation of HRM policy goals places considerable onus on front-line supervision. However, the general lack of support for, and training of, supervisory employees is likely to impede, rather than facilitate, any 'transformation' to HRM.

The contradictions within HRM are most apparent at the level of actual practices, with simultaneous advocacy of workforce attributes such as individualism and teamwork; commitment to a job and flexibility; the development of a strong culture and adaptability (Legge, 1989: 34–7). The conceptual difficulties inherent in these contrasts provide a reference point for many of the following chapters. It is worth noting here, however, that such contradictory tendencies are not only confined to those companies adopting HRM in half measure. The empirical cases discussed by Delbridge and Turnbull (Chapter 4) and Sewell and Wilkinson (Chapter 6), would generally be seen by advocates of HRM as 'successful' or 'exemplar' cases of HRM. In identifying the tension between individualism and teamwork, for example, what these cases demonstrate is the need for a redefinition of HRM, for despite any surface similarity with the textbook checklists of HRM policies, these cases could certainly not be described as operating a form of 'developmental humanism'.

The internal contradictions which beset HRM are well illustrated by the issue of employee commitment. For proponents of HRM, commitment represents a key dimension; the explicit or implicit assumption underpinning this is that highly committed workers are more productive. Leaving aside for the moment Guest's (1987: 573) discussion of 'commitment to what', and assuming that management wants its employees to be committed to the goals of the organization, it is evident that at several points the broader pursuit of an HRM strategy will act to undermine this securing of commitment. Sewell and Wilkinson, for example, contrast the rhetoric of mutual commitment and trust espoused by HRM with actual work experience in an 'excellent' Japanese company in the UK. Here, workers are subjected to the closest scrutiny which is then used as a basis for distinguishing individuals from their peers on matters of the smallest detail. Surveillance and low trust are also features of the supermarkets considered by Ogbonna (in Chapter 5). Again, notwithstanding a management rhetoric of HRM, the reality of work for the checkout operators was clearly very different. Similarly, in their investigation of the clothing industry – a further example of a low-wage, highly cost-competitive industry largely reliant on a female workforce – Lloyd and Rawlinson (Chapter 11) show HRM to have little *practical* bearing on the management of labour.

Conflicts are apparent too where organizations have attempted to introduce more flexible working arrangements and performance-related pay. The problems with flexibility stem partly from the tensions between different sources of flexibility. As Blyton and Morris argue (Chapter 7), while 'soft' forms of HRM encourage employee development in part through learning a broader range of skills (functional flexibility), 'hard' forms of HRM advocate the securing of greater variability in the volume of labour, thereby providing management with greater scope to match labour input to demand fluctuations. In addition, however, conflicts exist *within* each of the major sources of flexibility. For example, the danger exists of securing high levels of functional flexibility at the cost of other organizational objectives such as stability, continuity and cohesion; likewise, forms of numerical flexibility potentially clash not only with the objective of securing employee commitment but also with establishing and sustaining high quality output and group cohesion.

Performance-related pay, retitled Reward Management to emphasize the more purposeful and 'objective achieving' focus of HRM, would seem not only to have failed to yield high levels of commitment in many organizations, but also to have perpetuated a longstanding tradition in wage and salary administration of 'muddling through'. As Ian Smith points out (Chapter 10), while a strategy for reward may need to be part of a wider human resource development strategy, reward in itself is not

sufficient to promote human resource contributions to corporate improvement. Evidence suggests that reward may be secondary to other,
non-pecuniary elements. More importantly, however, individual reward
systems could well act to undermine cooperation, teamwork and even
individual motivation – all key elements of HRM.

These and other conflicts and contradictions evidenced by the different
contributors underline the problematic status of HRM as a coherent
concept. Rather than seeing this as a pretext for abandoning the notion of
HRM altogether, however, the evidence presented would seem to support
a more careful circumscribing of HRM, and a clearer definition of its status
as a set of management practices (with strengths and weaknesses also
evident in other sets of practices) rather than a more general theory of
management. In so doing, the relationship between HRM and the
longstanding core issues of labour management – issues of power, control,
conflict, resistance, dependence, consent and so on – is made clearer.
HRM is one of a series of approaches management may take to secure the
levels of compliance and cooperation it requires; different sets of
circumstances will influence the adoption of one approach over others,
while changing circumstances will encourage a shift from one to another
and, possibly, the creation of new practices and approaches. The last
decade in Britain has undoubtedly produced circumstances favourable to
the rise of an HRM rhetoric, and the adoption (though often in partial
form) of HRM practices in a number of work organizations. As we argue in
the final chapter, however, the contradictions within, and limitations of,
HRM make it all the more urgent that we return to the core issues (rather
than direct our gaze only to the different practices) of labour management,
in order to further our understanding of contemporary work and
employment relations.

Plan of the Book

The collection is divided into four main sections. Following this Introduction, Part One examines various aspects of the emergence of HRM. This
includes an exploration of the different conceptual strands of the HRM
debate, and the important consideration of the true status of HRM, as a
'map', a 'model' or a 'theory'. A widely held argument in the HRM
literature is that its growth in the last decade has been driven, to a
significant degree, by the need to respond to intensifying levels of
competition in general, and the competitive pressures emanating from
Japanese companies in particular. Aspects of these general and specific
sources of competition, and their links with HRM, are considered in the
other two chapters forming Part One.

In Part Two, many of the core dimensions of HRM – relating to culture,
quality, flexibility and reward management, for example – are considered.
In addition, the implications of HRM policies under conditions of

decentralized management structures, their significance for the role of supervisors, and the relationship between HRM and the adoption of new technology, are examined. These chapters examine in detail the many contradictions, both external and internal, which emerge when organizations attempt to implement HRM-type policies.

The two chapters in Part Three assess HRM from the standpoint of both managers and trade unions. While the chapter on managerial attitudes draws on recent results from a nation-wide longitudinal study, the implications of HRM for trade unions are explored through a comparison of three different patterns of response by three major UK unions. The main contribution in Part Four places HRM within a broader context by examining the underlying implications of the HRM rhetoric and its place within broader political and ideological developments characterized as the Enterprise Culture. Broader questions are raised not only about the deeper meaning of HRM (or at least the objectives and assumptions underpinning it) but also about the issues thereby raised for management education. In the final chapter we argue that, on the basis of the evidence presented throughout the book, it is essential that the analysis of HRM be located within the wider problematic of labour management and the conflicts inherent in capitalist employment relations.

References

Batstone, E. (1984) *Working Order*. Oxford: Blackwell.

Beer, M., Spector, B., Lawrence, P., Mills, Q. and Walton, R. (1984) *Managing Human Assets*. New York: Free Press.

Beer, M. and Spector, B. (1985) 'Corporatewide transformations in human resource management', in R.E. Walton and P.R. Lawrence (eds), *Human Resource Management: Trends and Challenges*. Boston: Harvard Business School Press.

Daniel, W.W. and Millward, N. (1983) *Workplace Industrial Relations in Britain*. London: Heinemann.

Dastmalchian, A., Blyton, P. and Adamson, R. (1991) *The Climate of Workplace Relations*. London: Routledge.

Dubin, R. (1978) *Theory Building* (revised edn). New York: Free Press.

Fombrun, C., Tichy, N.M. and Devanna, M.A. (1984) *Strategic Human Resource Management*. New York: John Wiley.

Fowler, A. (1987) 'When chief executives discover HRM', *Personnel Management*, January: 3.

Guest, D. (1987) 'Human resource management and industrial relations', *Journal of Management Studies*, 24 (5): 503–21.

Guest, D.E. (1989a) 'Human resource management: its implications for industrial relations and trade unions', in J. Storey (ed.), *New Perspectives on Human Resource Management*. London: Routledge. pp. 41–55.

Guest, D.E. (1989b) 'Personnel and HRM: can you tell the difference?' *Personnel Management*, January: 48–51.

Guest, D.E. (1990) 'Human resource management and the American dream', *Journal of Management Studies*, 27 (4): 377–97.

Guest, D. (1991) 'Personnel management: the end of orthodoxy?' *British Journal of Industrial Relations*, 29 (2): 149–76.

Hendry, C. and Pettigrew, A. (1990) 'Human resource management: an agenda for the 1990s', *International Journal of Human Resource Management*, 1 (1): 17–44.

Kanter, R.M. (1984) *The Change Masters*. New York: Simon & Schuster.

Keenoy, T. (1990a) 'HRM: a case of the wolf in sheep's clothing?' *Personnel Review*, 19 (2): 3–9.

Keenoy, T. (1990b) 'HRM: rhetoric, reality and contradiction', *International Journal of Human Resource Management*, 1 (3): 363–84.

Kelly, J. (1990) 'British trade unionism: change, continuity and contradictions', *Work, Employment and Society*, 4, Special Issue, May: 29–65.

Legge, K. (1989) 'HRM: a critical analysis', in J. Storey (ed.), *New Perspectives on Human Resource Management*. London: Routledge. pp. 19–55.

MacKay, L. and Torrington, D. (1986) *The Changing Nature of Personnel Management*. London: Institute of Personnel Management.

Marginson, P., Edwards, P., Martin, R., Purcell, J. and Sisson, K. (1988) *Beyond the Workplace: Managing Industrial Relations in the Multi-establishment Enterprise*. Oxford: Basil Blackwell.

Millward, N. and Stevens, M. (1986) *British Workplace Industrial Relations 1980–84*. Aldershot: Gower.

Peters, T.J. and Waterman, R.H. (1982) *In Search of Excellence: Lessons from America's Best-Run Companies*. New York: Harper & Row.

Poole, M. (1990) 'Editorial: HRM in an international perspective', *International Journal of Human Resource Management*, 1 (1): 1–15.

Sisson, K. (1990) 'Introducing the *Human Resource Management Journal*', *Human Resource Management Journal*, 1 (1): 1–11.

Skinner, W. (1981) 'Big hat, no cattle: managing human resources', *Harvard Business Review*, 59 (5): 106–14.

Storey, J. (ed.) (1989) *New Perspectives on Human Resource Management*. London: Routledge.

Storey, J. and Sisson, K. (1990) 'Limits to transformation: human resource management in the British context', *Industrial Relations Journal*, 21 (1): 60–5.

Torrington, D. (1989) 'Human resource management and the personnel function', in J. Storey (ed.), *New Perspectives on Human Resource Management*. London: Routledge. pp. 56–66.

Walton, R.E. (1985) 'From control to commitment in the workplace', *Harvard Business Review*, March–April: 76–84.

PART ONE: THE EMERGENCE OF HRM

2 HRM: A MAP, MODEL OR THEORY?

Mike Noon

Age seems to have raised the status of Human Resource Management (HRM). In the United States the Harvard version started life as part of an MBA syllabus in 1981, became a modestly named 'map of HRM territory' (Beer et al., 1984) and then developed into the 'Harvard model', with the editor of the recently launched *International Journal of Human Resource Management* proclaiming it to be 'the most influential and most familiar approach so far as the international scholarly and business communities are concerned' (Poole, 1990: 3). As a model it implicitly, and minimally, promises either a descriptive analysis or a prescriptive agenda for the management of people: a status that Beer et al. have never claimed for HRM. Their original intention was to develop 'a framework for thinking and managing human resources that general managers will find useful' (Beer et al., 1984: x) driven by the desire (academically led) and the need (market inspired) to develop a course at Harvard Business School. At best, although unstated, their claim might be that the Harvard framework is a prescriptive model.

A UK version of HRM, based largely on the Harvard framework, has been developed by Guest (1987, 1989) who modifies the concepts and gives it the status of a 'theory' with the commendable scholarly intention 'to develop a set of testable propositions and finally to arrive at a set of prescriptive policies' (Guest, 1987: 510).

Consequently, for some practitioners and academics, HRM is a full-blown management theory with practical implications, whilst for others it remains an uncertain and imprecise notion. Overall there is a general lack of clarity as to what HRM means for both the practitioner and the academic. For example, at practitioner level we can point to organizations that have merely changed the name plaque on the personnel manager's door to human resources manager (Armstrong, 1987) in contrast to organizations which have undertaken fundamental change in line with HRM prescriptive policy (see, for example, Sparrow, 1991). Likewise we are faced with explaining organizations that have always used HRM-type policies, yet persist in describing the practice as personnel management – the most obvious example in the UK being Marks & Spencer.

In the academic world, similar confusion is evident. Books are changing their titles from 'Personnel Management' to 'Human Resource Management' with very little change of content. In the UK there are now university chairs in HRM, yet there has never been a chair in Personnel Management. Some UK business schools appear to be using HRM as a convenient 'catch all' label embracing the separate disciplines of industrial relations, organizational behaviour and personnel management, which contrasts starkly with courses in HRM or the sort of programme propounded by Harvard. Likewise, the editor of the *Human Resource Management Journal* uses the term 'in the most general of senses to refer to the policies, procedures and processes involved in the management of people in work organizations' (Sisson, 1990: 1). Generally, academics in the United States have a more liberal attitude to the terminology and use HRM interchangeably with personnel management. This may suggest there is little difference between the two labels; however, there is still a debate in the US as to what HRM is – Thomas (1988), for example, contrasts the interpretations of Schein (1987), Kochan et al (1986), Walton (1987) and Grenier (1988).

Much of the confusion may arise because of the ambiguous pedigree of HRM: it can be traced back to the Organizational Development (OD) proponents of the 1970s (Iles and Johnston, 1989), human capital theory in the 1960s (Hendry and Pettigrew, 1990), Drucker in the 1950s (Armstrong, 1988) or even earlier. As Springer and Springer (1990: 41) suggest: 'The history of HRM in the United States may be said to start when NCR Corporation established a separate personnel office in the 1890s.'

Legge (1989) attributes much of the confusion about HRM to a failure to compare normative models of personnel management with HRM and then examine the practices of both. Furthermore, she identifies inconsistencies and tensions within HRM which compound the uncertainty of the model. This chapter argues that such an analysis can be taken further. We should examine the conceptual construction of HRM to determine its worth and resolve the question of whether HRM is a map, a model or a theory.

This is not just a case of semantics: it *does* matter which label we attach since each carries with it different expectations, and important philosophical and practical implications. As a model or theory, HRM is elevated to a position of scholarly and practical importance in terms of its analytical and predictive powers, whilst as a map it only lays claim to being a diagnostic tool aimed mainly at practising managers. Beer et al. (1984) do not argue that their 'map' constitutes a model, but those who have followed (supporting and criticizing) in their footsteps have been less cautious in their terminology. The reasoning, albeit implicit, does have logic: the 'map' seeks to represent the relations within a firm (determinants and consequences of HRM policies) and these isomorphic properties would constitute the status of a 'model' (based on Kaplan, 1964). Likewise, those who give the HRM 'map' the status of theory could point to commentators such as Dubin (1978) who treat the words 'model' and 'theory' as synonymous.

This chapter takes the Dubin approach as a way of analysing the conceptual elements of HRM. It examines the Harvard framework and its UK derivative to consider the status that HRM deserves in current management thought. If HRM constitutes a management theory (also read model) then it deserves serious attention which, after critical evaluation, may justify the status of theory. If it does not 'measure up' as a theory, then what is it?

The Elements of a Theory

Drawing from the work of Dubin (1978), Cohen (1980) and Bacharach (1989) we can argue that a theory consists of units whose interaction allows us to forward propositions about their relationships. These units are represented by constructs or concepts at the abstract level, whilst at the empirical (observable) level they are represented by variables. Likewise propositions can be operationalized as hypotheses, stating a relationship between variables. The theory is bounded by assumptions which have been informed by values and by ontological and epistemological considerations. This overview is represented by Figure 2.1.

To consider whether HRM constitutes a theory we can focus in some detail upon each of these elements of an idealized theory. We can look for weaknesses and contradictions to reject the theory's status, and strengths and consistencies to support it. The analysis will first examine the units and relationships, evaluating HRM in terms of plausibility and utility. The examination will then broaden out to consider the boundaries, as constituted by spatial and temporal considerations, and the underlying assumptions with particular reference to the approach to human nature and ontology.

Units and Relationships

The Harvard 'map' (see Figure 2.2) focuses upon the HRM policy choices and suggests that managers are influenced and constrained by stakeholder interests and situational factors. Management policy choices affect the human resource outcomes (commitment, competence, congruence and cost-effectiveness – the four Cs), which in turn affect long-term consequences. And to complete the process, the consequences will feed back to affect stakeholder interests, situational factors and policy choices. Interestingly, there is no feedback loop suggested at the policy or outcome stage, thus the relationships are uni-directional. The framework does display units and suggests relationships, but the authors are careful not to claim this as a model or a theory. Less cautious are some UK academics; for

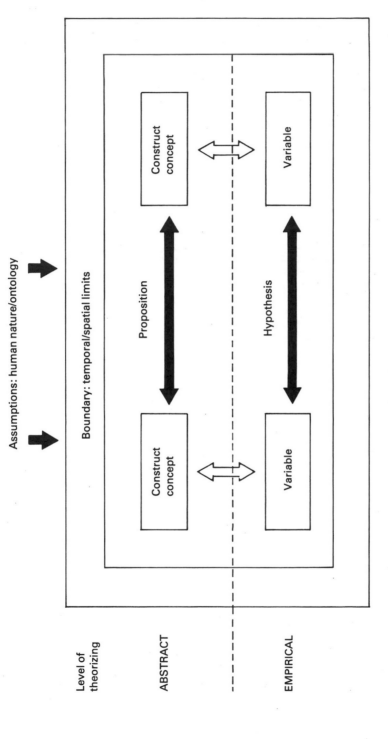

Figure 2.1 *Components of a theory*

Source: Based on Bacharach, 1989 and Dubin, 1978

example, Poole (1990: 2) refers to 'the original Harvard model'. Whilst features of such a 'model' could be identified at the abstract level – the concepts being the stakeholder interests, situational factors, HR policy choices, HR outcomes and long-term consequences, and the propositions being the causal links and feedback – the related variables and their associated hypotheses are not developed in sufficient detail for an empirical investigation to take place. All Beer et al. (1984) offer are prescriptive guidelines: how to do it, not how it is done.

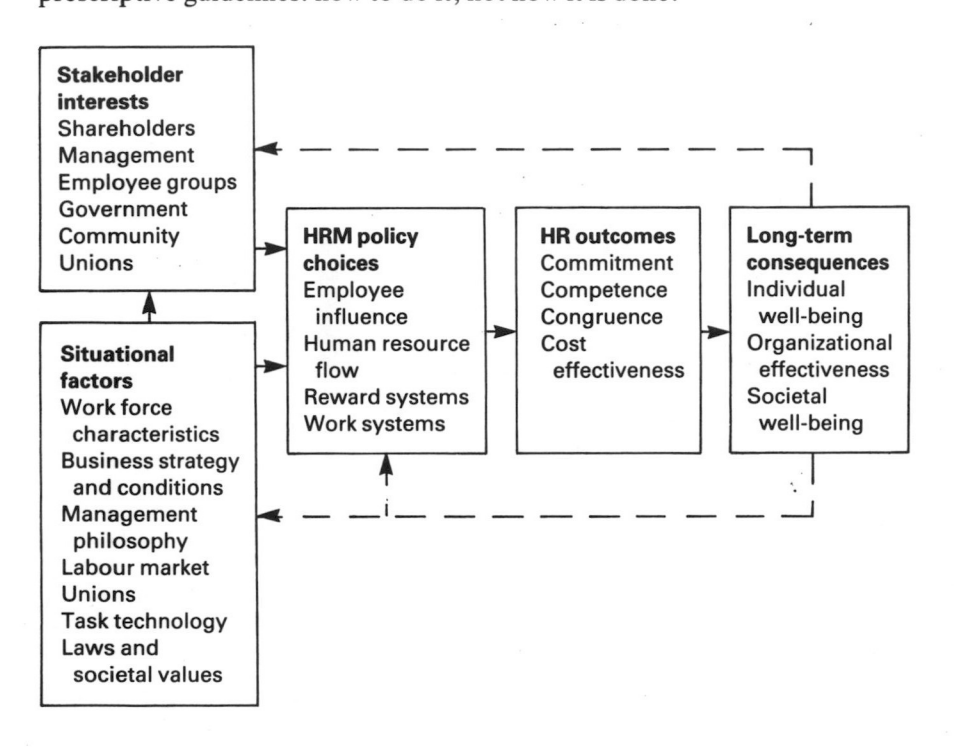

Figure 2.2   *Map of the HRM territory*

Source: Beer et al., 1984

Guest (1987) draws heavily from the Harvard framework to develop the 'bare bones' of a theory (see Figure 2.3). He adopts similar terminology to link policy with human resource outcomes and organizational outcomes, but suggests this needs to be 'cemented' by supportive leadership, a strong culture and a conscious strategy. This element of strategy seems to stem from yet a different US version of HRM, developed by Tichy et al. (1982), which is more concerned with the role human resources play in strategic management of the business. Borrowing from both versions, Guest synthesizes a UK version and arrives at the proposition, 'if an organization utilises the policy areas listed in pursuit of the four HRM policy goals in a

HRM policies	Human resource outcomes	Organizational outcomes
Organization/ job design		High Job performance
Management of change	Strategic integration	High Problem-solving Change
Recruitment, selection/ socialization	Commitment	Innovation
Appraisal, training development	Flexibility adaptability	High Cost-effectiveness
Reward systems		
Communication	Quality	Low Turnover Absence Grievances
	Leadership/culture/strategy	

Figure 2.3 *A theory of HRM*

Source: Guest, 1989

supportive organizational context, then positive outcomes should ensue'
(Guest, 1989: 50). By his own definition, he constructs a normative
'theory' of HRM.

So what about the variables and hypotheses? These seem to constitute
the flesh of Guest's theoretical skeleton, and as such are beyond his
concern. This may be a logical way of proceeding. After all, the variables
associated with just one of the HRM policies are likely to be numerous,
and the possible relationship to the outcomes plentiful, so, if all the
variables of the 'theory' were taken into account, its complexity would be
awe-inspiring. This takes us to the heart of the problem: a theory, in order
to make a contribution to knowledge, should be both comprehensive and
parsimonious (Whetten, 1989). It is highly likely that the HRM 'theory'
meets the first condition, because of its all-embracing approach, but
therein lies its weakness: it is perhaps too comprehensive. Parsimony, the
second condition, requires that factors which add little to the value or
understanding of the theory are eliminated, but without developing
variables and hypotheses to examine the empirical value of the theory, it is
difficult to jettison any without threatening its comprehensiveness. There
is, consequently, a tension between comprehensiveness and parsimony
which can be mediated only by testing the theory. Therefore, the abstract

reasoning depends upon the empirical work for validating the descriptive and predictive power of the model. As Dubin suggests, 'A theoretical model is a scientific model if, and only if, its creator is willing to subject it to an empirical test. Otherwise it falls in the realm of philosophy or theology' (1978: 12).

Thus, HRM may be a new management 'philosophy' (or judging by the fanatical fervour with which some people have adopted it, a management theology) but much work is still needed to develop the empirical units for analysis in order to establish HRM as a management theory – more of which below.

Evaluation of HRM

The problem with a theory is that it is only limited by the imagination and so logically it is possible and legitimate to build a theory of, for example, faith healing that would conform to the canons of theory building (Dubin, 1978: 12). Therefore it is not enough to accept the concepts and propositions at face value; a theory must be evaluated against two criteria, plausibility and utility.

Plausibility has been identified by Weick (1989) as central to the theorizing process. Building on the ideas of Davis (1971), he suggests that the conjectures of theorists are 'tested' against already held assumptions distilled from past experience and will elicit one of four responses: that's interesting, that's absurd, that's irrelevant and that's obvious. It is the first response that the theorist is looking for because it suggests that the conjecture is challenging the already held assumptions in a plausible manner.

So are the conjectures raised by the HRM 'theorists' plausible? Judging by the alacrity with which some academics and practitioners have responded to HRM, the answer would seem to be in the affirmative. One indication is that two new UK based journals were launched in 1990 – *The International Journal of Human Resource Management* and the *Human Resource Management Journal* – although in the US the journal *Human Resource Management* has been in existence since 1972 when the editors changed its title from *Management of Personnel Quarterly* to reflect a broadening of its scope. In addition, the *Social Science Citation Index* reveals that 113 books and articles were published between 1986 and 1990 with 'human resource management' in the title. Of course, a citation count gives no indication of the credibility of the arguments and, as Guest (1987) points out himself, there are some well established textbooks that have been retitled to include HRM, but have been changed little in their content.

However, there are voices expressing the absurdity of some of the HRM contentions and the over-simplification of the issues (see, for example, Fowler, 1987; Keenoy 1990a, b). Others have pointed out that HRM is often stating the obvious and consequently is irrelevant. For example,

Armstrong (1987: 34) succinctly writes, 'When confronted with HRM we may feel rather like Molière's M. Jourdain, who exclaimed to his philosophy teacher: "Good heavens! For more than forty years I have been speaking prose without knowing it."' But stating the obvious does have its uses because what may be obvious to one person may be obscure to another. Thus we might hear a boardroom executive exclaim, 'Well I'd never have thought of building people into the strategic plan.' What is 'obvious' to some is that HRM seems to be 'good/sensible personnel management', but since there has never been a 'theory' of personnel management as such, it has led UK commentators into discussing whether HRM is merely repackaged personnel management. The debate is somewhat parochial, however, given that HRM is used in the US as a generic term to cover a range of 'people management' issues.

It is also useful to look within HRM to assess its logical consistency as an indicator of plausibility. Legge (1989) suggests that HRM suffers from three inherent contradictions: individualism versus cooperation; commitment versus flexibility; and a strong culture versus adaptability. It is worth exploring and expanding upon these issues. First, there is an underlying emphasis on the individual: his or her contribution to the work process, potential for development and identity within the company. At the same time, HRM stresses the importance of congruence throughout the organization and thus policies are adopted which develop teamwork, quality circles, functional flexibility and cooperation. The contradiction is evident: a firm might introduce systems of individualized reward – performance-related pay, merit pay, fast-tracking – to enhance individual motivation, performance and commitment, but this might undermine cooperation between workers within the organization (as they are competing with each other) and therefore threaten congruence (see Smith, Chapter 10, this volume).

Second, HRM emphasizes high performance, quality and commitment, but there may be occasions when these are incompatible. For example, quality performance may depend on building up expertise over a period of time, yet the firm's requirement for functional flexibility (for congruence and cost reasons) may reduce competence levels. Thus, workers may be more widely skilled, yet their competence in these skills may be poor because they have less chance to develop specialized knowledge of the work process over time. In addition, if the responsibility for allocation of work is left to teams, then informal specialization may occur to improve one's individual performance and the team's overall performance, through the collective specialism of its members. Moreover, employees may resent the dissonance created between commitment to the task (encouraged by the individually-based performance management mechanisms discussed above) and commitment to the company (encouraged through the rhetoric of culture and the rewards of promotion and employment security) (see Ogbonna, Chapter 5, this volume). More explicitly, the notion of commitment may be totally undermined by factors outside the control of the committed workers. IBM, one of the best-known 'HRM companies', illustrates the vulnerability of the workforce to such exogenous factors. The organization was renowned for its employment security but was recently placed in the position of reducing its US workforce by 4.5 per cent (10,000 jobs) because of deteriorating performance in the slowing US economy (*Financial Times*, 6 December 1989). Likewise, Hewlett-Packard has been placed in a similar position due to market changes, and is restructuring and rationalizing its workforce as a cost-cutting exercise (*Financial Times*, 22 March 1991). As Whipp (Chapter 3, this volume) demonstrates, the ever more pervasive forces of competition make the attainment of HRM goals such as employment security increasingly difficult to achieve.

Third, Guest's HRM 'theory' stresses a strong culture to encourage shared values, create meaning and elicit commitment, yet there is equally an emphasis on flexibility and adaptability. Brunsson (1982) has suggested how a strong company ideology can constrain change, thus the ideology that might become enacted in an HRM company can prevent adaptation to changing circumstances (market, economic, political, social, etc.). This would suggest that the HRM 'theory' company becomes self-gratifying – the 'policy choices' become ideological nostrums which close off the system. This may have compounded the problems faced by Hewlett-Packard as it has struggled to adjust to rapid changes in the computer industry – particularly the shift in demand towards standardized products (*Financial Times*, 22 March 1991).

As further evidence of the problems of logical consistency in HRM, Hendry and Pettigrew (1990) point out the deficiencies in relation to what has become a key component: strategy. They state, 'Ironically, when HRM theorists have borrowed strategy concepts it has often been without regard to the actual behaviour of firms' (1990: 32). This suggests that the strategy–structure–HRM link is far from a simple causal relationship, particularly since HRM can contribute to strategy through the development of culture, and that structural change can precede strategy. Thus, Hendry and Pettigrew warn against 'treating the design of HRM systems in an overly rational way' (1990: 35).

We can expand the HRM critique by questioning the unitarist assumptions underlying HRM. Is is really plausible to assume a congruence of interests? Keenoy (1990b) reminds us that Fox (1966) condemned unitarism as a naive view of organizations. Whilst unitarist values may be held by organizational members, 'differential competing interests are an inevitable feature of *any* social institution characterized by the division of labour and a hierarchy of authority' (Keenoy, 1990b: 381). Thus agency, informed by values, may be represented by 'HRM policy choices', but these are structurally constrained by the demands of capitalism. We may want the world to be flat, but it is round, has been repeatedly proven so, and it would be a brave theorist who would announce otherwise.

There is a poignant caveat to the plausibility test, and that is that theories may be construed as plausible if they serve an individual's self-interest – particularly career objectives. As Weick states, 'It is a thin line from *that's interesting* to *that's in my best interest*, from *that's obvious* to *that's what managers want*, from *that's believable* to *that's what managers want to hear*' (1989: 528). It is this hard-nosed reality that leads to the second theory evaluation issue: utility.

Utility can be examined in two ways: theoretical utility and instrumental utility. The first applies to the extent to which the theory can explain and predict. Guest (1987) is keen to avoid the trap of prediction without explanation and draws upon evidence from behavioural science theorists, the Quality of Working Life (QWL) movement and OD specialists. However, in terms of the predictive utility of the theory, he openly acknowledges a paucity of data and argues for more research to assess the impact of HRM (1987: 317), a legitimate call for empirical work to help assess theory. In a later article he reviews the empirical evidence from the USA, which 'suggests either that HRM has not been extensively applied or that where attempts have been made to apply it, it has failed to solve these problems [faced by US companies in the 1980s]' (1990: 390). One might suppose that this seriously undermines the utility of the 'theory', but Guest concludes that 'any failure lies less in the theory of HRM than in its piecemeal or inappropriate application' (1990: 390). One is reminded of the old journalistic dictum, 'Why let the facts get in the way of a good story!' In short, the predictive utility of the 'theory' relies on the relatively sparse case study evidence of successful applications. This is not to suggest that theory cannot be built from case study research (see, for example, Eisenhardt, 1989) but HRM 'theory' does not have that pedigree.

The lack of empirical work to support the 'theory' can be linked back to the problems with developing variables and hypotheses noted above. The 'theory' as it stands may be just too broad for it to be tested adequately. Clearly this limits its utility, and importantly raises questions about whether it can be 'disproven'. Bacharach (1989) argues that falsifiability is an important evaluative criteria and that if a theory is constructed in such a way that it is impossible to be disproven then it must be viewed with some scepticism. Guest, obviously sensitive to this notion, has argued that research 'must move from description of HRM cases to theory testing' (1990: 395). Empirically this is possible both longitudinally and across industry – demonstrated by the work of the Centre for Corporate Strategy and Change at the University of Warwick (for an overview see Hendry and Pettigrew, 1990) – but the agenda is enormous.

Instrumental utility is concerned with the 'real world' practicalities of the 'theory' – or put more bluntly, the 'can I use it to get what I want?' approach. HRM might be an attractive proposition for a personnel manager seeking to augment his or her managerial influence in the boardroom and on the shopfloor. For example, consider the personnel manager, traditionally excluded from the boardroom, who might be seeking access to the strategic decision-making process under HRM

(Armstrong, 1987; Torrington, 1988). European survey evidence (Brewster and Smith, 1990) suggests that personnel representation at board level has been increasing, but that this does not necessarily ensure involvement in the development of corporate strategy. In the UK there is little evidence to suggest that HRM means access to strategic decision-making for personnel managers; rather it points to an increasing role for management accountants (for an exposition of this argument see Armstrong, 1989; Purcell, 1989). At the operational level, HRM might be seen by the line manager as a way of avoiding the personnel department and getting on with the job – Oliver and Lowe (1991) report evidence of this attitude in a UK computer company, in contrast to a more central role for personnel in comparable American and Japanese companies. Equally cynically, HRM might be seen by managers as a way of ensuring worker compliance; thus HRM becomes 'human resource manipulation' (Labour Research Department, 1989: 8), nothing more than 'a covert form of employee manipulation dressed up as mutuality' (Fowler, 1987: 3).

The emergence and development of HRM during the 1980s is not particularly surprising given the changing (largely declining) role of organized labour in the USA (see, for example, Kochan et al., 1986) and the UK (see, for example, Kelly, 1990). In such an industrial relations context, the instrumental utility offered to employers should not be overlooked. Theory cannot divorce itself from the political agenda, and theory builders must be sensitive to the political/instrumental utility of their work, if not the morality.

The Boundary

So far, the discussion has focused on the components of HRM 'theory', but equally important for any critical evaluation is an examination of the assumptions which define the boundaries of the theory. Bacharach argues that 'spatial and temporal boundaries restrict the empirical generalizability of the theory' (1989: 500); in other words, how widely can the theory be applied – over different sectors, different countries, different periods in time? A theorist and researcher should be careful in drawing the boundaries. The consequence being that detailed and elaborate studies/ theories have low generalizability because they tend to be specific (narrow boundaries) whilst abstract and broadly bound theories can be generalized in spite of the lack of detail (Bacharach, 1989). Ironically, therefore, the more we attempt to generalize, the less precise we become and the greater the appeal the theory may have; perhaps this explains the interest in HRM 'theory'.

In recognizing the limitations of unbounded theory, Guest has suggested that 'Even in those contexts where market conditions are favourable to HRM, making it desirable in theory [sic], it may not be feasible in practice' (1989: 50) unless five conditions are met: strong corporate leadership, strategic vision, technological/production feasibility, employee/industrial relations feasibility and innovative personnel departments. Guest continues, 'These are formidable constraints. In part they lead to the conclusion that many organizations would be unwise to pursue a full HRM strategy' (1989: 51). The strong implication is that HRM 'theory' is bounded such that its relevance is for growth industries, using high technology, with a predominantly white-collar workforce, traditionally non-unionized and espousing a strong corporate image (see, for example, Lloyd and Rawlinson, Chapter 11, this volume). Guest's 'theory' begins to lose generalizability. Moreover it suggests that HRM may be an 'outcome' which is contingent on specific market circumstances, thus it becomes a statement of what is desirable management practice. In addition, Guest notes the importance of the political context and concludes, 'the unitarist implications of human resource management could only begin to have an appeal following a much more radical shift of ownership and control in industry' (1987: 520).

The Assumptions

An underlying tension permeates the assumptions that inform HRM because of a contradiction in the perspectives on human nature it embraces. Sullivan (1986) suggests that Western management theory has traditionally taken one of four views of human nature: democratic, totalitarian, modern and hermeneutical. It is the two categories which presuppose human beings to be malleable that concern us: modern man (sic) and hermeneutical man (sic). Modern man can be influenced by manipulating the 'laws' (physical, psychological and social) which determine the process of being. Hermeneutical man, however, is self-bound rather than law-bound and consequently he or she *creates* organizational reality and structures rather than *responds* to them. The implications for the management of people are profound: modern man is a human *being* for whom work offers experiences to be *endured*, with emphasis lying on the exchange of *value*; hermeneutical man is a human *becoming*, interacting with others through work to achieve *lived experiences* through exchange of *meaning*.

The dichotomy and the consequent tension is also present in the underlying HRM assumptions. On the one hand it lays claim to a pedigree which encompasses Theory Y (McGregor, 1960), aspects of the QWL movement (Walton, 1973) and OD techniques (Bennis, 1966), whilst on the other hand it employs concepts from goal-setting theory (Locke, 1978), expectancy theory (Vroom, 1964) and human asset accounting (Giles and Robinson, 1972): self-expression and high trust are backed up with direction and low trust. Likewise, it uses cultural artifacts (symbols, heroes, rituals and so forth) and so implicitly accepts the importance of exchanged meaning, yet employs these to manipulate and manage the 'reality' experienced by the actors. Simultaneously, a behavioural control system (exemplified by personality tests and appraisal techniques, see Townley, 1989) ensures 'good fit' of personnel which regulates the meaning and limits the range of experiences achievable through interaction. HRM uses the language of individual self-fulfilment and self-creation but sets the boundaries to both. A human being *becomes* only within the confines of a managed reality.

At ground level this manifests itself in the form of a gap between rhetoric and policy. For example, Kochan et al. (1986) stress the importance of the Theory Y approach and high-trust relationships, then demonstrate how this was undermined at Xerox by imposing a control system for absenteeism more appropriate to a Theory X attitude to management. HRM 'theory' therefore may be striving for a type of postmodern interpretation of human nature: lived experiences through meanings constructed by others. But it is in an ontological tug-of-war: on the one side pulls reality as a concrete process, and on the other pulls reality as a symbolic discourse, ably assisted by social construction. We are unlikely to have a satisfactory theory whilst the white handkerchief oscillates.

Conclusion

The discussion reveals that we cannot easily dismiss HRM 'theory' because it does display some of the features of an adequate theory, but when we delve deeper it is clear there are some serious deficiencies. It is built with concepts and propositions, but the associated variables and hypotheses are not made explicit. It is too comprehensive, failing the parsimony criteria, which consequently presents problems with testing. The lack of general application of HRM 'theory' suggests either that practitioners have some doubts, or that its shortcomings in terms of testability prevent adequate empirical studies from being undertaken, so its plausibility might also be questioned. Moreover, there are notable dissenting voices in the academic community who condemn it as being obvious, absurd or irrelevant. In terms of logical consistency there are a number of notable contradictions which, coupled with the paucity of evidence, raise questions about its utility. Fundamentally, tensions are evident in the assumptions which inform the 'theory' such that it is founded on paradox.

If we take Dubin's (1978) approach to theory building then we would dismiss HRM 'theory' because it fails on two counts: first, in terms of 'adequacy' because of the logical inconsistencies; and second, in terms of 'reality' because it does not model the empirical world, or at least cannot adequately be tested as being able to do so. Defenders of HRM 'theory' might question these strict criteria or argue that theory should be interpreted in a far more liberal manner, or that it is merely a semantic device. The danger of accepting this view is eloquently expressed by Bacharach (1989: 512):

> If theorists don't take the rules of theory seriously, individually they will continue to cling to theories in almost cultist fashion. Getting beyond this clinging behavior, which tends to drive theorists from fad to foible, demands a precise discourse, one which allows theorists to focus on the specific strengths and weaknesses of particular theories.

The scrutiny offered in this chapter suggests that HRM 'theory' may well be neglecting important aspects of theory building. It might be more appropriate to describe it as a 'mimic theory', but why not be faithful to Beer et al. (1984), the originators of the idea, and describe it as a map or framework for analysis?

Even if it continues to be described as 'theory', a sobering comment on the significance of management theories in general is offered by Nehrbass (1979). He argues that, traditionally, academics have pursued theories and philosophies that have little relevance for practitioners, and as a consequence the ideas are often dismissed as 'naive or nonsensical'. He suggests that academic management theory can often be a product of values and ideology. For those of us who are not vehement positivists this is not a disturbing notion – it merely affirms that we should accept our subjectivity and test our theories rigorously to preserve academic integrity.

Guest (1990) has already identified the importance of values in the perpetuation of HRM by linking it to the 'American dream'. This echoes the comments of Legge (1989) who suggested that HRM might be interpreted as a response to the rise of the 'New Right' – embodying the values through its rhetoric. If HRM is really an ideological response to a particular value system, then we should examine the meaning and morality of HRM, as well as the 'theory' (see Keenoy and Anthony, Chapter 14, this volume).

If HRM is labelled a 'theory' it raises expectations about its ability to describe and predict. Academics are therefore disappointed to discover the sparse empirical evidence to substantiate the status of HRM, and quick to point to the contradictions embedded in the 'theory'. On the other hand, practising managers may welcome HRM 'theory' for its prescriptive utility. These people are less likely to be concerned with its internal consistency or theoretical beauty, and more likely to focus on its tool-kit utility. More explicitly their questions will be less related to those raised in this chapter, but more utilitarian in nature. They will look into the HRM tool kit to see whether there is a policy to fit the particular personnel maintenance work at hand.

Conversely, among both the academic and practitioner communities there will be those for whom the visionary and holistic language of HRM is seductive. Belief in HRM is not based upon deconstructing theory or looking for proof, but on faith. The HRM prophets guide the way to business improvement, harmonious employee relations, customer care and societal well-being: the promised land for advanced capitalist economies. Those who like the message and have faith, follow.

Overall, the danger of reconceptualizing HRM as a theory is that it raises its status and denies its history. The UK version owes much to the work of Beer et al. (1984) who were devising a 'map' to guide general managers through the people-management components of their MBA course. These historical roots should not be forgotten. Coupled with the paucity of empirical evidence and internal contradictions, they can have a particularly humbling effect on those who claim that HRM is the 'management theory' to take us into the next century.

Note

I would like to thank Tom Keenoy for his valuable comments on an earlier version of this chapter.

References

Armstrong, M. (1987) 'Human resource management: a case of the emperor's new clothes?' *Personnel Management*, August: 31–4.
Armstrong, M. (1988) *A Handbook of Personnel Management Practice*. London: Kogan Page.
Armstrong, P. (1989) 'Limits and possibilities for HRM in an age of management accountancy', in J. Storey (ed.), *New Perspectives on Human Resource Management*. London: Routledge. pp. 154–66.
Bacharach, S.B. (1989) 'Organizational theories: some criteria for evaluation', *The Academy of Management Review*, 14 (4): 496–515.
Beer, M., Spector, B., Lawrence, P.R., Mills, D. and Walton, R.E. (1984) *Managing Human Assets*. New York: Free Press.
Bennis, W. (1966) *Changing Organizations*. New York: McGraw-Hill.
Brewster, C. and Smith, C. (1990) 'Corporate strategy: a no-go area for personnel?' *Personnel Management*, July: 36–40.
Brunsson, N. (1982) 'The irrationality of action and action rationality: decisions, ideologies and organizational actions', *Journal of Management Studies*, 19 (1): 29–44.
Cohen, B. (1980) *Developing Sociological Knowledge: Theory and Method*. Englewood Cliffs, NJ: Prentice-Hall.
Davis, M.W. (1971) 'That's interesting', *Philosophy of the Social Sciences*, 1: 309–44.
Dubin, R. (1978) *Theory Building* (revised edn). New York: Free Press.
Eisenhardt, K.M. (1989) 'Building theories from case study research', *The Academy of Management Review*, 14 (4): 532–50.
Fowler, A. (1987) 'When chief executives discover HRM', *Personnel Management*, January: 3.
Fox, A. (1966) 'Industrial relations and industrial sociology', Research paper 3, *Royal Commission on the Trades Unions and Employers Associations*. London: HMSO.
Giles, W.J. and Robinson, D.F. (1972) *Human Asset Accounting*. London: Institute of Personnel Management and Institute of Cost and Management Accountants.
Grenier, G.J. (1988) *Inhuman Relations: Quality Circles and Anti-Unionism in American Industry*. Philadelphia: Temple University Press.
Guest, D. (1987) 'Human resource management and industrial relations', *Journal of Management Studies*, 24 (5): 503–21.
Guest, D. (1989) 'Personnel and HRM: can you tell the difference?' *Personnel Management*, January: 48–51.
Guest, D. (1990) 'Human resource management and the American dream', *Journal of Management Studies*, 27 (4): 377–97.

Hendry, C. and Pettigrew, A. (1990) 'Human resource management: an agenda for the 1990s', *International Journal of Human Resource Management*, 1 (1): 17–43.

Iles, P. and Johnston, T. (1989) 'Searching for excellence in second-hand clothes?: a note', *Personnel Review*, 18 (6): 32–5.

Kaplan, A. (1964) *The Conduct of Inquiry*. Aylesbury, Bucks: Intext Books.

Keenoy, T. (1990a) 'HRM: a case of the wolf in sheep's clothing?' *Personnel Review*, 19 (2): 3–9.

Keenoy, T. (1990b) 'Human resource management: rhetoric, reality and contradiction', *International Journal of Human Resource Management*, 1 (3): 363–84.

Kelly, J. (1990) 'British trade unionism 1979–89: change, continuity and contradictions', *Work, Employment and Society*, 4, Special Issue, May: 29–65.

Kochan, T.A., Katz, H.C. and McKersie, R.B. (1986) *The Transformation of American Industrial Relations*. New York: Basic Books.

Labour Research Department (1989) 'HRM – human resource manipulation?' *Labour Research*, August: 8–9.

Legge, K. (1989) 'Human resource management: a critical analysis', in J. Storey (ed.), *New Perspectives on Human Resource Management*. London: Routledge. pp. 19–40.

Locke, E.A. (1978) 'The ubiquity of the technique of goal-setting in theories and approaches to employee motivation', *Academy of Management Review*, 3 (3): 594–601.

McGregor, D. (1960) *The Human Side of Enterprise*. New York: McGraw-Hill.

Nehrbass, R.G. (1979) 'Ideology and the decline of management theory', *Academy of Management Review*, 4 (3): 427-31.

Oliver, N. and Lowe, J. (1991) 'UK computer industry: American, British and Japanese contrasts in human resource management', *Personnel Review*, 20 (2): 18–23.

Poole, M. (1990) 'Human resource management in an international perspective', *International Journal of Human Resource Management*, 1 (1): 1–15.

Purcell, J. (1989) 'The impact of corporate strategy on human resource management' in J. Storey (ed.), *New Perspectives on Human Resource Management*. London: Routledge. pp. 67–91.

Schein, E.H. (ed.) (1987) *The Art of Managing Human Resources*. Oxford: Oxford University Press.

Sisson, K. (1990) 'Introducing the *Human Resource Management Journal*', *Human Resource Management Journal*, 1 (1): 1.

Sparrow, P. (1991) 'Developing a human resource management strategy: International Computers Ltd.', in K. Legge, C. Clegg and N. Kemp (eds), *Case Studies in Information Technology, People and Organizations*. Oxford: NCC Blackwell. pp. 109–18.

Springer, B. and Springer, S. (1990) 'Human resource management in the US – celebration of its centenary', in R. Pieper (ed.), *Human Resource Management: An International Comparison*. Berlin: de Gruyter. pp. 41–60.

Sullivan, J.J. (1986) 'Human nature, organizations, and management theory', *Academy of Management Review*, 11 (3): 534–49.

Thomas, R.J. (1988) 'What is human resource management?' *Work, Employment and Society*, 2 (3): 392–402.

Tichy, N.M., Fombrun, C.J. and Devanna, M.A. (1982) 'Strategic human resource management', *Sloan Management Review*, 23 (2): 47–61.

Torrington, D. (1988) 'How does human resources management change the personnel function?' *Personnel Review*, 17 (6): 3–9.

Townley, B. (1989) 'Selection and appraisal: reconstituting social relations?', in J. Storey (ed.), *New Perspectives on Human Resource Management*. London: Routledge. pp. 92–108.

Vroom, V.H. (1964) *Work and Motivation*. New York: Wiley.

Walton, R.E. (1973) 'Quality of working life: what is it?' *Sloan Management Review*, Fall: 11–21.

Walton, R.E. (1987) *Innovating to Compete: Lessons for Diffusing and Managing Change in the Workplace*. San Francisco: Jossey-Bass.

Weick, K.E. (1989) 'Theory construction as disciplined imagination', *The Academy of Management Review*, 14 (4): 516–31.
Whetten, D.A. (1989) 'What constitutes a theoretical contribution?' *The Academy of Management Review*, 14 (4): 490–5.

3   HUMAN RESOURCE MANAGEMENT, COMPETITION AND STRATEGY: SOME PRODUCTIVE TENSIONS

Richard Whipp

The social and economic ferment of the past decade has brought the subjects of new forms of management and competition to widespread attention. Nowhere has the interest level been higher than in the area of the management of people and its supposed link to competitive performance. More precisely, it is often assumed that the adoption of HRM will enhance performance. The main aim of this chapter is therefore to examine current views on HRM and competition. At the same time, the chapter will suggest an alternative way of appreciating the role of human resources in the competitive process. Practical illustrations will be drawn from the UK automobile and book publishing industries.

The chapter has three sections. The first tackles the problem of competition and strategy. Contemporary conceptions of competition are deeply rooted within the political and economic context of the UK. Political imperatives have created fertile conditions for the growth of an assertive breed of managerial texts. Competition scholars have been equally active given the topicality of the subject (Porter, 1981). Their rational assumptions have resulted in an over-simplification of the nature of competition, stressing structures at the expense of processes. What is proposed here is an alternative approach to competition based on: the combined social and economic character of industries and firms; the intensely subjective social constructions which condition competitive relations (Weick, 1987); and above all, the highly uncertain outcomes of the competitive process (Barney, 1986; Schumpeter, 1950).

In a similar way, the processes by which strategic changes are made seldom move directly through neat, successive stages of analysis, choice and implementation. Given the powerful internal characteristics of the firm it would be unusual if they did not affect the process: more often they transform it. Seldom is there an easily isolated logic to strategic change. Instead that process may derive its motive force from an amalgam of economic, personal and political imperatives. The aim of this chapter is to use such an appreciation of strategic and competitive processes to explore the productive tensions within the term Human Resource Management.

An institutional, processual understanding of competition and strategy quickly puts into perspective any notion of HRM as a privileged route to competitive salvation. Section two therefore draws on a European scholarly tradition to construct a more critical notion of the potential and limits of HRM. The application of over-rational, linear programmes of HRM as a means of securing competitive success is shown to be at odds with experience both in the UK and elsewhere. In practice, the uncertainty of the competitive process is matched by the fragility of many HRM techniques. The often intangible social, political and educational dimensions of the competitive process are simply not amenable to straight-forward control. The assumption that HRM can be easily linked to competitive performance is misplaced. The impact of human resources on competitive performance is altogether more indirect and fragile.

The third section uses research conducted over the last five years in the UK automobile and book publishing sectors. The purpose is to illustrate the way an institutional conception of competition and strategy can reveal the uncertain role of HRM in the performance of companies.

Competition and Strategy

In order to understand the nature of competition and strategic change these readily familiar terms require careful specification. Strategic change and competition are joint and inseparable processes. These processes occur at multiple levels across time (Whipp, 1987). In other words, these processes move forward within their firm, sector and national contexts. Such processes are structured by a trinity of forces. These include not only the objective decisions of managers using information derived from their competitive environment; they also embrace the subjective learning (Langlois, 1986) and political dimensions which operate both in and outside the firm (cf. Rasanen, 1989; Romme, 1989).

The competitive and strategic behaviour of a firm cannot therefore be understood solely by reference to the industry structure model (Porter, 1980, 1985), a model which underlies much of the thinking in the emerging HRM literature. The role of the national economy and a wider conception of the social and economic relations of the sector are vital (Hollingsworth and Lindberg, 1985: 4–6; Lodge and Vogel, 1987). The competitive performance of a firm hinges therefore on the recognition that businesses compete not merely against one another but *at the same time* within the sectoral and national/international structures and relationships (Whipp, Rosenfeld and Pettigrew, 1989).

A number of differences are apparent between the orientation of this chapter, based on the composite dimensions of strategic change and competition, and more orthodox views (see Pettigrew and Whipp, 1991: ch. 1 for a more detailed account). One of the most critical contrasts is with the way traditional economics concentrates on the singular competitive traits of a firm. Even the 'new competition' writers (Abernathy et al., 1980) emphasize one key base of competition related to technology. Here it is argued that the competitive performance of an enterprise is the result of a collection of abilities. One must appreciate therefore the plurality in the bases on which a firm competes and above all their process of creation. Seldom is there a single base. Most firms develop many layers of competences which explain their overall competitive strength. These may combine both price and non-price characteristics, human and technical resources. Moreover, the sectoral and national conditions in which a firm operates and hence the bases on which it competes are quintessentially unstable.

This multi-level and dynamic view of competition is greatly strengthened by uniting it with a processual understanding of strategic change. The ability of an enterprise to compete within the prevailing settings relies on two qualities: the capacity of the firm to identify and understand the competitive forces in play and how they change *over* time, linked to the competence of a business to mobilize and manage the resources necessary for the chosen competitive response *through* time.

How strategy arises, what conditions its formation and, above all, how it is carried out are non-trivial issues. Apparently objective technical decisions over markets, finance or products are deeply influenced by the social and political texture of the firm. Business strategy, far from being a straightforward rational phenomenon, is in fact interpreted by managers according to their own frames of reference (Johnson, 1987). Strategy does not just concern senior management. Analyses of strategic management should be oriented accordingly. It is the limits to managerial action which are as telling in understanding the outcome of strategic changes as the assumed breadth of their discretion.

One is concerned therefore with both the intended content of a given strategy and the way it is shaped by the interior forces of the firm, and therefore the unintended outcomes. That content is made up of not only commercial and financial objectives but also the less obvious tacit knowledge of the decision-makers. These vital personal or group frames of reference are in part derived from the internal life of the firm, including the historical development of its structure, culture and politics. Such features do not only inform the actions of management; others inside the organization can in turn use them for their own purposes during official attempts at major strategic changes (Whipp, Rosenfeld and Pettigrew, 1989). The ability to see strategy in terms of a process cannot be emphasized too strongly. Along with other researchers (Hampden-Turner and Baden-Fuller, 1989; Mintzberg, 1978; Quinn, 1988) we conclude that one of the defining features of the process is ambiguity.

The general implication of this framework is overwhelming. The process of strategic change and competition is not to be likened to a linear, sequential assembly line of investigation, choice and implementation. Competition and strategic change must be seen together as a compound process (cf. Van de Ven, 1986: 599). An appreciation of this point can be used to both highlight the weaknesses of the early conceptions of HRM, and at the same time, suggest ways of developing more creative possibilities within the HRM project.

Human Resource Management

The army of human resource management commentators continues to grow apace. However, as this section will show, the gap between rhetoric and practice in HRM is partly explained by the emphases of the commentators. The second objective is to show how the processual and multi-level orientation, outlined in the previous section, is a possible step forward in both conceptual and practical terms.

Managing People

Interest in the management of people is longstanding (Hobsbawm, 1974). A number of schools of thought have arisen each attempting to address what were seen as the essential problems of their time. Reviews of the succession of approaches (Merkle, 1980) show how each variant reflected the social and economic conditions from which it emerged. The identification of such patterns is significant. It not only helps to explain the appearance of new initiatives such as human resource management in the 1980s, it also puts them into perspective. Rather than being seen as somehow the ultimate or most highly developed form of managing the workforce, such innovations are attempts to meet particular historical circumstances. Analysis of management attempts to control work has revealed the extent of the influences in operation (Whipp, 1988, 1990a). Studies of industrial conflict alone have uncovered a complex set of interlocking factors in their explanations (Thompson, 1983).

Many have argued that new forms of organization are required to meet the new circumstances of the 1990s. In view of the passing of the largely US auto industry model of mass production, the label post-Fordist has been used to denote the new principles of organization. The keynotes include the division of large corporations into multiple internal businesses; greater use of temporary employment contracts; the retention of a small core of highly skilled employees; extensive contracting-out of services; and the further separation of research, design and production. It is unsurprising therefore that new modes of workforce management such as HRM have been advocated in such circumstances, or that they have been heavily influenced by the apparent commercial success of Japanese companies which espouse HRM techniques (Pascale, 1990; Delbridge and Turnbull, Chapter 4, this volume).

The UK

One of the major problems with such writing relates to national context. Differences in legal, institutional and political frameworks dilute the relevance of the monolithic post-Fordist and HRM notions. More especially, the deeply-embedded characteristics of the firm and its management within national boundaries cannot be ignored. After all, British management has been recognized as failing to adopt the US principles of mass production and corporate organization in the post-war era (Marginson et al., 1988). It is entirely logical, therefore, to expect a distinctive response on the part of UK management to the technological and market changes of the past decade. Nowhere has this been more apparent than in the area of human resource management.

The argument that the UK has experienced lower growth than its main competitors due to the shortcomings in managerial techniques and the training of employees is hardly new. Economic retardation has been attributed historically to the choice made by UK employers and managers to retain their imperial and specialist markets (Elbaum and Lazonick, 1986), thus obviating the need to develop corporate organization on the US scale, and allowing the maintenance of the largely nineteenth-century employment arrangements of piecework and indirect control of labour. Some economists in the late 1980s (see Crafts, 1988) argue that supply side defects explain the low growth of the UK economy. These include inappropriate plant size, a shortfall of research and development and inadequate education and training allied to problems with the structure and conduct of industrial relations. On the evidence of the 1980s there has been little reduction of this historic 'training lag' (Constable and McCormick, 1987; Handy, 1987).

These findings are important in their own right but combining them with the work of other social scientists gives them even greater force. Both sets of writers confirm the long-term weakness of workforce management in the UK. Beyond this, though, these conclusions not only provide the vital national context in which UK firms operate, they are vital to understanding why abstractions of what HRM 'should be' fail to appear in practice at the level of the firm. The following section will tackle such problems directly.

Appearance and Reality

Given the shortcomings of workforce management in the UK and the immediate challenges of successful overseas competitors, it was to be expected that a new 'best practice' labelled HRM should be enthusiastically embraced by some. The demonstration effect of Japanese entry to Western domestic markets has been outstanding.

A stream of writing flowed throughout the 1980s. The central themes included: the striving to achieve an improved 'fit' between strategic planning and the difficult areas of people management (Beer et al., 1984; Walton, 1987); the belief that 'excellent' businesses relied on corporate culture (Peters and Waterman, 1982); and the recognition by Porter that HRM was an integral part of the value chain at firm level (Porter, 1985). Subsequently, a body of commentary has tried to elaborate the contribution which personnel policies could make to strategy (for a comprehensive treatment of these developments see Guest, 1987, 1991). The major differences in economic and social circumstances notwithstanding, evangelists for the US-based HRM approach have been numerous; the rhetoric of HRM has slipped into managerial parlance. Herein lies the problem. Considerable evidence is available which confirms the scale of the task if HRM is to become firmly rooted in UK business and elsewhere.

Case studies completed in the 1970s showed just how alien was the notion of strategy in the industrial relations and personnel functions across different industries (Whipp and Clark, 1986). Subsequent survey research in the 1980s has deepened our knowledge. There have been marked changes in certain aspects of work. One example is flexibility (Atkinson and Meager, 1986; Curson, 1986; Blyton and Morris, Chapter 7, this volume). Other research suggests that beyond these fragmented actions the development of full-blown personnel planning is still rare (see Sisson, 1989).

Many proponents of HRM have continued to espouse the integration of human resources into strategic management almost without reference to such deep-seated problems. Guest (1987) suggests that the main aim of HRM is to foster commitment from individuals to the success of the company through a quality orientation in the performance of individuals, departments and the total organization. Human resource management is also said to relate to the total set of knowledge, skills and attitudes that firms need to compete. It may involve concern for and action in the management of people including: selection, training and development, employee relations and compensation. Yet whilst much effort has gone into constructing this ideal type, nothing like comparable attention has been devoted to assessing (1) the intellectual consistency of such 'models' (see Noon, Chapter 2, this volume), or (2) to what extent a shift from traditional personnel management in the UK to an HRM approach is possible.

In terms of the first point, there is no simple direct connection between HRM and competitive performance. The human resource is but one of the potential assets within the ensemble of capacities of any one firm. Given what we have established of the multiple bases of competition in any industry then there are many ways which the human resources of a company can help or hinder the creation of those bases.

With respect to the second point, the research on which this chapter is based maintains that, in practice, the development of an HRM approach within a firm cannot be assumed. By the same token, neither can its positive contribution to competitive performance be taken for granted. The process by which human resources are developed such that they can contribute to the ability of the organization to accomplish strategic change and generate a competitive base is more often accomplished on paper than in reality. The attempts to move directly to an HRM approach are often condemned to failure both because of their inherent difficulty but even more so because of the context of British practice. Companies in our research who have attempted to develop such an approach and used it to help generate some limited form of competitive advantage share a central characteristic. The common denominator is the fragility and imperma- nence of HRM techniques, in spite of the extent of the attention devoted to their introduction.

Nowhere is this better illustrated than in the area of learning. The role of knowledge is paramount in the creation of differential advantage amongst firms. Learning can become the central means of creating, maintaining and regenerating that knowledge. An HRM approach can be a vital means of developing that learning capacity. Yet achieving this in practice can be problematical in the extreme. It is therefore an excellent example of the productive tensions within the central institutions of the HRM approach; it exemplifies their potential yet at the same time their impermanence and fragility.

Writers from a variety of backgrounds have given support to the importance of knowledge in economic relations in general (Hodgson, 1988; Loasby, 1988; Nelson and Winter, 1982). Some emphasize the great difficulty of exposing the knowledge contained within the procedural repertoires of organizations (Hedberg, 1981; Jelinek, 1979; Winter, 1987: 161, 171). Two things must be stressed. First, any company develops over time its own distinctive knowledge base. That base contains both technical and social knowledge. What becomes critical is the extent to which the knowledge base of a firm matches changing competitive conditions. Altering such a composite base is not simple. Second, the ability to learn is crucial. Learning is seen here as not just the acquisition of new knowledge by the individual. Rather it refers to how those within firms collectively change their knowledge, values and shared mental models of their company and its markets.

The two company examples which follow will show how it is the ability to shed outmoded knowledge, techniques and beliefs, as well as learn and deploy new ones which enables firms to carry out new strategies. The ability to do so faster and more effectively than your competitors may well become 'an almost priceless competitive advantage' (cf. de Geus, 1988: 71). In reality, the creation of such a capacity – a central part of an HRM approach – is far from straightforward and in no way can be taken for granted. It requires a rich array of creative and supportive action at all levels of an organization, the ability of those involved to work with prolonged periods of ambiguity or seeming *ad hoc* adjustments and, above all, the capacity to identify and exploit the opportunities for learning which arise.

The Automobile and Book Publishing Industries

Automobiles

After the post-war decades of replacement demand the 1970s altered the character of competition in the UK auto industry fundamentally. The British manufacturers were ill-equipped to withstand the shock. The 1980s witnessed a painful recovery in the face of the new performance standards set by other international volume producers.

The twin oil shocks of 1973–4 and 1979 were traumatic for the British automobile industry; it was still dealing with unresolved, long-term deficiencies when the shock waves struck. The problem set became infamous: unrationalized company form, lack of investment, under-developed production automation and marketing (see Whipp, 1990b). These problems gave rise to weak products, indifferent quality, outdated distribution, high manufacturing costs and poor labour relations. Import penetration rose from 6 per cent in the late 1960s to 40 per cent by 1975. In the 1980s, car manufacturing still fell in output terms well below the general trend of the index for total manufacturing industries. Moreover, the recovery in output between 1986–89 was linked with record annual trade deficits in cars from 1982 (reaching £6.11 billion in 1988). In the 1980s the industry had made immense efforts to re-orient itself to a new set of competitive standards. The apparent use of Japanese production techniques by new producers such as Nissan, Honda and Toyota has increased the pressure on the existing producers' efficiency. By 1989 Japanese investment in the UK auto industry was running at £1.81 billion. By the mid-1990s Japanese car-makers will represent approximately a third of UK car output.

At the same time performance by Japanese car manufacturers in the world auto industry have called into question almost every conventional assumption behind the existing business of car production in Europe and the USA. Japanese producers have achieved a unique synthesis of 'just-in-time' production with 'total quality control'. The national structure of suppliers and producers within a single group has resulted in much cheaper products but with higher quality levels than any other competitor. This competitive disparity between the Japanese producers and the rest of the world will dominate the industry for the next decade.

Jaguar

The experience of Jaguar Cars has been as traumatic as that of the UK auto industry. That experience falls into three main periods. From 1945 to 1968, domestic market dominance in luxury saloon and sports class cars was matched by a consistent record of 50 per cent of output being exported. The E-Type model of 1964 and the award-winning XJ6 of 1968 were outstanding examples of Jaguar's products. Suspect product reliability notwithstanding, Jaguar's strengths were incremental engineering innovation linked to competitive pricing. In this era the firm was dominated by its founder and chief executive William Lyons.

The erosion of this record between 1972 and 1980, when Jaguar was owned by British Leyland (BL), was marked. The 1979 Series III XJ6 was disfigured by quality and reliability defects. Production fell from 32,000 to 14,000 between 1974 and 1979. Jaguar was profitable in 1974 but by the end of 1979 losses were calculated to be running at £4 million per month. In 1980 Jaguar was given a year's notice of closure by BL unless the unit broke even. A new managing director, John Egan, was appointed in the same year. The turnaround in Jaguar's performance has been exceptional (see Whipp, 1990b) with the transformation of virtually every aspect of the company's operation. Jaguar was successfully floated on the Stock Exchange in 1984.

Survival and the reconstruction of the company was achieved. Problems for the company occurred during the attempt to grow as an independent entity. Turnover continued to rise but profits fell from £97 million in 1987 to £47.5 million in 1988. Having only just rebuilt the company after a decade of neglect to meet the competitive bases of the 1980s, Jaguar simply did not have the resources necessary for the competitive demands of the 1990s. The management's attempt to find a 'protective' buyer of their choice in late 1989, failed. The Department of Trade and Industry waived its Golden Share, and this enabled Ford to proceed with a hostile £1.6 billion bid in November 1989. That the growth and independence ambitions of the late 1980s could be thwarted so swiftly gives us an important confirmation of the fragility of the newly created strategic and the HRM skills of 1980s.

Jaguar in 1980 was a classic case of the negative inheritance of UK engineering companies. It was forced to create a personnel function virtually from scratch. In view of the workforce's resistance to change, resulting from over a decade of intense adversarial relations, a series of preparatory actions had to be taken. This included the use of the survival crisis of 1980–81 to indicate the need for both business and people change, the years to 1984 to reveal the full extent of the huge gaps in the company's knowledge base and, all the time, the use of a variety of opportunities to raise an identification with HRM techniques among both workforce and management.

The national attention which Jaguar subsequently received from HRM professionals was not entirely due to the creation of its HRM approach. What was critical was the way the management had to mobilize a range of secondary features to try to ensure the use of such HRM techniques. Jaguar did not raise up HRM as a new god to replace the old engineering deity which had so distorted the company's vision in the past. What stands out is the amount of action taken across the company to ensure even the introduction of certain basic HRM principles.

Jaguar of course supplies a striking example of the linkage of HRM to business needs and changes at the level of intention. HRM was a core concern of the survival, regeneration and growth strategies. Jaguar's ability to assess the environment, lead change (in the collective sense) and implement change would have been stillborn without that link. Less well known though are the situational and *ad hoc* features and the role they played. These included the realization from 1982 that world-class engineers were unable to assess purchase costs in relation to their projects. The mobilization of external influences, such as the constant comparisons with competitor training and skill levels, is equally overlooked by others. The linking of HRM activities with existing and emergent institutions is shown in the range of complementary activities (for example, 'open-learning' and J-days).

Jaguar's ultimate problem has been in its lack of capital resources to release the full potential of its technical and human assets by comparison to world standards. In the 1970s Jaguar was the epitome of UK manufacturing, with both poorly developed personnel management and a weakened knowledge base. Minimal formal management systems under Lyons had done little to develop the reliance on piecework, spot bargaining at shopfloor level and personal regulation by Lyons of the salaried staff. The assumption of responsibility for industrial relations management by BL from 1975 created further problems. The industrial relations problems of BL have become legendary. BL was faced with the task of rationalizing twenty-five manufacturing companies employing 80,000 people across sixty plants. All had previously been competitors. Whilst attempting such a huge feat the company was faced with unprecedented levels of inflation and a resurgent shopfloor-based unionism. The problem for Jaguar workers was that they saw their craft, specialist production differentials fly in the face of the need for corporate plant comparability.

Equally damaging was the way the conflict between Jaguar and BL did nothing to improve the growing weaknesses in the knowledge base of the Browns Lane assembly plant. Although still sound in product design, the limitations in production, project management, quality and marketing were deepening. Action by BL exacerbated the deficiencies. Sales is a clear instance. Jaguar had relied heavily on Henleys and its dealers in the south of England to handle certain difficulties associated with new products. This knowledge was lost when divisional sales took away the Henleys franchise with the assumption that luxury and volume models could be sold equally well in the mass market Austin and Morris showrooms. Starved of major investment Jaguar simply did not have the resources to develop its repertoire of basic techniques. It was this neglect which forced the Jaguar management under Egan to replace virtually every building on the Browns Lane site in the 1980s.

The attempt by the Egan regime to move away from the traditional UK industrial relations approach and to build up an HRM orientation had a central source. As in the case of Peugeot Talbot, it was the chief executive who championed the move. Given his experience in introducing such techniques at Massey Ferguson, both the commitment and the practical knowledge were there to guide such a process. The approach was a long-term one. It was based on the wholly realistic recognition of the entrenched values and behaviour patterns of decades. Once through the survival year, the chief executive set an apparently extreme goal: 'to become the finest car company in the world'. The statement was designed to shift the standards and sights of the company above the preoccupations of the UK car industry. World standards were now to be applied in all spheres from engineering through to human resources.

This provided a vital means of raising HRM consciousness among senior management. The problem was that these conditioning features would not legitimate nor establish an HRM style in one go. It has been a constant feature of the work of the board and the newly-created personnel function after 1981 that they have had to re-work the message and apply it regularly, albeit in different ways. Each phase of survival, regeneration and growth has required short-term targets to advance the application of HRM in practice. As the personnel director recognizes, there was no assumption that the adversarial mentality would disappear overnight as the series of shopfloor disputes between 1985 and 1988 confirmed. This is part of the reason for the elaborate communication structure which has been built up since its first vital role in the 1980 survival phase. The same attitude to adversarial relations was true in inter-departmental terms. A personnel manager notes how:

> friction, conflict, disagreement is healthy in any organization. The word objective is the one that has been missing. You have conflict in achieving results. What we have worked on is ensuring that behind all the debates and disagreements, we all know what the end result should be. What we have enabled ourselves to do is actually develop a healthy rivalry based on a common goal as opposed to individual camps looking at their own results rather than the company's results.

It is entirely consistent with this recognition of the difficulty of moving progressively from an industrial relations to an HRM orientation that such extensive effort has been expended under what we categorize as secondary supportive activity. Action taken during the regeneration phase illustrates how Jaguar management did not raise HR development as an end in itself. The reverse was true. Specific HR initiatives were justified by reference to the business objectives which they could serve.

The BL board had voted £200 million to the XJ40 car and AJ6 engine projects in February 1981 on the strength of the company's improved performance. Jaguar's aim was to use this investment to begin the transformation of the company's technology base. This in turn required a major recruitment campaign of engineering staff if there was to be any long-term possibility of competing with the German luxury producers' technological strength. The 450 engineering force of 1980 was insufficient. So began the recruitment of staff in the product and manufacturing areas which by 1986 had added 500. The problem of integrating such a large number of new employees was considerable, hence the introduction of selection tests and induction programmes in Jaguar after years of stable numbers in engineering. The programme of investment meant that engineering staff now had to spend large sums of money. Their inexperience, given the starvation of funds under BL, necessitated a training initiative in commercial and negotiating skills.

Given that the company's main goal was to be free-standing, then a series of human resource changes which would support this objective were required. New treasury, legal and company secretariat functions were added which were needed to mount the privatization initiative. Other individual appointments were made to improve planning capacity. The overhaul of the company salary structure was required in order to meet current market rates.

The human resource approach was deepened in a number of ways. Manpower planning, in the light of the profound changes in the company's commercial approach, was developed with a five-year horizon. A 'hearts and minds' programme was initiated. The aim was to organize a range of events for employees and their families to revive the pride in belonging to Jaguar. An Open Learning Scheme was introduced covering a range of specialist and more general education subjects. The commitment was to each employee receiving five days of training a year. The basic formula in developing the human resource was one of: (1) making changes in the human resource area which were required by the capital investment programme of 1981, which at the same time would (2) facilitate the structural changes necessary for improved competitive performance beyond privatization.

As the evidence of the Open Learning Scheme and the hearts and minds programme indicates, Jaguar has had to develop a rich mixture of HR changes and linked institutions. Central to the regeneration strategy was the adjustment of the payment system. The adoption of measured daywork by BL was a disaster. The scheme was disliked by management and workforce alike. It destroyed worker responsibility and in Jaguar's case resulted in a loss in productivity of around 20 per cent. Instead, the new management introduced a bonus scheme for both hourly paid and staff employees. This was not on an individual but a plant and company basis. The use of bonus payments consolidated into higher basic pay levels led to a tripling of productivity and the movement of Jaguar's pay rates towards the top of the range in the UK car industry. An employee share scheme and profit-sharing, linked to PAYE, were developed as an integral part of the privatization plan.

The ability of Jaguar to retain the knowledge generated by such periods of intense change is highly prized, as other car companies have sometimes found to their cost. The way GM observed the mistakes of Ford in relying on mass production techniques alone in the 1920s and then went on to combine successfully assembly line manufacture with multi-divisional management is a classic case of such learning. The need for Jaguar has been to capture and maintain the major improvements in its business during a sequence of accelerated and intense transformation. The danger is that the pressures of such a process could mean that new techniques or approaches are lost along the way: they are then especially costly to rediscover and recreate at a later date. The company is achieving this, and not always consciously, by a combination of: values sponsored by the chief executive, new internal relations which facilitate learning and the use of formal development programmes.

At the highest level the chairman (until his departure in 1990) clearly espoused a personal learning philosophy. This comes out most clearly in the way he drew on techniques learned from his time with General Motors and Massey Ferguson. This was particularly evident in the way he created his senior management team *before* attempting to tackle the horrendous problems that Jaguar faced in 1980: a direct outcome of his previous experience. Even more important has been the way he has sought to create a learning philosophy at all levels of the organization.

In many ways the pressures of the survival and regeneration phase of Jaguar's development made learning a necessity. People had to be able to learn new techniques and assume whole new areas of responsibility across the break-even period and, for different reasons, during the re-creation of Jaguar's full complement of departments. The career of a human resources manager is indicative, in the way he returned to Jaguar as head of the training function in 1980, went on to assume responsibility for internal communications and then embraced office services and special facilities. In his view this was entirely consistent since 'the chairman does believe that most people can learn most things'.

The greater problem has now arisen of how to sustain this general approach to learning through the growth stage. This is especially relevant when the company has so many new entrants, notably in engineering. Individual and group learning seems to be advancing by use of both the new inter-departmental relations and formal development approaches.

Since product quality has become of paramount importance to Jaguar's policy it is an excellent illustration of how the new structures and relations within the company are being used to ensure that hard-won improvements are not squandered. The barrage of activities to improve quality between 1980–84 served their purpose in re-establishing Jaguar in the luxury car market. Thereafter the problem has been one of sustaining the requisite high levels of attention to quality appropriate to the ideal of the 'world's best car company'.

The use of what Rex Marvin (chief vehicle design engineer) calls 'feedback loops' is one answer. In his view the need in vehicle engineering is for 'constant repetition of the message' of quality. Yet this has to be kept fresh as a message if it is in effect to be constantly re-learned by those in post and by new entrants. It is here that the new web of relations with those at other points in the production chain assumes such importance. In other words engineers are exposed to dealers who are best able to demonstrate the lesson of what quality failings mean in the eyes of the customer. The visit of the UK and continental dealers to Browns Lane in September 1986 prior to the launch of the XJ40 was a case in point. The quarterly meetings of Jaguar's service managers from around the world (known in house as the 'hottest, coldest, fastest and largest') is particularly instructive. Their continual dialogue with the engineers, in Marvin's terms, closes the feedback loop very directly.

Post-project audits and follow-up exercises between departments are similar devices to achieve the same end. New technology, such as CAD/CAM or the computer programmes used in critical path analysis also have an in-built potential for recording vital information associated with certain new techniques and projects.

Running alongside these new relationships is of course a major investment in a human resource development programme which is an integral part of Jaguar's business policy. At the heart of that approach is a commitment to formal off-the-job training. Of the £15 million per annum HRM budget £10 million is spent on training. Moreover the combination of business and human resource planning has meant that steps have been taken which avoid the disruption which can dilute the benefits of wider group learning. Examples include the ability to plan recruitment initiatives which balance hiring outsiders with the training of in-house employees; similarly staff development programmes have been designed to build succession paths and minimize turnover (the current rate is 3 per cent).

A number of points are worth emphasizing from Jaguar's experience. The first relates to the huge efforts required merely to 'catch-up' with the conventional personnel practices of other companies in the 1980s. Overcoming the inherited problems of the UK engineering sector with regard to the management of people took virtually a decade. Second, it is noticeable how HRM techniques were not developed to fit the company's strategy. Rather, Jaguar in the early 1980s developed its capacity to think strategically and use HRM concepts and practices, in parallel. It is the need to mobilize such a range of conditioning work and supportive secondary mechanisms which stand out. Nonetheless, by the end of the 1980s, even a company such as Jaguar – held up to be the epitome of how to foster an HRM approach – found it hugely difficult to make such an approach count in terms of competitive performance. Managing both the strategic and competitive processes in the face of new world standards proved ultimately to be beyond its capabilities. Such problems are seen even more intensely in the book publishing industry.

Associated British Publishers (ABP)

The small size of the book publishing industry – around 1 per cent of those employed in manufacturing industry – is apparent. However the stature of the industry is best judged by the significance of its product. Not only are

685 million books sold each year, the book is one of the major bearers of the cultural record of society.

According to *Euromonitor* there are only 200 publishers whose principal business is book publishing. There is a pattern of concentration among those 200. Prior to the series of mergers and take-overs of the mid-1980s, the top eleven book publishers accounted for 62 per cent of the market. In spite of its small size the British book industry has a high level of output by international standards New title output stood at just under 50,000 in 1985. On the other hand, buying levels had remained virtually static in the UK when compared to the growth in demand for other consumer goods. Over 30 per cent of the industry's output is currently exported. ABP exemplifies the UK book industry's high levels of exports given the small sales base offered by the domestic market. In 1983 31 per cent of ABP's sales came from export. ABP and others have been faced with the difficulties posed by the strength of sterling and the weakness of the dollar in the early 1980s. Bookselling has been caught up in the consumer boom and the so-called 'retail revolution' of the mid-1980s. The environment is intensely competitive. The outcome for publishers is equally dramatic. Standards for delivery times, for example, especially through 'tele-ordering', are much higher, with a reduction from around the old level of four weeks to ten days. Publishers now need to be able to handle smaller orders more frequently.

Associated Book Publishers (ABP) contained the Methuen, Chapman and Hall and Eyre & Spottiswoode imprints. In 1964 the modern form of ABP was created by Sweet & Maxwell's acquisition of the company. The ABP name was retained as a means of signalling Sweet & Maxwell's expansion away from purely legal publishing. The attempt to create three publishing divisions down to 1973 (law, trade and academic) proved to be difficult. Linking ABP's inherited interests in Canada and Australia was a major problem and the merger process in Australia was only completed in 1970. The period between 1973 and 1980 was dominated by fire-fighting in the face of inflation. The 1973–74 recession hit the specialist publishing hard. The academic and scientific lists were cut by 40 per cent. Attempts to enter the mass paperback market from 1976 were brought to an abrupt halt by the second oil crisis.

The 1980s for ABP have been dominated by three main episodes. First was the appointment of an outsider to head the UK operations. Alan Miles, from Weidenfeld & Nicolson, was able to supply a vital internal restructuring and much-needed financial controls. Together with the up-turn in demand for consumer goods in the mid-1980s, these actions led to a clear improvement in short-term performance. The second episode of the 1980s began in 1985 when ABP acquired Routledge & Kegan Paul PLC, Croom Helm Ltd and Pitkin Pictorial. ABP's long-term problem of developing wider successful publishing to match its legal division's strength remained. The third centred on the acquisition of ABP in 1987 by International Thomson. It was the historically high premium prices which bidding companies were paying for publishers in 1986–87 which proved decisive. The 730p a share cash offer represented a total cash price of £210 million.

If Jaguar, as one of the supposedly successful examples of the use of HRM, found it difficult to put such an approach into practice, then the problems found in UK book publishing were even greater. Moreover, whilst Jaguar was able at least to develop an *ad hoc* means of collective learning, ABP could not. At ABP the extent of the fire-fighting required in the 1970s, and then the slump in the company's fortunes in 1980, meant that less time was left for consideration of human resource planning compared to Jaguar. Most attention was given to the increasing require- ments of employment legislation and the plant-based bargaining at Andover (its distribution centre) with SOGAT and ASTMS members. The smallness of the personnel function meant that there was only one training officer.

Training rested on the notions of apprenticeship inherent in the progression of editorial, sales and production staff along accepted career ladders. In the case of the editorial function this started with: 'secretarial'/ personal assistant work, followed by desk editing, junior editorial roles helping commissioning editors, before becoming a commissioning editor in charge of a list.

Greater use was made of Book House from 1981 and their introductory and basic courses in publishing. Those making transitions to managerial responsibility faced many challenges. The conclusion of a sales manager, with experience across the divisions since 1976, is indicative:

> I found that the most difficult. I went from managing a small team of people to being given something like fourteen people to manage and that I found very hard . . . you do it by trial and error and it doesn't feel so good.

When ABP considered forming a separate UK board, one of the arguments against doing so was the lack of appropriate training of the divisional directors.

Compared to Longman, one of its main UK competitors, ABP was unable to alter its knowledge base as extensively. The traditional industrial relations approach of its personnel department was not able to act as the catalyst for change in the same way as at Longmans. The new managing director of ABP UK in 1980 noted how the principal strength of the business lay in the professionalism of its staff. There was an undoubted commitment, especially on the editorial side to their subject, their lists and their authors. The culture of ABP was founded on the quality and integrity of its publishing. The law lists through to the University Paperback series of Methuen or the Arden Shakespeare editions were united by this common denominator. The quality of the titles was widely accepted in the trade.

Yet, in relation to Longman, this adherence to editorial integrity was in danger of being maintained somewhat at the expense of increasing commercial requirements. The position is best summed-up by a divisional director. He noted how:

> Most of us came into publishing because we liked the idea of books or the subject behind the books. Most of us did not come into publishing because we were business people to make money.

David Croom realized the feeling behind the approach very quickly after the merger with ABP in 1985. He noted how ABP editors when considering a potential book asked: 'Is it worthy of my list?' Croom Helm editors asked: 'Is it worthy of my ratios?' The less accelerated development of precise awareness of other publishers' strengths and practices was apparent to the new senior management who entered from 1980. The dominant legal division had formed, of necessity, a sharp picture of its direct competition as a result of the attacks on Butterworth and Sweet & Maxwell between 1980–86 from abroad. In other words the legal editors appear to have been working with a full awareness of the incursion of Oyez and Longman followed by the American Commerce Clearing House and specialists such as Colleys in tax law. In contrast, a senior editor in the academic division in 1987 almost rejected the notion of direct competition as untenable since:

> I am not aware of the competition. How can we be? My problem is in visualizing the competition. It's so easy to get into publishing, there are so many publishers doing it that in a way you don't look over your shoulder. If it were toothpaste there are only about ten brands and you can study them intensively . . . I'm very interested to see what other publishers are doing but by the time they've done it, it's too late because the lead time in publishing is so long.

Other leading publishers elsewhere found it hard to construct meaningful data on competition in such a fragmented and under-researched industry.

Many of the internal characteristics of ABP were fully expressed in its culture. The hallmarks were devolvement and the pursuit of quality. In many ways the strength of these aspects of its culture tended to restrain ABP's solution to the puzzle of how to expand the total business when compared to Longman. ABP apparently did not establish ABP as a singular identity. In practice booksellers and others in the trade relate to Sweet & Maxwell or Chapman and Hall. At Longman the company name overshadows the list names (for example, Oliver & Boyd) completely. At ABP the identification with the imprint was encouraged.

Similarly, allowing the adherence to quality to become so dominant among editorial staff ran the risk of obscuring the need to develop the business. It is significant that in the reforms from 1980 quality was to remain paramount. A new structure of controls was to liberate growth. The new UK managing director wished to introduce more detailed controls but controls geared to the quality of books commissioned. He saw that the results of the business were the aggregate of the success of individual books. New routines would not of themselves solve problems but they should provide the environment necessary to encourage the growth of the entrepreneurial function. Compared to Longman there was more of a view that the system would generate growth.

In Longman's terms ABP's ability to learn from its experience was less developed. It is interesting to compare the extensive efforts made by Longman to explain 'what sort of company we want to be' to its staff with their relative cautious emergence in ABP. As one manager at ABP observed:

> the company's called ABP and yet the products (from each of the eight divisions) by which it might be recognized are called something different. That has had an effect and we have been slow in correcting it.

It is clear that improvements were made in the operation of the divisions and these were retained. The reporting forms and budget systems not only gained acceptance through their immediate relevance (for example, in revealing cash flow deficiencies). By their very nature they became self-reinforcing. Put simply, the monthly and yearly repetitions ensured increasing familiarity at editor level with the help of the divisional accountants. Elsewhere the mechanisms for learning from past successes or mistakes did emerge but did not develop over the longer term so much as at Longman. In 1979, the need was identified for 'post-mortem' forms to be completed for each book. This way there was less chance of failed projects being left unrecorded or taken-for-granted.

Challenges to these operating assumptions came inadvertently through the merger with RKP and Croom Helm in 1986. The need to integrate the two organizations into the academic division provided an opportunity for the staff to reassess their preferred ways of working. In the words of an editor of the Methuen academic list the coordination of the publishing process on her list was the responsibility of the production manager:

> who spends most of her life working out how to knit these things together for better or for worse. It was really highlighted when we started to acquire other companies which caused us to reflect on how they did it and how you did it and what was the best way to make a path through these.

Common Themes

Although from very different sectors, Jaguar and ABP provide similar evidence of the contradictions between current HRM rhetoric and everyday practice. That evidence appears in a number of forms.

First, it is noticeable how both companies could not hope to link strategic thinking with human resource planning. Strategic management itself was simply absent before the 1980s, as in many UK firms. The depth of analysis of the competitive forces in both industries in the UK was at best uneven and at worst shallow. The claim that UK firms are well positioned to adopt something called 'strategic human resource management' looks decidedly suspect (Hendry et al., 1989). Secondly, both organizations had barely developed, even by the end of the 1970s, what commentators now call a personnel management approach. A reactive, less structured stance was the natural response to the highly unstable environment of the UK and the relative absence of a mature management science, of the type at least found in the USA.

Thirdly, where attempts were made to improve business performance through alterations in the way people were managed, they proved to be fragile, unstable and highly difficult to sustain. The generation of a learning capacity was a case in point.

Learning is seen here as not just the acquisition of new knowledge by the individual. Rather it refers to how those within firms collectively change their knowledge, values and shared mental models of their company and its markets, as Jaguar showed in the early 1980s. Learning goes way beyond training, embracing structural adjustment, the use of experimentation, the development of new language and the reshaping of values. Learning seen as a spiral process is useful, moving through cycles of observation, reflection, hypothesizing, experimentation, action. Knowledge then has to be codified and diffused within the organization and entrenched knowledge and beliefs broken down (Hedberg, 1981). The spiral metaphor allows for movement both up and down and even blockages to the process which may produce immobility or even regression, as in the case of ABP. The relation between such learning and strategy formation and implementation is reciprocal. As the Jaguar and ABP examples show, it is the ability to shed outmoded knowledge, techniques and beliefs as well as to learn and deploy new ones which enables firms to carry out strategies.

Just this one area of the human resource management approach highlights both the limitations yet ultimate potential for HRM in the UK and European context. As Jaguar and ABP show, the need is for more understanding of such unpredictable, iterative processes of learning by doing. Organizations will continuously attempt to comprehend their fundamentally altered environments in the 1990s and create appropriate styles of managing their people. Academics and practitioners alike therefore, will have the chance to create a more robust intellectual and practical model of HRM (cf. Lloyd and Sveiby, 1989; Pucik, 1988).

Conclusion

The main findings of this chapter are two-fold: one concerns the way human resource management, strategy and competition are conceived; the other, the way they may be understood in practice.

Competition is, above all, a process not a state. That process is informed by the combined social and economic character of given markets as well as the often intensely subjective perceptions of those involved. Equally, the processes by which strategic changes occur rarely conform to the pattern of analysis, choice and execution beloved of Industrial Organization economists. The process is often 'illogical', in their terms, given the interplay of chance, personal motives and political imperatives within the firm. Both competition and strategic management are highly volatile, creative processes which conventional structural-based thinking fails to capture. Nowhere is this more relevant than with regard to the management of people.

The hope that HRM can be easily linked to the competitive performance of a firm is illusory. In the UK at least there is a real danger that the HRM label is being applied to firms inaccurately. In practice, the disarray of the competitive process is mirrored by the fragility and impermanence of many HRM instruments. The social, political and educational forces of the competitive process are seldom susceptible to such control. The assumption that HRM can be easily linked to competitive performance is misplaced.

If simple notions of HRM as a direct means of achieving competitive success do not work at the conceptual level, then neither do they work in practice. An appreciation of the more European, critical tradition of the social relations of the workplace – a tradition which thrives on multidisciplinary approaches and tackles directly the richness of social, political and economic context (cf. Thompson, 1983) – makes one sceptical of the claims of much in the prescriptive North American HRM literature. In UK conditions, and especially in view of the emerging relations within the European trading block, to put such uncritical faith in a North American inspired model of HRM is unwise.

The experience of Jaguar cars in the 1980s is instructive. As with many UK manufacturing firms, Jaguar's inheritance was not rich in strategic analysis or even basic personnel techniques. Even in a company seen as one of the most adroit at escaping that inheritance, the unpredictability of the competitive process proved overwhelming. In the last three years of the 1980s, swift alterations in both demand and political expediency resulted in the company being taken over by Ford. In ABP at the same period, the injunctions of the HRM advocates to make personnel policies an integral part of strategic planning would have been equally implausible.

Care has been taken, however, not to reject the notion that human resources can contribute to competitive performance. Using the example of the knowledge base of an organization, it has been possible to show how a learning capacity can help to develop that base in the hope of matching changing competitive conditions. Yet at the same time it was pointed out, as with many HRM techniques, how difficult that is in practice. The range of actions necessary, the sensitivity of such techniques over time and hence the high level of uncertainty over their ultimate competitive significance was apparent. At both the conceptual and practitioner levels, the impact of human resources on competitive performance is highly conditional, indirect and often as unpredictable as the process of competition itself.

The creation of an HRM approach based on learning cannot occur overnight. What is involved is a much longer-term learning process which poses a series of questions for an organization. The route to such learning is made easier if a group of conditioning features is first introduced. This involves the raising of a general consciousness of the benefits of HRM in relation to the business needs of the firm. Enforced alterations in both business and people aspects of the organization can produce a receptive context for HRM change. Thereafter, the mechanisms for confirming such HRM initiatives are often discovered and exploited opportunistically. Such actions can be conducive to the survival of the initiatives. These acts include: the mobilizing of external influences which confirm the link between business needs and the means HRM can supply, through to the creation of linked institutions and structures which demonstrate the credibility of HRM policies (cf. Pettigrew and Whipp, 1991).

The role of knowledge is paramount in the way an HRM approach can help create competitive advantage. That knowledge has both technical and social components. What becomes critical is the extent to which a company's knowledge base matches changing competitive conditions through learning. Learning here is seen as not just the acquisition of new knowledge. It also relates to how those within a firm collectively change their values and shared mental models of their company and markets. Indeed it is the ability to shed outmoded knowledge, techniques and beliefs, as well as to learn and deploy new ones, which enables firms to carry out given strategies.

This chapter has revealed a number of tensions within the HRM field; such tensions are seen as productive. Indeed, the possibilities for both academics and practitioners alike are striking. At the conceptual level the opportunity exists for constructing frameworks of HRM which not only build on the more demanding notions of HRM and competitive strategy as an unpredictable yet immensely creative process, but which also harvest the growing crop of independent and critical empirical accounts of the way people are being managed in current circumstances. What is required, perhaps, is writing which attempts to capture such creativity within the process of HRM, as Handy (1989) has done in the area of organizational forms or Zuboff (1988) with respect to information technology and people. The task is momentous in its own right. Yet the results can be of timely practical benefit to those with the responsibility of managing people in the 'age of surprises' (*Fortune*, 1988) of the final years of the century.

References

Abernathy, A.J., Clark, K. and Kantrow, A. (1980) 'The new industrial competition', *Harvard Business Review*, September–October: 69–81.

Atkinson, J. and Meager, N. (1986) *Changing Patterns of Work*. London: NEDO.

Barney, J.B. (1986) 'Types of competition and the theory of strategy: towards an integrative framework', *Academy of Management Review*, 11 (4): 791–800.

Beer, M., Spector, B., Lawrence, P., Mills, Q. and Walton, R. (1984) *Managing Human Assets*. New York: Free Press.

Constable, J. and McCormick, R. (1987) *The Making of British Managers*. Corby: BIM.

Crafts, N. (1988) 'British economic growth before and after 1979: a review of the evidence', Centre for Economic Policy Research, London, *Discussion Paper 292*, November.

Curson, C. (ed.) (1986) *Flexible Patterns of Work*. London: IPM.

de Geus, A. (1988) 'Planning as learning', *Harvard Business Review*, March–April: 70–4.

Elbaum, B. and Lazonick, W. (1986) *The Decline of the British Economy*. Oxford: Clarendon Press.

Fortune (1988) 'Managing now for the 1990s', 26 September.

Guest, D. (1987) 'Human resource management and industrial relations', *Journal of Management Studies*, 24 (5): 503–21.

Guest, D. (1991) 'Personnel management: the end of orthodoxy?' *British Journal of Industrial Relations*, 29 (2): 149–76.

Hampden-Turner, C. and Baden-Fuller, C. (1989) 'Strategic choice and the management of dilemma', Centre for Business Strategy, *Working Paper no. 51*.

Handy, C. (1987) *The Making of Managers: A Report on Management Education, Training and Development in the United States, West Germany, France, Japan and the UK*. London: NEDO.

Handy, C. (1989) *The Age of Unreason*. London: Hutchinson.

Hedberg, B. (1981) 'How organizations learn and unlearn', in D. Nystrom and W. Starbuck (eds), *Handbook of Organizational Design, 1, Adapting Organizations to their Environments*. Oxford: Oxford University Press. pp. 3–27.

Hendry, C., Pettigrew, A.M. and Sparrow, P. (1989) 'Linking strategic change, competitive performance and human resource management: results of a UK empirical study', in R.M. Mansfield (ed.), *New frontiers of Management*. London: Routledge. pp. 195–220.

Hobsbawm, E. (1974) *Labouring Men*. London: Weidenfeld & Nicolson.

Hodgson, G. (1988) *Economics and Institutions*. Cambridge: Polity Press.

Hollingsworth, J.R. and Lindberg, L. (1985) 'The governance of the American economy: the role of markets, clans, hierarchies and associate behaviour', IMM, Wissenschaftszentrum Berlin.

Jelinek, M. (1979) *Institutionalizing Innovation: A Study of Organizational Learning Systems*. New York: Praeger.

Johnson, G. (1987) *Strategic Change and the Management Process*. Oxford: Basil Blackwell.

Langlois, R.N. (ed.) (1986) *Economics as a Process: Essays in the New Institutional Economics*. Cambridge: Cambridge University Press.

Lloyd, T. and Sveiby, E. (1989) *Managing Knowhow*. London: Bloomsbury.

Loasby, B. (1988) 'Long-range formal planning in perspective', in J.B. Quinn, H. Mintzberg and R.M. James (eds), *The Strategy Process*. Engelwood Cliffs, NJ: Prentice-Hall. pp. 89–94.

Lodge, G. and Vogel, E. (1987) *Ideology and National Competitiveness: An Analysis of Nine Countries*. Boston, MA.: Harvard Business School Press.

Marginson, P., Edwards, P., Martin, R., Purcell, J. and Sisson, K. (1988) *Beyond the Workplace: Managing Industrial Relations in the Multi-establishment Enterprise*. Oxford: Basil Blackwell.

Merkle, J. (1980) *Management and Ideology*. London: University of California Press.

Mintzberg, H. (1978) 'Patterns in strategy formation', *Management Science*, 24 (9): 934–48.

Nelson, R. and Winter, S. (1982) *An Evolutionary Theory of Economic Change*. Cambridge, MA.: Harvard University Press.

Pascale, R. (1990) *Managing on the Edge*. London: Viking.

Peters, T.J. and Waterman, R.H. (1982) *In Search of Excellence: Lessons from America's Best-run Companies*. New York: Harper & Row.

Pettigrew, A. and Whipp, R. (1991) *Managing Change for Competitive Success*. Oxford: Basil Blackwell.

Porter, M. (1980) *Competitive Strategy*. New York: Free Press.

Porter, M. (1981) 'The contributions of industrial organisations to strategic management', *Academy of Management Review*, 6 (4): 609–20.

Porter, M. (1985) *Competitive Advantage: Creating and Sustaining Superior Performance*. New York: Free Press.

Pucik, V. (1988) 'Strategic alliances, organisational learning and competitive advantage: the HRM agenda', *Human Resource Management*, 27 (1): 77–93.

Quinn, J.B. (1988) 'Managing strategies incrementally', in J.B. Quinn, H. Mintzberg and R.M. James (eds), *The Strategy Process: Concepts, Contexts and Cases*. Englewood Cliffs, NJ: Prentice Hall. pp. 671–78.

Rasanen, K. (1989) 'Sectoral roots and strategic change: the case of Finnish corporations: 1973–1985', Paper presented to the 9th EGOS Colloquium, July, WZB Berlin.

Romme, G.L. (1989) 'The dialectics of closing and opening in strategy formation', Paper presented to the Workshop on 'Making History/Breaking History', EIASM, Leuven.

Schumpeter, J.A. (1950) *Capitalism, Socialism, and Democracy*, 3rd edn. New York: Harper.

Sisson, K. (ed.) (1989) *Personnel Management in Britain*. Oxford: Basil Blackwell.

Thompson, P. (1983) *The Nature of Work*. London: Macmillan.

Van de Ven, A. (1986) 'Central problems in the management of innovation', *Management Science*, 22 (5): 590–607.

Walton, R. (1987) *Innovating to Compete: Lessons for Diffusing and Managing Change in the Workplace*. San Francisco: Jossey-Bass.

Weick, K. E. (1987) 'Substitutes for corporate strategy', in D.J. Teece (ed.), *The Competitive Challenge: Strategies for Industrial Innovation and Renewal*. Cambridge, MA.: Ballinger. pp. 221–34.

Whipp, R. (1987) 'A time to every purpose: an essay on time and work', in P. Joyce (ed.), *The Historical Meanings of Work*. Cambridge: Cambridge University Press. pp. 210–36.

Whipp, R. (1988) 'Work and social consciousness', *Past and Present*, 119, May: 132–57.

Whipp, R. (1990a) *Patterns of Labour: Work and Social Change in the Pottery Industry*. London: Routledge.

Whipp, R. (1990b) 'Managing technological changes: opportunities and pitfalls', in M.A. Dorgham (ed.), *International Technology Management*. Geneva: Inderscience. pp. 90–108.

Whipp, R. and Clark, C. (1986) *Innovation and the Auto Industry: Product, Process and Work Organisation*. London: Frances Pinter.

Whipp, R., Rosenfeld, R. and Pettigrew, A.M. (1989) 'Culture and competitiveness: evidence from mature UK industries', *Journal of Management Studies*, 26 (6): 561–86.

Winter, S. (1987) 'Knowledge and competence as strategic assets', in D.J. Teece (ed.), *The Competitive Challenge: Strategies for Industrial Innovation and Renewal*. Cambridge, MA.: Ballinger. pp. 159–84.

Zuboff, S. (1988) *In the Age of the Smart Machine: The Future of Work and Power*. New York: Basic Books.

4   HUMAN RESOURCE MAXIMIZATION: THE MANAGEMENT OF LABOUR UNDER JUST-IN-TIME MANUFACTURING SYSTEMS

Rick Delbridge and Peter Turnbull

The emergence of Human Resource Management (HRM) in the 1980s, and the growth of a new vocabulary of 'people management', has coincided with the emergence of Japan as the leading industrial nation in the world economy. Alongside the 'excellence' movement (Peters and Waterman, 1982), a major impetus to the development of HRM in North America has been the crisis of American management brought on by its failure in the face of Japanese competition (Hendry and Pettigrew, 1990: 18), as illustrated by the flood of Japanese imports in the 1970s and a wave of direct Japanese investment in the 1980s in the face of US protectionism. Britain has experienced a similar process, albeit with a time-lag, and discussion of the 'Japanization' of British industry is now commonplace (see Oliver and Wilkinson, 1988).

In addition to the spur of market competition, Japanese companies have played a more direct role in the emergence of HRM as 'role models' for the West, a new 'Type J' organization characterized by extraordinary levels of worker commitment, effort and, above all, company loyalty. As Keenoy (1991: 376) notes: 'Japanese companies, alongside IBM, provide the model for "traditional HRM".' Thus, in contrast to the (often fruitless) search for companies that practise HRM in Britain and North America, recourse can always be made to 'best practice' among Japanese competitors (for example, Alston, 1986; Guest, 1987: 518; Ouchi, 1981; Townley, 1989: 100). While the now familiar maxim 'People are the company's most important asset' is often little more than an empty cliché in the West, for the Japanese corporation it appears to be a fundamental operating principle. For example, a recent report by the Japan Institute of Labour identified human resources development as being the greatest concern of Japanese management (over 85 per cent of the respondents cited it as a key issue), ranking above the reinforcement of marketing and sales operations, the creation of new products and services, and the introduction of new technology, equipment and machinery (see Amaya, 1990). Developing human resources was also identified as the most pressing concern for the future. More importantly in the context of HRM, the Japanese 'commitment to people' is *strategically integrated* with the overall business objectives of the organization:

> the Japanese commit more than lip service to their concern for human resources. *They back it up with a well-integrated system of strategies and techniques that translate ideology into reality.* (Robbins, 1983: 68, emphasis added)

The aim of this chapter is therefore to explore 'Japanese-style' HRM in more detail and to evaluate the extent to which this provides a 'blueprint' for Western companies. The objectives of Japanese personnel policies were identified by Thurley (1982: 38) as being performance, motivation, flexibility and mobility, secured through an array of complementary policies such as self-appraisal and feedback, consultation, status/grading progress, organizational bonuses, job rotation and retraining, transfer policies, self-education, organizational redesign and even company housing. To this list could be added quality circles, single status, company uniforms and the morning work-out complete with company song.[1] In short, the Japanese corporation appears to embrace all the essential policy goals of HRM identified by Guest (1987) and others, namely high levels of commitment and quality, flexibility and strategic integration, and these objectives are bound together with a very strong 'cement' in the form of an all-embracing organizational culture. Moreover, as the Japanese company hires 'the whole person' (Naylor, 1984: 34–5) and develops each individual through its 'humane' HR strategy, the approach is represented as being employee-centred, with the emphasis on 'human resources' and the utilization of individual talents resonant of McGregor's Theory Y. Indeed, Pascale and Athos (1982: 192–3) have taken the Japanese model to argue that companies should lay claim to more than workers' 'mind and muscle', that they should intrude upon their personal lives and deeper beliefs.

However, during the early 1980s in particular, emulation of Japanese-style HRM practices on a piecemeal or *ad hoc* basis produced only limited results, as the experience of many Western companies with quality circles clearly testifies (Bradley and Hill, 1987; Dale and Lees, 1986; McGraw and Dunford, 1987). What was often overlooked was the 'strategic link' or 'fit' between HRM policies and a particular system of manufacturing, namely just-in-time (JIT). Japanese-style HRM practices did not arise in a vacuum, nor were they concerned with worker emancipation. Rather they were the essential 'software' needed to support the 'hardware' of JIT.

When analysed in this context a contradiction emerges between the rhetoric of JIT and the reality of work under such regimes. Evidence from both Britain and America suggests that the experience of work under a JIT system involves work intensification, very little autonomy for the individual, a more complete system of management control and a concomitant decline in trade union (and worker) bargaining power. Team working, job rotation and flexibility are not the means of releasing the untapped reserves of 'human resourcefulness' by increasing employee commitment, participation and involvement, as the 'soft' versions of HRM suggest (Keenoy, 1990: 3). Rather they are the tools of work intensification and heightened management control. The emphasis is almost exclusively on the *management*, or more precisely the *maximization*, of human resources, involving an instrumental approach which is coherently integrated into corporate business strategy. As the following section demonstrates, this is not so much a question of choice as necessity, since the JIT system increases the dependency of management on the workforce by removing all elements of slack or waste in the system. It therefore requires a more systematic approach to the (conflict-free) management of labour in order to avoid potential disruption. However, an elaboration of the JIT system illustrates that HRM is invariably of the 'hard' variety identified by Guest (1989), and as such involves a unitarist style of management with a diminution of worker control and autonomy.

Just-in-Time and HRM – The Strategic Link

The superior efficiency of JIT over conventional (Western) methods of production is now widely recognized and well documented. In the motor industry, for example, the birthplace of JIT, the comparison between Japanese assemblers and their North American and European competitors is startling. The average assembly time per vehicle of Japanese motor manufacturers in Japan is less than seventeen hours compared with over twenty-five hours for North American manufacturers and over thirty-six hours for European assemblers. Similar differences apply to quality, the utilization of factory space and inventory levels (Womack et al., 1990: 92). Unsurprisingly, JIT is increasingly associated with 'best practice' in manufacturing as a whole, as the *Management Today* review of 'Britain's Best Factories' over the past three years aptly illustrates (Caulkin, 1988, 1990; Ferguson, 1989). Of the sixteen companies identified as 'Britain's Best', ten operated a JIT system and all sixteen had some form of Total Quality system in operation.[2] Total Quality Management (TQM) is essential for the effective utilization of JIT as any defective units, in the absence of stocks, would bring production to an immediate halt, although clearly not all companies that apply TQM operate on a JIT basis. Nonetheless, for many firms the question appears no longer to be *whether* to introduce JIT, but *how*. The adoption of these systems is seen as an imperative to survival (Womack et al., 1990).

JIT is basically aimed at securing time economies in the circuit of capital and new ways of extracting productivity improvements from the labour force (Turnbull, 1988: 8). Throughput is increased by eradicating waste and increasing the quality of output, such that the exact quantity of (defect free) goods are produced just-in-time for sale in the market; sub-assemblies are produced just-in-time for final assembly; and bought-out parts and materials arrive from outside suppliers just-in-time to be made into sub-assemblies. In short, production is *pulled* through the factory in accordance with the configuration of final market demand, and every stage of the production process is geared 'to produce instantaneously, with perfect quality and minimum waste' (Bicheno, 1987: 192).

The techniques of JIT have been described in great detail (for example, Monden, 1983; Schonberger, 1982) and include the minimization of inventory levels with a reliance on demand pulling products through the system rather than production pushing them; a total quality drive toward zero defects in order to prevent waste; the reduction of set-up times to improve flow and responsiveness to the market; standardization of work tasks to eliminate uncertainty in the manufacturing process; a drive for continuous improvement that relies heavily on employee input; and the organization of production into teams, frequently through the reorganization of the plant layout into 'manufacturing cells' based on 'group' rather than 'functional' technology. Clearly, many of the HRM 'software' techniques are subsumed under the 'hardware' of the manufacturing system itself, such as teamworking (cellular manufacture or group technology) and employee involvement (continuous productivity improvement and zero defects). The strategic integration of HRM is in fact a precondition of the JIT system.

JIT is a very fragile production system, highly susceptible to the quality of output, the accuracy of scheduling, the efficiency and reliability of equipment and, above all, the efficiency and input of the workforce. As already noted, the absence of stocks means that any defective parts bring production to a halt (hence the need for TQM), as would any breakdown of machinery (hence the preference for preventative maintenance performed on line by production workers). Employee flexibility and the willingness of employees to respond to the requirements of the production process become paramount, as the conception and execution of work tasks are apparently 'rejoined' and responsibility moved down to the shopfloor. Thus, just as conventional (mass) production has been laid to rest by the new 'lean production' of the Japanese, so-called because it uses less of everything, including labour, so too has the old Fordist dictum that 'What workers want is more money, what they need is tight supervision.' According to Womack et al. (1990), 'lean production' not only recognizes the potential input of shopfloor workers, it is actually *dependent* on their contribution if the system is to operate smoothly and ever more efficiently. Consequently, the workers are not just rewarded financially but are provided 'with the skills they need to control their work environment' (1990: 101). It is this image of the future, of the factory 'populated almost entirely by highly skilled problem solvers whose task will be to think continually of ways to make the system run more smoothly and productively' (1990: 102), that appeals to both production engineers and human resource managers. This view of JIT, or lean production, is clearly a 'positive-sum' scenario, as what is good for the company is good for the workforce. This satisfies yet another precondition for 'successful HRM' (Guest, 1987: 512).

Unfortunately the rhetoric and reality could not be more incongruous. The management of labour under a JIT regime is based squarely on compliance, blame and stress, producing an oppressive working environment accessible only to the young and/or the fit. Moreover, the system is dependent on some variant of enterprise (or non-) unionism, and contingent on superimposing collaborative goals over the distinct interests of workers (Clarke, 1990; Robertson et al., 1991). Conformity with the goals of the organization takes precedence over any form of worker emancipation or industrial democracy (management through compliance); apparently high-trust employment relations are contradicted by tight surveillance, strict discipline and quality control procedures which seek to identify (and often publicly humiliate) the 'guilty' worker (management through blame); and the extreme standardization of jobs, with no individual variation, belies any notion of worker empowerment or multi-skilling as work is continually intensified (management by stress).

Human Resource Maximization

Shortly after Nissan announced its intention to manufacture cars at Washington (north east England) in 1985, the secret of Japan's success, the so-called 'Japanese tripod' of teamwork, quality consciousness and flexibility, was revealed to the human resource managers of Britain through the pages of *Personnel Management*. According to the new Personnel Director of Nissan Motor Manufacturing UK, workers at Nissan regard themselves as part of the team (and company), quality is emphasized in actual work, and the employee's genuine involvement in the company through teamworking and quality leads naturally to flexibility, the third leg of the tripod (Wickens, 1985). The result, according to the company, has been to create a 'harmonious and productive working environment' (*Guardian*, 8 September 1987). However, the link between harmony and productivity is brought into question on two different, but inter-related counts. First, although distinctive production methods and workforce skills have been clearly linked to productivity in Japan, no such link is evident for loyalty, commitment or even 'corporate culture' (Dunphy, 1986). Nor do Japanese HRM policies generate higher levels of worker satisfaction (Briggs, 1988; Dunphy, 1986). Second, and relatedly, the key role of HRM as a strategically integrated sub-system of JIT is to make workers feel *obliged* to contribute to the economic performance of the organization and to identify with its competitive success, and to do so predominantly by means of coercion (Delbridge et al., 1991). The 'tripod of success' is more appropriately labelled a 'tripod of subjugation', as there is far more to Japanese-style HRM practice than simply teamwork, quality consciousness and flexibility.

Teamwork – Management Through Compliance

The Japanese put great store by working as a group and achieving *wa* – group harmony and consensus. Work itself is organized around groups rather than individuals such that the unit of production is generally 'the team', a group based on a 'manufacturing cell' within which workers are responsible for actual products rather than a single process. It is essential for JIT production that these groups work efficiently and without disruption, and to this end Japanese firms spend considerable time, effort and money on recruitment, induction and 'socialization', the essence of which is to achieve conformity throughout the workforce. The team itself then takes over in the management of compliance, with the key role assigned to the team leader.

The easiest way to get a compliant workforce is to recruit one.[3] At the Mazda plant in Flat Rock, Michigan, for example, applicants underwent a five-stage series of tests before formally being offered a job. The recruitment procedure consisted of an application form, written aptitude tests, personal interviews, a group problem-solving assessment, and simulated work exercises over a period of many weeks (Fucini and Fucini, 1990: 50–6). The process of weeding out 'druggies, rowdies and unionists' is typical of Japanese firms elsewhere, and invariably results in a 'green' workforce to match the site of the plant. The end result of the recruitment process at Flat Rock was a young workforce (average age 31 years old), a very inexperienced workforce (70 per cent with no previous factory experience of any kind) and a male-dominated workforce (over 70 per cent). More generally, the emphasis is on *behavioural traits* rather than technical competence (Townley, 1989: 95–6; White and Trevor, 1983: 103, 124), as the Personnel Director of Komatsu in north east England made clear: 'Our approach to recruitment has been specific and rigorous. We haven't necessarily taken on the most skilled people, but the ones who have the right attitude to team working and flexibility' (quoted in Gabb, 1988: 78–9).

Once selection has taken place the company embarks upon the socialization of its new recruits. At a Japanese TV manufacturer in Britain, for example: 'Key British production personnel initially are exposed to manufacturing operations in Japan and finally return as converts. They not only spread the word, they show modelled behaviour patterns' (Reitsperger, 1986a: 79). 'Intensive induction', as Alston (1986: 168) puts it, is intended 'to develop them into loyal employees', with initial training dominated by 'personality development' and attempts to inculcate the company's history and purpose. The objective is to 'fuse' the individual and the company by imposing collaborative (company) goals over the distinct interests of workers. The result, as Nakane (1970) notes, is that 'in most cases the company provides the whole social existence of a person, and has authority over all aspects of his life'.[4]

The standardization of the workforce continues on the line through the day-to-day experiences of teamworking. These teams, as Buchanan (1987) points out, are fundamentally different from the autonomous work groups espoused in the 1960s and 1970s. Rather than 'stand alone' autonomous groups, Japanese work teams are fully integrated, and are an integral part of the JIT system, and as such the problems the team addresses are technological and strategic rather than moral and operational (Buchanan, 1987). The end result is a loss of autonomy as any changes to the production process must be agreed by the team and senior management *before* they are introduced. The Mazda training manual, for example, states that:

> For all work we perform in the workshop, a work procedure sheet has been provided . . . If the operator changes the work procedure at his discretion, he may put the process before and after that process in jeopardy, or increase the cost . . . Therefore *the operator should always observe the specified work procedure faithfully*. If you have any doubts, you may propose a change to the team leader and should *never change the work procedure at your discretion*. (T&GWU, 1989, original emphasis)

Effectively, then, collective autonomy is limited to task *design* as opposed to task *execution* (Klein, 1991), demonstrating that it is only in defining the question or problem that Japanese management seek to obtain consensus (MacMillan, 1985). Thus, once a suggestion is made, implementation is at *management's* discretion, and only those changes that improve efficiency and flow are adopted. The net result is the standardization of work tasks through 'team consensus', which reduces all work in the factory to 'routine variety' (Robertson et al., 1991). Suggestions on health and safety or 'humanizing' the workplace are more often ignored (Fucini and Fucini, 1990).

If teamworking under a JIT system involves a loss of control over the work process rather than worker autonomy, and leads to conformity with standardized work tasks rather than individual initiative, why do workers participate in such a system? A frequent explanation is 'life-time employment' and seniority-based payment systems which 'tie' the worker to the firm and produce a virtually closed internal labour market and very limited inter-firm mobility (for example, Briggs, 1988). But the structure and organization of work teams, and the inter-personal relations that develop within them, also play a crucial role. The former can be illustrated in the case of Iveco-Ford, a UK truck manufacturer which recently introduced a new supervisory structure to replace the old foreman system. Management recognized that 'people on the shopfloor had a detailed knowledge of the operation and we want to tap into this in a co-ordinated way' (T&GWU, 1989). To achieve this a new 'Coordinator' position was introduced to bridge the role of foreman and hourly paid operatives, with each Coordinator (team leader) responsible for volume, quality, minor maintenance, operator training, process checks, allocating jobs at the start of each shift and reporting on lateness, sickness and absenteeism. Team leaders become the 'eyes and ears' of management on the shopfloor and provide a direct means of communication with the workforce. The aim is to keep the teams small (one Coordinator for every ten shopfloor workers at Iveco-Ford for example) so that they develop their own identity and pull together to solve problems – management's problems (Labour Research, 1989: 8). At Iveco-Ford, as at many other companies, this form of work organization is seen as a direct challenge to independent trade unionism, by-passing the more usual channels of communication and reinforcing 'the company message' (see also Martinez Lucio and Weston, Chapter 13, this volume). As Nissan managers are keen to point out, 'He who communicates is King' (Smith, 1990: 10; Wickens, 1987), and team leaders become the 'King-pins' of each team (and in the process oust the shop steward, the 'lynch-pin' of the trade union). Control is thereby returned to the line, as Guest (1987: 512) and other proponents of HRM recommend, but the effect of team leaders is to wrest collective autonomy from the group. In reality, decisions are effectively dictated by the next 'customer' in the supply chain or defined by management (for example quality standards).

Equally important is the fact that by organizing workers into teams and making these teams accountable for their own performance, firms operating a JIT system are able to impose a 'customer ethos' on the workforce and harness the peer pressure of fellow team members to ensure compliance with company objectives. As the *Financial Times* (7 September 1985) pointed out, teamworking has become the new 'Holy Grail of management: the replacement of class struggle with the struggle for markets. No longer us workers against them management, but us Company X against them Company Y people.' To this end, in becoming a member of the 'corporate family' the employee must accept an invasion of his or her private life as the distinction between personal time and company time becomes blurred. Mazda workers in America, for example, are told that if a neighbour is having trouble with a Mazda car they are to apologize on behalf of 'their' company and try to solve the problem. Even inside the factory there is the motivation to meet the requirements of downstream 'customers' on the shopfloor. Any failure to supply the 'customer' just-in-time with perfect quality goods is noticed immediately in the absence of buffer stocks and brings an immediate response. Thus the objective is not simply to illustrate to the worker that he/she has 'let down' a fellow team member, but to bring peer pressure to bear *within* the team, as a team leader at a UK engineering firm explains:

> he makes his endshield and passes it on to the next bloke who's got to put the screws in and he says 'You stupid bastard it's got no bloody thread in there' . . . the final assembly of the whole product is within 50 yards of him. So he's immediately going to go over there and give him a bollocking. (quoted in Oliver and Davies, 1990: 562–3)

The pressure of one's peers extends to other aspects of work such as attendance, as there is often no cover for absentees under a JIT system and other team members (or the team leader) must cover for the absent worker. A list of absentees, and their reasons for absence, is frequently posted in a prominent position on the shopfloor to bring further pressure to bear in what has been described as 'an intensive ideological campaign' by management to illustrate to all employees how fellow team members are 'hurt by absenteeism' (Parker and Slaughter, 1988: 106). Even where the pressure on employees to attend work is matched by a 'paternalistic concern' for their welfare while off work sick, as at a Japanese TV manufacturer in the UK which sent employees flowers and insisted on visits by the employee's supervisor, these policies were implemented to 'hasten recovery' and ultimately reduce absenteeism. In other words, 'when they are thought to improve productivity and quality performance' (Reitsperger, 1986b: 577).[5] In sum, team work facilitates management's ownership of the workforce, both mind and body, and this invasion of the worker's psychological space tends to blur the distinction between voluntary and mandatory behaviour. The imposition of compliance through market relations (the customer ethos) and peer group pressure is nowhere more prevalent than in respect to quality control.

Quality Consciousness – Management Through Blame

Under a JIT system, the objective is to build quality into the *process* rather than simply inspect the quality of the *product*. This involves devolving responsibility for quality to the direct operators, with the consequent elimination of quality inspectors at the end of the process. Each team is expected to assume 'ownership' of the product(s) it produces, and each individual team member 'owns' the process(es) on which he or she works. Unsurprisingly, quality (and HRM) texts talk of worker 'empowerment' under TQM, and the image is one of high-trust employment relations. Again, reality is somewhat different (see also Sewell and Wilkinson, Chapter 6, this volume).

With no 'buffers' of any kind in the production process, either physical (for example, stocks) or temporal (for example, generous lead- or set-up times), uncertainty becomes ever more pronounced. In the West, managers have *accommodated* uncertainty through buffers, 'just-in-case' something goes wrong, whereas under a JIT system the task of management is *the elimination of uncertainty itself*. Standardization of the work process thus becomes essential, and this applies especially to quality control. With Statistical Process Control (SPC), for example, work itself is plotted on a graph, such that if the process exceeds upper or lower limits, or even shows signs of exceeding those limits, corrective action can be taken – *but always in accordance with prescribed problem-solving methods*. If anything, SPC tends to structure experimentation and therefore *reduces* the worker's freedom to make process changes. For the workers, then, the result is a feeling of 'low trust' (Klein, 1989: 64) and considerable stress. As Dawson and Webb (1989: 230) point out, this stress arises from: 'the responsibility for solving production faults, while watching the "daily rate" production targets slip further behind. There is also a paradoxical pressure concerning the appearance of "not working" while engaged in such attempts to fix the process.'

As quality is measured and monitored continually, problems can be traced to a particular team and even specific individuals. At one Japanese plant in Britain a combination of visual and electronic tests are used to identify faults which can be (and are) traced back to the 'culprit' on the line. Every defect attributable to an individual results in a speedy up-date of performance charts hanging above the operator's head, at the end of the line, and in the canteen. A 'black mark' for quality (which is how such faults are displayed) results in material penalties and ultimately the sack, in addition to a 'dressing down' from the team leader or production manager in front of other team members (Sewell and Wilkinson, 1991). It is hardly surprising, then, that workers automatically check all the parts they receive, 'knowing that any defects from their operations will be spotted and ultimately – and embarrassingly – traced to them' (Hayes, 1981: 62). Quality control is therefore not used simply to improve product quality, but to discipline the workforce. Quality charts in particular are part and parcel of a more extensive system of surveillance and monitoring which is used to ensure compliance (Delbridge et al., 1991).

The basis of quality control is therefore *management through blame*. As Shimizu argues, workers are encouraged to participate in the process of surveillance and to identify 'worthless, parasitical and superfluous persons (oneself included)' (quoted in Dohse et al., 1985: 127). At Nissan UK, for example, the company has a 'Vehicle Evaluation System' and a 'Neighbour Watch Scheme', described by Nissan managers themselves as a system of 'employee peer surveillance', which make it possible to trace faults to individuals. These 'faults' are exposed in quality circles, where small groups of around ten workers sit in a circle and where, as one worker described, 'if you'd done anything wrong you got put in the middle and shouted at' (quoted in Garrahan and Stewart, 1989). It is hardly surprising that many workers' experience of quality circles or suggestion schemes is one of 'information and control' rather than participation (for example, Taylor et al., 1991), or that workers 'participate' in such activities as a means of survival rather than out of any feelings of 'team spirit' or 'company loyalty'. But as such 'involvement' entails disciplining others by pointing out faults, 'a whole system of self-subordination begins to develop' (Garrahan and Stewart, 1989). In some Japanese corporations management has even set up internal 'spy rings' in which employees spy on each other (both during and outside working hours) and report any 'deviant' behaviour (Yamamoto, 1990).

The 'involvement' and 'participation' of workers in a JIT system is therefore not only closely prescribed but tightly controlled. *Responsibility* is devolved to the shopfloor *but not control*, which remains highly centralized in the hands of management. Employees are only required to participate in incremental improvements to product quality and process efficiency, which simply incorporates workers in the projects of capital without extending any real control or collective autonomy to the workforce (see Dawson and Webb, 1989: 236). As Schonberger (1982: 193), a leading exponent of JIT has argued: 'the Japanese out-Taylor us all – including putting Taylor to good use in QC-Circles or small group involvement activities'. Whereas Taylor (1947) sought to eliminate 'systematic soldiering', under JIT the objective is to eliminate 'waste', defined as all activities that add cost but not value to the finished product.

Flexibility – Management by Stress

When Nissan began manufacturing cars at Washington, the Saatchi and Saatchi advertising campaign declared, 'They don't half work.' Shortly after, workers were reported to have quit the company because of the frenetic work pace, which appears not to have slackened (*The Engineer*, 18 February 1988). In fact, because the JIT system is underwritten by *kaizen* (continuous improvement), whereby all elements of 'waste' are systematically and progressively eliminated, the work routine is continually intensified. Initially, all elements of 'pure waste' are eradicated, such as waiting time, stacking work-in-progress and non-value added operations such as walking any distance to collect tools or even shifting a tool from one hand to another.[6] The focus then shifts to increasing the net (value adding) operations performed by each worker, which is where flexibility enters the picture. Work is now *operator-paced* rather than machine-paced, which removes any 'free time' the worker may have previously enjoyed while the machine ran through its cycle. With flexible working and multi-machine manning, or operator time set to coincide exactly with cycle time, the worker must hasten from one task to the next. At the Mazda plant in Flat Rock, jobs require fifty-seven seconds of motion every minute, often for nine or ten hours a day (Fucini and Fucini, 1990: 148–53). Again, the purpose or outcome is not to enrich the job but to maximize the output of human resources.

The key to flexibility under a JIT system is in fact standardization, which allows *no* individual variation. The training manual of CAMI, for example, a joint venture between GM and Suzuki in Canada, declares: 'The standardized operation shows the best method of performing every operation in a process which any associate must strictly observe in doing the job' (quoted in Robertson et al., 1991). In other words, the aim is to eliminate *all* variation within production, and then to enforce strict adherence to the procedure. Every operative must perform the job in exactly the same way, and it becomes 'necessary to have machines that even a newly hired, unskilled labourer will be able to become fully proficient on within three days' (Monden, 1983: 58). Assembly work is therefore routinized, with each job broken into small components and each task performed within a very short cycle time. When combined with flexibility and job rotation this produces a work pattern characterized by routine variety, such that while jobs are not homogenized, the abilities of the workers are. Each multi-*task* worker is now interchangeable, and none is irreplaceable.

The aim of standardization (the 'one best way'), however, is to facilitate *kaizen* ('is there a better way?'), whereby:

> employees are not merely encouraged but *expected* to identify process problems, intervene in production to rectify them and suggest changes in the organization of production to prevent their recurrence. Far from simply improving the quality of working life, this widening of responsibility creates extra stress. (Dawson and Webb, 1989: 236)

JIT has consequently been labelled 'crisis management' (Domingo, 1985) and more appropriately 'management by stress' (Parker and Slaughter, 1988). As a manager at a US engine plant that has recently switched to a JIT system noted: 'It is not [any longer] a 30-day time span, it is a 3-minute time span . . . they have targets every day. It used to be that you could loaf a little bit, and other days you knew you were under the gun. Now you're under the gun all the time' (Klein, 1989: 64). Or, as a worker at Lucas Electrical, a UK automotive components manufacturer, put it, 'the rhythm of work is so constant. We now work flat out all the time, rather than when we want to.' The loss of collective and even individual control over the work process, combined with 'flexible work intensification', produces high levels of stress, which is heightened by the visibility of daily production targets displayed on light boards which 'count down' during the shift, reinforced by bar charts which display individual performance task-by-task, and monitored in some factories by photoelectric cells and floor mat censors to ensure that workers comply exactly to management instructions (Monden, 1983).

Management by stress is clearly heightened by such 'visibility' and 'accountability', and is compounded by the use of peer pressure to achieve conformity. Individual workers become isolated and experience feelings of distrust and fear, even towards fellow workers: 'Today some [Japanese] transplant workers complain that there is no one to take their side. Everyone in the new transplant organization seems to be "they", both fellow workers and union representatives' (Rehder, 1990: 91). At NUMMI, the General Motors/Toyota joint-venture in California, workers complain that: 'You can't trust the person working next to you. You want to put your confidence in them, but then they'll turn you in' (assembly worker, quoted in Parker and Slaughter, 1988: 222).

As many observers have noted, if there is a flaw in the JIT system, then it is 'the toll exacted from workers in company plants and suppliers' (Cusumano, 1985: 305). Workers are not only expected to work as fast as they can wherever they can, but in the words of an Iveco-Ford shop steward are 'expected to apply the whip to their own backs', with the Coordinator there 'to help them along' (T&GWU, 1989). Workers at CAMI in Canada have found that once they '*kaizen*-out' a job, they then find themselves overworked, as management find it very easy to fill up the time the workers have saved with 'their' improvements (Robertson et al., 1991). Yet another misconception of Japanese-style HRM can thus be laid to rest. As Dohse et al. (1985: 128) point out, JIT is 'not an alternative to Taylorism but rather a solution to its classic problem of the resistance of workers to placing their knowledge of production in the service of rationalization'.

Conclusions

As has been demonstrated, the HRM practices utilized to support and augment a JIT production system, which are increasingly identified with 'best practice' in the West, are clearly of a 'unitarist-instrumental' variety or what in Britain is simply referred to as 'hard' HRM. Such policies may be linked to economic efficiency and productivity but not to an improvement in the quality of working life for employees. In fact, the practices of teamwork, quality consciousness and flexibility which characterize such HRM strategies are in essence the means by which the workforce is controlled, through a mixture of stress, peer pressure, surveillance and accountability. Moreover, this style of HRM facilitates the regulation of work through the employment of a standardized workforce which is ultimately *forced* to conform to managerial requirements. The rhetoric may be of employee involvement, development and autonomy but the reality is workers operating under clearly defined (and dictated) managerial guidelines, under constant surveillance, and solving managerially defined problems without the time, resources or power to input developments which may qualitatively improve their work experience.

Increasingly, JIT production methods are equated with 'efficient' management production techniques which *must* be applied in Western companies if they are to remain competitive (for example, Womack et al., 1990). The adjective 'Japanese' thus creates an imperative for introducing changes in working practices (Graham, 1988: 73–4), whether those changes are linked to a JIT system or not. For the introduction of HRM in general (Guest, 1990), and JIT in particular (Holloway, 1987: 159), the most important factor has been the defeat or at least the 'taming' of organized labour. Even Taiichi Ohno, the founder of JIT, 'considered his success in controlling the union to have been the most important advantage Toyota gained over its domestic and foreign competitors' (Cusumano, 1985: 307).

Guest (1989) has argued that HRM is not necessarily anti-union. Of the four goals of HRM identified in an earlier paper, Guest (1989: 43–4) sees only flexibility and high commitment as potentially problematic for trade unions, the former being accentuated by the multi-union structure of many British firms and the latter presenting a challenge to the maintenance of 'dual allegiance' (to the company and the trade union). With JIT, however, the challenge to independent trade unionism runs much deeper, and the argument that workers no longer *need* collective representation is a dangerous justification for enterprise or non-unionism. The HRM practices associated with JIT challenge the very basis of trade union representation, communications and activity, through such developments and practices as company advisory boards for 'collective bargaining' and grievance handling, teamworking and the substitution of team leaders for shop stewards as the 'representative' of team members, and individual merit or reward systems which intensify peer pressure and individual competition and undermine group identification and collective solidarity.

The need for independent collective representation is increasingly recognized, and realized, by shopfloor workers themselves at Japanese transplants in Britain and North America, as evidenced by the emergence of (unofficial) shopfloor resistance (Fucini and Fucini, 1990), as is the challenge posed to trade unions by the adoption of JIT by indigenous manufacturers (Morris, 1991; T&GWU, 1989; Turnbull, 1988). In particular, although the 'Japanese Way' is setting new standards in quality and productivity, the resulting excessive human costs (Rehder, 1990: 97) are being challenged as unacceptable, even in Japan.[7] There is growing evidence that employees' health and safety is an early victim of the system. Repetitive strain injuries are one example of the human cost of JIT, with more serious injuries also more common (Beynon, 1984; Grunberg, 1986). The fact that workers may be (relatively) well paid, have single status, a company canteen, *inter alia*, does not negate the need for independent representation. It is often remarked that Japanese workers are tied to 'their' company by 'golden chains' (Muto, 1986), enjoying substantial benefits but unable to transfer to another company without the loss of earnings or other benefits (as they would automatically be placed at the bottom of the hierarchy). Thus, life-time employment can be more like a life-time sentence, or more accurately a 'prime working life' sentence. The pernicious nature of work under a JIT regime, with its high stress and few off-line indirect positions, means that workers invariably do not 'survive' as long in the factory environment. In Japan, older workers are often transferred to a subsidiary or customer company (with loss of earnings and benefits), a practice known as *amakudari* (literally 'descent from heaven'). Workers at companies such as Ford UK are now more likely to be 'spent-out' as they are forced to work longer on the line, with fewer opportunities for 'progress' to off-line jobs (Morris, 1991), and are now presented with the 'option' of voluntary early retirement at the age of 55 years. It is not uncommon for workers under a JIT system to offer this simple advice: 'Don't fall ill, don't grow old, and above all don't get tired.'

In contrast to Britain and North America, in countries where labour representation has been more difficult to displace, the utilization of human resources is more akin to a 'developmental humanism' and JIT has been explicitly rejected. At the Saab-Valmet plant in Finland, for example, buffers are not allowed to fall below twenty minutes of work because, as one manager put it, 'Scandinavian respect for the workers' quality of life requires that the worker have the ability to work quickly for a few minutes in order to take a small personal break without stopping the line' (quoted by Klein, 1989: 65). The 'social democratic' model of work organization, in which HRM is based on a humane development of human resources, is not incompatible with industrial efficiency. High-wage economies/industries with strong union representation can still compete in world markets if they make use of 'economies of scope' provided by new technology (and a workforce capable of using such technology) to produce high value, high quality products. Streeck (1987) has actually demonstrated that the institutionalized structure of trade unions and social democratic rights in countries such as Sweden and West Germany have both facilitated a strategic approach to corporate decision-making and have compelled firms to adopt more progressive (non-Taylorist) forms of work organization. The crucial choice is therefore between forms of work organization which extend and deepen democratic representation and economic efficiency, compared to those such as JIT where economic efficiency is premised on the restriction of worker autonomy, discretion and democratic representation.

Notes

1. Accounts such as these of Japanese-style HRM are based almost exclusively on the practices of large corporations. Life-time employment, company housing and the like are restricted to (core) members of the large corporations within a 'dual economy' in which a larger number of workers do not enjoy such 'benefits' (see Kendall, 1984).

2. The companies reviewed ranged from manufacturers of earth moving equipment and car components to manufacturers of computers, DIY electrical goods, TV sets, photocopiers and electrical distribution boards.

3. This principle is frequently extended to the recruitment of the most 'appropriate' trade union.

4. The male pronoun is empirically correct as the vast majority of 'core' workers employed by Japanese corporations are men.

5. Given the importance of regular attendance under JIT financial incentives are also brought to bear. Rover, for example, recently announced that productivity bonus schemes were to be progressively phased out in favour of a new bonus scheme related to the performance of the company as a whole, with qualification for the bonus being attendance related.

6. At one South Wales electronics plant owned by a Japanese multinational corporation, for example, a saving of 0.85 seconds on the standard time was achieved by removing the need for operators to turn around and bend down to pick up parts.

7. A recent circular from the Ministry of Labour in Japan warned companies not to enforce too strict an adherence to JIT because of the social and other costs involved. In particular, the Ministry has warned against excessive overtime.

References

Alston, J.P. (1986) *The American Samurai: Blending American and Japanese Managerial Practices*. New York: de Gruyter.
Amaya, T. (1990) *Recent Trends in Human Resource Development*. Tokyo: Japan Institute of Labour.
Beynon, H. (1984) *Working for Ford* (2nd edn). Harmondsworth: Penguin.
Bicheno, J. (1987) 'A framework for JIT implementation', in C. Voss (ed.), *Just-in-Time Manufacture*. London: IFS. pp. 191–204.
Bradley, K. and Hill, S. (1987) 'Quality circles and managerial interests', *Industrial Relations*, 26 (1): 68–82.
Briggs, P. (1988) 'The Japanese at work: illusions of the ideal', *Industrial Relations Journal*, 19 (1): 24–30.
Buchanan, D. (1987) 'Job enrichment is dead: long live high performance work design', *Personnel Management*, May: 40–3.
Caulkin, S. (1988) 'Britain's best factories', *Management Today*, September: 58–80.
Caulkin, S. (1990) 'Britain's best factories', *Management Today*, November: 60–89.
Clarke, S. (1990) 'The crisis of Fordism or the crisis of social democracy?' *Telos*, Spring: 71–98.
Cusumano, M.A. (1985) *The Japanese Automobile Industry*. Cambridge, MA: Harvard University Press.
Dale, B.G. and Lees, J. (1986) *The Development of Quality Circles*. Sheffield: Manpower Services Commission.
Dawson, P. and Webb, J. (1989) 'New production arrangements: the totally flexible cage?' *Work, Employment and Society*, 3 (2): 221–38.
Delbridge, R., Turnbull, P. and Wilkinson, B. (1991) 'Pushing back the frontiers: management control under JIT/TQM factory regimes', Paper presented to the 9th Annual Labour Process Conference, UMIST, April.
Dohse, K., Jurgens, U. and Malsch, T. (1985) 'From "Fordism" to "Toyotism"? The social organization of the labour process in the Japanese automobile industry', *Politics and Society*, 14 (2): 115–46.
Domingo, R. (1985) '"Kanban": crisis management Japanese style', *Euro-Asia Business Review*, 4 (3): 22–4.
Dunphy, D. (1986) 'An historical review of the literature on the Japanese enterprise and its Management', in S.R. Clegg, D. Dunphy and S.G. Redding (eds), *The Enterprise and Management in East Asia*. Hong Kong: Centre of Asian Studies, University of Hong Kong. pp. 343–68.
Ferguson, A. (1989) 'Britain's best factories', *Management Today*, November: 68–96.
Fucini, J.J. and Fucini, S. (1990) *Working for the Japanese: Inside Mazda's American Auto Plant*. New York: Free Press.
Gabb, A. (1988) 'Komatsu makes the earth move', *Management Today*, April: 77–81.
Garrahan, P. and Stewart, P. (1989) 'Working for Nissan', Paper presented at the Conference of Socialist Economists, Sheffield Polytechnic, July.
Graham, I. (1988) 'Japanization as mythology', *Industrial Relations Journal*, 19 (1): 69–75.
Grunberg, L. (1986) 'Workplace relations in the economic crisis: a comparison of a British and a French automobile plant', *Sociology*, 20 (4): 503–29.
Guest, D. (1987) 'Human resource management and industrial relations', *Journal of Management Studies*, 24 (5): 503–21.
Guest, D. (1989) 'Personnel and HRM: can you tell the difference?' *Personnel Management*, January: 48–51.
Guest, D. (1990) 'Human resource management and the American dream', *Journal of Management Studies*, 27 (4): 377–97.
Hayes, R.H. (1981) 'Why Japanese factories work', *Harvard Business Review*, July–August: 57–66.

Hendry, C. and Pettigrew, A. (1990) 'Human resource management: an agenda for the 1990s', *International Journal of Human Resource Management*, 1 (1): 17–43.

Holloway, J. (1987) 'The red rose of Nissan', *Capital and Class*, 32: 142–64.

Keenoy, T. (1990) 'HRM: a case of the wolf in sheep's clothing', *Personnel Review*, 19 (2): 3–9.

Keenoy, T. (1991) 'Human resource management: rhetoric, reality and contradictions', *International Journal of Human Resource Management*, 1 (3): 363–84.

Kendall, W. (1984) 'Why Japanese workers work', *Management Today*, January: 72–5.

Klein, J.A. (1989) 'The human cost of manufacturing reform', *Harvard Business Review*, March–April: 60–6.

Klein, J.A. (1991) 'A re-examination of autonomy in the light of new manufacturing practices', *Human Relations*, 44 (1): 21–38.

Labour Research (1989) 'HRM – human resource manipulation?' *Labour Research*, August: 8–9.

MacMillan, C.J. (1985) *The Japanese Industrial System*. New York: de Gruyter.

McGraw, P. and Dunford, R. (1987) 'The strategic use of quality circles in Australian industrial relations', *Journal of Industrial Relations*, 29 (2): 150–68.

Monden, Y. (1983) *Toyota Production System*. Atlanta, GA: Industrial Engineering and Management Press.

Morris, B. (1991) 'New technology and old industrial relations at Ford Dagenham: change, continuity and conflict', Paper presented to the 9th Annual Labour Process Conference, UMIST, April.

Muto, I. (1986) 'Class struggle in post-war Japan', in G. McCormack and Y. Sugimoto (eds), *Democracy in Contemporary Japan*. Sydney: Hale & Iremonger. pp. 114–37.

Nakane, C. (1970) *Japanese Society*. Berkeley: University of California Press.

Naylor, P. (1984) 'Bringing home the lessons of Japanese management', *Personnel Management*, March: 34–7.

Oliver, N. and Davies, A. (1990) 'Adopting Japanese-style manufacturing methods: a tale of two (UK) factories', *Journal of Management Studies*, 27 (5): 555–70.

Oliver, N. and Wilkinson, B. (1988) *The Japanization of British Industry*. Oxford: Basil Blackwell.

Ouchi, W.C. (1981) *Theory Z: How American Business can meet the Japanese Challenge*. Reading, MA: Addison-Wesley.

Parker, M. and Slaughter, J. (1988) *Choosing Sides: Unions and the Team Concept*. Boston: Labor Notes.

Pascale, R.T. and Athos, A.G. (1981) *The Art of Japanese Management*. New York: Simon & Schuster.

Peters, T. and Waterman, R. (1982) *In Search of Excellence*. New York: Harper & Row.

Rehder, R.R. (1990) 'Japanese transplants: after the honeymoon', *Business Horizons*, January–February: 87–98.

Reitsperger, W.D. (1986a) 'Japanese management: coping with British industrial relations', *Journal of Management Studies*, 23 (1): 72–87.

Reitsperger, W.D. (1986b) 'British employees: responding to Japanese management philosophies', *Journal of Management Studies*, 23 (5): 563–86.

Robbins, S.P. (1983) 'The theory Z organization from a power-control perspective', *California Management Review*, 25 (2): 67–75.

Robertson, D., Rinehart, J. and Huxley, C. (1991) 'Team concept: a case study of Japanese production management in a unionized Canadian auto plant', Paper presented at 9th Annual Labour Process Conference, UMIST, April.

Schonberger, R.J. (1982) *Japanese Manufacturing Techniques: Nine Hidden Lessons in Simplicity*. New York: Free Press.

Sewell, G. and Wilkinson, B. (1991) 'Someone to watch over me: surveillance, discipline and the capitalist labour process', Paper presented to the 9th Annual Labour Process Conference, UMIST, April.

Smith, G.B. (1990) 'Co-makership: the Japanese success story in a British environment', *International Journal of Quality and Reliability Management*, 7 (2): 7–14.

Streeck, W. (1987) 'Industrial relations and industrial change: the restructuring of the world automobile industry in the 1970s and 1980s', *Economic and Industrial Democracy*, 8: 437–62.

T&GWU (1989) 'Lessons from Langley for Ford: co-ordinators, group leaders and teamworking', Report prepared by Mike Gosling for the Transport & General Workers' Union 1/1107 Dagenham Branch, June.

Taylor, B., Elger, T. and Fairbrother, P. (1991) 'Work relations in electronics: what has become of Japanisation in Britain?', Paper presented to the 9th Annual Labour Process Conference, UMIST, 10–12 April.

Taylor, F.W. (1947) *The Principles of Scientific Management*. New York: Harper & Row.

Thurley, K. (1982) 'The Japanese model: practical reservations and surprising opportunities', *Personnel Management*, February: 36–9.

Townley, B. (1989) 'Selection and appraisal: reconstituting "Social Relations"?' in J. Storey (ed.), *New Perspectives on Human Resource Management*. London: Routledge. pp. 92–108.

Turnbull, P.J. (1988) 'The limits to "Japanisation" – just-in-time, labour relations and the UK automotive industry', *New Technology, Work and Employment*, 3 (1): 7–20.

White, M. and Trevor, M. (1983) *Under Japanese Management*. London: Heinemann.

Wickens, P. (1985) 'Nissan: the thinking behind the union agreement', *Personnel Management*, August: 18–21.

Wickens, P. (1987) *The Road to Nissan*. London: Macmillan.

Womack, J.P., Jones, D.T. and Roos, D. (1990) *The Machine That Changed the World*. New York: Rawson Associates.

Yamamoto, K. (1990) 'The "Japanese style industrial relations" and an "informal" employee organization: a case study of the Ohgi-Kai at T. Electric', University of Tokyo, Institute of Social Science *Occasional Paper No. 8*, December.

PART TWO: DIMENSIONS OF HRM

5 ORGANIZATION CULTURE AND HUMAN RESOURCE MANAGEMENT: DILEMMAS AND CONTRADICTIONS

Emmanuel Ogbonna

One of the key aspects of Human Resource Management is its association with the creation and maintenance of a 'strong' organizational culture. This has become the cornerstone of employee relations strategies in many companies in the 1980s and the underlying assumption is that managing culture is an effective method of generating competitive advantage. However, HRM also emphasizes other methods of generating advantage over competitors which are not necessarily compatible with creating 'strong cultures'. For example, HRM stresses the importance of 'high-trust' relations yet the desire to generate and maintain the behaviours that management considers necessary may require close scrutiny of employees; this may be interpreted as a lack of trust. Although there remain important concerns about the notion that culture can be managed, there are nonetheless important contradictions and dilemmas in HRM which need to be explored. This chapter highlights some of these contradictions and dilemmas.

The approach will be to locate the concept of culture in the HRM literature, addressing the controversial notion that culture is manageable. This literature will be examined from both critical and prescriptive angles, highlighting the problems with the concept of HRM and especially the management of culture. The case of Capro Stores (codenamed) will then be presented to describe the attempts by a major UK supermarket to develop an HRM policy based on the management of culture. The chapter concludes with an examination of the success or otherwise of HRM in general and in the UK supermarket industry in particular, highlighting the problems with HRM and the management of culture.

Can Culture be Managed?

The question of whether culture is manageable has given rise to widespread controversy. Smircich (1983) identifies two distinct approaches to this debate based on Burrell and Morgan's (1979) paradigmatic framework; culture as something an organization *is* and culture as something an organization *has*. These two stances, which appear to be mutually exclusive, have dominated not just the research on organizational culture but also explorations of the very nature of the concept.

Many writers have proposed models of changing culture which are consistent with the tenet that organizational culture can be managed. One of the most elaborate was posited by Silverzweig and Allen (1976) whose 'normative systems' model presents a good summary of the main focus of writers on cultural change. The model is built around the premise that people form shared values when they come into a sustained period of interaction, where there are a set of norms and expectations which, whilst not written, constitute a major influence on their actions as members. It also assumes that the culture of individuals is not merely shaped by that of the organization, they are also capable of influencing and shaping the culture of which they are part. The model thus contends that the behaviour of individuals and of the organization can essentially be changed by altering the environment within which the behaviour occurs. The long-term consequence of this is a change in the values guiding behaviour. The model, which consists of four stages, is described by its proponents as adaptive to organizational needs. The implication is that as the organization's environment changes, its culture can correspondingly change to accommodate the new environment. The model demonstrates the importance of HRM policies in changing organizational culture. Indeed, Silverzweig and Allen (1976) identify eight critical variables on which the success of the model depends. These variables are often to be found in the HRM literature and include leadership, performance and reward systems, and training and orientation.

Although Silverzweig and Allen's (1976) model has formed the intellectual inspiration for many writers on managing organizational culture, there remain important questions on its validity. For example, the model seeks to measure the extent to which organizational culture has been assimilated by individual members. It suggests that survey instruments may be relied on in assessing participants' understanding of the prevailing organizational culture, but this must cast some doubt on the reliability of the information revealed. Indeed, it would appear that if a questionnaire is used to elicit the extent to which the culture of the organization is understood, the results may be misleading. This is because the questions asked may reflect only the investigator's values or preconceived notions of the organization's culture and these may not necessarily be consistent with either the dominant culture or the culture of different sub-units in the organization.

There is also the problem of operationalizing the 'laboratory' experiment through the 'normative systems workshop' whereby staff are expected to participate as though in their ordinary work situation. The involvement of staff in the 'normative systems workshop', however, may not reproduce their true behaviour in an ordinary work setting and so may not achieve the objective of them experiencing the desired culture. For example, while employees may be willing to cooperate initially, since they are the focus of managerial and research attention, once this condition changes, they may go back to their familiar routine. This point is illustrated by the so-called 'Hawthorne effect'.

Furthermore, scrutiny of the work of other writers who take their intellectual lineage from the normative model, reveals a number of questions on managing culture. For instance, Schein (1985) identifies three levels of the cultural phenomena in organizations as follows:

1. On the surface are the overt behaviours and other physical manifestations (artifacts and creations).
2. Below this level is a sense of what 'ought' to be (values).
3. At the very deepest level are those things that are taken for granted as 'correct' ways of coping with the environment (basic assumptions).

Graves's (1986) analysis of changing culture shows that such change can also be directed at three levels but highlights the distinction between changing behaviours and changing deeper level values which, by implication, is changing culture. The question remains as to what this distinction really is and to what extent it can be made in practice. Could it not be that models which purport to change culture are simply extending the behavioural change strategies found in the literature? To illustrate, Sathe's (1985a) model of changing culture highlights that changing behaviour is an important step in changing culture, and Graves's (1986) attempts to delineate cultural from behavioural change. But behind the rhetoric lies the suspicion that these are simply disguised packages of behavioural change. However, we should be wary of fundamental (deep-seated) cultural issues. For example, Sathe (1985a) warns of the danger of relying on behavioural modification techniques, insisting that these would only lead to changes in outward behaviour but would not lead to change in the inner consciousness of the individual. The former is a temporary change in culture and the latter a permanent change. To this end, proponents of HRM will argue that consistency in internal HRM policies will not only generate sharedness of values but also could potentially develop trust, as people feel that their treatment is fair and consistent (Beer et al., 1985). However, if a permanent change in behaviour is the yardstick for measuring cultural change, then it is possible that *some* behavioural change techniques *can* generate such change. Furthermore, Sathe's (1985a) line of reasoning, while sensible, raises a fundamental dilemma. For if we accept that culture can be changed, reliance on techniques which guarantee *permanent* or even deep-rooted change itself becomes an impediment to future change. This point is crucial and will be taken up later.

Almost all the models of managing culture emphasize the need to control HRM and other variables considered critical to the success of any attempt to change culture. Of these, leadership has received the widest attention as the single most important factor in changing culture. For example, Katzenbach, a McKinsey partner, was quoted by Thackray (1986: 70), to have stated that it is very difficult for a company to 'achieve broad cultural change without new leadership'. Graves (1986) suggests that changing culture requires change in leadership at the top, a point which is consistent with Sathe (1985a, b), Silverzweig and Allen (1976) and Tichy (1982), among many others. The justification for changing the leaders of organizations is that they epitomize the prevailing culture; they may hold strong values which block attempts to change culture. It should be noted, however, that new leadership is not a guarantee that employees, as many writers assume, will conform to the desired values displayed by the leaders. This assumption is flawed in two major respects. The first is that it ignores the influence of informal group norms and other forces outside the control of the individual, or indeed the organization; these can be powerful determinants of behaviour especially when they are in conflict with organizational norms. Secondly, new leadership does not on its own guarantee employee conformity. As Robbins (1987) demonstrates, there are specific conditions for the acceptance of the new leader's values: the leader must establish a clear alternative vision of what the organization can be; there must be respect for the leader's ability; and the leader must have the power to enact the alternative vision. In other words, the new leaders must be distant enough so as not to see things through the eyes of their predecessors, yet they must understand the organization well enough to be able to develop alternative directions. This dilemma sums up the difficulty in managing culture.

Communication is another variable which has been widely cited as a necessary prerequisite to managing culture. Graves (1986), for example, stresses the need to communicate the level of culture that managers wish to change. Hence, organizations are advised that when changing only behaviour, employees could be told of the need for their fundamental attitudes and values to remain unchanged. Silverzweig and Allen (1976) highlight the importance of information and communication in modifying the existing culture, and Sathe's (1985a) model emphasizes the necessity for managerial conviction and credibility in communicating the new patterns of values and beliefs that organizational members are expected to adopt. Wilkins (1984) also shows that efficient communication of positive organizational stories can help to shape culture. The problem here is that communication is presented as if it were something that managers can effectively control and this is patently not the case, since unintended meanings are often put across. This problem is compounded by the fact that receivers (employees) would often be biased in their interpretation of information. Further, while managers may not encourage the spread of negative stories, they are often the ones that employees remember the most. Communication difficulties are likely to be heightened where there are strong and perhaps conflicting sub-cultures. This is because communication essentially depends on shared meanings, and a multiplicity of cultures is likely to produce a multiplicity of meanings which will inevitably reduce the extent to which values are shared.

The preceding discussion shows that there remain important questions surrounding the assumption that culture can be managed. However, a key element of HRM policy is the management of organizational culture. It is important to locate the concept of culture in the HRM literature identifying how writers suggest or imply that culture can be managed.

Culture and HRM

The link between organization culture and HRM has not been clearly developed in the literature. This is despite the widespread remarks by researchers linking the two concepts (Armstrong, 1987; Beer et al., 1985; Legge, 1989; Wilkins, 1984). Such a link is potentially useful and could add to our understanding of both concepts. The absence of a link is due in part to the lack of a developed theory of HRM (see Noon, Chapter 2, this volume) and one which clearly differentiates it from personnel management. Although many writers have questioned the validity of claims that HRM is a concept distinct from personnel management (Armstrong, 1987; Fowler, 1987; Legge, 1989), it nonetheless appears that it is a concept whose time has come and which is probably here to stay (Gapper, 1991). Indeed, judging from the recent proliferation of articles, books and journals, HRM is no longer in danger of being 'talked' into existence (Guest, 1987); it has already been *written* into existence.

An important issue to be considered in building an HRM philosophy is related to what Guest (1987) identified as the goal of integration. He notes that there are four elements of such integration. These elements can be broadly grouped into 'external' and 'internal' integration. 'External' integration would refer to the relationship between HRM and the organizational environment. The argument is that HRM should take centre stage in the strategic planning process if the organization is to realize its full potential. This centrality is heightened as the organizational environment becomes increasingly turbulent. As Tichy (1982: 72) observes: 'The technological, economic and demographic changes of the 1980s are pressuring organizations to use more effective Human Resource Management.'

A development of this stance is found in the current movement in the literature towards Strategic Human Resource Management where the emphasis is on generating an effective link between HRM and strategy (Fombrun et al., 1984; Hendry and Pettigrew, 1986; Lengnick-Hall and Lengnick-Hall, 1988).

'Internal' integration concerns those factors which are within the organization and are deemed to be relatively easily controlled. This covers the other three elements identified by Guest, including the need for HRM policies to be consistent and to feed through to strategic plans, the need to elicit line management commitment to practising HRM, and the need for employees to become an integral part of the organization. It is this last point that Beer et al. (1985) describe as 'congruence'. They note the necessity for HRM policies to integrate not only the goals of management and employees but also other interest groups, including the community and the employees' families. Notwithstanding the problematic nature of attempting to integrate these varied and often conflicting interests, this posits HRM as an holistic concept and firmly embracing the welfare dimension of personnel management.

The second goal of HRM identified by both Guest and Beer et al. is that of generating commitment. This is probably the most contentious aspect of HRM, since the objective is to encourage individual employees to be committed to their work and the organization. The origin of this line of reasoning can be traced back to early approaches to motivation, with the underlying assumption that a committed worker, rather like a satisfied worker, is likely to be a more productive worker. HRM proponents, however, go beyond the type of job satisfaction that early motivation theorists sought to generate. There is greater emphasis on mutuality of interests as the major driving force behind the generation of commitment. For example, Walton (1985) sees HRM as promoting the collective interests of employers and employees, and as such has the potential to elicit commitment which will not only be manifested in the form of increased profitability for the organization but also improved well-being and development of individual employees. In a similar vein, Beer et al. (1985) observe that increased commitment has the potential of not only increasing profitability but also employee self-worth and dignity. There are clearly dangers, however, in assuming that commitment to the organization will *necessarily* be in the interest of the employee and employer (Iles et al., 1990). There is also the multiple and often conflicting nature of employee commitment which may be problematic. For example, people can at the same time be committed to their work, trade union, profession and/or an informal group in the organization to which they belong. They can also be committed to other roles outside of the workplace. These points will be elaborated in the case study presented below.

The third objective of HRM is described by Guest as flexibility/ adaptability. This is based on the realization that HRM policies need to be flexible and adaptive if they are to achieve the goal of 'strategic fit' already highlighted. The external environment plays a major role in the formulation of organizational strategies and advocates of strategic human resource management contend that HRM policies should be developed in harmony with these strategies. The resulting internal HRM policies must be flexible so as to adapt to changes in the organizational environment. The extent of volatility in the firm's external environment will determine the extent of flexibility required to remain competitive. The theory of the 'flexible firm' propagated by Atkinson (1984) highlights the issue of flexibility as an important part of managing human resources especially in a competitive environment (see Blyton and Morris, Chapter 7, this volume).

The last objective identified by Guest is that of quality. This fits closely with what Beer et al. describe as 'competence'. The notion here is that HRM advocates the recruitment and retention of high calibre employees in the belief that this will feed into the products and services of the organization. This is manifest in the movement to total quality management (TQM) which has become prevalent in many manufacturing and service organizations. TQM is measured in terms of both the perception of the final customer and the people who work in the organization, each of whom is given an 'internal' customer (Ogbonna and Wilkinson, 1988; Ogbonna, 1990).

It has been asserted that culture is an important organizational attribute which must be managed (Kilmann, 1982; Ray, 1986). Legge (1989: 28) observes that HRM 'emphasizes the management of culture as a central management activity', while Armstrong (1987) notes that the management of culture is an essential element of HRM. Indeed, the achievement of HRM objectives requires the management of the organizational value system (culture) and this requires skilful implementation, since different cultures will require different HRM practices (Fombrun, 1983). For instance, to generate trust and commitment, an organization would need to emphasize the importance of these attributes in its employee relations philosophy, as well as utilizing appropriate policies to reinforce them. Further, organizations wishing to generate and sustain 'strong cultures' would need to pay particular attention not only to their HRM policies to ensure that they are supportive of the culture they wish to develop, but should also ensure that they are consistent and feed through to strategic planning. It is the perception of this consistency over time which may give rise to a strong culture.

It has been observed by Beer et al. (1985) that organizations need to develop a clearly stated 'management philosophy' (read culture) which will form the guiding framework from which HRM policies will be developed. They contend that where this philosophy is strongly articulated by senior managers, the resulting HRM policies are likely to be internally consistent, hence encouraging the future development of a 'strong culture' by moulding the belief system of employees and future managers. They point out that the consequence of not having a clearly articulated belief system will be that: 'short-term pragmatic consideration would dominate HRM policy decisions rather than simply influence them. The result would be inconsistent new policies and the erosion of the philosophy' (Beer et al., 1985: 29–30). In a similar vein, Wilkins (1984) demonstrates that many organizations develop 'statements of philosophy' which denote their stance on the management of human resources. He contends that the difference between successful (excellent) and less successful companies is that successful companies have a system of passing down organizational culture to new participants who adopt the statements of philosophy as if they were communicated directly by the executives who originally articulated them.

It is the HRM policies that give credence to the philosophy and help support positive organizational stories which Wilkins sees as a major tool of transmitting and sustaining culture.

Where an articulate philosophy is present, Wilkins (1984) observes that HRM can create an environment which encourages the development of a 'strong' organizational culture. He illustrates this point by citing examples of three HRM policies: selection, development and reward, and retention. The case of Capro stores, described below, illustrates that other HRM policies are in practice perceived to contribute equally to the shaping of organizational culture. This said, a brief explanation of how some of the widely cited HRM policies can shape organization culture will be useful.

Selection is probably the most widely cited HRM policy that facilitates the management of culture. The level of importance attached to selection is not surprising since it provides an entry point into the organization and the opportunity for both the individual and the organization to establish a psychological contract. To this end, Tichy (1982) notes that organizations using HRM policies to develop a 'strong culture' pay close attention to this process. The objective is to develop the selection process so that only people whose values are consistent, or could be made consistent, with the dominant values of the organization are employed. By employing 'like-minded' people, organizations are able to increase the strength of their culture and reduce the possibility and consequences of undesired behaviours.

Once the 'desired' people are recruited, proponents of HRM argue the importance of a system of intense socialization and development. Here, HRM policies concerning training and development can be designed to inculcate in employees those attitudes which are 'in tune' with the desired organizational culture. It is also possible for the performance and reward scheme to recognize only those employees who have shown loyalty and whose values are consistent with those of the organization, hence an internal promotion policy must be selective and act as a reinforcement to the company culture.

From the foregoing discussion, it is clear that there is a link between organizational culture and HRM. It has been demonstrated that an important goal of HRM is the management of organizational culture to achieve competitive advantage. Proponents of HRM promoting this view do so on the assumption that organizational culture can be managed, but the question remains as to whether managing organizational culture is simply an ideal which falls short of reality. The following section summarizes current thinking in the area.

The Reality of Managing Culture

As already indicated, the key argument of researchers who see cultural change as impossible is that organizational members are seldom aware of their culture because it operates at a subliminal level. It is taken for granted and, for the most part, acts as an objective reality never to be questioned. Viewed as deep-seated attitudes, culture appears difficult to change, but the management of culture does not have to be concentrated solely at this level. In fact, judging from the comments of some of the most widely cited researchers on the subject, one has to be sceptical as to the prospect of achieving 'deeper level' change. As Deal and Kennedy (1982: 164), the authors of *Corporate Cultures*, acknowledge: 'Let's be candid about this, we don't know this area better than anyone else. Cultural change is still a black art as far as we are concerned.' And Waterman, the co-author of *In Search of Excellence*, commenting on the popularity of the book, was reported to have stated: 'It's not a bible you know!' (Piercy, 1987: 11). One implication is that 'deeper level' change is more difficult to achieve and it may be easier to concentrate on the more observable behavioural changes. The culture that may be managed is the manifestly observable behaviours *not* the unobservable deep-seated attitudes of individuals.

The argument here is that behavioural change often precedes cultural change since culture is an adaptive learning process which responds to the needs of the people (Schein, 1984, 1985). However, there is scepticism as to whether deeper level values are as susceptible to change as the more visible manifestation of culture. Gagliardi (1986), for instance, questions the logic implied by the work of Schein and many others that as organizational members learn to adapt to their environment they replace their existing values with new ones. Deep-rooted values, he argues, are by definition entwined with the deepest level of human cognition and changing them is often not considered by people since such change invigorates anxiety and people are often reluctant to try, since there is no guarantee that changing deep-rooted values will solve organizational problems. In other words, deep-rooted values remain intact while surface behaviours may change in response to environmental pressures.

Other writers have noted that the results of managing culture are often unanticipated (Krefting and Frost, 1985), implying that although organizational culture rather like the culture of societies can and does change, its direction and impact *cannot* be precisely controlled. This line of reasoning appears convincing when it is considered that for anyone attempting to change culture to be taken seriously, he or she needs to have a vision of what the new culture will be like. Unfortunately, many managers are often unsure of what they want to change and are unlikely to be able to formulate visions of the future, which in itself is characterized by uncertainty and ambiguity. Indeed, far from analysing and planning the future of their organizations, managers tend to be reactive, dealing with problems as they arise (Mintzberg, 1975).

To summarize the discussion so far, the literature on managing organizational culture is confusing. There are clearly two ways in which culture is treated in relation to change. There are those who treat culture as behaviour and there are those who treat it as values and taken-for-granted assumptions. The consequence of this confusion is that there is no conceptual model which convincingly demonstrates how change in deeper-level values should be attempted. This is despite the fact that much of the literature accepts such a change as constituting cultural change. Instead, what we are presented with are haphazard treatments of cultural change which either equate it to behavioural change, or simply assume that behavioural change will in the long term lead to cultural change.

The adoption of HRM philosophy based on the management of culture is thus plagued with problems. On a theoretical level, HRM seeks to manage culture through changing deep-rooted values, yet an examination of the literature suggests that what is being achieved is more likely to be a change in the observable behaviour of employees. It therefore becomes necessary to explore the wider contradictions and dilemmas in HRM and, particularly, the management of culture. This will be done by presenting the case of a major UK supermarket whose practices and philosophies approximate those of HRM.

The Capro Case

Capro was established as a food retailer in the 1960s. It is now ranked among the top five UK supermarkets. It pioneered superstore development in the UK with the opening of its first superstore in the mid-1960s. The company's basic philosophy was to stock goods in large quantities and 'sell them cheap'. This was very successful in the 1970s when price was seen as a major factor in consumer purchasing decisions. However, in the 1980s, in addition to price, quality, convenience and service were perceived by the industry as the keys to competitive advantage. Capro acknowledged this late and was behind its competitors. Since the mid-1980s, Capro has rapidly developed as will be demonstrated later. The typical Capro store employs about 350 people. The store management team is headed by a general store manager to whom a number of managers report. The stores report to and are supported by regional offices, directly controlled by the head office.

Capro's Corporate Strategy

In the 1970s and early 1980s, there were a series of speculations concerning the supermarket industry. It was claimed that the industry would reach saturation point by the 1990s. Capro reacted by pursuing an extensive diversification strategy. It merged with a major furniture retailer and acquired another. It also started an experiment in car retailing through its superstores. This diversification moved the company away from its area of distinctive competence (food retailing) and there was very little synergy to be gained, given the different nature of the three companies. It was seen by industry experts and observers as a failure. Consequently, it was not long before the company realized its mistake and decided to dispose of its interests in the other companies. This decision marked a turn in the corporate strategy, from diversification back to specialization. Having decided to concentrate on its core business of food retailing, several improvements were made in this narrow sector. These changes have proved financially satisfactory and Capro's profit margin now compares favourably with the highest in the industry. As part of this change process, a number of operational strategies have been implemented in an attempt to close the gap between the company and its competitors.

Store Redesign and Development   A strategic initiative was taken by the company in the wake of the results of an extensive commissioned survey, which revealed that customers preferred locational convenience and better service to the offer of mere competitive price. As one senior manager put it: 'People tend to shop through convenience in terms of location and the general image they have about the business.' In addition, the geographical area covered by Capro stores generated a weakness which the management needed to overcome. Until 1984, most Capro stores were located in the north of England. This was despite the fact of high unemployment and a generally depressed economic climate in the north. Many of the stores, which were mainly built in the 1960s, were also out of date and were largely built for the convenience of the company rather than the customer. Accordingly, the management decided to locate most new store developments in the south of England, particularly the south east, and to redesign the stores to satisfy customers' demands for convenience.

Competitive Strategy   Until recently Capro's fundamental goal was short-term profit maximization and every decision-making activity was driven by this goal. The decision to build large superstores in the 1960s was not to do with offering customers choice among competing products but to enable the company to obtain the benefits of economies of scale, hence competitive advantage in price. One senior manager, recruited in 1984 to direct the company's new strategies, pointed out that in the past, management did not realize that to make money the company had to provide a range of goods and services. He went on: 'they stocked individual lines that provided big margins, instead of a range of different products . . . they were offering the products they wanted not the ones the customer actually wanted'. Another senior store manager, who has been with the company for thirteen years, provided the following historical account of its competitive strategy: 'Thirteen years ago, customer service was way down our list of priorities. The company was only interested in getting the shelves filled. We didn't deal with customer complaints . . . and we used to say no to them most of the time.' This manager went on to describe the job of a manager thirteen years ago as to 'run the store in the best way', which was to 'stock at the cheapest price, sell at the cheapest price with minimum overheads to maximize profits'. While profit maximization is still an important objective at Capro, management's focus is now long term rather than short term with its competitive strategy now combining price with better customer service, which includes the stocking of a wide range of products, the provision of choice, and better and more convenient stores.

Customer Service The company's efforts to improve customer service are demonstrated by its customer care programme which has become a permanent feature of the organization. The approach was to retrain all its employees in order to change their attitude towards the customers. The customer care training reinforces the view that the customer comes first and deserves the best service. This is seen as an ongoing programme and to highlight its importance, senior managers visit all the stores to determine the one which offers the best service in a 'store of the year' competition. Employees in the winning store are offered financial rewards and the store is profiled in the company's in-house magazine, giving members a psychological boost.

An important part of the customer care programme is that staff are encouraged to be friendly. What is significant, though, is the debate on the so-called 'smile campaign'. The majority of the staff interviewed by the author, especially the front-line staff in direct contact with the customers, are unhappy about being told to put on a smile for the customers. They claim that they are sometimes reprimanded by their supervisors for not smiling, a point which one supervisor's comments confirm: 'We are able to detect when a check-out operator is not smiling or even when she is putting on a false smile . . . we call her into a room and have a chat with her.' The check-out operators' allegation is denied by one senior manager who points out that they are encouraged to smile but not forced to do so. The two claims, although conflicting, have one thing in common: employees are being requested to suppress their private emotions and offer the customer a friendly smile. This task is not always easy, especially when customers have problems which can not be appeased with a smile. As one store manager explained: 'They [the operators] are told to smile all the time and if the customer has a particular problem then they should try and get them through the check-out and contact a supervisor or manager to deal with it.' One check-out operator indicated that she has got the message: 'We are given customer care training when we join the company and as an ongoing thing. We are told to smile all the time and that the customer is always right.' Nonetheless, responses from a majority of operators interviewed suggest that their job is becoming more difficult because the attempt to increase the level of service offered by a store is directly associated with the increase in the number of difficult customers they have to deal with.

Control and Technology As part of the strategy to concentrate on developing Capro stores, the company has embarked on policies which will enhance management control. One indication of this can be seen in the centralization of operations. The old philosophy of 'pile it high, sell it cheap' required entrepreneurial managers to be successful. This is because they had to deal with suppliers on a local level and the profitability of each store partly depended on the manager's negotiating skills and ability. Centralized distribution has now been introduced at a huge cost which the company believes is a worthwhile investment.

Associated with the centralized distribution system is the introduction of electronic point of sale (EPOS) and electronic fund transfer at the point of sale (EFTPOS). These two technologies have transformed the ways supermarkets are run. More control can now be exerted from head office with the up-to-the-minute data which is provided. The sales data of every branch is used to plan distribution at the central warehouse and as stocks are automatically replenished, the head office buyers rely on the data provided by EPOS on the sales of particular lines; this provides a useful negotiating advantage. The managers are thus freed from the routine task of ordering stock, to concentrate on human resource management. EPOS can also be deployed in the planning of daily staff requirements. It can provide accurate information on the busiest days and times of the week which the manager can feed into human resource flexibility planning.

The reaction of the check-out operators towards EPOS is mixed. Many see it as useful in improving customer service since the time it takes customers to go through the check-out is reduced. Others think that it adds to the monotony and difficulty already experienced on the job. As one operator puts it: 'Sitting down all day and passing products through the scanner can be very boring.'

Human Resource Management

Capro believes that the *commitment* of its employees is required if long-term strategic objectives are to be achieved. There is greater emphasis on staff welfare and development now than in previous years and the role of the personnel department is better appreciated by senior management. Indeed, the name of this department has been changed from 'personnel' to 'human resource management' and a new head of that department with full director status has been appointed to further develop consciousness of the importance of effective management of human resources among senior managers. Ironically, while designations of staff at the head office concerned with the implementation of the new profile have been changed to human resource managers, those of the staff at store level are still 'personnel officers'. A senior manager in this department spelled out the company's emphasis on HRM: 'We believe that if we have to achieve this philosophical change, we have to change our personnel policies and increase the profile of our personnel department.' The following reveals the changes that have been made to Capro's human resource policies.

Staff Training and Development The company has placed a greater emphasis on training its staff. This emphasis became necessary with the new strategies and the associated expansion to the south east of England. As the company moved south, it found too many companies chasing too few staff; the 'good' staff were almost impossible to recruit as many companies were after them. A decision was made to develop people within the company. Today it is generally believed within Capro that effective staff training is a prerequisite to success in the supermarket industry. This is demonstrated by the customer service training which all staff in Capro undergo.

Senior management's attitude is that greater emphasis should be directed to managerial staff who are then encouraged to train the staff under them. This, according to one senior manager, is because 'the training of low-level staff is a complete waste of resources if their managers are not actually supporting what the organization wants'. An example of the efforts made to achieve this objective is the special customer service programmes which have been designed for managers, who are then expected to convey the message to their subordinates. As part of the training initiative, there are now staff training officers throughout Capro stores. They help to administer the customer care programme as well as programmes for training staff to be efficient in their present jobs and preparing them for the future.

Promotion from Within Capro's senior head office managers like to think that they recruit or encourage the recruitment of what they call 'like-minded' people. Once recruited, efforts are made to keep them within the organization. One way of doing this is by encouraging managers to identify staff with potential who are then developed within the organization. Many employees within the company have benefited from the policy of internal promotion. The feeling, particularly among super-visors and junior store managers, is that anyone who is sufficiently interested in his or her job could be promoted to any level he or she aspires to. However, in the case of senior store managers, progression appears to be slow. This is despite senior head office management's insistence that there is a shortage of managerial staff. For example, the next promotion for a senior store fresh foods manager is to become a general store manager and have his or her own store. This is not easy as one such manager explains:

> You have to be nominated to go before an assessment panel and there are only two assessment panels each year. We have about 500 senior managers in our stores and only 24 can go on the panel each year and only about four can get their own store.

This contradicts senior head office management's expression of a shortage of managerial manpower and highlights a major flaw in the 'strong culture' movement. This will be taken up again, below.

Communication and Staff Involvement The need to improve staff communication in Capro became a priority when, in 1984, it came second (Inland Revenue was first) in a MORI 'worst ever' contest for internal communication. Employees are now privy to some previously confidential information about the performance of the company. Indeed, the company has taken a lead in this respect with its 'employee report'. This is now produced with the annual report and is short, well illustrated and written without the usual financial jargon often associated with such reports.

At store level, weekly and monthly sales data are available for staff to see and these are displayed on staff notice boards in some stores where the managers have a preference for informality. There is also a store council which provides an opportunity for workplace consultation; management also appears to attach considerable importance to team briefings where employees are kept informed of management's activities. This is a two-way process where the head office management expects feedback from employees. Store managers, in conjunction with regional officers, thus appear keen to encourage staff to contribute ideas and respond to information coming from head office.

Apart from the methods described above, an important means of involving staff in company activities is through the 'employee of the month/year' and 'store of the month/year' competitions. Staff are encouraged to nominate people who have helped colleagues or customers beyond the call of duty. Marks are awarded to the people nominated and the person with the highest mark becomes the store's employee of the month. The highest scoring employee of the month becomes the employee of the year and goes forward with employees in other stores to determine Capro employee of the year. The store of the year contest is won by that store judged by a senior head office management team to have offered the best service to its customers. The winning employees and the employees in the winning store are given financial rewards as well as the psychological boost resulting from their success.

Capro's Organizational Culture

In the old Capro, there was no systematic approach to developing an appropriate culture to support management strategies. Nevertheless, a culture supportive of price and cost sensitivity emerged. To be sure, the 'pile it high sell it cheap' philosophy meant that the company was working on tight margins and always seeking to minimize overheads. The staff were paid a minimal wage, with little or no training, were given cheap overalls and told to get on with their jobs. The type of culture that prevailed in the company is most accurately depicted by the managers who experienced it. One senior store manager who had been with the company for over ten years explains the type of values they were encouraged to share: 'In 1979, the philosophy was to fill the shelf and sell the stock . . . this went to extremes. The controller will visit the store on Saturday afternoon and if your shelf is not filled, you'll literally be in hot water.' Another manager who experienced the old culture confirmed this point citing the same 'Saturday afternoon' example in relation to the check-out: 'If you have queues all the way back . . . the controller will congratulate you.' He contrasted this with the current customer service initiative where the manager has to ensure that queues are kept to a minimum.

The importance that management attach to developing a strong culture to sustain Capro's new strategic vision is demonstrated by the efforts made in this direction. In 1988, the company commissioned a firm of management consultants to advise on ways of matching corporate strategies, culture and HRM. Another important move was the recruitment of new directors, especially a human resource director. This is linked to the high profile that is now given to the management of human resources in the organization. It is interesting to note that the new directors believe that creating the appropriate corporate culture is an essential prerequisite to success. The recruitment of new directors and senior store managers with a new vision tends to support the popular belief in the organizational culture literature, that top and senior management are critical factors in the development and change of organizational culture.

The loyalty of staff and their sense of belonging to the company may be enhanced or motivated by the offer of a range of welfare benefits. For example, there is a 10 per cent staff discount on goods purchased in Capro stores and the company obtains discounts for its staff on goods purchased in many other stores. There is also a share participation scheme where staff are allocated free shares in the company in appreciation of their efforts the previous year. Other benefits include a Pension Scheme, Savings Related Share Option Scheme, and Death Benefit Grant. There are also staff social clubs subsidized by the company, while every branch is encouraged to organize sporting or other social events. This is mainly to raise money for charity since every store has its own pet charity. Many employees suggested to this author that these benefits indicate that the company cares for staff welfare. It is clear that management assumes that many employees are willing to work hard since there is a perceived relationship between performance and reward.

Capro is now totally committed to developing an organization culture that will be supportive of present and possible future strategies. The extent to which the company has succeeded or will succeed in creating the type of strong culture it would like is, however, debatable.

Discussion

So far in this chapter, the link between HRM and culture has been demonstrated. It has been pointed out that one of the central tenets of HRM is the management of organizational culture and creating a 'fit' between the internal and external organizational environment. The case of

Capro stores has also been presented as an example of an organization that has apparently taken HRM philosophy on board while pursuing a competitive advantage and creating a 'strong culture'. However, when the case is compared to the theoretical foundations underpinning HRM models, a number of contradictions and dilemmas emerge. The final section of this chapter examines the extent to which Capro has succeeded in achieving HRM ideals based on the management of culture. In particular, the contradictions and dilemmas inherent in HRM and the management of culture are highlighted.

HRM and Culture: Contradictions and Dilemmas

The case study shows that Capro has consciously decided to manage its culture to fit its strategic direction. The realization that a strong culture was needed came with the new strategic initiative which emphasized the importance of developing a customer service ethos. This required employees to behave in ways that demonstrated to the customer that the company cares. Indeed, the objective has been to develop HRM policies that will facilitate the generation of a 'strong culture' and thus competitive advantage. Although Capro has attempted to change its culture at the three levels identified in the literature (Graves, 1986; Schein, 1985), it appears that it has only succeeded in doing so at the more visible behavioural level. To be sure, the case study does not indicate that employees have taken on board the *values* and assumptions espoused by senior management, yet there is evidence that they are conforming to the required behaviour. When it is considered that the company has sought to implement many of the prescriptions of HRM and the management of culture, it becomes necessary to explore why value internalization has not been achieved.

There are two crucial points to be considered in attempting to explain the lack of empirical support for the success of HRM in the management of culture. First, as noted above, much of the literature on organizational culture perceives change of deep-rooted values as a change of organizational culture. For example, Schein (1984, 1985), who is probably the most cited author on the subject, largely concentrates his analysis on deep-rooted values and beliefs. It is this deeper level that Sathe (1985a, b) refers to as culture. However, if this is so, cultural change is nothing more than an excursion into the unknown (subliminal) which may or may not yield the desired result. The key concern is that the cultural change described in the literature may be at the observable behavioural level rather than the subliminal level. At the very best, many attempts to change culture are only successful at the overt behavioural level. It is possible that overt behaviour may generate deep-rooted values over time but attributing this to the initial change programme may be an over-simplification.

Second, HRM may be fraught with contradictions and dilemmas that may make the management of culture and the achievement of other HRM objectives difficult. To explore this point, it is important to compare Capro's 'ideal' HRM objectives with the contradictions and dilemmas experienced while seeking to attain the objectives (Table 5.1).

Table 5.1. *HRM at Capro*

Ideal HRM Goals		Contradictions and Dilemmas
Quality and service	vs	Difficult customers
High trust and commitment	vs	Surveillance, female workers
Cultural similarities across stores	vs	Rapid expansions/takeovers
Strong internal labour market	vs	High labour turnover, high % of part-time, drop in numbers of young people

Quality and Service The new culture which Capro's management attempted to create was one in which employees were expected to behave deferentially towards customers – to smile, to maintain eye contact, etc., and generally be responsive to customer needs. This is despite the increase in the number of irate customers they are expected to deal with. There is clearly a contradiction in being expected to smile and be friendly to a customer who is rude and abusive; yet this is what management expect. As one check-out operator explains:

> We do get a lot of customers moaning and groaning and that's where we can get nervous. We are supposed to look after the customers but some can be very rude . . . you have to keep all that inside you; you are not allowed to let it out and this adds to the stress of the job. You can easily let your emotions out on the next customer who still expects you to smile.

Another operator cites a specific situation they can get into with customers:

> The worst thing is that while I am at the till trying to be as fast as I can, I can hear the customers moaning that I am slow . . . There are times when I just want to look up angrily and tell them to shut up but I have to be busy and keep smiling.

Many check-out operators expressed similar feelings. Some of them have, however, devised ways of coping with this difficult aspect of their job. One described herself as a good actress admitting that she puts up an act to satisfy management's demand: 'We are told to smile all the time . . . sometimes it is very difficult . . . I succeed because I try to put up an act . . . My mother thinks I'm very good at it and that I should have been an actress.' One can expect to find many 'thespians' in supermarkets like Capro but by far the most common method of coping with difficult customers is by discussing them while sitting together in the canteen during breaks and away from the customers. The day's difficult customers are discussed and operators seek solace by making rude remarks about them privately. There are nonetheless many operators who find it difficult to manage their emotions in the face of difficult customers.

High Trust and Commitment Another area of contradiction is HRM's emphasis on generating trust and commitment based on the mutuality of interests (Walton, 1985). A number of factors and practices make the attainment of this 'ideal' difficult. For example, many front-line employees in retailing, and particularly supermarkets, are older women who come to work with instrumental attitudes ('for the money') which helps to maintain or improve a certain quality of family life. Many of them are committed not to the organization but to their families. Indeed, many claim to have rejected promotional opportunities on the grounds that the long hours would conflict with family demands. Many managers, recognizing this, expressed their preference to take on younger people who are more likely to be committed to a career with the organization; however, management were constrained because the older female labour offered the best flexibility (another HRM policy objective). The dilemma is either to employ a group of people from which a proportion are likely to be career-minded and hence committed to the organization, or to maintain a policy of flexibility which offers substantial cost savings. It is clear that most companies in this sector will go for the latter.

There is also the problematic nature of 'high-trust' relations which HRM proponents have put forward. The idea is that if employees are trusted they are likely to be responsive. Nonetheless, the reality, as revealed by the Capro case, is that of close scrutiny, surveillance and tighter control of work. There is always a member of the management team behind the tills, especially during busy hours, and some stores have TV monitors in the manager's office which enable them to observe the behaviour of staff on the shop floor. Not displaying the desired behaviour can result in being called into the manager's room 'for a chat' and supervisors have been trained to detect operators not smiling or putting up a false smile. Occasionally, senior head office managers arrive at a store unannounced to monitor the behaviour of staff and there are also random visits by bogus shoppers employed by the company. This constant surveillance reinforces the threat of sanctions for undesired behaviour thereby keeping the workers on their toes and preventing them from expressing their true feelings to the customers.

Cultural Similarities Across Stores The recruitment of 'like-minded' people and the encouragement of an internal labour market are both HRM policies which companies are encouraged to pursue if they wish to develop strong cultures. There are, however, factors which may make the achievement of this objective difficult, as the Capro case reveals. The key factor is the relatively low wages in the industry. There is a high rate of staff turnover and this is not surprising considering that supermarket jobs are not only poorly paid but unglamorous, monotonous and frequently intense. Consequently, supermarkets do not usually attract 'high quality' staff and may not necessarily be in a position to be selective. This notwithstanding, the predicted change in the composition of the UK workforce will mean that even more older women will be coming back into the labour market. As has been pointed out already, older women with family commitments are less likely to be committed to the organization.

Even if a policy of recruiting only 'like-minded' people can be effectively implemented, there is still an inherent danger that HRM may become an enabling strategy for discrimination. People come to an organization with values which may, while reflecting the values of the wider society, embody aspects of their ethnic values and beliefs. In a multi-ethnic society, there is a high risk that the values adopted within the organization will be those of the mainstream society which may reflect conscious or subconscious prejudices. Selective recruitment policies may help to reinforce these prejudices and there is even a danger that such policies may be in breach of the legislation on discrimination.

Internal Labour Market　Equally, the emphasis on internal labour market presents a dilemma for HRM. The policy of promoting people from within will undoubtedly strengthen the culture of the organization as new store openings provide promotion opportunities for employees especially at supervisory and managerial levels. However, evidence from Capro indicates that the pace of change presents problems. As one senior manager at the head office explains, the company is growing so quickly that it cannot grow the requisite number of staff within. A new superstore requires about fifty supervisors and thirty managers. Inevitably, a number of people would need to be recruited externally which could threaten the strength of the culture.

While the last point seems sensible on the surface, interviews with senior assistant store managers whose next promotion is to become store managers running their own stores reveals a different leitmotif which contradicts the whole emphasis on developing a strong culture. It would appear that at senior store managerial level it is the desire to recruit new people with new ideas that is the major driving force behind the decision of head office managers. It is felt that many managers who have been with the company for a long time will tend to have acquired values which are inconsistent with those that are now espoused in the organization. The company is thus frequently unwilling to promote such people to the positions of general store managers because it is feared that they will run the stores in the 'old ways'.

The above point raises an interesting question about 'strong organizational cultures' which HRM advocates encourage. A strong culture has been defined as that in which core values are widely shared, intensely held and clearly ordered (Robbins, 1987; Sathe, 1985a, b). This definition is problematic in many respects. That a strong culture organization is one in which 'core values are widely shared' ignores the influence of strong multiple and often conflicting sub-cultures; 'intensely held' contradicts the notion that culture can be changed in tandem with organizational strategy; and 'clearly ordered' assumes that the subconscious, where values are embedded, can be ordered. These problems sum up the opaqueness of the concept of culture.

Conclusion

This chapter has reviewed some of the important linkages between HRM and culture. It has demonstrated that both HRM and culture are problematic concepts struggling to gain academic credibility. In particular, the contradictions and dilemmas of HRM have been presented. Many of the contradictions and dilemmas will apply irrespective of the organization and the industry though some will undoubtedly be industry-specific.

The most important aspect of HRM appears to be the emphasis on managing organizational culture. This is because the achievement of HRM policy objectives is dependent on managing internal and external organizational culture. The assumption is that organizational culture can be managed. The Capro case, however, illustrates that managing culture is no more than an ideal which is difficult to attain. In this case, management was only able to generate behavioural compliance from an indifferent workforce. As a result, changes in the visible manifestations of culture were observable while values and assumptions remain intact. This said, it would be wrong to conclude that HRM and culture are no more than passing fads. Instead, a crucial question needs to be posed: does it matter to managements whether or not the behaviours generated are based on internalized values? It would appear that arguments about value internalization are often academic and many managers in organizations attempting cultural change like Capro are happy to be generating behaviours concomitant with their chosen strategies. After all, it can be argued that HRM itself has a connotation of instrumentality, hence only the end result matters. If this is so, then HRM may have become the latest addition to the array of strategies that legitimate managements' attempts to tighten their control over the workers. One can only spare a thought for check-out operators and wonder whether training on acting skills and the management of emotions will not be mutually beneficial.

References

Armstrong, M. (1987) 'Human resource management: a case of the emperor's new clothes?' *Personnel Management*, August: 30–5.
Atkinson, J. (1984) 'Manpower strategies for the flexible firm', *Personnel Management*, August: 28–31.

Beer, M., Spector, B., Lawrence, P., Mills, D. and Walton, R. (1985) *Human Resource Management: A General Manager's Perspective*. New York: Free Press.

Burrell, G. and Morgan, G. (1979) *Sociological Paradigms and Organizational Analysis*. London: Heinemann.

Deal, T. and Kennedy, A. (1982) *Corporate Cultures*. Reading, MA: Addison Wesley.

Fombrun, C. (1983) 'Corporate culture, environment and strategy', *Human Resource Management*, 22 (1/2): 139–52.

Fombrun, C., Tichy, N.M. and Davanna, M.A. (1984) *Strategic Human Resource Management*. New York: John Wiley.

Fowler, A. (1987) 'When chief executives discover HRM', *Personnel Management*, January: 3.

Gagliardi, P. (1986) 'The creation and change of organizational cultures: a conceptual framework', *Organizational Studies*, 7 (2): 117–34.

Gapper, J. (1991) 'An idea whose time has come', *Financial Times*, 28 January.

Graves, D. (1986) *Corporate Culture*. London: Frances Pinter.

Guest, D.E. (1987) 'Human resource management and industrial relations', *Journal of Management Studies*, 24 (5): 503–21.

Hendry, C. and Pettigrew, A. (1986) 'The practice of strategic human resource management', *Personnel Review*, 15 (5): 3–8.

Iles, P., Mabey, C. and Robertson, I. (1990) 'HRM practices and employee commitment: possibilities, pitfalls and paradoxes', *British Journal of Management*, 1: 147–57.

Kilmann, R.H. (1982) 'Getting control of corporate culture', *Managing (USA)*, 2: 11–17.

Krefting, L.A. and Frost, P.J. (1985) 'Untangling webs, surfing waves, and wildcatting: a multiple-metaphor perspective on managing organizational culture', in P.J. Frost, L.F. Moore, M.R. Louis, C.C. Lundberg and J. Martin (eds), *Organizational Culture*. Beverly Hills, CA: Sage. pp. 155–68.

Legge, K. (1989) 'Human resource management: a critical analysis', in J. Storey (ed.), *New Perspectives on Human Resource Management*. London: Routledge. pp. 19–40.

Lengnick-Hall, C.A. and Lengnick-Hall, M.L. (1988) 'Strategic human resources management: a review of the literature and a proposed typology', *Academy of Management Review*, 13 (3): 454–70.

Mintzberg, H. (1975) 'The manager's job: folklore and fact', *Havard Business Review*, July–August: 49–61.

Ogbonna, E. (1990) 'Organization culture and strategy in the UK supermarket industry'. PhD dissertation, Cardiff Business School, University of Wales.

Ogbonna, E. and Wilkinson, B. (1988) 'Corporate strategy and corporate culture: the management of change in the UK supermarket industry', *Personnel Review*, 17 (6): 10–14.

Piercy, N. (1987) 'Marketing concepts and marketing action, the role of organizational culture, structure and process in implementing marketing change', Cardiff Business School, Working Paper in Marketing and Strategy.

Ray, C.A. (1986) 'Corporate culture: the last frontier of control', *Journal of Management Studies*, 23 (3): 251–97.

Robbins, S.P. (1987) *Organization Theory*. Hemel Hempstead: Prentice-Hall.

Sathe, V. (1985a) 'How to decipher and change corporate culture', in R. Kilmann, M.J. Saxton and R. Serpa (eds), *Getting Control of the Corporate Culture*. San Francisco: Jossey-Bass. pp. 230–61.

Sathe, V. (1985b) *Culture and Related Corporate Realities*. Hoomwood, ILL: Irwin.

Schein, E.H. (1984) 'Coming to a new awareness of organizational culture', *Sloan Management Review*, 25: 3–6.

Schein, E.H. (1985) *Organizational Culture and Leadership*. San Francisco: Jossey-Bass.

Silverzweig, S. and Allen, R.F. (1976) 'Changing the corporate culture', *Sloan Management Review*, 17 (3): 33–49.

Smircich, L. (1983) 'Concepts of culture and organizational analysis', *Administrative Science Quarterly*, 28 (3): 339–58.

Thackray, J. (1986) 'The corporate culture rage', *Management Today*, February: 66–9, 114.

Tichy, N.M. (1982) 'Managing change strategically: the technical, political and cultural keys', *Organizational Dynamics*, Autumn: 59–80.

Walton, R.E. (1985) 'Towards a strategy of eliciting employee commitment based on policies of mutuality', in R.E. Walton and P.R. Lawrence (eds), *Human Resource Management Trends and Challenges*. Boston: Harvard Business School Press. pp. 35–65.

Wilkins, A.L. (1984) 'The creation of company cultures', *Human Resources Management*, 23 (1): 41–60.

6 EMPOWERMENT OR EMASCULATION? SHOPFLOOR SURVEILLANCE IN A TOTAL QUALITY ORGANIZATION

Graham Sewell and Barry Wilkinson

The following passage is taken from James Rule's book, *Private Lives and Public Surveillance*.

> Every action of a client would be scrutinised, recorded and evaluated both at the moment of occurrence and for ever afterwards. The system would collate all information at a single point, making it impossible for anyone to evade responsibility for his past by fleeing from the scene of earlier behaviour . . . Any sign of disobedience – present or anticipated – would result in corrective action . . . apprehension and sanction would occur immediately. By making detection and retaliation inevitable such a system would make disobedience almost unthinkable. (Rule, 1973: 37)

It is representative of a particular consciousness that emerged in the 1960s and 1970s which was concerned with drawing the public's attention to the insidious growth of the collection and storage of personal information by the state and its agents, enabled by developments in the use of information technology. Although the state has always exercised the right to collect information relating to its citizens[1] – indeed, could not successfully operate in its present form without such a right – it has been the steady emergence of computer-based technology in everyday life which has focused minds on two related fears: the possibly pernicious nature of certain types of surveillance and information gathering in civil society and use and abuse of information generated by such activities. As it now seems that some kind of contact with information technology during our lives is almost inevitable for all of us there appears to be a level of acceptance for certain types of personal information like health records, bank accounts or the electoral roll to be held on computerized systems. In the light of this seemingly inexorable encroachment of computerized information systems into our lives the debate has now shifted towards issues like placing limitations on who has access to information, increasing the security of systems, or minimizing the threat to civil liberties which derives from new techniques like the ability to cross-match data files.[2] The Data Protection Act of 1984 has gone some way towards providing a degree of statutory protection against some of the most obvious abuses of personal data stored on electronic media but concerns remain very much alive.

We mention these points briefly in order that we might highlight what we see as a significant omission in the wider debate over the use of information technology in the gathering of personal/personnel information and its storage, manipulation and retrieval. Although concern relating to these aspects of information technology extends across its impact on most sections of civil society, the use of mechanisms of individual surveillance and control in the industrial, commercial or service workplace have remained relatively unexplored. This omission may seem natural when discussing highly coercive industrial regimes that invoke a vision of an earlier authoritarian age of capitalism but with the current trend towards the use of management practices which collectively we know as Human Resource Management, where the rhetoric of cooperation, trust and the existence of common goals and objectives are to the fore, it is also an omission which can no longer be ignored.

In our own research exploring the role played by information systems in supporting new manufacturing and management techniques like 'Just-in-Time' and 'Total Quality Management' we have been struck by the intensive level of personal surveillance directed at individual members of the workforce which appears to accompany the necessary organizational changes needed to underpin such developments. Within the broader rubric of a critical perspective on human resource management it is our intention in this chapter to explore the nature of such surveillance as a key component of Total Quality Management and contrast its accompanying rhetoric of empowerment, trust and mutual dependency with the shopfloor reality of pervasive regimes of constant electronic and peer group scrutiny, the combined effects of which echo the principles identified by Rule (1973) in our introductory passage.

Human Resource Management: Commitment, Trust and Responsibility?

> Insofar as they provide an umbrella title for a broad range of disciplines such as organizational sociology and psychology, industrial relations and personnel management, the currently favoured use of the words 'human resource management' can be considered as being relatively uncontroversial. However, for some (e.g. Guest 1987) human resource management or HRM is a coherent and distinct concept which integrates the aforementioned disciplines and appears to usher in an approach to the management of employees which emphasises employee commitment and involvement and a relatively caring concern for employees while simultaneously integrating [human resource] policy with strategic business objectives. (Keenoy, 1990: 1)

Looked at in this light, HRM becomes an ambitious project promising a shift in the personnel managers' Janus-like role where they are obliged to balance competing interests and establish 'psychological contracts' (Torrington and Hall, 1987) to one where care and concern for people goes hand-in-hand with the pursuit of profit supported by the maximum utilization of human assets. Apparently unconstrained by notions of irreconcilable conflicts or fundamental differences of interest, for its proponents, HRM appears to offer a means of resolving problems associated with the contradictions of capitalism and the dysfunctions of bureaucracy and hierarchical organization.

A central plank of HRM is the deployment of a number of techniques and practices which, according to its supporters, enables it to effect the heroic achievement of spanning the gulf between the corporate interests of a company and those of its employees. These include the careful selection and induction of employees which contributes to the establishment of a homogeneity of values, a pay and appraisal system which integrates individual and strategic company interests, and a carefully designed internal labour market which gives employees an interest in the long-term success of the organization; in other words, exactly the sort of 'good' personnel practice documented in, and advocated by, countless personnel management textbooks. However, there is considered to be an extra dimension, and it is this 'Factor X' which distinguishes HRM from classical personnel management.

The additional dimension relates to the generation of commitment, trust and responsibility which is held to arise when employees' values fall into line with the employer's 'organizational' values, a congruence which is achieved through the exercise of HRM techniques and practices. Of these, the existence of charismatic or 'transformational' leadership is crucial, along with the fostering of an organizational culture which is characterized by widely shared and strongly held implicit and explicit values (Armstrong, 1987; Legge, 1989). Organizations held up as models of this 'strong' version of HRM, which extends beyond concepts of sound personnel management, are typically the 'excellent' North American companies and the large Japanese corporations (see also Delbridge and Turnbull, Chapter 4, this volume). For Peters and Waterman (1982), excellent companies have 'great leaders' who can 'create enthusiasm' and 'unleash excitement'; they are 'hands-on' manager, role model and hero all in one. Further, the company becomes a 'community' to which people 'belong'; employees are 'members' of a wider social, cultural and even spiritual group which echoes an earlier, idealized age. Witness the rhetoric of a manager in an 'excellent' company:

> Companies like 3M have become a sort of a community centre for employees, as opposed to just a place of work. We have employee clubs, intramural sports, travel clubs and a choral group. This has happened because the community in which people live has become so mobile it is no longer an outlet for the individual. The schools are no longer the social centre for the family. The churches have lost their drawing power as social-family centers. With the breakdown of these traditional structures, certain companies have filled the

void. They have become sort of mother institutions. (Peters and Waterman, 1982: 261)

However, as Peters and Waterman go to some lengths to remind us, an ordinary company can be engineered into an excellent one. Furthermore, charisma is not an intrinsic human gift but is a commodity which can be bought (or learned). Indeed, both the main proponents of 'excellence' have amassed personal fortunes convincing people that these assertions are a matter of fact.

Continuing in a similar vein to that of Peters and Waterman, Pascale and Athos turn their attention to the lessons that can be learnt by Western organizations from their Japanese counterparts. They advocate the role of the organization as providing a source for 'meanings' and 'superordinate goals' for its employees:

> By accident of history, we in the West have evolved a culture that separates man's spiritual life from his institutional life. This turn of events has a far-reaching impact on modern Western organizations. Our companies freely lay claim to mind and muscle, but they are culturally discouraged from intruding upon our personal lives and deeper beliefs.
>
> What is needed in the West is a 'Spiritualism' that enables a firm's superordinate goals to respond truly to the inner meanings that many people seek in their work – or, alternatively, seek in their lives and could find at work if only it were culturally acceptable.
>
> Western institutions are, in fact, backing into this role . . . most major firms describe these activities as 'Human Resource Management' instead of 'personnel' . . . some of our most outstanding companies have long acknowledged a larger role in the lives of their employees and foster greater interdependence among them. All are remarkably 'Japanese' when we look at them closely. Their success may have important implications for Western organizations in the future. (Pascale and Athos, 1982: 192–3)

All this is reminiscent of Elton Mayo and the human relations school which emerged in the United States in the 1930s, when managers were told they might improve productivity and resolve organizational conflicts by good leadership and communication. Rose describes such an ideology as being particularly seductive:

> What, after all, could be more appealing than to be told that one's subordinates are non-logical; that their uncooperativeness is a frustrated urge to collaborate; that their demands for cash mask a need for approval, and that you have a historic destiny as a broker of social harmony. (Rose, 1975: 124)

Human Resource Management, then, like the old human relations movement, envisions a greater, more pervasive role for the organization in both the working and non-work life of individuals, a role which is pursued particularly keenly in contemporary Japan. For the purposes of this chapter our focus is on working life, although the reader may deduce some of the broader implications of our critique of this vision.

Within organizations, HRM is presented as a method of 'releasing untapped reserves of labour-resourcefulness by facilitating employee responsibility, commitment and involvement' (Keenoy, 1990: 4). Here HRM implies a new form of organization which transcends bureaucracy and the role of the employee as a 'cog in the machine' or 'mere subject of exploitation'. The excellence literature provides a popular account of the idealized new form: organizations should be relatively flat, small 'profit' or 'accountability' centres should be set up, responsibility should be pushed to line management or 'team leaders' at the point of production or service delivery, and everyone should have a customer, whether internal or external, to ensure quality by exerting a form of consumer sovereignty on the relationship. These help to give organizational members a sense of 'ownership' leading to 'commitment' and, therefore, the possibility that management may 'trust' the work force (Robson, 1988). Supported by a culture in which employees' values reflect those of the organization, the implication is that eventually workers will be in the position to become self-managing.

The total quality management literature takes these ideas further and is, by most accounts, a fundamental and necessary element within the HRM project. A number of names recur in this literature to the extent that the likes of Philip B. Crosby, W. Edward Deming and Joseph M. Juran have now achieved near-mythological status among quality specialists. Indeed without any hint of irony Oakland (1989) refers to them as the 'Total Quality Gurus'. Central to Deming's thesis is that through improving quality, costs decrease because there is less wastage and correction. Further, he argues that through meeting the requirements of the customer, a larger market share will ensue, leading ultimately to lower prices and improved competitiveness (Deming, 1982). Clearly, in order to extend beyond the enunciation of mere platitudes a mechanism or mechanisms are needed which enables Deming's vision of 'zero defects' to be, if not achieved, then approached. In most of the TQM literature the approach advocated centres around the belief that the delegation of responsibility for quality to the point of production is the essential component of any total quality system – a process referred to by Juran (1979; Juran and Grunya, 1980) as 'worker empowerment'. Within the total quality organization work teams become accountable to their 'customers', whose requirements must be met. Indeed, the popular 'Customer is King' philosophy is inherent to TQM (the equivalent Japanese phrase being 'The honourable customer is God'!) (Lillrank and Kano, 1989). Continuous improvement or *kaizen* activities comprise a further component of the total quality philosophy, emphasizing everyone's responsibility to continuously seek out and solve problems in the production process. Finally, and overarching these ideas, is the principle of developing a pre-emptive as opposed to reactive approach to quality. If the goal of zero defects is to be achieved, then potential defects and their sources must be anticipated and corrective action taken before the event.[3]

A principal component of TQM, that of ceding a degree of responsibility to the shopfloor, resonates strongly with the ideals of HRM. Indeed, the degree of commonality between the TQM and HRM literature is striking – both have been held up as a means of providing job enrichment, with the associated assumption that through giving employees more responsibility they will become increasingly committed to the organization. And on the surface, job enrichment may be apparent. Employees work in teams which are in themselves mini-organizations having their own responsibilities towards their customers. This can entail job enlargement as the team takes on responsibility for quality (through the self-inspection principle) and for routine maintenance and fine tuning of the production schedule. Workers are thereby 'empowered', and are given the resources (training, equipment, etc.) necessary to achieve their goals and to continuously increase their own effectiveness and productivity within the domain of their responsibility. Generally, the whole organization is characterized by delegation: workers are trusted to produce quality goods in the absence of bureaucratic control procedures.

The relatively flat organizational form and enhancement of responsibilities at the level of the team has led some authors to point to the total quality organization as being 'organic' as opposed to 'mechanistic'. It becomes a place where 'the informal "densities of social interaction" get direction and objectives, which are equal to, or at least supportive of, those of the formal organization' (Lillrank and Kano, 1989: 103). TQM, then, has been characterized as a form of organization in which employees can be trusted and 'empowered' to take on more responsibilities in a context of HRM practices which ensure a homogeneity of values. However, this view has not gone uncontested. For example, it has been suggested that the Japanese style of human resource management and their typical style of organizational structure 'increases [top management's] control while giving the impression of lessening it' (Robbins, 1983: 67; Kirkpatrick et al., Chapter 8, this volume). This is because the procedures associated with selection, socialization and appraisal militate against employees pursuing alternative interests, and because top management have greater control of information in the absence of a proliferation of the layers of bureaucracy. Similarly, Muetzelfeldt (1989) argues that a centralization of power simultaneously occurs along with the delegation of responsibility, a process which he terms 'devolutionism'. For Muetzelfeldt, devolutionism

> is an effective political strategy for those who wish to centralise organisational power and simultaneously incorporate workers . . . into those power relations. This is because it appears to devolve and disperse power throughout the organisation, giving the impression that it contributes to industrial democracy. (Muetzelfeldt, 1989: 16).

Our own study of the shopfloor experience of workers who were simultaneously subject to the espoused theory and practice of both HRM and TQM would support such critical perspectives which see 'empowerment' and trust as rhetoric and the centralization of power and control as the reality.

The Shopfloor Experience of Total Quality

The Anatomy of a Total Quality Organization

During the course of our research we were particularly struck by the activities of one company which had developed a sophisticated approach to its quality management programme within its UK plant. In the context of a research project which examined the role of management information systems in supporting just-in-time and total quality operations in a number of diverse manufacturing and service settings, it was this case study which provided us with some of the most thought-provoking material that we have come across. Of particular interest was the novel application, in a mutually supportive role, of both total quality and human resource management practices. As a manufacturer of mass-market consumer electronics, the plant is particularly suited to the application of just-in-time.[4] When this is considered along with the following facts – it is Japanese-owned; it makes wide use of team-based working; senior management speak enthusiastically about extending 'responsibility' to the shopfloor; it has a flattened organizational structure; it makes great play in addressing *all* employees as 'members'; it has a common uniform and cafeteria; indeed exhibits many of the attributes associated with excellent companies – then there may well be a danger of this case being presented as something of an 'ideal type'. However, one of the most striking things about the case is the selective, pragmatic and incremental manner in which this position has been developed to augment what is an unremarkable production process characterized by standardized and repetitive tasks. Furthermore, all this is in a factory which was originally British-owned, then ran as a joint venture before finally coming under the full control of the Japanese partner whilst still retaining many of the management and shop floor personnel from those earlier days. Starting from this base the company has actively sought to develop a culture of cooperation, trust, open communication and participation within and between all levels of the management and shop floor workforce. Furthermore, as will become evident as this chapter proceeds, one of the aspects of the company's operations identified by management as a principal beneficiary of this type of HRM perspective is in the domain of quality management.

This UK plant of 'Kay Electronics'[5] is one of several within the company located throughout the world which manufactures a broadly similar range of consumer electronics products to supply local markets. This activity principally involves the final assembly of components and sub-assemblies on a modular basis. However, the main value-added activity of the plant centres around the insertion of discrete and integrated electronic components on to printed circuit boards (PCBs). It is these PCBs which provide the main source of manufacturing variation as their configuration depends on the technical standards of the destination market for the final product. PCB assembly consists of two main stages. First, core (non-variable) components are automatically mounted on the board, then the individual variable components are inserted by hand. This is the most labour-intensive section of the plant and, as the biggest potential source of in-process errors, is subject to the most active quality programme. It is on the manner in which this quality programme imposes on the PCB shop workforce, both at the collective level of the team and at the level of the individual, that we now wish to focus.

Manufacturing standards for the entire plant are established at the corporate headquarters in Japan. For each new product industrial engineers derive an overall notional standard manufacturing time based on an aggregation of derived standard times relating to relevant sub-assembly operations. These standard times form the basis of manufacturing manuals which then have universal applicability throughout the corporation. The loading of every plant is based on these figures with each plant being obliged to achieve these standard manufacturing times to within plus 5 per cent variance.[6] Thus, the day-to-day activities of the PCB shop itself, like all other parts of the factory, are dominated by the need at least to achieve the externally imposed notional standard times for each particular board, thereby satisfying daily volume and quality requirements.

Physically, the PCB shop comprises a number of product-based cells which are organized around a U-shaped conveyer belt. Each cell is staffed by a team comprising between forty to forty-five members who are led by a team leader with support from two senior members. The positions of team leader and senior member represent the top status and responsibility levels within the internal labour market of the shop floor with accession to these ranks being based on experience and exemplary performance.[7]

Within the limits set by the daily production targets, teams, and especially team leaders, have a great deal of discretion in the way the labour resources are deployed across the cell. Three main tasks must be covered – manual insertion, visual inspection of the boards and electronic circuit testing – and each morning the team meets to discuss the production plan for the shift and then decide who works where for that day. Once the total number of members available to the team has been ascertained then each individual is assigned to a station within the cell where they will usually stay until the end of the shift. In addition to being able to accommodate any minor fluctuations in the production plan, the team must be able to absorb any absenteeism of its members within itself.[8] As in best HRM practice, members are strongly encouraged to obtain more than one skill and those that do are rewarded by advancing within the company's payment structure. Indeed, multi-skilling is effectively essential for the successful operation of the team approach as members are expected to be able work at any station within the cell and must be able to cover each other not only for general absenteeism but also for unscheduled absences during the shift.

One of the most important aspects of the team system as it operates at Kay is illustrated by the way in which individuals are encouraged to improve personal and team performance. Members are constantly made aware by management that production targets should be considered as being somewhat arbitrary and representative of the *minimum* levels which should be attained and that they should seek to make innovations which increase their own productivity or quality performance. Team meetings then provide the forum where any process innovations can be shared with other members and, if suitable, adopted across the team. Not only is this approach consistent with TQM's emphasis on continuous improvement but it can also can be seen as a pragmatic means of responding to increased demand in products from a plant that has been running at capacity since Kay took over control.

The focus of the quality programme in the PCB shop is primarily directed towards the manual insertion activity where the principal concern is that of misinsertion. This concern derives from the fact that manual insertion requires a great deal of dexterity as it involves a member picking up small electronic components and placing their wire connectors in pre-drilled holes on a circuit board as it traverses in front of them on a conveyor belt. In the period of the traverse time across one station members are expected to perform anywhere between six and fifteen insertions, depending on the size and complexity of the components. After manual insertion, visual inspection identifies many of these problems which are recorded and, if possible, immediately rectified by the inspectors. When boards reach the end of the line they are then subjected to two further electronic tests which identify most of the insertion faults missed by the visual inspection. The electronic tests are used to trace the individual responsible for the faulty insertion and it is not uncommon for them to be called from the line to rectify it before the boards are passed on to the next manufacturing stage, an act which is sometimes regarded within teams as being humiliating. On a daily basis the results from these three tests are combined with data generated by a further four tests which are undertaken between the PCB shop and the final despatch area to provide detailed information about the quality performance of the team and its individual members. Not only is all the information relating to the team, including quality performance, absenteeism, conformity to standard times and production planning targets stored on electronic media, but it is also prominently displayed to be visible to all members regardless of their physical position in the cell. These displays invariably form the basis for much of the discussion at the daily team meetings.

During the period of our research at Kay a significant extension of the use of quality information was made. Production specialists from Kay's corporate headquarters spent a month in the plant implementing a system of highly visible displays based on 'traffic light' cards suspended above their heads from the production line superstructure. Depending on their quality performance on the previous shift as indicated by information supplied by the visual and electronic tests, the cards are at either green (no misinsertions), amber (between one and four misinsertions) or red (four or more misinsertions). Thus, in addition to providing the individual member with a reminder that they must improve their performance, it also relays that information to the wider audience constituted by the team.

The Challenge of Quality Monitoring

The form of manufacturing organization employed by Kay Electronics, as described in the previous section, represents an interesting synthesis of what might be described as traditional and new approaches. The traditional is represented by the use of a manufacturing technology dominated by a linear assembly process governed by the speed of a conveyor belt. This traditionalist perspective would be reinforced by a superficial analysis of the individual production tasks performed by members whilst on the line which suggests a highly regularized and repetitive set of tasks that are followed on the basis of externally derived standard times.[9] However, this regularization of production tasks is off-set by ceding much of the responsibility for the day-to-day management of the line to flexibly skilled members who comprise the team – a form of responsible autonomy (Friedman, 1977). Additionally, as senior managers argue in best HRM-fashion, members are further empowered as they have a real ability to improve the operation of the team through seeing the process innovations they are encouraged to make implemented more widely across the cell and, perhaps, throughout the entire corporation.

For the use of the term 'empowerment' of members to be meaningful there must be a genuine shift in the locus of power away from management and to the shopfloor.[10] Indeed, genuine empowerment is not without risks for management as it could eventually undermine the legitimacy of management (the 'Who needs management anyway?' question). However, even a more limited form of empowerment – the 'devolutionism' as described by Muetzelfeldt (1989) – reveals an interesting contradiction in the nature of organizational power: delegation is itself a double-edged sword, which can actually increase the power of the delegating agency, so long as it can legitimate and retain its authority, and undermine it if the obedience of the delegated agents cannot be assured. As Clegg puts it: 'to increase the power of the delegating authority does not mean authorising delegated others and delegated authorities cannot be guaranteed to be the loci of wholly predictable and controlled agency, other than if they are totally obedient' (Clegg, 1988: 108). In short, even though limited empowerment may bring positive benefits (perhaps, for example, greater productivity) it also bestows on the workforce the potential ability to undermine the efficient operation of the plant. Given that multi-skilling and flexible deployment actually extend the domain of the labour process over which an individual worker can extend direct influence, this risk is compounded as a worker has greater scope to 'throw a spanner in the works'.

Although the issue of (dis)obedience may naturally lead one to focus on its unfavourable connotations, it must not be overlooked that the creation of a climate of discretion may not only imply that workers have the opportunity to diverge from management-defined norms negatively. By the same token, opportunities can exist to make positive divergencies. As Clegg argues: 'discretion need not entail dissent: it may be organizationally creative, productive and reproductive' (Clegg, 1988: 108).

We would not wish to argue that this creativity is a unique product of delegation – witness what has respectively been described as 'goldbricking' (Roy, 1952) or 'making-out' (Burawoy, 1979; Roy, 1969) where workers have attempted to use their own ingenuity to marginally improve their working conditions within traditional production regimes. Rather, we consider the argument to revolve around the question of how management harnesses this creativity so as to benefit capital accumulation whilst simultaneously minimizing the opportunities for disruption.

Quality Monitoring in Operation

Committed advocates of HRM would argue that, once common goals are established, the issue of disobedience recedes as workers no longer need to defend a 'frontier of control' behind which they jealously guard the hard-won benefits of 'making-out' but can pass them on in return for an increase in mutual benefit throughout the organization. However, and despite a rhetoric of responsibility and common objectives, we have found that the management of Kay Electronics have been reluctant simply to rely on the goodwill of its workforce on these matters but have developed a disciplinary mechanism, based on the surveillance and control capacities of its quality monitoring system, which is used to identify both positive and negative divergences from management defined norms which are then acted upon accordingly.

Although mechanisms of surveillance and control in an industrial setting can be formal or informal, mechanized or manual, and operate instantaneously or with a delay, after Dandeker (1990), optimum surveillance must cover all the activities of every individual within (and, perhaps ideally, without) the plant[11] and provide instantaneously up-dated information to a central point commanded by an elite controlling group. We will now continue by exploring how the quality monitoring system used by Kay goes some way to approaching this ideal in the name of continuous improvement and total quality.

Although the surveillance of members at Kay explicitly focuses on their quality performance, the issue is also closely related to their personal productivity as the number of faults made by an individual is an indicator of their ability to cope with the speed of the line. Indeed, the possible contradiction in the relationship between speed and quality is captured in a comment made by a member who said: 'When you're interviewed [for the job] they ask you what's the most important – quality or quantity? They want you to say quality, but when you get on the line you see they want both. You can't have both.'

The challenge for management, then, is to establish a dynamic balance between production volume *and* production quality – a situation which the form of surveillance employed by Kay goes a significant way towards achieving through its ability to identify individual members' performance in relation to that of the team. Thus, if the traffic lights constantly indicate that someone is regularly either under-performing (card always on red when others are green) or out-performing (card always on green when others are amber or red) then management can take appropriate steps to identify the reason. The usual action taken if out-performance is identified is to examine that member's activities to establish whether they have made a process innovation (for example effecting two- rather than one-handed insertion for a particular component) which could become a new standard to be tested by speeding up the line and observing how other members adjust to the situation. Similarly, if the under-performance of an individual is identified then managers are equally keen to establish the reason. The primary concerns are if the members concerned need more training or if problems outside the factory may be affecting their performance whilst at work. Counselling by the team leader or further training usually follows but the ultimate sanction of dismissal faces continual transgressors.[12] If all cards are either on red or green it suggests that the line is either too fast or too slow for everyone, begging the question of where the balance between quality and quantity should be set. It appears that the extent of the amber zone (one to four errors) has been set by management to represent a level of performance where the number of errors are acceptable but which also creates a climate where all members are constantly made aware of the need to make improvements – an approach which Slaughter (1987) describes as management by stress.

The 'Panoptic Gaze' of Quality Monitoring and the Social Disciplining Force of the Team

As we have already asserted, the delegation of responsibility associated with HRM would be insupportable unless its positive benefits can be guaranteed. In this light, the effectiveness of Kay's quality system is not simply restricted to its ability to indicate the existence of a problem but also extends to its ability, in a form reminiscent of the Panopticon (Foucault, 1977), to exert a disciplinary force which operates directly on the subjectivity of individual members. In attending work, members are consenting to be subject to a system of surveillance which they know will immediately identify their divergence from norms and automatically trigger sanction or approval. As Rule (1973) has indicated, the risk of instantaneous detection resulting in immediate action makes the member less likely to transgress. Thus, for Foucault, the principal effect of a system of surveillance is that it induces in the member, a state of consciousness and permanent visibility that assures the automatic functioning of power . . . surveillance is permanent in its effects, even if it is discontinuous in its action . . . the perfection of its power should tend to render its actual exercise unnecessary . . . its architectural apparatus should be a machine for creating and sustaining power relations independent of the person who exercises it. (Foucault, 1977: 201)

As Foucault continues, the subject,

should be caught up in a power situation of which they are themselves the bearers . . . [the Panopticon is] a machine for dissociating the see/being seen dyad: on the peripheric ring, one is totally seen, without ever seeing; in the central tower, one sees everything without being seen. (Foucault, 1977: 202)

The final sentence is a reference to the original conception of the Panopticon as an architectonic machine which *sequestrates* subjects (isolates them in time and space) in a series of cells located around a central observation tower. This is all very well in a prison (the Panopticon's original inspiration) but such an arrangement becomes less tenable in a socialized production process involving a division of labour.[13] If Taylorism embodies a desire to minimize the worker's domain of activity in time and space (in a form closely akin to that of sequestration) then job enlargement and teamwork represents the opposite of this and demands a new form of surveillance unconstrained by the limitations of a physical architecture (Sewell and Wilkinson, 1991). We would argue that it is the emergence of what Zuboff (1988) describes as the 'Information Panopticon' which has created the opportunity for the disciplinary power of the Panoptic gaze to be exercised in the context of job enlargement and 'empowerment'. In this sense, the solitary confinement of Taylorism has been superseded by the electronic tagging of the Information Panopticon.

If the self-managing effect which stems from the disciplinary force exerted by the Information Panopticon acting on the subject provides a superior supportive framework for a team-based labour process, then the teams themselves provide their own complementary disciplinary force through peer group scrutiny. Although in replacing the 'relays' of a Weberian bureaucratic hierarchy, electronic surveillance provides management with a vertical information and control system within a flattened organizational structure (Sewell and Wilkinson, 1991), even the most meticulously designed systems of surveillance may not provide total coverage in practice. For example, it became clear at Kay that members would often counter the impact of misinsertions being attributed to them by asserting that the component had been dislodged further down the line by a subsequent operation. Nevertheless, it was still identified as a problem within the team and one which they had the collective responsibility to rectify. Thus, through team-based organization, members are made to be aware of other members' mistakes and, within the forum of the team meeting, are required to develop measures to tackle them. The personal effect of this form of peer group scrutiny was vividly demonstrated by one member who said: 'OK, so no one likes to have a red card hanging above their head but it's when you see other people with red cards when yours is green that it really gets to you.'

The combination of the cards and the selective display of both individual and team performance indicators (quality, productivity, absenteeism, etc.) enables the team to identify those members who 'aren't up to it'. This creates a climate where a horizontal disciplinary force, based on peer scrutiny, operates throughout the team as members seek to identify and sanction those who may jeopardize its overall performance.

Given the apparently profound impact that these mechanisms of surveillance, discipline and control have throughout Kay, one might assume that they form the focus for much debate and no little resistance within the factory. However, in terms of general resistance to the operation of both the horizontal and vertical disciplinary mechanisms at play, we found little evidence at Kay that either formed any kind of focus for dissent. For example, perhaps the most obvious way to subvert the effectiveness of the quality monitoring would be for the team to act concertedly by agreeing to work up to a maximum line speed set by themselves (it is the team leader who controls the speed of the line during a shift), by purposely misinserting components or, ultimately, sabotaging the quality monitoring systems themselves. However, at Kay it was clear that, despite being all too aware that they were being subjected to the scrutiny of a managerially imposed disciplinary mechanism, members put up little opposition to its operation. This lack of opposition can be related to the rigorous application of the selection, induction and industrial relations practices described earlier – perhaps a personnel manager's quest to identify potentially 'docile bodies' in advance.

The institutionalized acceptance of managerial prerogatives is further illustrated by the fact that the initial implementation of the system and subsequent 'improvements' to its functioning, such as the introduction of the traffic lights, have *never* formed the subject for bilateral negotiations between management and members' representatives. Indeed, when asked how they felt about the imposition of the card system the most common response we elicited from the members was a seemingly unquestioning acceptance of their operation – 'just another part of the job' forming an inevitable extension of the managerially imposed control system to be accepted along with all other terms and conditions. Furthermore, it may be salutary for the individuals taking part in any course of prospective resistance to note that even if any collective action were to take place, it would have to face the possible challenge of being undermined by the quality monitoring system's ability to identify even the smallest possible divergencies from the norm made by particular individuals, who could then be singled out by management for dismissal.

Conclusions

It seems that everywhere in business Human Resource Management departments are emerging from the husks of former Personnel departments. This trend is also being followed in academic settings – what British business or management school would be complete without its HRM section? Both these developments are not surprising given that the promises of HRM as enunciated by its principal proponents are so appealing. Indeed, we believe that the espoused benefits which derive from the practising of HRM appear so seductive that, like the member at Kay, HRM itself cannot escape the minutest scrutiny – the emerging orthodoxy cannot go unchallenged. We have made a detailed study of a company which is proud of its record of taking workers from what, traditionally, was a confrontational industrial setting and 'empowering' them in an HRM 'laboratory'. Our conclusions as to how these practices impact on the shop floor are in contrast with the common rhetoric of HRM.

The flattened organizational structure of HRM demands that individuals exercise a degree of self-management, as does a total quality orientation. But do such self-managers possess any real degree of empowerment? The answer is 'yes', but only in a highly circumscribed form. At Kay the team does have some responsibility – for deploying itself throughout the cell; for achieving and then improving on quality performance; and for resolving other issues that are internal to the team – but the responsibility for establishing all the overall production norms still resides with management. In this light, Kay's empowerment is much more closely akin to Muetzelfeldt's devolutionism. Self-management is not supported, and its benefits are not passed on, as part of an act of consent between the members and the team, or the team and the management, but are instilled and perpetuated by a system of surveillance and control that acts directly on the subjectivity of the workers. Thus, the management roles associated with the relays needed to maintain discipline and order within Weberian bureaucracy have not been superseded but internalized within the workers themselves.

In a discussion centring on (em)power(ment) and discipline, it is inconceivable that we could not be drawn to the work of Michel Foucault. Hoy (1986) suggests that Foucault is less concerned with defining the nature of power *per se*, but rather with showing us where to look for it. We looked for the power at Kay and found its realities reflected in the operation of the quality monitoring system. Furthermore, it was Foucault's assertion that unexercised power relations exist everywhere but can only be understood in the context of their direct action on the individual subject. The analogy is akin to that in physics and the relationship between *potential* and *kinetic* energy. Here objects remain static in relation to each other when a system is in equilibrium but will assert their relative potential powers when that equilibrium is disturbed. Within Kay, the existence of a superstructure of surveillance, controlled by management, provides them with a mechanism through which they can exercise potential power but it is not until the equilibrium is disturbed through a member making an error that he or she is withdrawn from the line in view of the whole team to perform a repair, or is dismissed from the company, that the power of management becomes overt. It is the individual member's knowledge of this potential sanctioning which underpins the disciplinary force of the quality monitoring system and supports self-management.

But what are the wider implications of this research for the human resource management project? Based on our evidence of Kay, we argue that a serious questioning of the theory and practice of HRM should take place, especially in relation to the dynamics of the power relations which it seeks to influence and manage. We acknowledge that the evidence presented here could be perceived as being limited in scope by being confined to a single case study, albeit in a company that many HRM experts would be happy to cite as an exemplar of best practice. However, Kay is just the most advanced case of the shopfloor surveillance phenomenon we came across in our research to date and we have identified similar practices in operation in other UK, Japanese and US plants (for example, in the UK plant of one of Kay's Japanese competitors, in a British-owned electronics plant and in Peugeot's Ryton plant where the shop floor is even divided up into 'Surveillance Areas'). Work on other sectors where the rhetoric of HRM is common currency, most notably in forms of retailing (Austrin, 1991; Fuller and Smith, 1991; Ogbonna, 1990), also demonstrates that similar manifestations of the surveillance phenomenon exist elsewhere. We believe that any critical analysis of HRM must embrace the issues raised by this growing body of research.

We reserve our final comments for the subjects of Kay's Power/ Knowledge mechanism – the members themselves. They operate within the context of contradictory signifying systems. On the one hand, the rhetoric of HRM preaches commitment based on trust, a culture based on equality and a unity of goals backed up by practical measures which try to minimize differences (most notably uniforms which do not reflect a hierarchy, a single union deal and a common cafeteria). On the other hand, they are subjected to the closest scrutiny which is used to distinguish them from their peers on matters of the minutest detail. No wonder they do not have a clearly formed position relating to the role of workplace surveillance as it affects them individually and collectively. However, once consciousnesses have encompassed this, the issue of surveillance can enter the arena of industrial politics. Returning to our original theme, ethical concerns for the impact of computer-based surveillance should be extended to the industrial (and commercial) workplaces where the implementation of systems such as those used at Kay can now be the focus of debate and negotiation. Indeed, in those companies that profess to practise it, if the rhetoric of HRM is not to appear hollow then this surely must be an urgent consideration.

Notes

The authors gratefully acknowledge the financial support of the joint committee of the Economic and Social Research Council and the Science and Engineering Research Council.

1. One only has to think of items like the British Census, which has continued virtually uninterrupted since 1801, through the Domesday book, back to the head counts of the Roman Empire and beyond to appreciate the state's zeal in the collection of information concerning its individual citizens.

2. 'Cross-matching' refers to the ability for information from records in one database to be compared with that in others in order to establish unforeseen links. This facility has proved to be particularly attractive to police and security forces, a feature which is often seen as a matter for concern.

3. Statistical process control is increasingly used as a method of anticipating the moment when the quality of a repetitive process is likely to become unacceptable (see Oakland, 1986).

4. See Sewell (1990) for a discussion of the manufacturing and market conditions most suited to the application of these practices.

5. 'Kay Electronics' is, of course, a fictitious name.

6. Plants on the Japanese mainland are not allowed this level of leeway. One British manager within Kay felt that this was a tacit admission on behalf of top management that British workers were not considered to be as able as their Japanese counterparts.

7. Significantly, only one of the management team had risen through the ranks after starting as a member on the shop floor.

8. There is an absolute minimum level of staffing beyond which the team could not operate a normal shift. If this threshold is reached then the team leader must 'beg' spare members from other teams.

9. Perhaps even Taylor himself would have been excited by the possibilities presented by the PCB shop?

10. Although this is clearly a truism, we are concerned that it is a test which has seldom been applied in practice.

11. Yamamoto (1990) describes how workers in one Japanese factory are encouraged to investigate colleagues' lives outside the company if it is suspected that this may be affecting their performance. This can even lead to workers being followed home by work mates!

12. To put the issue of quality in perspective, if a member makes more than twenty identifiable insertion errors in an average of 10,000 individual repetitions during a working month then they are put on probation for the following month. If this level of performance is recorded again in the probationary month the member receives a written warning. If the situation persists for any three consecutive months then the member is dismissed.

13. Mellossi and Pavarini (1981) have argued that the earliest industrial labour process was, indeed, modelled on forced prison labour. Furthermore, Perrot (1979) argues that the architecture and shop floor design of early French factories mirrored that of eighteenth-century prisons.

References

Armstrong, M. (1987) 'Human resource management: a case of the emperor's new clothes?' *Personnel Management*, August: 30–5.

Austrin, T. (1991) 'Flexibility, surveillance and hype in New Zealand financial retailing', *Work, Employment and Society*, 5 (2): 201–21.

Burawoy, M. (1979) *Manufacturing Consent*. Chicago: University of Chicago Press.

Clegg, S.R. (1988) 'Radical revisions: power, discipline and organizations', *Organization Studies*, 10 (1): 97–116.

Dandeker, C. (1990) *Surveillance, Power and Modernity*. Cambridge: Polity Press.
Deming, W.E. (1982) *Quality, Productivity and Competitive Position*. Cambridge, MA.: MIT Press.
Deming, W.E. (1986) *Out of Crisis*. Cambridge, MA.: MIT Press.
Foucault, M. (1977) *Discipline and Punish: The Birth of the Prison*. London: Allen Lane.
Friedman, A. (1977) *Industry and Labour: Class Struggle at Work and Monopoly Capitalism*. London: Macmillan.
Fuller, L. and Smith, V. (1991) 'Consumers' reports: management by customers in a changing economy', *Work, Employment and Society*, 5 (1): 1–16.
Guest, D.E. (1987) 'Human resource management and industrial relations', *Journal of Management Studies*, 24 (5): 503–21.
Hoy, D.C. (1986) 'Power, repression, progress', in D.C. Hoy (ed.), *Foucault: A Critical Reader*. Oxford: Blackwell.
Juran, J.M. (1979) *Quality Control Handbook*. New York: McGraw-Hill.
Juran, J.M. and Grunya, F.M. (1980) *Quality Analysis and Planning*. New York: McGraw-Hill.
Keenoy, T. (1990) 'HRM and work values in Britain', Paper presented at the Second International Conference of the International Society for the Study of Work and Organizational Values, Prague, 19–22 August.
Legge, K. (1989) 'HRM: a critical analysis', in J. Storey (ed.), *New Perspectives in HRM*. London: Routledge.
Lillrank, P. and Kano, N. (1989) *Continuous Improvement: Quality Control Circles in Japanese Industry*. Michigan: Ann Arbor.
Mellossi, D. and Pavarini, M. (1981) *The Prison and the Factory*. London: Macmillan.
Muetzelfeldt, M. (1989) 'Organization as strategic control', Paper presented at the 3rd APROS Conference on Organizations, Technology and Culture, ANU, Canberra, 14–16 December.
Oakland, J.S. (1986) *Statistical Process Control*. London: Heinemann.
Oakland, J.S. (1989) *Total Quality Management*. Oxford: Butterworth-Heinemann.
Ogbonna, E. (1990) 'Organizational culture and organizational strategy in the UK supermarket industry'. PhD dissertation. University of Wales, Cardiff.
Pascale, R.T. and Athos, A.G. (1982) *The Art of Japanese Management*. Harmondsworth: Penguin.
Perrot, M. (1979) 'The three ages of industrial discipline in nineteenth-century France', in J.M. Merriman (ed.), *Consciousness and Class Experience in Nineteenth Century Europe*. London: Holmes & Meier.
Peters, T. and Waterman, R.H. (1982) *In Search of Excellence*. New York: Harper & Row.
Robbins, S.P. (1983) 'The theory Z organization from a power-control perspective', *California Management Review*, 25 (2): 67–75.
Robson, M. (1988) *The Journey to Excellence*. Wantage: MRA International Ltd.
Rose, M. (1975) *Industrial Behaviour*. Harmondsworth: Penguin.
Roy, D. (1952) 'Quota restriction and goldbricking in a machine shop', *American Journal of Sociology*, 57 (5): 427–42.
Roy, D. (1969) 'Making out: a workers' counter-system of control of work situation and relationships', in T. Burns (ed.), *Industrial Man*. Harmondsworth: Penguin.
Rule, J.B. (1973) *Private Lives and Public Surveillance*. London: Allen & Lane.
Sewell, G. (1990) 'Management information systems for JIT production', *Omega*, 18 (5): 451–64.
Sewell, G. and Wilkinson, B. (1991) 'Someone to watch over me: surveillance, discipline and the just-in-time labour process', Paper presented at the 9th International Conference on the Labour Process, UMIST, Manchester, 10–12 March 1991 (forthcoming in *Sociology*).
Slaughter, J. (1987) 'The team concept in the US auto industry: implications for unions', Paper presented at ERU Conference on the Japanization of British Industry, UWIST, Cardiff, 20–22 September.

Torrington, D. and Hall, L. (1987) *Personnel Management: A New Approach*. London: Prentice-Hall.

Yamamoto, K. (1990) 'The "Japanese style industrial relations" and an "informal" employee organization: a case study of the Ohgi-Kai at T. Electric', University of Tokyo, Institute of Social Science Occasional Paper No. 8, December.

Zuboff, S. (1988) *In the Age of the Smart Machine*. New York: Basic Books.

7   HRM AND THE LIMITS OF FLEXIBILITY

Paul Blyton and Jonathan Morris

The purpose of this chapter is to examine the relationship between workforce flexibility and HRM. Though widely viewed as a key component of HRM, this relationship is flawed at two levels: first, a number of contradictions are identifiable between the pursuit of flexibility and other HRM objectives; second, marked internal contradictions exist within the flexibility concept itself. Combined, these make the relationship between HRM and flexibility highly problematic. It is argued that only by significantly changing the way many managers are pursuing greater flexibility will they begin to resolve the difficulties that they currently face in simultaneously trying to pursue flexibility and other HRM practices.

HRM and Flexibility: Establishing the Links

In searching (sometimes in vain) for the core elements of HRM, several writers have highlighted the importance of workforce flexibility. In Legge's (1989) critical analysis of the HRM concept, for example, she argues that proponents of HRM champion the workforce as a 'source of competitive advantage, that . . . may be tapped most effectively by mutually consistent policies that promote commitment and which, as a consequence, foster a willingness in employees to act *flexibly* in the interest of the "adaptive organization's" pursuit of excellence' (1989: 25, emphasis added). Similarly, Guest (1987, 1989) identifies 'flexibility among employees' as one of four central policy goals of HRM (the others being the integration of human resource issues into strategic plans, high commitment and high quality). Likewise, for Storey (1989: 3) 'new patterns of working' – particularly various forms of flexibility – figure prominently in the developments which have given rise to the change in terminology from 'personnel management' to 'human resource management'.

Underpinning this linkage of HRM and flexibility is the argument that HRM posits a closer connection between business strategies and personnel policies and practices. In a market environment characterized by both increased competition and greater turbulence, a key requirement of strategic planning is to achieve both cost efficiency and adaptability. One of the ways this feeds through to human resource issues is the pursuit of greater workforce flexibility, in which the labour force is utilized more effectively, not least through being more responsive to fluctuations and shifts in both the nature and level of demand, and changes in technology and production processes.

This view is particularly consistent with 'harder' versions of HRM. Storey (1989: 8) summarizes the 'hard' version in terms of its emphasis on 'the quantitative, calculative and business-strategic aspects of managing the headcounts resource'. Under this approach, flexibility would potentially represent a strategy based on making more adjustable the volume of labour, the position of job boundaries and/or the structure of remuneration, in order to reduce labour costs and increase labour utilization. For proponents of 'softer' versions of HRM too, however, flexibility also represents a potentially important dimension. Under this approach – which Storey (1989: 8) characterizes as placing more emphasis on communication, motivation and leadership – flexibility is seen to contribute to an approach to create, for example, more fulfilling jobs through the acquisition of a broader range of competences and responsibilities, or more convenient jobs through the development of more flexible working time arrangements.

As we review briefly below, various factors in the last decade have given rise to an increased emphasis on flexibility. As argued elsewhere in this volume, however, in the private sector at least, one pervasive influence behind the growth in interest in both HRM and flexibility has been the need to respond not just to general increases in levels of competition, but specifically to those levels of productivity and competitiveness achieved by Japanese companies over the past twenty years (see Whipp; Delbridge and Turnbull, Chapters 3 and 4, this volume). Interpretations of the effective use of labour in Japan have emphasized both the continued use of temporary workers as a buffer against demand fluctuations and the maintenance of permanent employment relationships among other groups, based on the reciprocal exchange of job security for acceptance of internal mobility within the organization (Dore, 1986). For Dore, the Japanese life-time employment system, while appearing a potential source of *rigidity*, in practice yields high levels of *flexibility*, due to this willingness of employees to accept internal mobility and new technology.

What is significant in this, however, is the inclusion in the Japanese system of both task-related flexibility (in its emphasis on the internal mobility capacity of its permanent workers) and numerical flexibility (secured through the use of temporary workers). In the HRM literature such flexibility distinctions tend to be left implicit. Yet given the linkage between HRM and business objectives and strategies, it would seem that as well as developing a versatile workforce to adapt to market developments, human resource managers are also required to be sensitive to fluctuations in market demand, responding by varying the number of workers employed and/or their working hours. Hence, potentially at least, human resource managers will be seeking to utilize several, rather than a single approach to workforce flexibility. The significance of this will become clear in the following pages.

In addition to the effect of the Japanese productivity 'miracle', several other factors can be identified which have encouraged the increasing attention paid to workforce flexibility over the last decade. We have examined these in more detail elsewhere (Blyton, 1992b; Blyton and Morris, 1991) and it is necessary only to summarize the main ones here. They include:

1. a series of developments perceived to be intensifying levels of competition in product markets, including: a growth in international trade in goods and services; growth in the activity of newly industrializing countries; the continued productivity gains achieved in Japan; increased liberalization of trade in Europe and North America; and deregulation policies increasing competition in various public sectors;
2. more volatile and less predictable product markets due partly to an intensified search for competitive advantage via new product development;
3. the effects of world recession in the early 1980s, resulting in widespread reductions in workforce levels and subsequent re-casting of job boundaries;
4. the impact of new technologies which in many cases have undermined the logic of existing job boundaries and job classifications;
5. the effects of different labour market conditions – in some areas, slack labour markets and high unemployment allowing organizations to utilize numerical flexibility strategies; in others, tight labour market conditions encouraging greater investment in training of existing workforces to provide adequate coverage of tasks;
6. a weakened trade union movement in the UK and elsewhere which has enabled employers to pursue changes in traditional job boundaries and the extension of practices such as sub-contracting, formerly successfully resisted by unions in many areas of work;
7. state intervention and deregulation policies which have acted to reduce the amount of protection afforded to employees by legislation or trade union influence.
8. changes in labour supply, in particular the growth in female participation in the labour force, many seeking (or prepared to accept) part-time employment.

Many of these factors are relevant not only to understanding the growth in emphasis on workforce flexibility; several are also crucial to understanding the growth of the HRM project itself. For example, in both the UK and US, the generally unitary nature of HRM and its frequent espousal of individual 'employee' rather than collective 'industrial' relations, must be interpreted partly in the light of trade union movements seriously depleted in terms of aggregate membership and influence. Similarly, increases in competition appear to have engendered an accelerated search for competitive advantage from all aspects of organizational activity, including labour activity. In this context of increased attention to sources of efficiency and profitability, HRM has been championed as a more explicit linkage of workforce issues with strategies to achieve competitive gain. Yet, while the concepts of HRM and flexibility may have sprung in part from a common set of circumstances, the contribution of workforce flexibility to HRM is in practice far from unproblematic. Indeed, a closer examination both of the notion of workforce flexibility, and the degree of consistency between flexibility and other dimensions of HRM, reveals several points of contention. The tendency in some countries and work organizations to pursue flexibility via different forms of 'precarious' employment contract, raises particular questions about the consistency of various aspects of flexibility within a broader strategy of human resource management.

The remainder of this chapter explores these issues further and seeks to identify possible ways in which a redefined flexibility could be both more equitable and make a more positive contribution to future employment practice. It must be said, however, that we remain sceptical of the willingness of many organizations in the UK and elsewhere to shift away from what Boyer (1988) and Rojot (1989) among others characterize as short-term, 'defensive' flexibility strategies and engage more fully in the longer-term developments implicit in the ideas underpinning 'strategic' human resource management. To establish the basis for this concluding discussion, however, it is necessary first to review the notion of flexibility itself and then to identify the potential contradictions both within flexibility and between the search for greater workforce flexibility and the pursuit of HRM.

The Notion of Flexibility

Rather than a single 'flexibility' debate, there has in recent years been a series of debates, varying considerably in their levels of analysis and ways in which the term has been employed. Flexibility itself conveys notions of adaptability, pliability and responsiveness to change. As such, it has been utilized variously to interpret changes in policy and practices taking place within individual organizations, as well as in inter-organizational relationships, national labour markets and supra-national economic strategies. From Regulation and Flexible Specialization theories to analyses of labour recruitment, utilization and reward patterns, the notion of flexibility has gained a particular, though conceptually problematic, significance over the past ten years. For our present discussion it is the application of flexibility within and between organizations which is the most pertinent. Here, flexibility has been used to encapsulate a wide range of developments in organizational structures, product and process strategies and, particularly, employment and job practices. In this area of work and employment few, if any, of the changes discussed under the flexibility umbrella are unique to the current period. Indeed, this has been a source of considerable scepticism about the value and validity of the flexibility argument (Pollert, 1991). For Hakim (1990) and others, however, it is the increased *pace* of change and the heightened significance placed on workforce flexibility which marks out the present from earlier periods.

In the current debate, four potential sources of flexibility have attracted most attention.

1. *Functional* or *task* flexibility, referring to the adaptability and mobility of employees to undertake a range of tasks and/or employ a variety of skills and thereby respond more effectively to changing production requirements and technological developments.
2. *Numerical* flexibility, generally used to denote management's ability to vary the amount of labour in response to changes in levels and patterns of demand. Strategies to effect this include use of short-term, casual and temporary contracts and 'hiring and firing' policies (that is, reliance on the external labour market), together with externalizing work through the use of sub-contractors.
3. *Temporal* flexibility, involving varying patterns of hours worked in response to changing patterns of demand or, in some cases, employee needs. Like task and numerical flexibility, a central management objective behind temporal flexibility is to increase the extent to which labour time is fully utilized.
4. *Wage* flexibility, based on a shift away from uniform and standardized pay structures towards more individualized systems containing a greater element of variability, dependent upon performance.

Though increasingly widely used, the flexibility argument suffers from a number of theoretical and empirical shortcomings. The frequent prescriptive nature of its application, the conceptual issues of what should and should not be included as indicators of flexibility, the heterogeneity of those different elements, the evident gulf between the rhetoric and empirical reality of flexibility, the lack of detailed evaluation of the needs and consequences of introducing greater flexibility and the widespread failure to consider conflicts of, or at least competing interests over, how flexibility should be introduced, have detracted from the overall analysis, measurement and evaluation of flexibility (Pollert, 1991). And yet it remains the case that in spite of these shortcomings, flexibility has represented a key issue, if not *the* key issue, in employment relations in several industrial societies over the past decade. Summarizing recent trends in European industrial relations, for example, Baglioni (1990: 12) concluded that labour flexibility has become 'the employers' new frontier' in the management of labour. Evidence from Europe, North America and Australia attests to the increased significance being attached by management to securing greater flexibility in the use of labour (Baglioni and Crouch, 1990; Blyton and Morris, 1991; Boyer, 1988; Laflamme et al., 1989; OECD, 1989).

In seeking to characterize the different emphases given to flexibility in different national contexts, several commentators have summarized general developments in terms of variously labelled (though in practice often closely related) bipolarities. Among the most important of these taxonomies have been those distinguishing between 'defensive' and 'offensive' forms of flexibility (Boyer, 1988) and the associated distinction between 'short-term' and 'long-term' forms of flexibility (Rojot, 1989). Defensive flexibility strategies are characterized primarily as largely *ad hoc*, short-term and opportunistic responses to fluctuations in demand, with flexibility representing a low labour cost response to market changes. Numerical flexibility – particularly the use of temporary workers and those hired on short-term and other precarious contracts – is identified particularly with this form of response. In contrast, 'offensive' or 'long-term' flexibility strategies are characterized as those where more proactive human resource measures are taken to adapt to market and other changing circumstances, and in which emphasis is placed more on achieving an adaptable rather than a low-cost labour force. Functional flexibility, particularly where this entails investment in training employees to undertake a broader range and level of tasks, is central to these notions of offensive and long-term flexibility.

Other analyses of flexibility have made similar distinctions, for example between 'precarious' and 'non-precarious' forms of flexible employment (Rodgers, 1989), and between 'internalization' and 'externalization' flexibility strategies: internalization referring to an increase in the flexibility of internal work arrangements (through temporal and functional changes for example) while externalization denotes either an increased use of the external labour market (for example, through temporary contracts or 'hire and fire' policies) and/or the use of external organizations to undertake sub-contract work (Brunhes, 1989). In Britain, where the 'flexible firm' model has attracted both most of the discussion as well as much criticism of its conceptual and empirical shortcomings, the pursuit of functional flexibility among 'core' work-groups is contrasted with the numerical flexibility located in the 'periphery' (Atkinson, 1984; Malloch, 1991; O'Connell Davidson, 1991; Pollert, 1988).

In Europe, managerial (and macro-economic) strategies in Sweden and Germany have been identified primarily with the pursuit of greater functional flexibility, while in contrast, Britain has been seen as a country giving much greater prominence to achieving higher levels of numerical, and to a lesser extent wage, flexibility (Brunhes, 1989). Reasons for these patterns include the tight labour market conditions in Sweden, the stronger job protection provisions afforded by legislation both in Germany and Sweden, the prior development of extensive vocational training, and the greater support among trade unions for additional training and changes in work practices. In Britain on the other hand, unresolved shortcomings in training provision continue to hinder the development of functional flexibility. This continued under-investment in training is part of a wider management approach to flexibility, which appears to be viewed primarily as a means of reducing labour costs. Such a view has inevitably led to more attention being directed to those aspects of flexibility relating to the volume of labour than to longer-term investment in training and qualifications, which necessarily underpin greater skill flexibility. In addition, greater union and worker protection of traditional job boundaries in the UK, an absence of legislation over job security and prevailing labour market and labour supply conditions, can all be seen to have facilitated a greater emphasis on numerical rather than functional forms of flexibility. In short, the UK approach is characterized more by cost minimization than productivity enhancement.

An example from our own current research would appear to support this pattern. In the UK steel industry in the 1980s, labour flexibility was sought primarily in the increased use of sub-contractors (Fevre, 1987). Only in recent years have the first serious efforts begun to be made to introduce greater inter-craft flexibility which, in some management quarters at least, is viewed as a necessary first step to a reduction in the craft/operator distinction and the growth of teamworking practices. In the German steel industry on the other hand, multi-skilled training has been more extensively introduced into the vocational training system for craft workers, while in certain companies at least (notably Hoesch) there have been significant developments in multi-trained groupworking arrangements taking place over several years (Blyton et al., 1992; Franz and Lichte, 1989; Morris et al., 1992).

Despite the foregoing comments, however, it would be wrong to see these national characterizations of flexibility as anything other than generalized summaries. In practice, organizations are unlikely to pursue only a single source of flexibility. This is also reflected in national legislation. The Employment Promotion Act in Germany, for example, is designed to increase managers' ability to recruit temporary labour. Indeed, in comparing flexibility policies across Europe, Walsh comments that 'in Europe, policy-makers see European industrial competitiveness relying largely on improvements in the functioning and efficiency of labour markets through the removal of rigidities, including reducing job security, weakening the social institutions surrounding the labour market and encouraging greater variety in working hours, contracts and pay' (1991: 351). Thus, even those countries in which conditions appear fertile for the growth of task flexibility, various stimuli exist for the simultaneous extension of numerical forms of flexibility.

Boyer's (1988) conclusions support this. While pointing to national variations in flexibility due to particular socio-economic and environmental factors pertaining to a country, he also identifies a convergence of flexibility strategies in relation to, for example, moves away from rigid hierarchies of skills and jobs. Similar patterns have been identified in North America, particularly in the automobile industry (Holmes, 1991; Katz, 1985). Just as it is possible to identify numerical flexibility strategies in those countries which have been identified principally with task flexibility, so too in countries such as the UK, which have been primarily associated with numerical flexibility, it is evident that many organizations are also pursuing greater task flexibility via measures such as reduction in job classifications and job boundaries, teamworking and more broad-based training programmes. Yet it is in this simultaneous pursuit of different sources of flexibility, and more generally in the different bipolar taxonomies of flexibility, that a key contradiction within the flexibility concept itself lies. For while some aspects of flexibility (such as training for skill flexibility) are predicated on a close and continuing attachment by employees to their work organization, other aspects (utilizing temporary, fixed term and other precarious forms of employment, for example) are based more on a model of limited attachment. Nor is it likely that over a long period, or on any sizeable scale, these two sources of flexibility can be satisfactorily secured at the same time. Continued emphasis on short-term employment with limited prospects for advancement, for example, will tend to militate against the general acquisition of job competences.

We return to these contrasting features of flexibility again in the next section, but before this, two further points need noting concerning potential contradictions within the flexibility concept. First, there are several possible points of conflict between the advocacy of flexibility as part of broad national economic programmes and the pursuit of flexibility within individual work organizations. This is not simply a question of clashes resulting from long-term approaches being emphasized at one level while short-term flexibility is being pursued at another. Even where the aspect of flexibility is a shared one, potential contradictions between different levels can arise. Grahl and Teague (1989), for example, have noted that in the area of occupational qualifications, the needs of organizational and broader labour market flexibility potentially conflict. Within work organizations, the move to more internal, firm-specific skill training and assessment of competence, is widely seen as an important step to establishing greater task flexibility by breaking away from the 'rigidity' of national and formalized systems of skills certification, such as those embodied in traditional craft apprenticeship systems. At national level, however, where labour mobility represents an important aspect of flexibility, this mobility is more likely to be enhanced by standardized and transferable qualifications than by firm-specific training and competence measurement (Grahl and Teague, 1989: 93).

Second, advocates of flexibility run the danger of overstating the value of adaptability and responsiveness to change, and thereby simultaneously understating the importance of stability and continuity within organizations (Standing, 1986). This in part reflects the over-simplified vocabulary which tends to be used and a tendency to juxtapose 'flexibility' with 'rigidity' (the former portrayed in terms of adaptability, the latter conveying notions of fixed attitudes and procedures and a lack of responsiveness to change). In many (often prescriptive) treatments of flexibility there is a clear failure to recognize that too high a degree of flexibility will potentially undermine the basis of organizational cohesion. In the same way, over-emphasis of the importance of multi-skilling and task flexibility could conceivably lead to an under-recognition of the value of specialization, and the job specific knowledge and experience gained as a result of working on the same task for a sustained period.

Flexibility and HRM – Sources of Contradiction

As we noted above, a number of commentators have identified workforce flexibility as a central plank in the definition and objectives of HRM. Yet as we have also discussed, flexibility is not a unidimensional concept but rather incorporates several contrasting elements. This lack of homogeneity is also the key to several (though not all) potential conflicts and contradictions between flexibility and HRM. In as much as the emphasis of HRM is placed on the long-term planning and integration of personnel policies within broader business objectives, it is the longer-term elements of flexibility – in particular the development of greater skill flexibility – where the two concepts appear to be at their most consistent. The investment in training implicit in at least some forms of functional flexibility, coupled with the longer time horizon (that is, not simply a response to short-term market fluctuations) makes functional flexibility more consistent with the precepts of HRM, compared to many of the forms of numerical flexibility.

Here, then, is a central problem with flexibility and HRM. At one level the two concepts appear to be developing in unison, indeed spurred on in countries such as the UK and USA by common facilitating conditions of weakened unionism and governments actively supporting managerial prerogative. However, just as elsewhere in this volume there is serious questioning of the extent to which consistent HRM policies are in fact being pursued, so too in regard to flexibility. Reality appears at odds with much of the rhetoric. In particular, in the UK at least, there is limited evidence of firms pursuing flexibility *strategically*. Hakim's (1990) analysis, for example, found few firms explicitly adopting a 'core/periphery' strategy in relation to their use of labour. This absence of strategy is also suggested by the restricted development of longer-term sources of flexibility in Britain, notably skill flexibility. In the craft areas, the available evidence indicates marginal or modest rather than root and branch changes taking place (Cross, 1988). This suggests either that flexibility changes are being successfully resisted by the workforce, that training and other requirements are inadequate to bring full task flexibility to fruition, or that skill flexibility does not form part of a core strategy in many organizations, but rather is being pursued in a limited, tentative, *ad hoc* and piecemeal fashion (Elger, 1991). Thus, while skill flexibility may be consistent with at least some other aspects of the HRM argument – particularly those characterized as 'soft' HRM – the evidence is that these functional forms of flexibility are not in fact being vigorously pursued.

Given its facility as a short-term response to demand conditions, it is not surprising that evidence is available in the UK of the expansion of at least one form of numerical flexibility, sub-contracting (Marginson, 1991; Morris and Imrie, 1991), though certain other sources of numerical flexibility such as temporary working appear to be remaining fairly stable (Casey, 1991). At a number of points this search for lower labour costs via numerical flexibility is prone to clash with various objectives espoused under HRM. Prominent among these are possible conflicts between flexibility and both the pursuit of higher levels of employee commitment and the securing and maintenance of high quality output. First, it may be anticipated that those on temporary or otherwise precarious contracts, and possibly many workers sub-contracted to organizations, will conceivably display lower levels of commitment to the work organization than those enjoying greater job security, particularly where there is little prospect of increased permanent employment in the organization. This lack of attachment will be exacerbated if temporary, sub-contracted and other groups are also denied access to company share-ownership schemes, performance bonuses and the like, which are specifically designed to build up employees' identification with the company.

Harmonization of employment conditions has also been identified as a potentially important issue for the generation of greater shared identification. Such a policy is consistent with other HRM precepts including the importance of building unitary and strong organizational cultures, in which all employees are encouraged to identify with the organization's success. Some aspects of flexibility, notably reductions in job classifications, could well act in support of a broader development of harmonization. Yet in pursuing other sources of flexibility, the outcome could well be *less* rather than more harmonization. By utilizing different forms of employment contract – for example, temporary and fixed term employment, sub-contracting, annual and variable hours agreements, and individualized pay arrangements – numerical, temporal and wage flexibility may contribute to greater workforce heterogeneity and a shift away from, rather than towards, greater harmonization of terms and conditions of employment.

Second, given the relevance of training and competence for achieving high quality output, those employed on short-term contracts, who almost by definition receive relatively little training, are less likely to achieve consistently high levels of quality production compared to their permanent counterparts. In some cases, the difficulty for managers of simultaneously employing people on precarious (and often poorly paid) contracts and, at the same time, seeking commitment and high quality output, has been recognized. Morris (1987), for example, found that the associated problems have resulted in Japanese companies in Europe showing a considerable reluctance to hire non-full-time permanent workers. In those few instances where part-time or temporary workers have been hired, the conditions offered to the former, and the amount of training and subsequent access to permanent employment made available to the latter, tend to be far higher than is typically associated with part-time and temporary positions in British companies.

The issue of management maintaining control over quality of output is also relevant to the increased use of sub-contracting. By externalizing work, the principal organization potentially compounds its difficulties of maintaining quality standards and more generally retaining control and coordination of the production process (Rubery et al., 1987). This problem relates both to the sourcing of components and to the sub-contracting of those activities (such as specialized maintenance tasks) which have a direct bearing on the production process. Such problems of quality and coordination are not *inevitable* consequences of buyer–supplier relations, however. Studies of these relationships in Japan, and among Japanese firms in Britain, indicate the extent to which collaborative and long-term relationships can be established which yield both coordination and quality (Trevor and Christie, 1988; Morris and Imrie, 1991). Such relationships, however, have proved far from straightforward to replicate among non-Japanese companies. Turnbull's (1991) study of the automotive components industry, for example, found a continuation of low-trust, 'arm's length' relationships despite the clear benefits accruing to those overseas competitors who had achieved closer relations between buyers and suppliers.

These problems of maintaining adequate quality levels are not necessarily confined to numerical flexibility. For instance, unless any cross-task training is fully adequate, and the scope for recognizing individual aptitude and experience sufficiently accommodated within job rotation or team-working schemes, the potential exists for at least some employees spending part of their working time engaged on work for which they are not fully competent. Indeed, in our current steel project mentioned above, at least one steel plant in Germany was found to have abandoned its practice of having craft workers being also engaged in production because of the lower output and quality levels achieved by the mixed craft/production teams (Blyton et al., 1992). In the same way, wage flexibility based on performance-related pay systems could engender the same sort of output and quality problems previously associated with earlier forms of performance-related pay based on piecework. Many piecework payment systems in the past were seen to encourage employees to maximize the quantity of their output, without paying sufficient regard to levels of quality, wastage and so on. Introduction of final quality checks and payment only for defect-free production sought to rectify this. Likewise, current systems of performance-related pay are likely to avoid similar problems only if they adequately build quality into their measurement criteria of performance.

Conclusion

In the way in which they have been conceptualized and discussed over the past decade, both HRM and flexibility share a number of common shortcomings. Both contain a marked diversity in their constituent elements, both owe their development in important part to the particular political and economic conditions of the 1980s, both suffer from an evident gap between an overly-prescriptive rhetoric and an empirical reality, and both tend to offer too managerialist a view of the employment relationship which perceives change as essentially the consequence of managerial will, thereby failing to take sufficient account of the ways in which other interest groups, historical experience and the wider social, economic and political environment, condition and constrain that change process.

Given these problems, it is hardly surprising that various points of conflict and contradiction are identifiable both within flexibility and HRM, as well in the relationship between them. In part these are due to the distinctive elements within each concept. Thus, the divergence between long- and short-term forms of flexibility is paralleled by the 'soft' and 'hard' distinctions in HRM, the former emphasizing more the long-term maximization of human potential, the latter giving sharper focus to the shorter-term control of the labour resource (Storey, 1989; Noon, Chapter 2, this volume). Further, it is not only time-scale which varies here. The longer-term view of both HRM and flexibility appear to offer more positive, proactive and humanitarian approaches to productivity gain than the shorter-term views: productivity enhancement rather than cost minimization.

Even if we accept that the main thrust of the debate on HRM appears to favour a longer-term and strategic perspective, the reality in Britain at least is that much of the interest in workforce flexibility is currently focused on short-term responses, primarily cost-driven and introduced in a more or less *ad hoc* manner. There is scant evidence either of any concerted extension of functional flexibility generally, or even the pursuit of functional flexibility strategies among key workers. Further, as we have agreed, the HRM goals of improved employee commitment, quality of output and harmonization will potentially be undermined by the introduction of different forms of flexible work and employment patterns. More generally, both short- and long-term forms of flexibility potentially clash at several points with other organizational objectives such as continuity and stability.

Despite these problems, if HRM is concerned with the effective matching of human resource with business strategies, flexibility is likely to remain a central feature of HRM thinking, as organizations respond to changing markets and technologies. What then are the possibilities for reconciling the contradictions between flexibility and HRM? This is a large issue and we can only begin to address it here. A core issue, however, would seem to be a failure in the way both concepts have been discussed, to recognize the plurality of interests existing within the workplace and the need to acknowledge *reciprocity* as a basis for building long-term relationships. The analysis of both flexibility and HRM has to date suffered from a widespread over-readiness to adopt a managerial perspective which ignores the distinct interests of employees. The HRM literature, for example, has spent much time concerned with management *securing* commitment, quality, and so on, but far less – indeed almost nothing – on what is being *offered* to employees in return for making this additional commitment. The implicit unitary assumption is that all groups share a common perception of, and identification with, the organization's (financial) success. Further, all too frequently, management appears to be adopting the vocabulary of commitment without recognizing the two-way nature of commitment, and the need to support their call for higher employee commitment through improved job security, high quality terms and conditions of service, and prospects for career advancement. The weakness of many labour markets over the past decade, and the corresponding weakening of trade union influence, has facilitated this one-sided development of HRM.

The same can be seen in regard to flexibility. Labour market conditions, reinforced both by a state withdrawal from labour market regulation and by unions operating in reduced circumstances, have enabled management to use flexibility not only to transfer product market uncertainties onto employees, but more generally to define flexibility in ways which match managerial objectives rather than ones which could represent possible areas of common ground with employees, in relation to work and employment patterns. Elsewhere we have discussed temporal flexibility as one potentially fertile area for this common ground to be identified (Blyton, 1992a). Similar reciprocity is also required in other areas of flexibility – for example, in regard to skill enhancement – if they are to contribute positively to other HRM policy goals.

Thus we are arguing that for HRM and flexibility to persist as key concepts in work and employment relationships, greater recognition must be given to the view that a high quality, flexible and committed workforce can only be achieved and sustained over a significant period if the overall employment relationship is based on a more equitable reciprocity. It is not enough for management to claim flexibility and commitment simply in terms of the organization's 'needs' for low-cost, competitive production. As particular national examples (Sweden and the FRG, for example) indicate, it *is* possible to develop flexibility and human resource policies in systems which operate with high wages, legislated employment protection and an acceptance of the legitimacy of trade union and employee influence. We would hold that in the longer term, HRM and workforce flexibility are *only* sustainable if they also provide the income, security and prospects for advancement which match the increasing demands being placed upon the workforce.

References

Atkinson, J. (1984) 'Manpower strategies for flexible organisations', *Personnel Management*, August: 28–31.

Baglioni, G. (1990) 'Industrial relations in Europe in the 1980s', in G. Baglioni and C. Crouch (eds), *European Industrial Relations: The Challenge of Flexibility*. London: Sage. pp. 1–41.

Baglioni, G. and Crouch, C. (eds), (1990) *European Industrial Relations: The Challenge of Flexibility*. London: Sage.

Blyton, P. (1992a) 'Flexible times? Recent developments in temporal flexibility', *Industrial Relations Journal*, 23 (1): 26–36.

Blyton, P. (1992b) 'The search for workforce flexibility', in B. Towers (ed.), *Human Resource Management*. Oxford: Blackwell. pp. 295–318.

Blyton, P. and Morris, J. (1991) 'A flexible future: aspects of the flexibility debates and some unresolved issues', in P. Blyton and J. Morris (eds), *A Flexible Future? Prospects for Employment and Organization*. Berlin: de Gruyter. pp. 1–21.

Blyton, P., Franz, H.W., Morris, J. and Bacon, N. (1992) *Work Reorganization in the UK and German Steel Industries*. Final Report, London: Anglo-German Foundation.

Boyer, R. (ed.) (1988) *The Search for Labour Market Flexibility*. Oxford: Clarendon Press.

Brunhes, B. (1989) 'Labour flexibility in enterprises: a comparison of firms in four European countries', in Organisation for Economic Cooperation and Development (ed.) *Labour Market Flexibility: Trends in Enterprises*. Paris: OECD. pp. 11–36.

Casey, B. (1991) 'Survey evidence on trends in "non-standard" employment', in A. Pollert (ed.), *Farewell to Flexibility?* Oxford: Blackwell. pp. 179–99.

Cross, M. (1988) 'Changes in working practices in UK manufacturing 1981–88', *Industrial Relations Review and Report*, 415, May: 2–10.

Dore, R. (1986) *Flexible Rigidities*. London: Athlone.

Elger, T. (1991) 'Task flexibility and the intensification of labour in UK manufacturing in the 1980s', in A. Pollert (ed.), *Farewell to Flexibility?* Oxford: Blackwell. pp. 46–66.

Fevre, R. (1987) 'Subcontracting in steel', *Work, Employment and Society*, 1 (4): 509–27.

Franz, H.W. and Lichte, R. (1989) *Study of the Vocational Training Requirements in the European Iron and Steel Industry*. Dortmund: Sozialforschungsstelle.

Grahl, J. and Teague, P. (1989) 'Labour market flexibility in West Germany, Britain and France', *West European Politics*, 12 (2): 91–111.

Guest, D.E (1987) 'Human resource management and industrial relations', *Journal of Management Studies*, 24 (5) : 503–21.

Guest, D.E. (1989) 'Human resource management: its implications for industrial relations and trade unions', in J. Storey (ed.), *New Perspectives on Human Resource Management*. London: Routledge. pp. 41–55.

Hakim, C. (1990) 'Core and periphery in employers' workforce strategies: evidence from the 1987 ELUS Survey', *Work, Employment and Society*, 4 (2): 157–88.

Holmes, J. (1991) 'From uniformity to diversity: changing patterns of wages and work practices in the North American automobile industry', in P. Blyton and J. Morris (eds), *A Flexible Future? Prospects for Employment and Organization*. Berlin: de Gruyter. pp. 129–56.

Katz, H.C. (1985) *Shifting Gears: Changing Labour Relations in the US Automobile Industry*. Cambridge, MA: MIT Press.

Laflamme, G., Murray, G., Belanger, J. and Ferland, G. (eds) (1989) *Flexibility and Labour Markets in Canada and the United States*. Geneva: International Institute for Labour Studies.

Legge, K. (1989) 'Human resource management: a critical analysis', in J. Storey (ed.), *New Perspectives on Human Resource Management*. London: Routledge. pp. 19–40.

Malloch, H. (1991) 'Strategic management and the decision to subcontract', in P. Blyton and J. Morris (eds), *A Flexible Future? Prospects for Employment and Organization*. Berlin: de Gruyter. pp. 191–210.

Marginson, P. (1991) 'Change and continuity in the employment structure of large companies', in A. Pollert (ed.), *Farewell to Flexibility?* Oxford: Blackwell. pp. 32–45.

Morris, J. (1987) *Japanese Manufacturing Investment in the EEC: The Effects of Integration*. Report to DG 1, EEC, Brussels.

Morris, J., Blyton, P., Bacon, N. and Franz, H.W. (1991) 'Beyond survival: the implementation of new forms of work organisation in the UK and German steel industries', *International Journal of Human Resource Management*, 3 (2): 307–29.

Morris, J. and Imrie, R. (1991) *Transforming Buyer–Supplier Relations: Japanese Style Industrial Practices in a Western Context*. London: Macmillan.

O'Connell Davidson, J. (1991) 'Subcontract, flexibility and changing employment relations in the water industry', in P. Blyton and J. Morris (eds), *A Flexible Future: Prospects for Employment and Organization*. Berlin: de Gruyter. pp. 241–58.

OECD (Organisation for Economic Cooperation and Development) (ed.) (1989) *Labour Market Flexibility: Trends in Enterprises*. Paris: OECD.

Pollert, A. (1988) 'The "flexible firm": fixation or fact?' *Work, Employment and Society*, 2 (3): 281–316.

Pollert, A. (1991) 'The orthodoxy of flexibility', in A. Pollert (ed.), *Farewell to Flexibility?* Oxford: Blackwell. pp. 3–31.

Rodgers, G. (1989) 'Precarious work in Western Europe: recent evidence', in G. Laflamme, G. Murray, J. Belanger and G. Ferland (eds), *Flexibility and Labour Markets in Canada and the United States*. Geneva: International Institute for Labour Studies. pp. 145–62.

Rojot, J. (1989) 'National experiences in labour market flexibility', in Organisation for Economic Cooperation and Development (ed.) *Labour Market Flexibility: Trends in Enterprises*. Paris: OECD. pp. 37–60.

Rubery, J., Tarling, R. and Wilkinson, F. (1987) 'Flexibility, marketing and the organisation of production', *Labour and Society*, 12 (1): 131–51.

Standing, G. (1986) *Unemployment and Labour Market Flexibility: The United Kingdom*. Geneva: International Labour Organisation.

Storey, J. (ed.) (1989) *New Perspectives on Human Resource Management*. London: Routledge.

Trevor, M. and Christie, I. (1988) *Manufacturers and Suppliers in Britain and Japan*. London: Pinter.

Turnbull, P. (1991) 'Buyer–supplier relations in the UK automotive industry', in P. Blyton and J. Morris (eds), *A Flexible Future? Prospects for Employment and Organization*. Berlin: de Gruyter. pp. 169–90.

Walsh, T. (1991) 'The reshaping of "flexible" labour? European policy perspectives', in P. Blyton and J. Morris (eds), *A Flexible Future? Prospects for Employment and Organization*. Berlin: de Gruyter. pp. 349–64.

8 DECENTRALIZATION: FRIEND OR FOE OF HRM?

Ian Kirkpatrick, Annette Davies and Nick Oliver

One of the central tenets of human resource management (HRM) is that responsibility for personnel issues be devolved to line management, and that organizational sub-units operate with a high degree of autonomy. Many organizations are currently decentralizing for business-strategic reasons, and superficially this would seem to offer opportunities for HRM practices to spread. However, for those wishing to promote HRM, decentralization may prove to be a two-edged sword. This chapter explores why.

In recent years a growing number of academics and practitioners have viewed human resource management as a new enlightenment in personnel work. A new role is prophesied for personnel professionals who have been traditionally excluded from business policy decisions and 'isolated' from other executive managers (Guest, 1982). There is no shortage of definitions of the term HRM in the literature but perhaps the most comprehensive has been proposed by Guest, who put forward an ideal type model in which HRM is described as 'a set of policies designed to maximize organizational integration, employee commitment, flexibility and the quality of work' (Guest, 1987: 503), with a view to maximizing business effectiveness. Guest further argues that HRM demands a series of interconnected changes in values, organizational structure and job descriptions. These are necessary given the dual objective of integrating human resource policies both 'internally', to achieve consistency, and 'externally' with strategic planning.

Fundamental to HRM is a unitary set of values or 'holistic' philosophy which underpins managerial action and promotes 'the development of all aspects of an organizational context so that they encourage and even direct managerial behaviour with regard to people' (Beer et al., 1985: 4). It is precisely this 'holistic' philosophy of employee development, relying on the active agency of line managers which most clearly differentiates HRM from conventional models of personnel management. In this chapter the feasibility of implementing an ideal-type model of HRM under conditions of decentralization is explored.

There is now a great deal of evidence showing a general trend towards the decentralization of management and organizational structures (Channon, 1982). Such structural changes have resulted, according to Goold and Campbell (1986) because of the emergence of large diversified companies: 'As firms diversify they move away from being functionally organised towards a divisional structure in which responsibility is pushed down to business unit and profit centre managers' (Goold and Campbell, 1986: 1).

Evidence of these structural changes comes from a study of 144 of the largest 500 UK companies by Hill and Pickering (1986). Their conclusion was that now virtually all major UK companies operate with decentralized organizational structures. The trend towards decentralization has led to the restructuring of some corporate personnel functions, forcing them to relocate within divisions or smaller operating units (Evans and Cooling, 1985). Traditionally, personnel played the role of guardian and monitor of core policy, concerned with the need to promote order, equity and consistency, in effect 'one of the last remaining centralizing forces' (Hendry, 1990: 93). However, the more an organization pursues decentralization the more superfluous this role becomes. Using a case study of a multinational oil company, this chapter examines the dynamics of this process. First, however, the HRM 'package' requires a fuller description.

A Normative Model of HRM

Guest's (1987) ideal-type model is used to characterize the HRM package as it is 'the most serious and constructive attempt to provide analytical clarity' (Keenoy, 1990: 372) in a complex debate. Guest identifies four key goals of HRM namely integration, commitment, flexibility and quality. These goals are based on the assumptions of needs theory, unitarism and individualism, which many observers, including Guest himself, have questioned (Storey, 1989). Central to the model is an assumption that, if these goals operate simultaneously, then one might expect human resource policies to result in improved business performance. To understand how this occurs it is necessary to describe these goals in more detail.

First there is the goal of integration, which, according to Guest, should operate on four levels. The first level is an integration of human resource policy with strategic planning. Recently Legge has reconceptualized this as a contingent 'external' fit (Legge, 1989). The next level is an integration of internal processes, derived from 'the need for human resources policies to cohere with other areas of policy and secondly, within themselves' (Guest, 1987: 512) achieving a form of vertical integration closely associated with the strategic dimension. The third level comprises the central idea of integrating human resource policies within the management process emphasizing the 'attitudes and behaviour of line managers' as 'their recognition of the importance of human resources and the need to engage in practices which engage this understanding is critical' (Guest, 1987: 512). This level of integration has been described as the strongest element of HRM (Armstrong, 1989). According to Legge it is this notion of HRM as a

central managerial activity, in effect 'the discovery of personnel management by senior executives' (Legge, 1989: 29) which most clearly differentiates it from personnel management. Ultimately, HRM is about line
managers enacting personnel policies within their existing, albeit enlarged,
role by having already incorporated a philosophy which sees the employee
as an asset to be developed rather than a cost to be minimized. The final
level of integration is that of congruency, or the identity of interest
between employee values and business goals (see Ogbonna, Chapter 5, this
volume).

From these notions of integration Guest talks about the goal of
commitment, its importance based on 'the assumption that committed
employees will be more satisfied, more productive and more adaptable'
(Guest, 1987: 513). Adaptability and flexibility constitute the third goal of
HRM and Guest describes the importance of flexibility within systems and
structures as well as in terms of job content. Such flexibility, it is argued,
only becomes 'feasible if employees at all levels display high organizational
commitment, high trust and high levels of intrinsic motivation' (Guest,
1987: 514). The last goal of quality, both in terms of staff, work
performance and public image should of course develop from the other
three, but will also demand good communications and effective management systems.

It can be concluded from the above discussion that the normative model
consists of two inter-related elements, the 'developmental' and the
'operational'. The former stresses the need for long-term employee
centred policy choices designed to improve commitment and involvement
while the latter specifically refers to the integration of personnel and line
management (including also the need for short-term responses to
uncertainty). In theory at least, there may be no reason why these two
elements of the model should not complement each other in a virtuous
circle. In support of this logic, Legge (1989) introduces the notion of 'tough
love', that is 'management care that doesn't shy away from tough
decisions': 'Development, flexibility and adaptability are defined by the
organization and in its own interests. The company's interests and those of
its employees are equated' (Legge, 1989: 34).

However, this ideal-type model relies on a particularly strong assumption of line management already having incorporated the HRM philosophy
(particularly its developmental side) in the first place. Without this the
operational and developmental aspects will fail to complement each other
and could even start to form a vicious circle. Any experimentation of HRM
techniques would then be piecemeal and opportunistic efforts, doomed to
failure without any 'underlying accepted standard of treatment for
employees beyond pure short term commercial logic' (Purcell, 1987: 546).
It is precisely because HRM relies upon this incorporation of values (or
culture) at all levels that contradictions may often arise in practice. In the
remaining sections of this chapter we examine the context of the
decentralized organization, and investigate the occurrence of such contra-

dictions in an arena where management action is constrained by both structural and attitudinal factors.

Decentralization and the Prospects for HRM

In order to discuss the prospects for HRM in a decentralized context, a number of separate issues will need to be considered. First, what factors are likely to influence the extent to which an organization pursues decentralization? (Decentralization in this context refers to a greater separation of decision-making power between corporate office and operating divisions/units). Secondly, what characteristic behaviours are displayed by organizations which have pursued various degrees of decentralization? Finally, what are the implications of this trend towards decentralized structures for the role of personnel managers and the replacement of the traditional personnel role with some variation of the HRM model?

Factors Influencing Decentralization

If the structure/strategy mix and the extent of decentralization of large firms is itself mediated by a variety of contingencies (Chandler, 1962; Galbraith and Kazanjian, 1986), how is this process explained? Purcell and Alhstrand (1987) refer in their studies to an interplay between first and second order strategies, first order being concerned with basic goals and direction, and second order with issues of organizational structure and the internal distribution of decision-making power. Second order strategy determines the degree of autonomy and control between corporate office and operating division/units. This interplay functions as a 'normative cascade', in which 'decisions on the scope of activities and goals will lead to decisions on organizational structure and internal control mechanisms' (Purcell and Alhstrand, 1987: 6). Linked to this are issues such as the extent and direction of diversification. For example, a first order strategy of diversification into unrelated product markets might well generate a second order strategy of greater decentralization (more divisional/unit autonomy), whereas a strategy of related diversification would demand less decentralization (more internal synergy/integration with less unit autonomy). There are also third order strategies which relate to employee relations issues – the degree to which these influence the first and second order strategy is discussed later.

'Types' of Decentralized Organization

So far we have identified a number of forces which help explain why organizations have pursued decentralization to a greater or lesser extent. What, however, are the characteristics displayed by these relatively decentralized organizations? Goold and Campbell (1986) refer to at least three possible types, namely strategic planning, strategic control and financial control firms which vary on a continuum of low to high decentralization respectively. These ideal types also display totally different behavioural responses to the market. Financial control companies, on the highly decentralized end of the continuum, typically place more emphasis on the application of short-term financial performance targets to business units, allowing for a greater level of autonomy, characteristic of 'portfolio' style management (Purcell, 1989). In contrast, strategic planning, or 'critical function' (Sisson and Scullion, 1985) organizations lay more stress on internal integration and synergy, with higher levels of corporate office involvement in the management of operating divisions, playing a kind of 'developmental' role. Although these typologies are a useful tool for our analysis, more recent work by Hill and Hoskisson has shown that:

> As firms grow by vertical integration or related diversification, they will become increasingly constrained by information processing requirements to focus on attaining financial economies, [and that] under conditions of either high or increasing uncertainty, vertically integrated firms will focus on realizing financial economies. (Hill and Hoskisson, 1987: 338)

Given this, it seems that despite the plurality of arrangements possible, even in those firms we may expect to display the characteristics of strategic planning, the pressures of cost minimization eventually lead to a form of decentralization more in line with financial control.

Decentralization and the Role of Personnel

There is growing evidence that the role of the personnel function at corporate level in large organizations is in decline (Hunt and Lees, 1987; Purcell and Alhstrand, 1987). The 1985 Workplace Industrial Relations Company Level Survey (Marginson et al., 1988a) shows a marked fall in the number of personnel and industrial relations directorships compared to the earlier, more comprehensive, Workplace Industrial Relations Survey (Millward and Stevens, 1986). This view is also supported by Evans and Cooling who argue that:

> The staffing of many central personnel functions has fallen as organizations have decentralized and reduced the significance of corporate policy functions. More personnel specialists have often been added to the divisions or operating companies, with greater responsibility for developing personnel policies at this level. (Evans and Cooling, 1985: 17)

A note of caution is necessary here lest we convey the impression that all personnel departments have suddenly been decentralized in this way. Decentralization is a matter of degree and has reached different stages of development in different organizations; clearly some personnel departments will have maintained certain corporate functions. Furthermore, Marginson et al. (1988b) argue that the process of decentralization is itself confusing and traumatic, often without any clearly definable separation between corporate and operational decision-making. This suggests that many organizations are transitional 'half-way house configurations' in which personnel is neither fully decentralized nor totally centralized. A great many corporate personnel departments are still playing their traditional role of monitoring and instructing operating units on core policy. Certain corporate functions may also maintain 'dotted line' relationships with personnel departments in operating units while at the same time limiting their own role to one of providing internal consultancy services (Evans and Cooling, 1985). However, this will operate on a continuum so that, 'The great majority of enterprises which devolved profit responsibility, by designating lower levels as profit centres, were significantly less centralized than the small number of enterprises which did not' (Marginson et al., 1988b: 242). In this sense it is therefore still justifiable to talk about a clear trend towards decentralizing personnel.

This debate supports the idea that personnel is losing its strategic role, but closer inspection reveals a more complex picture. Research by Purcell and Alhstrand (1987) considered how far HR policies, which they describe as third order strategy, are taken into account when first and second order strategies, which basically determine organizational structures, are decided. The 'critical choices' concerning human resources which need to be made as part of third order strategy include:

1. the structure of collective bargaining;
2. the organization of personnel;
3. issues of corporate culture (style);
4. internal labour markets.

In looking at the interplay between these different levels of strategy Purcell and Alhstrand conclude that in the majority of cases third order strategy is rarely considered when first and second order decisions are made, suggesting that personnel is being excluded, not only from the process but also as an issue worth consideration. Usually third order strategies are mere derivatives, made to fit into the framework of decisions taken higher up. For example, the decentralization of industrial relations: 'Is best explained not by strategic thinking by corporate employee relations executives, but by the need, and sometimes the forced need, to fit the institutions and procedures of IR into the mould created by second order strategy' (Purcell and Alhstrand, 1987: 7).

What has been described looks like a general decline of personnel's strategic role in all cases. However, as mentioned above in our description of different types of decentralized structures, the strategic influence of personnel, and by implication the possible role for strategic HRM, will vary. It might be helpful to consider how this works at the two extremes on a continuum of relative decentralization. First, within strategic planning organizations the existence of a clear 'institutional style' based on the need for internal synergy and integration may preserve some strategic influence for personnel in areas like manpower planning, internal labour markets and corporate culture. These are typically the so-called 'excellent' companies described by Peters and Waterman (1982) who 'stick to their knitting' and pursue long-term employee development goals. Secondly, financial control organizations, at the opposite end of the continuum, are those firms who adopt a more pragmatic approach and in which the greater level of decentralization to operating divisions/units is likely to exclude personnel from any kind of strategic role. Moreover, it is in financial control firms that third order strategies are most likely to be pragmatically slotted into first and second order decisions. This results largely from the strict financial disciplines imposed by corporate offices on local management who are responsible for meeting short-term performance targets. Interference by centralized personnel departments would be seen as nothing less than an incursion on the autonomy of operating/division/unit general managers who face a variety of distinct problems in competing in different end markets. This pressure creates a further impetus to devolve personnel issues from the strategic to the level of the operating units, linking policy closely with the specific human resource needs and short-term goals, and, if possible, avoiding comparability between different operating units. In short: 'Portfolio planning tends to drive out, or at least drive down, questions of style and non-economic issues and positively encourages different approaches to employee relations within different segments of the business' (Purcell 1989: 76).

Such moves obviously carry implications for the clear, consistent and corporate-wide approach to personnel issues implied by the pure model of HRM, in areas such as pay, conditions and internal labour markets. Thus, devolution may undermine the role of the personnel function as the guardian of the 'institutional style' at a corporate level. However, a similar function could be developed at business-unit level, if there is sufficient development pressure at that level to support it. This contingency approach to measuring the strategic input of personnel is fairly convincing, but how far is it really the case? If Hill and Hoskisson (1987) are correct in their assertions of a trend towards cost-minimization in all highly decentralized firms, then we can only assume that even strategic planning firms will be forced to consider ways of devolving their personnel departments, and in doing so, reduce their strategic role. This seems a gloomy forecast not only for personnel departments but also for the alternative HRM model.

Decentralization in Practice – The Case of MNOC

This case study records how the personnel function of a large multinational oil company (MNOC) responded to strategies of organizational decentralization. It describes how personnel, which decentralized its own structure, tried to develop an HRM strategy, and the problems they encountered.

The data on which the case is based were gathered by one of the authors during a period of employment with the company in its personnel function.

MNOC's UK operations are divided into three key sectors, production/exploration (upstream), distribution/marketing (downstream) and chemicals, all under the umbrella of a well staffed corporate HQ (including a personnel function). The three sectors, decentralized in the mid-1970s, are now effectively businesses (divisions) in their own right. However, MNOC remains vertically integrated, from the initial exploration of oil through to its production, refining and final sale/distribution. Therefore, like all its competitors, MNOC retains an intricate matrix structure with various integrating systems to manage this complexity.

Despite this interdependency, in an effort to cut costs and improve efficiency, the downstream business of MNOC decided in the early 1980s to further decentralize into smaller semi-autonomous Operating Companies. As a result a number of distinct businesses were established in refining, supply, marketing and sales, each responsible for their own performance. Although these operating companies would never be allowed to stand or fall on their short-term financial results alone, their managers do 'simulate' many of the difficulties experienced by those in firms which are run in this way. Since its reorganization the downstream company has successfully defended its market share (in some cases expanded it), while at the same time improved efficiency by cutting its workforce by half.

Personnel Organization

The personnel function of MNOC is well resourced and has a reputation for excellence. As the guardian of a world-wide internal labour market incorporating most levels of management it has considerable influence. Traditionally it was seen as a highly centralized 'stand alone' function, based primarily within large corporate offices, administering the MNOC's 'paternalistic' package of employee benefits, terms and conditions. It also played the conventional role as mediator, or as a source of arbitration between line managers and disaffected employees. Until the late 1980s the downstream company had a large corporate personnel function responsible for most core services, resourcing and the employee relations needs of that sector. However, following the restructuring of the business, personnel found itself 'one step behind' and, after conducting an in-house review, decided to decentralize its own organization.

The Review Process and HRM

Lasting over two years the review process identified a need for personnel to move from a functional to an integrated structure 'to ensure the personnel resource is appropriately dedicated to the different segment needs'. To achieve this change four key objectives were agreed:

1. to ensure that Personnel made a strategic contribution;
2. to improve professional support to line managers;
3. to transform the perceived role of personnel;
4. to improve personnel systems.

These objectives implied a radical departure from personnel's traditional role, 'changing our stance from a largely reactive, centralized function to a more integrated, enabling, strategic function'. All agreed that existing human resource policies had failed to focus clearly enough on business strategy. Moreover, if personnel was to move with the times, and regain its perceived loss of credibility, it had to offer something new. They had to develop a more proactive, 'client based' approach, which could 'add value' to the business and reduce overhead costs. With the restructuring of the business, personnel had a 'clear opportunity' to develop a 'stronger human resource input', and concentrate on the 'human resource aspects of our business strategies'. Clearly the function had adopted a great deal of HRM rhetoric in their optimistic analysis of the situation.

The driving force behind this HRM rhetoric was a complete reorganization of personnel and its integration within the operating companies. This involved relocating existing staffs to new 'mini-personnel departments' in each operating company, while at the same time devolving work and streamlining the corporate function. Obviously this meant gradually shifting the balance of power within the personnel function in similar fashion to the rest of the business. Central to this redistribution of power was a change in reporting relationships. The new mini-personnel departments, headed by a human resources manager, were now directly accountable to the Operating Company general manager. Although they retained a 'dotted line' (indirect) reporting relationship with the rest of the function, their key loyalties were now expected to lie with the business. At corporate level, the role of 'administering the rules' was to be gradually displaced by one of offering specialist consultancy advice to line managers and mini-personnel departments. In this new world personnel was 'atomized', and placed on the front line along with the management of the Operating Companies.

Personnel in the Pursuit of the HRM Panacea

To illustrate how personnel experienced decentralization and made moves towards implementing HRM we will focus on a typical business in the 'downstream' operations of MNOC. This business is primarily involved in sales and marketing, with mainly office-based white collar staff. Within this business there had been a further decentralization to several departmental managers, each responsible for a specific niche of the wholesale oil market. Although it is hard to generalize, the cultural 'values' of staff in this Operating Company were broadly similar to the rest of the UK section of the MNOC, especially in their expectation of paternalistic management styles and 'cradle to the grave' attitudes toward job tenure. However, as one would expect, this operating business also had elements of its own distinct sub-culture. This was 'sharper', more cost-conscious and indi-vidualistic. Prior to its reorganization Operational Company management had only experienced the personnel function from a distance; there was generally little understanding, appreciation or even interest in what personnel did.

Personnel Objectives

The strategic 'direction' of HRM policy is decided by corporate manage-ment and then passed through a series of networks who mediate and 'fine-tune' specific policy initiatives. Currently this strategic human resource 'direction' is to develop individual commitment by encouraging employees to become 'contributors' rather than 'job holders'. In doing so they have authorized a number of changes in appraisal/reward systems and in corporate culture more generally. These policies are now in the process of being applied to the specific conditions of the decentralized Operating Companies. It is important to stress, however, that although the development of some policy is left to the discretion of the mini-departments, most 'strategic' policy decisions are cascaded down the organization, allowing very little room for manoeuvre at the point of application.

The mini-personnel department in the Operating Company set itself specific objectives about how it intended to change the personnel management process, along the lines of an HRM model. These were:

1. Educating line managers. This involved providing the line with more user-friendly information about personnel policy and procedure. In turn it suggested a need to improve the efficiency of 'core' personnel services which were now the responsibility of mini-departments.
2. Improving personnel effectiveness in 'core' areas such as resourcing, career planning, employee relations and general services. By effective-ness was meant developing a role of providing specialist 'consultancy' advice in support of line managers. Personnel had to become more service, or customer oriented.
3. Helping line managers take on more 'personnel' work, increasing their involvement in such areas as recruitment and selection, appraisals, communications and most importantly, transferring staff development costs onto line budgets.
4. Promoting a more systematic approach towards manpower planning, goal setting and appraisals.
5. Developing flatter structures to achieve more flexibility and capability for change.

All the above objectives were underpinned by a general philosophy reflected in a newly acquired rhetoric. The personnel role had now changed, becoming part of the business and not separate from it. It was put to staff: 'that their line manager is the primary point of contact between employees and the company and that Personnel's principal role is to advise and enable the line manager to manage their own staff'.

Being directly involved in the management team, personnel searched for ways of promoting these ideas as well as introducing 'corporate policies' within the Operating Company. There was also evidence of personnel trying to fit into the line culture by using a similar language as a way of gaining credibility and legitimizing their role. On paper, at least, personnel did this by adopting a rhetoric of HRM; in many of the specific policy choices one can see the increasing emphasis on integration, and on individual development. The issue of how far this shift to HRM would eventually undermine the long-term future of the mini-personnel department was not even considered. Simply meeting those objectives (outlined above) was thought to be a considerable task in itself. It appears that personnel was using its new position, decentralized into the business, as an opportunity for embarking on stage one of a move to HRM.

The Problems of Normative HRM for Decentralized Personnel Departments

As in the case described here, as a result of decentralization many personnel departments have been located within a new 'space' within their host organizations in which some have attempted to redefine their role by employing the language, and to some extent the practices, of HRM. The case described above showed the clear take-up of HRM rhetoric amongst the personnel professionals within the operating units, a finding which echoes that of other research (Evans and Cooling, 1985; Mackay, 1987). Increasingly, personnel professionals are using the language of business needs, cost-effectiveness and the need to devolve more personnel work to the line. Taken to their logical conclusion, many have already commented that such policies of integration can only herald the demise of the personnel department or at best leaving one consisting of: 'a mass of "clerk of the works", performing routine administrative work for a newly self-confident line management, whilst a few elite "architects" of strategic human resources policy continue to operate at the corporate headquarters level' (Armstrong, 1989: 155).

This process of absorption of the personnel function into operating units, and perhaps into line management itself, is clearly consistent with Guest's ideal type of HRM. In this respect, contemporary corporate restructuring seems to support HRM. However, the short-term perspective at business unit level pulls in precisely the opposite direction from the long term, developmental orientation of HRM. As we shall argue, this contradiction poses one of the most severe obstacles to the implementation of HRM within decentralized organizations..

Line Management: A Non-developmental Culture?

Guest, in putting forward his ideal-type model, recognized the difficulty of applying it within the British context. For example, its contradictory reliance on the agency of personnel specialists when clearly HRM implies 'giving Personnel away to line managers'. He also points to the underlying problem of HRM being 'difficult to practice, especially when it entails line management commitment' (Guest, 1987: 519). Our case evidence shows clearly how the pressure to achieve results in financial terms precluded the longer-term developmental activities relevant to the 'soft' motivation and commitment-oriented aspects of HRM.

As a consequence of decentralization, the Operating Company studied was now a profit centre with its own budget and it was expected to cover its own overheads. Many line managers argued that the less 'relevant' soft areas of policy should be dropped and personnel costs kept under control so that overheads could be kept down to a minimum. As a result, personnel in the operating unit fought an uphill battle to achieve credibility. They were literally in a position of having to convince line management of the need for a personnel department, let alone the relevance of human resource policy to the business. As the business achieved only low profit margins in a highly competitive market everyone found themselves under immense pressure to perform just to keep their heads above water. In this situation most issues were judged in quantitative, cost-conscious terms. Given that personnel's objective was to integrate human resource work into line management, this demanded recognition of the long-term and qualitative content of this work (as well as its short-term benefits to the business) and consequently posed a problem. The process required line management commitment in both time and energy. Personnel was therefore increasingly forced to justify itself using the same criteria of short-term cost effectiveness as everyone else. If this type of persuasion failed they would then be forced to impose change under pressure from corporate office channelled through the general manager. In a succession of policy areas, including the transfer of human resource costs, appraisals, staff consultation and Equal Opportunities policy, personnel received only grudging compliance from line managers who could not see the relevance of these policies and resented the fact that their time was being wasted on them. Some policies were accepted only half-heartedly, while other attempts to develop flatter structures were rejected completely. In short, personnel found itself in a vicious circle. While having to engage in day-to-day fire-fighting they were unable to convince the line that it should adopt more responsibility for personnel work or of the qualitative benefits of long-term human resource strategy.

This case supports a growing body of evidence of the type of culture generated by organizational structures which push financial responsibility down to relatively low levels. In addition to the short-termism that typically accompanies such structures, the nature, as well as the time scale, of decisions is likely to be framed by this context: 'Forced to concentrate on the economic consequences of his decisions the divisional manager comes to ignore their social consequences' (Mintzberg, 1979: 424).

If management had incorporated HRM's developmental goals *prior* to decentralization then perhaps decentralization could have fostered the development of HRM practices. Yet the problems run deeper than this. In the MNOC case, personnel was decentralized as a consequence of first/second order strategy, therefore the development of HRM was never specifically a strategic objective. In addition, before personnel even attempted to clarify its own objectives it had to contend with a number of problems arising from the trauma of decentralization itself. First, the reorganization process had occurred at a rapid pace and, on the whole, had been poorly planned and communicated. This led to high transition costs in the form of an initial drop in personnel services, made worse by resource constraints. It was difficult even to keep up with ongoing responsibilities, let alone develop a new approach. Neither was personnel given much time to consolidate; personnel was still expected to continue its participation in the wider world of policy networking within the company. More seriously still, personnel's reorganization had occurred at exactly the same time as the business was facing critical choices about the need to contract and rationalize. This traumatic environment created an added workload for personnel who had to devote time to managing a difficult process of adjustment with all its political and psychological implications, namely falling morale amongst staff fearful of redundancy and loss of job security. Therefore, even if line management had wished to develop HRM they had little time and few resources with which to do so. Therefore, as Legge (1978) and more recently Armstrong (1989) have argued, the promoters of HRM still face the 'dominant utilitarian values and bureaucratic relations of business culture' (Armstrong, 1989: 158). HRM may reform these values; more likely it will be subordinated to them. Characteristic of the business culture is an ethos in which hard, quantitive information is weighted more heavily than other forms of information, hence disadvantaging policies geared towards outcomes that are difficult to measure. Typically, personnel practitioners are forced to justify activities and policies in cost-effectiveness terms, to the detriment of innovative HRM activities. Normative HRM thus:

> Simply ignores the reality that the 'line manager' in the present-day company is becoming, before all else, a budget holder. This means that his or her performance is primarily evaluated in budgetary terms or return on investment targets, with short-term bonuses or long-term career progression often linked to these measures of performance with greater or lesser degrees of formality. (Armstrong, 1989: 164)

These problems may be particularly acute in British companies, which on the whole are managed to maximize (short-run) profits. Some support for this argument is provided by Oliver and Lowe (1991) in a comparison of three companies (one Japanese, one American and one British) in the UK computer industry. They found marked differences in the way in which HRM was enacted in each. In both the American and Japanese companies the HRM function (as it was labelled) were concerned with supporting business objectives, but in the context of relatively influential and well-resourced positions within their companies. The views of the managing director of the Japanese company stand in marked contrast to those of his British counterpart:

> In my view human resources is a strategic job . . . on every decision debated by the board I want to know the Human Resource Manager's input. (Managing Director of the Japanese Company)

> I came from a very large company where we had . . . a large personnel department that caused more problems than it solved. I think personnel departments are good, but we carry them. If I want a secretary, I'll hire a secretary. (Managing Director of the British Company, quoted in Oliver and Lowe, 1991: 19)

Although both the Japanese and American companies in the Oliver and Lowe study operated financial control via budgeting systems, the interviewees from these companies did not give any impression that such systems really 'drove' their companies, but rather that they set the constraints within which activities occurred. In the British Company the financial goals and targets were very much in evidence, and seemed to be the main device for integrating the activities of the various sub-units of the organization. Profit responsibility was pushed down to the lowest possible level and the model of the Hanson Trust was explicitly evoked in relation to this company's activities. In both foreign-owned companies the human resources function was granted considerable status and was allowed to make an input to strategic decisions. In the British Company there was no human resource department, and indeed senior managers showed some hostility to the idea of having such a department. Control of hiring in the British Company, as with other activities, is effected via the financial controls placed upon the business units. Human resource decisions were thus completely subordinated to financial planning and control rather than party to it. This is consistent with the views of Armstrong (1989) who argues that accounting and finance functions typically occupy a dominant position in British companies, relegating functions such as personnel to short-term, reactive roles. All the indications are that decentralization and relatedly the spread of the 'cost-centre' approach to management can only aggravate this situation. To conclude, even in adopting the rhetoric and attempting to implement some of the policy prescriptions of HRM, personnel will have a difficult time overcoming the contradictions between 'hard' and 'soft' goals and the inherent pressure towards short-termism created by decentralization.

Decentralization, Power and Ambiguity

Due to the complex, multi-faceted nature of the human resource policy-making process in MNOC there was some confusion over the boundaries between discretion and compliance at different levels. For example, a personnel manager at business unit level was likely to perceive his/her discretion over a specific policy area to be greater than would a corporate human resource manager. This is largely because of the confused and complex nature of the decentralization process. These boundaries were constantly changing over time as different levels articulated their interests more clearly. However, in the short term such confusion was typically interpreted as a conflict over loyalties, especially in the mini-personnel departments who still retained a dotted-line relationship with the rest of the corporate function. In order to pursue an HRM strategy in full, there was pressure for the mini-personnel departments to focus totally on the needs of their business. This posed a dilemma. Should these departments keep their eyes on the 'whole' organization or should they concentrate on integrating and meeting the specific human resource needs of their business? This dilemma manifested itself most clearly when the mini-department was under pressure to implement corporate policy, fit into manpower planning objectives and participate in the networking system all at the same time. This created some debate over what policies should be employed in the business unit, with specific needs, and which should be rejected. As the business in question operated with extremely tight profit margins, and as a consequence of decentralization was required to cover personnel overheads in its own budget, this inevitably created problems. This added to personnel's problem of achieving legitimacy in the business unit, since they seemed to contradict themselves. In one breath they talked about integration and meeting the needs of the business, yet in the next were seen to be advocating corporate policies and procedures which some line managers thought were not relevant to the needs of their business. Because decentralization had created these ambiguities, personnel found itself in a 'Catch 22' situation, ideologically unable to stand away from the line and impose policy, but also unable to develop a clear, relatively independent focus.

This second observation from the case points to a dilemma faced by many personnel departments within their new 'space' created by the process of decentralization. It concerns the level of discretion they hold over policy-making and the difficulty of spreading resources of time and energy between operational concerns (specific to their business unit) and any remaining corporate responsibilities. Although the evidence to date is limited, Hill and Pickering (1986) identify a marked ambiguity over discretion and accountability between corporate offices, divisional offices and operating subsidiaries as a consequence of decentralization. Such ambiguity reflects unresolved dilemmas between centralizing and decentralizing arguments and is linked to the issue of 'half-way house' configurations mentioned earlier (Marginson et al., 1988a). It creates strain over exactly what degree of decentralization has occurred, resulting in 'tension' which 'involves firms in a series of difficult choices and a careful balancing act, in which the balance tends to shift backwards and forwards over time' (Hendry, 1990: 93). This persistence of what amounts to varying and uncoordinated types of corporate intervention leads one to the conclusion that: 'A decentralization of structures is not necessarily associated with a devolution of genuine discretion' (Kinnie, 1989: 30).

This ambiguity affects personnel departments because it precludes clear focus on the task of addressing business objectives. This certainly occurred in the case of MNOC. It also implies that personnel must retain a foothold in more than one camp, thus having to serve more than one master simultaneously, with all the resource implications this is bound to entail. One might further argue that personnel can only hope to overcome the contradiction between the developmental, yet locally responsive aspects of HRM once they possess a clear remit and devote all their time and energy to the implementation of HRM at the level of the business unit/division. Otherwise they might be faced with an information overload which prevents them formulating clear objectives outside the day-to-day press-ures of fire-fighting.

Conclusions

The increasingly well-documented trend towards decentralization within large corporations has created both a challenge and a threat to personnel management. In one respect, despite their dissemination into the 'space' of the operating unit and corresponding loss of strategic influence, there is an optimism which is reflected in the increased uptake of a discourse of HRM. We argue that although this discourse is the way in which personnel departments are attempting to re-articulate a new role, it contains a fundamental and perhaps ultimately fatal contradiction. Many of the tenets of the HRM package are based on a long-term, developmental orientation, and indeed *require* this for their successful operation. Yet HRM also contains stipulations about being integrated with the (immediate) needs of the business and being 'close to the line'. Herein lies the rub: can the long-term aspects of HRM so central to its whole philosophy survive in a decentralized line environment dominated by short-term pressures? Our analysis suggests not.

References

Armstrong, P. (1989) 'Limits and possibilities of HRM in an age of management accountancy', in J. Storey (ed.), *New Perspectives on Human Resource Management*. London: Routledge. pp. 154–66.

Beer, M., Spector, B., Lawrence, P., Mills, D. and Walton, R. (1985) *HRM: A General Manager's Perspective*. New York: Free Press.

Chandler, A.D. (1962) *Strategy and Structure: Chapters in the History of the Industrial Enterprise*. Cambridge, MA: MIT Press.

Channon, D. (1982) 'Industrial structure', *Long Range Planning*, 15 (5): 78–95.

Evans, E. and Cooling, A. (1985) 'Personnel's role in organizational restructuring', *Personnel Management*, January: 14–17.

Galbraith, J.R. and Kazanjian, R.K. (1986) *Strategy Implementation: Structure, Systems and Process*. St Paul: West Publishing.

Goold, M. and Campbell, A. (1986) *Strategies and Styles: The Role of the Centre in Managing Diversified Corporations*. Oxford: Blackwell.

Guest, D. (1982) 'Has recession really hit personnel management?' *Personnel Management*, October: 36–40.

Guest, D. (1987) 'Human resources management and industrial relations', *Journal of Management Studies*, 24 (5): 503–21.

Hendry, C. (1990) 'The corporate management of human resources under conditions of decentralization', *British Journal of Management*, 1 (2): 91–104.

Hill, C.W.L. and Hoskisson, R.E. (1987) 'Strategy and structure in the multi-product firm', *Academy of Management Review*, 12 (2): 331–42.

Hill, C.W.L. and Pickering, J.F. (1986) 'Divisionalization, decentralization and performance of large UK companies', *Journal of Management Studies*, 23 (1): 26–50.

Hunt, J. and Lees, S. (1987) 'Hidden extras – how people get overloaded in takeovers', *Personnel Management*, July: 24–9.

Keenoy, T. (1990) 'Review article – human resource management: rhetoric, reality and contradiction', *International Journal of Human Resource Management*, 2 (3): 363–84.

Kinnie, N. (1989) 'The decentralization of industrial relations? – recent research considered', *Personnel Review*, 19 (3): 28–35.

Legge, K. (1978) *Power, Innovation and Problem Solving in Personnel Management*. London: McGraw-Hill.

Legge, K. (1989) 'HRM: a critical analysis', in J. Storey (ed.), *New Perspectives on Human Resource Management*. London: Routledge. pp. 19–40.

Mackay, L. (1987) 'Personnel: changes disguising decline?' *Personnel Review*, 16 (5): 3–12.

Marginson, P., Edwards, P.K., Martin, R., Purcell, J. and Sisson, K. (1988a) *Beyond the Workplace: Managing Industrial Relations in Multi-Plant Enterprises*. Oxford: Blackwell.

Marginson, P., Edwards, P.K., Purcell, J. and Sisson, K. (1988b) 'What do corporate offices really do?' *British Journal of Industrial Relations*, 26 (2): 229–45.

Millward, N. and Stevens, M. (1986) *British Workplace Industrial Relations – 1980–84*. Aldershot: Gower.

Mintzberg, H. (1979) *The Structuring of Organizations*. New Jersey: Prentice Hall.

Oliver, N. and Lowe, J. (1991) 'UK computer industry: American, British and Japanese contrasts in human resource management', *Personnel Review*, 20 (2): 18–23.

Peters, T. and Waterman, R. (1982) *In Search of Excellence*. New York: Harper & Row.

Purcell, J. (1987) 'Mapping management styles in employee relations', *Journal of Management Studies*, 24 (5): 533–48.

Purcell, J. (1989) 'The impact of corporate strategy on HRM', in J. Storey (ed.), *New Perspectives on Human Resource Management*. London: Routledge. pp. 67–91.

Purcell, J. and Alhstrand, B. (1987) 'Business strategy and employee relations structures', Paper presented to BAM Conference, Warwick University.

Sisson, K. and Scullion, H. (1985) 'Putting the corporate personnel department back in its place', *Personnel Management*, December: 36–40.

Storey, J. (ed.) (1989) *New Perspectives on Human Resource Management*. London: Routledge.

9 'LOCATING THE LINE':[1] THE FRONT-LINE SUPERVISOR AND HUMAN RESOURCE MANAGEMENT

James Lowe

A consistent theme of the HRM literature is the responsibility given to line managers for the management of the human resource. In contrast to the personnel management literature, it is argued that the 'personnel specialist' no longer assumes sole responsibility for the management of people. Instead, this is increasingly seen as being 'integrated' and shared with line management (Guest, 1987: 51). Sisson (1990: 5), for example, argues that 'the locus of responsibility . . . is now assumed by senior line management', while Poole (1990: 3) emphasizes that HRM 'involves all managerial personnel (and especially general managers)'. The role of line management is no longer restricted to monitoring and organizing production but also achieving the HRM policy goals of commitment, quality, flexibility and ultimately the profitability of subordinates. Thus it is implied, both implicitly and explicitly, that the role of line management is expanded or redefined so that it incorporates 'people responsibilities' rather than purely 'technical responsibilities'.

The references made to 'all managerial personnel' and 'senior line management' are important ones because they underline the fact that virtually all commentators have tended to overlook the role of the front-line manager or supervisor in the management of human resources. As Skinner (1981: 113) argues: 'The business schools neglect it [supervision], and economics, schedules, costs and time pressures allow careless and inhumane practices to characterize it.' In an international context, however, the 'supervisory problem', as it has become known, appears to be a peculiarly Anglo-Saxon problem. While other countries appear to have developed effective systems of supervision and employee management, many organizations in the UK and USA appear to have grappled unsuccessfully with the problem for many years. And yet it is in these countries that talk of HRM is most widespread, where there is now a greater emphasis on front-line management leading the 'transformation' to HRM, and where as a result the 'problem of supervision' is most likely to act as a constraint on new management initiatives. In fact, if supervisors are to accept greater responsibility for the management of their subordinates then several constraints are immediately apparent. Most important of these is the historically ambiguous role of the supervisor in modern (Anglo-Saxon) organizations, particularly the lack of managerial authority and status associated with the position. Related to this is the question of whether supervisors with low levels of education and/or training have the competence to discharge newly acquired responsibilities. Furthermore, if, as Guest (1987: 51) suggests, HRM must be 'given up' by personnel managers in order to be taken seriously then what implications does this have for the relative role, status and relationship which exists between production (line management) and personnel specialists? It is not only a question of 'locating the line' but how HRM is integrated into front-line supervision (Storey, 1987). Without such integration the achievement of HRM policy goals appears problematic.

This chapter addresses a number of these questions by outlining the historical connection between the responsibilities, authority and status of the supervisor with the personnel specialism. It rejects the notion that under personnel management the personnel specialist carries sole responsibility for managing the human resource and argues instead for a more precise definition of 'responsibility'. An analysis of various models of supervision is provided by examining the role of the supervisor in an international context with a discussion of the relative 'fit' under HRM and new forms of work organization. A case study of supervisors in a UK automobile manufacturer is then presented to illustrate some of the constraints faced by organizations attempting to redefine their supervisory systems consonant with an HRM strategy.

Responsibility and Supervision: The Rise of Personnel and the Fall of the Supervisor

To discuss whether responsibility for HRM is being relocated to the line, it is necessary to be quite specific about what is meant by 'responsibility'. Responsibility, according to the Collins English Dictionary, has three meanings: the first refers to the 'state or position of being responsible'; the second to 'a person or thing for which one is responsible'; and the third to 'the ability or *authority* to act or decide on one's own'. In the first two senses, 'responsibility' thus alludes to accountability and culpability while the third definition emphasizes the power and control exercised by the 'responsible' person. The difference in meaning here amounts to more than semantics for two reasons. First, it is apparent that when commentators refer to personnel specialists having sole responsibility for the human resource, they are ignoring the fact that line management is, and has always been, responsible (read accountable) for the performance of subordinates. Thus it is evident that when commentators refer to responsibility they are implying that the authority of line management over managing the human resource is increased through expanding line management's involvement in such areas as hiring, training, rewarding, appraising, punishing and firing subordinates.

Secondly, the question of whether more responsibility or authority for HRM is being relocated to the line has direct implications for the occupational status of line management itself and for the terms used in this chapter. A persistent theme of the literature relating to the 'supervisor' emphasizes the divorce between the responsibilities assigned to them and the lack of authority associated with the position (Child and Partridge, 1982; Patten, 1968). Thus the defining characteristic of a line *manager* as distinct from a line *supervisor* is that the former has authority to take decisions affecting subordinates (this is clearly a conceptual distinction because some organizations in practice use the title of supervisor for managerial positions). Thus, in order to locate the responsibility and authority of the line for the management of subordinates, it is necessary to trace the historical development of the modern supervisor, especially in relation to the personnel function.

The roots of the modern industrial supervisor can be traced back to a system of 'internal contracting' at the end of the nineteenth century (Gospel, 1983). Here the details of production, including the organization of work, management and control of labour was left to a sub-contractor, typically a skilled craftsman. The contractor had both total responsibility and authority for recruiting, selecting, training, paying, monitoring and disciplining employees and enjoyed a share of the profits. By the 1870s, the years of the 'Great Depression', the rise of 'new unionism' and new ideas on payment systems encouraged employers to move away from internal contracting towards a supervisory system that exerted more direct control over labour costs and the wage-effort bargain (Littler, 1982). Thus, in an uneven transition many contractors became employed as supervisors, performing largely similar functions but increasingly not employing their own labour and receiving a wage as a company employee (Gospel, 1983; Schloss, 1892). Nevertheless, the supervisor at this time could still be characterized as a 'man-in-charge' (Partridge, 1989), like Tressell's (1917/1955) character 'Hunter' in *The Ragged Trousered Philanthropist*, whose workplace authority meant considerable status. One reflection of this was higher pay levels compared to other manual workers and office staff (Pollard, 1968: 163–85; Williams, 1915: 283)

However, 'the traditional foreman's power started to be modified as soon as it emerged from the internal contract' (Littler, 1982: 87). From the 1890s there was increasing evidence that the power and authority of the supervisor was in decline. The increasing specialization of functions, encouraged by the ideas of Taylorism, fragmented decision-making over the wage-effort bargain, between supervisor, feed and speed inspector and rate fixer. This encouraged wide differences in terms and conditions between workers, often within the same factory, and stimulated 'leap-frogging', as an emergent shop steward movement increasingly challenged these variations. Thus, employers sought to gain more direct control over effort through the use of assembly line technology which allowed the pace and sequence of tasks to be planned from above. In this way technical control supplemented and to some extent superseded supervisory control (Edwards, 1979). In addition, the development of new piece rate payment systems encouraged the central determination of rate fixing, undermining the personal bargaining power of the supervisor (TUC, 1910: 25,29,47, 56). This development also helped stimulate the further growth of the shop steward movement (Cole, 1923: 14–15; Phelps-Brown, 1959: 290–2), which undermined the long-term position of the supervisor as both the unquestioned setter of effort norms and sole communicator/interpreter of management's policy.

At the same time the supervisor was also losing the right to hire and fire. Webb (1917: 21–3) charts the development of 'Employment Departments' which increasingly took on the responsibility for recruitment and selection so that it was no longer based on the 'personal choice and whim of the foreman' (Littler, 1982: 88). These developments heralded the emergence of the personnel function as a profession, with the establishment of the Institute of Welfare Officers in 1913. Shortly after the First World War, a Government Commission singled out the ruthlessness and arbitrary use of the foreman's power as one of the reasons for the high incidence of industrial conflict in the pre-war period (Child, 1969). The role of the welfare worker was therefore to curb and restrict the supervisors' (ab)use of their workplace power. Thus the genesis of the personnel function and its professional ideology lies to a great extent in its role as the organization's 'arbiter of justice' or 'acolyte of benevolence' (Torrington and Hall, 1987).

By the 1940s growing union organization in the UK and US had increased the negotiating and bargaining role of the personnel function. As trade unions became more widely recognized, organizations responded to the 'challenge from below' by adopting increasingly bureaucratic means of control (Edwards, 1979). Thus the personnel specialists became the 'policemen' of grievance and disciplinary procedures, acting as a 'contracts man' (Tyson, 1987) at times of negotiation and as. the principal organizational representative in resolving major industrial conflicts. These developments, however, had major implications for the supervisor for they ultimately reduced both the authority and role of the supervisor in the reward and punishment of subordinates.

This decline in the supervisor's status led to a narrowing of pay levels and a decline in promotional opportunities, as qualified engineers and accountants increasingly began to fill higher management positions. With the decline in pay, status and skill levels associated with supervisory jobs, some positions were now taken by unskilled workers, selected mostly on an *ad hoc* basis for their ability 'to cope with the job' rather than their technical and interpersonal abilities (NIIP, 1951). Wray (1949) also noted that supervisors, who were on the periphery of the management system, often lacked the opportunity to influence the managerial decision-making process. For these reasons writers in the US, like Roethlisberger (1945), began to talk of the supervisor as a 'man-in-the-middle', because of the role strain and conflicting demands the supervisor faced in reconciling the demands placed on them by management with those of their subordinates.[2] This was exacerbated by the fact that supervisors were increasingly representing two 'organizational families' (Mann and Dent, 1954): management's interest on the shopfloor as the first line of management, yet with an occupational background and work experience more reflective of the shopfloor, from where they had risen and which was therefore more in line with the subordinates they supervised.

The existence of grievance and disciplinary procedures reinforced the position of the supervisor as a 'man-in-the-middle' because this form of bureaucratic control allowed shop stewards to by-pass the supervisor, should they not gain a satisfactory decision. As Les, a shop steward, at Ford's Halewood plant explained, the predominant approach was to '"swear blind" and "fail to agree". Then we'd go up to the office and I'd . . . call him [the foreman] a stupid bastard in front of management' (Beynon, 1973: 143). In other words, shop stewards knew, and took advantage of the fact, that a disciplinary claim or grievance put in to procedure would be considered by the personnel specialist (as the 'arbiter of justice') in the light of precedent and wider organization policy rather than to suit the 'requirements' of the supervisor or to maintain the individual supervisor's authority. Supervisors thus faced the likelihood of having their decisions over-ruled on the advice given by the personnel specialist to their superior. In short, the supervisor becomes a 'pissing post' for shop steward demands (Hill, 1976), enduring pressure to maintain the standards established by their own personal authority within their respective 'local' section, while facing uncertain support from their superiors for their decisions (Beynon, 1973).

One result of the historical development of the supervisor's role, according to Child and Partridge (1982), is that in the UK at least, a career system has emerged with a social and educational gap between qualified managers and uneducated supervisors. Those promoted to supervisory positions in the UK experience 'career discontinuity' as the promotion to supervisor signals the end of future promotion opportunities (Child et al., 1983). In a contemporary context, this represents a severe limitation on the development of any HRM strategy. Not only are those employees supposedly responsible for carrying forward or effecting the transformation to HRM denied authority in their jobs, they themselves are unlikely to be committed to the organization, given the lack of support from more senior management and a career path which signals that they have reached the 'end of the road'. Can employees who are often alienated from the organization really be expected to infuse commitment in others?

HRM and the Supervisor

In the theoretical literature, a convergence seems to exist between liberal theorists of post-industrial society and Marxist theories of the labour process about how changes in work organization affect the supervisory role (Rose et al., 1987). On the one hand, post-industrialists argue that the supervisor will become an increasingly redundant role as 'the labour process becomes decreasingly proletarianized, requiring a higher proportion of workers with technical expertise, in occupations demanding less routinization of tasks and more responsibility' (Rose et al., 1987: 7). Thus workers will enjoy more authority to plan and allocate work assignments, responsibility for attaining organizational goals, and control over the pace and rewards of their labour. In this way, the coordinating and administrative functions of the traditional supervisor are delegated to the work team or individual employees and the close surveillance of workers no longer becomes necessary (Blauner, 1964; Dahrendorf, 1959; Mallet, 1963).

On the other hand, Marxist accounts reach the same conclusion, though paradoxically with a diametrically opposed analysis of the labour process. For writers like Braverman (1974) and Edwards (1979) it is deskilling which makes direct supervision progressively unnecessary as the traditional allocative, coordinating and control functions of the supervisor are incorporated into either the technology of the tasks themselves (so-called 'technical control') or organizational structures such as work roles, procedures, rules, discipline and job descriptions ('bureaucratic control') (Armstrong, 1986; Edwards, 1979). This conclusion is also supported by non-Marxist studies which have examined the implication of automation for supervisory roles (Crossman, 1960; Leavitt and Whistler, 1958). In contrast to these accounts, the literature on HRM suggests a more prominent and more important role for the supervisor. However, despite the importance attached to front-line supervision, there is to date no specific model of the supervisory role under HRM. In this context it is necessary to look to the research on supervision rather than HRM *per se* to determine whether any of the models suggested by this literature 'fit the bill'.

Child and Partridge (1982: 206) provide a taxonomy of basic design approaches to resolving the 'supervisory problem'. First, they argue that the role can be abolished by delegating 'disturbance-handling' activities to semi-autonomous workgroups, an approach which has been experimented with in Norway and Sweden with varying success. The second alternative is to maintain the role but make certain improvements, primarily by clarifying the role in organizational terms as a purely 'supervisory' job distinct from management so that supervisors develop a better understanding of their role and have realistic expectations about it. Thirdly, the role may be developed into a front-line managerial position. This would give the supervisor control over the main work parameters of their section including greater authority for human resource decisions, such as the selection, training and rewarding of subordinates, and for technical decisions over the scheduling of work, layout and choice of equipment. Fourthly, where supervisory roles are occupationally or professionally defined and primarily concerned with technical problems, a model of technical supervision is envisaged where the supervisor would delegate routine elements of the job to subordinates but function as a specialist advising and evaluating the work of others.

Other alternatives can be derived from comparative international analyses which have established that the 'supervisory problem' is a peculiarly Anglo-Saxon phenomenon (Lawrence, 1984). As already noted, it is in the USA and UK in particular where debates concerning HRM have been most pronounced, perhaps reflecting an historic 'failure' to manage the human resource effectively. More generally, the 'supervisory problem' may also be linked to the relatively low status of the production function in countries like the USA and UK (Lockyer, 1976; Nicholson, 1976; Weiner 1981). In countries where the status of the production function is held in far greater esteem, the supervisory 'class' occupy positions of high status. In Japan, for example, most supervisors have at least ten years' experience and benefit from greater access to higher levels of the management hierarchy than in the UK. In West Germany too, the *Meister* will have served a formal apprenticeship and will usually be a skilled worker with years of experience (NEDO, 1992). As such they are expected to have a detailed knowledge of their section, liaise with other departments and have a more direct involvement in training subordinates. They thus perform functions which would normally fall under the remit of specialist departments in the UK (Partridge, 1989). This is also reflected in the fact that German firms have a lower proportion of staff personnel compared to British firms (Maurice et al., 1980). Other comparative studies also indicate a greater preference for bureaucratic forms of control expressed by a higher incidence of formalization and procedures in UK organizations compared to French and German organizations of similar size (Child et al., 1983). Again this finding may reflect UK employers' attempts to compensate for the lower skills and calibre of their respective supervisory workforce as both Germany and Japan devote more resources and effort to technical training.

At the same time, this kind of evidence also supports the arguments of writers like Beynon (1973) and Anthony (1985) who argue that British management has deliberately kept the supervisor devoid of authority and used them as 'buffers' or 'scapegoats' in order to avoid responsibility for the management of employees. Indeed, the fact that the supervisory role has developed in this way in the USA and UK has led many to argue that it undermines organizational effectiveness (NEDO, 1992). The existence of an organizational and social gap between supervisors and management undermines competitiveness because it effectively separates the career manager from the realm of making things (that is, production) and the supervisor from influencing those who take decisions over planning, design and technology (Mant, 1979). To use Betts's (1980) distinction, the strategic control of production by management becomes poorly linked and integrated with the day-to-day operations under the control of supervisors.

In an international context, then, HRM can be regarded as an attempt to redefine and relocate the responsibility and status of the supervisor. In Child and Partridge's (1982: 206) taxonomy, the preferred model is to develop the role into a front-line managerial position (see Beer et al., 1985; and Guest, 1987), as is the case in Germany and Japan (Partridge, 1989: 216). Although there is as yet no explicit HRM 'model' of the supervisor, it is possible to construct the key features of supervisory systems under HRM from the burgeoning HRM literature. These features are summarized in Table 9.1. As illustrated, the wider features of the HRM model can be said to support the (re)location of human resource responsibilities onto the line. For instance, we might expect that under unitarist/high-trust conditions, where employees exhibit high levels of commitment, the delegation of authority for human resource management responsibilities to line managers would be greater than under pluralistic (unionized) conditions where low-trust relationships are more typical and where labour control represents a persistent problem. Under unitarist/high-trust conditions, a failure to follow policy or take professional decisions on HRM issues potentially poses less of a threat of widespread collective conflict within the organization. Indeed, the fact that employees show high levels of commitment enables the supervisor to adopt a 'coaching' rather than 'policing' management style (Walton, 1985), since the problem of gaining compliant effort levels from employees is less pronounced. Furthermore, companies pursuing cooperative, unitaristic labour–management relationships place emphasis on the early resolution of grievances and this in turn means that the supervisor plays a greater role in interpreting and solving industrial relations issues (Mallory and Mollander, 1989).

Related to this is the extent to which companies under HRM reinforce the line manager's position of authority over subordinates by focusing greater attention on the individual in terms of reward and performance measurement. At Hewlett-Packard, for example, a comprehensive 'management-by-objectives' system operates which underpins an essentially high-trust culture that relies on self-directed, 'committed' employees. Indeed, there is some evidence of a strengthening of authority relationships between supervisor and subordinate through the extension of appraisal systems to shopfloor workers (Long, 1986; Townley, 1989). Likewise, in the case of Nissan UK, the supervisor is the primary influence over the selection and induction of subordinates (Wickens, 1987: 91) and the company ensures that the supervisor is management's key (or 'king') communicator of company information. This reflects a deliberate strategy, and an explicit recognition, that a return to forms of 'personal' and informal control over subordinates is likely to be more flexible and more rapidly enforced by line management (supervisors) compared to systems which largely rely on bureaucratic/procedural forms of control. This can be

Table 9.1　*Stereotypes of personnel management and human resource management*

	Personnel	HRM
Time and planning perspective	Short-term, reactive, *ad hoc*, marginal	Long-term, proactive, strategic, integrated
Psychological contract	Compliance	Commitment
Employee relations perspective	Pluralist, collective, low trust	Unitarist, individual, high trust
Preferred structures systems	Mechanistic, centralized, defined roles	Organic, devolved, flexible roles
Roles	Specialist	Largely integrated into line management

(*Source:* Guest, (1987)

	Personnel	HRM
Supervisory system	'Man-in-the-middle'	Front-line manager
Predominant management style	'Policeman', overseer, enforcer	Coach, enabler, facilitator
Preferred method of labour control	Bureaucratic control	Personal control
Status, authority and pay differentials with nearest subordinates	Low	High
Career opportunities	Closed	Open

seen most clearly over questions of absenteeism and lateness at Nissan UK, as the Personnel Director Peter Wickens (1987: 100) explains: 'The key is the Supervisor . . . not the clock with a lateness control procedure administered by the Personnel Department. There is no substitute for the

Supervisor knowing his staff and having the ability to make decisions without reference to externally imposed bureaucratic procedure.' To reinforce the point, Wickens (1991: 3) has argued elsewhere that companies should learn to 'trust' and rely more on the experience and judgment of the supervisor, suggesting that: 'Company-wide policies and procedures, job evaluation, co-ordinated employee relations, systematic selection and promotion methods have all but eliminated the remaining responsibilities and authority of this beleagured individual [the supervisor].'

Under HRM, then, organic/devolved organizational structures or systems with flexible roles can be expected to predominate. But this makes labour control more problematic, since direct supervision of subordinates becomes more difficult, even though changes may occur within a context of strict monitoring of individual performance through developments in manufacturing information technology which could substitute some supervisory functions (see Sewell and Wilkinson, Chapter 6, this volume). As a result, additional means of regulating effort and performance become necessary and the need for greater compliance from employees necessitates a greater awareness of personnel policy by line management so that 'deviant' performance can be 'professionally managed'. In order to ensure consistency of practice across the organization or plant, and also that decisions taken by line management are consonant with personnel policy, it is necessary to develop and reinforce awareness of personnel policy through communicating with, and training, line management.

Training is also a key feature of the 'soft' aspects of HRM and this also has implications for the supervisory role. If (human) resource maximization is the *modus operandi* of HRM then we would expect the supervisor to become more involved in training generally. To ensure that employees' skills are maximized the supervisor's involvement may take a number of forms including a greater input in the design of appropriate training material so that the training needs identified by the supervisor can be met by the organization. Furthermore, the supervisor also has greater influence in determining which subordinates require training and ensuring that they are booked on appropriate courses. Lastly, the supervisors, in their 'coaching role', may also take a more proactive role in conducting more of the training themselves.

Whether HRM is successfully implemented, then, depends a great deal on the role performed by the front-line supervisor. This raises a number of issues relating directly to this debate. For instance, has line management the competence to manage the human resource? Does the supervisor have sufficient skills to be both aware and able to follow and implement personnel policy? Is the supervisor given adequate training in order to develop the necessary competence for managing subordinates? Does the supervisor have sufficient status and authority in the workplace to know that decisions concerning subordinates will be upheld and supported by superiors and/or the personnel department? Given that the supervisor's authority and discretion over human resource decisions are linked to the strength of shopfloor unionism, how will the adoption of HRM in general, and the integration of HRM with the line in particular, affect this relationship?

At the macro level, surveys suggest there is cause for concern rather than optimism. The BIM survey (1976) *Front Line Management*, for example, demonstrated that, as an occupational group, supervisors are an ageing population, lacking in educational and technical qualifications and typically poorly trained. Similarly, a more recent survey of 210 supervisors supports the notion that the supervisor continues to be a 'man-in-the-middle'; half the sample reported that they received no training or preparation, and nearly 70 per cent reported that their managers did not take enough interest in their personal development (*Works Management*, 1989, cited in Wickens, 1991: 1). The same study also found that 82 per cent of the sample were recruited from the factory shopfloor and that more than half did not expect to move higher up the managerial ladder. But it is at the micro level where the 'problem of supervision', and the constraints this imposes on HRM, are most acute. To explore these issues in more detail we now turn to the case of 'Hanwell' Motors.

Relocating the Line – HRM and Supervision at Hanwell Motors

Hanwell Motors is a multinational automobile company that has owned manufacturing and assembly plants in Britain for a number of years, and in the past has been widely regarded in the engineering industry for its training initiatives. The case plant currently employs approximately 6000 employees including staff. The author's contact with the case study company began in 1989 when he was employed in the Employee Relations department; since this time the author has maintained research links with the company (see Lowe, 1991, 1992). Over a three-year period this has involved over 100 interviews with shopfloor supervisors and production managers as well as a number of members of the personnel function. Faced with increasing competition from both foreign and domestic producers the plant has over the last ten years attempted to make several major cost and quality improvements. Many of these improvements follow closely the movement *towards* a just-in-time system of manufacturing. As Wilkinson et al. (1991) have shown, the conditions for the successful introduction of JIT and Total Quality Management (TQM) are frequently reliant on the implementation of HRM.

The use of the term 'human resource management' is not new within the case study company and certainly pre-dates the 1980s. However, the term is used interchangeably with 'personnel management' and this reflects the fact that for the practitioners working in this company 'HRM', as a set of practices or policies, is neither unique nor, for many, significant. The sub-unit of the training department responsible for implementing the supervisor and team leader training programs changed its name from 'salaried personnel development specialists' to 'human resource development specialist(s)' at the beginning of the program but like many companies this was done to give it a 'better image' and because it 'sounded better'. More important has been the movement toward a JIT system of production which has led to a number of changes within the plant and has affected the distribution of responsibility and authority on the shopfloor. A part of the company went through several internal reorganizations during the 1980s which involved expanding the production supervisor's 'line side' responsibilities. Supervisors assumed primary responsibility for quality control, housekeeping, cost control and preventative and line side maintenance of their production areas. In effect they have become 'mini-managers' of an integrated work area, although the plant's layout is of the conventional assembly and not modular type. At the same time the company has introduced teamworking and delegated many of the supervisor's traditional 'disturbance handling' responsibilities, like manning up and line balancing, to team leaders. The team leader is a newly created position reporting to the supervisor and is designed to assist the supervisor by relieving such day-to-day 'disturbances', leaving the supervisor 'free' to pursue more proactive, planning roles, such as implementing improvements to work processes, preventative maintenance and training subordinates.

Rather than reflecting a HRM strategy *per se* the expansion of supervisory responsibilities and increased spans of control (from an average twenty to forty subordinates over five years) was driven by centrally imposed financial targets which sought to achieve efficiency savings by reducing the number of supervisors. The redistribution of responsibilities has resulted in reduced labour costs for the company because the savings in 'supervisory headcount reductions'[3] more than off-set the increase in pay given to team leaders for performing their duties. Indeed, in 1991 the average supervisory salary (including overtime and shift allowances) amounted to approximately £25,000 per annum; thus the savings in supervisor's salaries were not insignificant. Furthermore, one personnel officer confided that the resultant reduction in labour costs was in effect subsidizing the company's team leader training program. In this respect then, the 'hard' cost features of HRM were the driving force behind the 'soft' training HRM initiatives taking place.

As a typical British brownfield site the plant's shopfloor workforce (including many production supervisors) was largely unskilled. Many lacked formal educational qualifications, the average worker at the plant having only one CSE grade three. Thus, the major organizational changes brought about by the redistribution of responsibilities and authority on the shopfloor raised the issue of the skill and competence of the plant's shopfloor staff. To address any skills gap that might develop the plant's training department was given the responsibility to develop and implement training and development programs for supervisors and team leaders so that they would have sufficient skills and abilities to cope with the new demands of their job. The plant enjoys considerable discretion in determining the content and methods of the training courses it conducts. This autonomy allows flexibility in meeting the local requirements of the company's various plants. Indeed, the delegation of training to plant level was believed to be so stark that members of the training department believed that they did not have a *corporate* training strategy.

With the above issues in mind, the plant's training department, with the aid of specialist consultants, developed a supervisory training program which aimed to bring production supervisors up to the technical skills level of maintenance supervisors. The program comprised of twelve weeks off-the-job training including an outward bound event. However, these courses were found to be impractical and unsatisfactory in terms of the results they achieved. First, production supervisors found the course too difficult: as one supervisor put it 'the technical stuff went right over my head' (fieldnotes). Secondly, the training program failed to prepare the supervisors with the necessary 'people management' skills that their new position required. As a result, a new training program with different supervisors was developed which reduced the training to four weeks off-the-job training. The emphasis on skill acquisition changed from technical to social skills development such as leadership, communication and team building, and the presentational skills of supervisors were brought to the fore. An important part of the training uses a well known method called Team Orientated Problem Solving (TOPS (8D)), a collection of eight techniques that allow supervisors to lead team problem-solving exercises. This training program at present has only been running for a few months but initial feedback suggests that it is more successful in achieving its training objectives than its predecessor.

The team leader training program is a ten-day training course which also focuses on the social skills development of the team leader. Little emphasis is given to technical skill development because every team leader is selected within the company and undergoes a series of tests, in particular numeric reasoning and knowledge of SPC, and an interview. Only upon demonstrating their technical abilities in this way can a shopfloor worker be selected for a team leader position.

The team leader training program begins with a 'business reality' module which emphasizes the ways in which shopfloor employees can significantly affect the company's operating costs. A typical example from this course is where participants learn from an accounts department representative that the annual total cost of employees' gloves to the company is £40 million. The attempt to inculcate 'cost consciousness' highlights again the fact that these 'soft' elements of HRM have a 'hard' underbelly. Other course modules include the role of the leader, equal opportunities, team building, communication and a line simulation exercise to develop planning and coordination skills. As the course outlines demonstrate, much of the content of the training focuses on the acquisition of social skills. According to the training manager of the plant, ten years ago the company made no provision for such training. Now the split between technical and social skill acquisition is roughly fifty-fifty.

Despite the need for substantial training and development of a large number of the plant's personnel, the training budget averaged around 1 per cent of the plant's turnover. Given the nature and extent of change that had taken place the training department believed this was an inadequate budget. Even so, in 1991 the training manager believed that these resources would be subject to reduction in the event of the recession continuing. Furthermore, the level of resources committed to training was relatively low compared to a comparable German plant owned by the company. With a more highly skilled workforce the German plant had set aside 2 per cent of its turnover for training.

The company's under-resourcing of training and development in its British plant is explained by a number of factors. A principal concern was that the retraining of a segment of largely unqualified personnel would be wasted given that in the low skilled British labour market it would be likely to lead to higher labour turnover as newly trained employees took their skills elsewhere. Secondly, a number of pressing demands like increased output/quality, coupled with high absenteeism and stoppages, and an existing low skill base encouraged short-term, knee-jerk reactions by management to solving the plant's problems. There was an emphasis on fire-fighting at the plant and this was exemplified by senior management becoming frequently involved in operational issues. Not only did this reduce the attention devoted to strategic matters (including training and preventative maintenance) it also, in some cases, reduced the effectiveness of the training itself. For instance, much of the training emphasized leadership skills and the taking of initiative on the part of supervisors but senior management's involvement in operational decisions often resulted in supervisors' decisions being over-ruled and thus impeded the learning process, inhibiting the outcome of the training itself (for more details of this, see Lowe, 1991).

The impact of HRM in terms of redistributing authority for subordinates away from personnel to line management, seemed limited. While some supervisors believed that personnel were 'getting quicker and quicker' in dealing with the more serious grievances and disciplines, a majority of the supervisors did not feel that they themselves exercised more authority over such issues. Indeed, as one supervisor explained, 'if it [a grievance or discipline] goes above you, then you've lost it'. Furthermore, the prevailing attitude of the production department was summed up by one production manager who described Personnel Department 'as the barnacle on the arse of progress', implying that Personnel placed 'undue' constraints on the production function over human resource issues. In short, the supervisor still appeared to be a largely unskilled 'pissing post' with the Personnel Department maintaining a separate and influential role over human resource issues.

Supervision and the Limits of HRM

Clearly, the case study material presented, by its very nature, is limited to the specific context of this automobile plant itself. As previous studies of the supervisor have highlighted, comparing supervisory roles across organizations is notoriously difficult due to differences in job classification systems and the tendency to define supervisory jobs purely on the basis of responsibility for labour control (Child and Partridge, 1982; Thurley and Wirdenius, 1973: 25–6). This makes surveys of occupational change in supervisory roles particularly problematic (Rose et al., 1987). Thus a survey (IRS, 1990) reporting that over half the sample of forty companies surveyed are attempting to change the role of the supervisor away from an 'overseer' role to more of a 'managerial position' along with more systematic training of supervisors comprising elements of 'managerial' programmes should be treated with caution.[4] Furthermore, a number of smaller samples of case studies into supervisory change (including an assessment of the implications of teamworking on supervisory jobs) have argued that the supervisor appears to be regaining both authority and status (IDS, 1987, 1988, 1991). These questionnaire surveys and case study synopses at best can only provide a cursory snapshot of *reported* change in supervisory practice. Case analysis conducted at the micro organizational level, in contrast, highlights the complexity of changes in supervisory roles and demonstrates some of the likely difficulties faced by all manufacturing companies in implementing HRM, and particularly relocating the responsibility and authority of the management of the human resource to the line.

The relatively low qualifications and skill levels of the case study company are fairly typical of British manufacturing industry. This undoubtedly constrains the likely restructuring of the supervisory role under HRM. Ironically, one of the claims put forward to differentiate HRM from personnel management is that it is directed towards managers as well as blue-collar workers (Legge, 1989). However, the survey evidence of management education and training does not seem to bear this out in practice. In fact it shows that management education and training in Britain is, by international standards, chronically under-resourced (Constable and McCormick, 1987). Mangham and Silver (1986), for instance, point out that 'over half of all UK companies appear to make no formal provision for the training of their managers'. Further, Handy et al. (1988: 11) point out that approximately half of Britain's younger managers have left education before degree level, concluding that 'British education and training is too little, too late, for too few.'

One of the results of the lack of management education and training is that it generates a managerial culture which downgrades the importance of training. For instance, Steedman and Wagner's (1987) comparative study of British and West German manufacturing sites in the kitchen furniture industry shows that British managers were not overly concerned by the fact that only about 10 per cent of the British workforce held any kind of vocational qualification compared to 90 per cent of the West German workforce who had undergone a three-year period of craft training. Furthermore, a 1987 Gallup poll found also that as many as 25 per cent of those managers surveyed thought that training was not important for their career (quoted in Keep, 1989). These attitudes are likely to feed through to the lower levels of the organization given that many line managers usually exercise considerable discretion in releasing and authorizing the training of subordinates. This was certainly the case at Hanwell's. Such attitudes clearly pose problems for the idea that under HRM line managers take a leading role in 'maximizing' their human resources.

As the case demonstrates the emphasis on managing human resources was primarily adopted as a means of overcoming or compensating for the lack of technical training and ability of the supervisors. Such an approach typifies the preference for supervisors in the UK (and also in the US) to 'concentrate on the personnel and human-relations aspects of the role rather than the task content' (Child and Partridge, 1982), and that 'this is partly a reflection of the prevailing management ethos' (Partridge, 1989: 215; see also Child, 1969; Mant, 1979). In contrast, in Germany and Japan supervisors demonstrate more task-centred leadership which is informed by greater technical knowledge (Partridge, 1989; White and Trevor, 1983). Thus, in these countries, the supervisor's higher skill levels and particularly technical ability allow them to initiate more easily continuous improvements to work processes, train subordinates and maintain important machinery. Thus they can operate on longer-term objectives and can fulfil more proactive planning roles than their UK/US counterparts. This again underlines the point that the 'supervisory problem' is primarily an Anglo-Saxon phenomenon and that 'human resource management' via relocating responsibility to the line and reasserting supervisory leadership of subordinates is being pursued as a competitive 'solution' (a 'quick fix') rather than a long-term strategy which also relies on developing the technical skills of the supervisor.

The success of HRM as a strategy which relies solely on upgrading the social skills of the supervisor (as opposed to one based on upgrading the technical skills of supervisors) would seem limited by the emergence of new organizational forms and logics. The adoption of JIT and Total Quality Management manufacturing practices enhance the need for supervisors' people *and* technical skills (Lowe, 1992). For instance, supervisors may now take a leading part in making continuous improvements to work processes. The principal rationale of these new organizational logics is to eliminate all forms of waste throughout the production chain, including work-in-progress and inventories of raw materials and supplies. Thus the need to produce 'right first time' is heightened as any disruptions to production of any kind, be they breakdowns, poor quality or a labour dispute, have more pervasive effects on performance (Oliver and Wilkinson, 1988). Therefore, the pursuit of flexibility and innovation is likely to enhance the supervisor's role in troubleshooting, training subordinates and more preventive maintenance (Little, 1985). Furthermore, as has been shown, the supervisor can have a critical bearing on the failure or success of organizational change (Weir and Mills, 1973). With many supervisors operating with less stocks and work-in-progress they become increasingly dependent on the quality and flow of materials from other areas. At the same time, it is likely that they will find it necessary to compete with other areas for scarce resources such as specialist maintenance services. The ability of the supervisor to represent their respective area at the boundary with other departments or areas with which they have a dependent relationship but little direct control becomes more crucial in determining the supervisor's own performance and that of their area. 'This, together with an ability to read the organization, to be able to locate sources of help and to be able to perceive the workplace as a network of informal as well as formal relationships, appear to be the skills the modern front line manager needs' (Mallory and Mollander, 1989: 44).

To pursue the role of a change agent, supervisors will ultimately have to become more immersed in the management system as a whole, demonstrating confidence and ability to relate, identify and communicate with higher management. As the case study has shown, in the UK the historical existence of a social and educational gap between the supervisor and management proper make it unlikely that supervisors can simply enter and mobilize the informal networks of the wider management system. The existence of this organizational and social gap also demonstrates the limitations of HRD programs designed to develop existing supervisors into staff with managerial skills. Reconnecting supervisors to the management hierarchy by retraining them with additional social skills is unlikely to lead to them mobilizing networks and using the interpersonal, political and representational skills required of their new roles. Only by reducing the educational and social differences between management and supervisory levels is such training likely to succeed. In Nissan UK this is partly achieved by hiring graduates to fill supervisory jobs and providing training facilities which allow non-graduate supervisors to attain formal educational qualifications (Wickens, 1987). In the US too, automobile manufacturers are beginning to recruit college graduates to supervisory positions and this seems to be paying off in that these supervisors appear to identify much more with management than their predecessors (Grimm and Dunn, 1986). To what extent the hiring of graduates in Britain to supervisory jobs provides a solution to the supervisory problem remains a matter of debate, however, especially given the historically low status of engineering and the production function in Britain which in the past has discouraged graduates from following careers in production (Mant, 1979; Weiner, 1981). Indeed, a 1985 study entitled 'Attracting the brightest students into industry' highlighted the poor image of manufacturing amongst schoolchildren, with 50 per cent reporting that industry was 'too routine and boring'. Starved of talent, typically under-paid and under-represented at Board level *vis-à-vis* its sister functions, production, in the words of one practitioner, represents the 'poor relation' of British industry (Wickens, 1987: 162).

The evidence presented in the case study, then, suggests that HRM as a strategy reflects a re-packaging and symbolic name change of the personnel function aimed at corporate level with the intention of re-emphasizing the status and professionalism of personnel practitioners (Armstrong, 1989). Indeed, the fact that survey evidence shows that senior management generally seem to have developed a greater awareness of certain human resource issues appears to demonstrate that the personnel profession has succeeded in presenting its case (see Poole and Mansfield, Chapter 12, this volume). This perhaps reflects the real agenda of HRM and underlines an apparent paradox in its prescriptions because, far from giving up control and relocating authority for human resources to the line, the status of the personnel function has always, and continues to, rely on the inability or lack of expertise of line management in managing their human resources. Thus, the progress of HRM at a strategic level may reflect not a loss of control but a further *weakening* of line management's responsibility for the human resource. In this sense, HRM could be said to represent a form of 'deviant innovation' as the values and norms of the function could be said to deviate from those necessary for organizational success (Legge, 1978). Certainly on the evidence of this case, the impact of HRM on the shopfloor in brownfield sites with a 'mature' supervisory system is likely to be extremely limited.

Conclusion

The role of the supervisor under HRM has been a neglected aspect of the literature. The supervisor has been characterized in both the UK and US, as a 'man-in-the-middle' because of the way the role has developed over time. While most analyses of the supervisor have tended to emphasize the 'redundancy' of the role, comparative analyses of the supervisors' functions and current changes in work organization encourage a different view: one which sees the supervisor as performing an important managerial role in both technical and human resource areas. As the case study demonstrates, however, brownfield sites in the UK are operating under several constraints in attempting to restructure supervisory roles, including a generally low technical and educational skill base, the historically low status of the production function, and a legacy of an existing cadre of supervisors who have been poorly selected, trained and rewarded. If the transition to HRM depends upon 'relocating the line', with personnel and HRM managers giving up control and placing it in the hands of supervisors who are unable and often unwilling to 'manage' their 'human resources' then the exercise looks certain to fail.

Notes

1. The title 'locating the line' comes from a paper given by John Storey to an Industrial Relations Research Unit workshop on HRM in 1987.

2. The male pronoun is used in the case of 'man-in-the-middle' because the term is historically derived and has conceptual meaning in the context of literature relating to the supervisor's status and authority in the workplace. Gender neutral language is adopted for the remainder of the chapter.

3. The term 'headcount reductions' is widely used in the case study company. See Keenoy and Anthony, Chapter 14, this volume, for a critique of the terminology of HRM.

4. This report makes no reference to non-response to its questionnaire. It might be suggested that in this case non-response is an important factor as it is likely to skew the result towards those organizations which have introduced changes to supervisory roles and therefore are not averse to advertising the fact, whereas non-respondents perhaps have an interest in maintaining silence about not implementing these changes.

References

Armstrong, P. (1986) 'Class and control at the point of production – foremen 1', in P. Armstrong (ed.), *White Collar Workers, Trade Unions, and Class*. London: Croom Helm. pp. 19–42.

Armstrong, P. (1989) 'Limits and possibilities for HRM in an age of management accountancy', in J. Storey (ed.), *New Perspectives on Human Resource Management*. London: Routledge, pp. 154–66.

Anthony, P.D. (1985) *The Foundation of Management*. London: Tavistock.

Beer, M., Spector, B., Lawrence, P., Mills, D. and Walton, R. (1985) *Human Resources Management: A General Manager's Perspective*. New York: Free Press.

Betts, P.W. (1980) *Supervisory Studies* (3rd edn). Plymouth: McDonald & Evans.

Beynon, H. (1973) *Working for Ford*. Harmondsworth: Penguin.

BIM (British Institute of Management) (1976) *Front Line Management*. London: BIM.

Blauner, R. (1964) *Alienation and Freedom*. Chicago: University of Chicago Press.

Braverman, H. (1974) *Labor and Monopoly Capital*. New York: Monthly Review Press.

Child, J. (1969) *British Management Thought*. London: Allen & Unwin.

Child, J., Fores, M., Glover, I. and Lawrence, P. (1983) 'A price to pay? Professionalism and work organization in Britain and West Germany', *Sociology*, 17 (1): 63–77.

Child, J. and Partridge, B. (1982) *Lost Managers*. Cambridge: Cambridge University Press.

Cole, G.D.H. (1923) *Workshop Organisation*. London: Hutchinson.

Constable, J. and McCormick, R. (1987) *The Making of British Managers*. London: BIM.

Crossman, E.R.F.W. (1960) *Automation and Skill*. London: HMSO.

Dahrendorf, R. (1959) *Class and Class Conflict in an Industrial Society*. London: Routledge & Kegan Paul.

Edwards, R. (1979) *Contested Terrain*. London: Heinemann.

Fletcher, C. (1969) 'Men in the middle: a reformulation of the thesis', *Sociological Review*, 17 (3): 341–54.

Fucini, J.J. and Fucini, S. (1990) *Working for the Japanese*. New York: Free Press.

Gospel, H. (1983) 'The development of management organization: a historical perspective', in K. Thurley and S. Wood (eds), *Industrial Relations and Management Strategy*. Cambridge: Cambridge University Press. pp. 91–110.

Grimm, J.W. and Dunn, T.P. (1986) 'The contemporary foreman status', *Work and Occupations*, 13 (3): 359–76.

Guest, D. (1987) 'Human resource management and industrial relations', *Journal of Management Studies*, 24 (5): 503–21.

Handy, C., Gordon, C., Gow, I. and Randlesome, C. (1988) *Making Managers*. London: Pitman.

Hill, S. (1976) *Dockers: Class and Tradition in London*. London: Heinemann.

IDS (Incomes Data Services) (1987) *Supervisors of Manual Workers*, IDS Study 386, May.

IDS (Incomes Data Services) (1988) *Teamworking*, IDS Study 419, October.

IDS (Incomes Data Services) (1991) *Supervisors*, IDS Study 479, May.

IRS Focus (1990) 'From overseer to first-line manager: the changing role of the supervisor', *IRS Employment Trends*, 476, November.

Keep, E. (1989) 'Corporate training strategies: the vital component?' in J. Storey (ed.), *New Perspectives on Human Resource Management*. London: Routledge. pp. 109–25.

Lawrence, P. (1984) *Management in Action*. London: Routledge & Kegan Paul.

Leavitt, H.J. and Whistler, T.L. (1958) 'Management in the 1980s', *Harvard Business Review*, 36 (6): 41–8.

Legge, K. (1978) *Power, Innovation and Problem Solving in Personnel Management*. Maidenhead: McGraw-Hill.

Legge, K. (1989) 'Human resource management: a critical analysis', in J. Storey (ed.), *New Perspectives on Human Resource Management*. London: Routledge. pp. 19–40.

Little, A.D. (1985) *The Strategic Benefits of Computer-Integrated Manufacturing*. Cambridge, MA: Arthur D. Little.

Littler, C. (1982) *The Development of the Capitalist Labour Process*. London: Heinemann.

Lockyer, K. (1976) 'The British production Cinderella: 2 – Effects', *Management Today*, June: 70–1.

Long, P. (1986) *Performance Appraisal Revisited*. London: Institute of Personnel Management.

Lowe, J. (1991) 'Teambuilding via outdoor training: experiences from a UK automotive plant', *Human Resource Management Journal*, 2 (1): 42–59.

Lowe, J. (1992) 'Manufacturing reform and the changing role of the production supervisor', *Journal of Management Studies* (forthcoming).

Mallet, S. (1963) *La Nouvelle Class Ouvrière*. Paris: Editions du Seuil.

Mallory, G.R. and Mollander, C.F. (1989) 'Managing in the front line: the changing role of supervisors', *Journal of General Management*, 14 (3): 35–45.

Mangham, I.L. and Silver, M.S. (1986) *Management Training: Context and Practice*. School of Management, University of Bath, ESRC/DTI Report.

Mann, F.C. and Dent, J.K. (1954) 'The Supervisor: member of two organizational families', *Harvard Business Review*, 32 (6): 103–12.

Mant, A. (1979) *The Rise and Fall of the British Manager*. London: Pan.

Maurice, M., Sorge, A. and Warner, M. (1980) 'Societal differences in organizing manufacturing units: a comparision of France, West Germany and Great Britain', *Organization Studies*, 1 (1): 59–86.

Miller, D. and Form, W. (1981) *Industrial Sociology*. New York: Harper & Row.

NEDO (National Economic Development Office) (1992) *What Makes A Supervisor World Class?* London: NEDO.

Nicholson, T.A.J. (1976) 'The British production Cinderella: causes', *Management Today*, June: 66–9.

NIIP (National Institute of Industrial Psychology) (1951) *The Foreman: A Study of Supervision*. London: Staples.

Oliver, N. and Wilkinson, B. (1988) *The Japanization of British Industry*. Oxford: Basil Blackwell.

Opinion Research and Communication (1985) 'Attracting the brightest students into industry', Committee for Research into Public Attitudes.

Partridge, B. (1989) 'The problem of supervision' in K. Sisson (ed.), *Personnel Management in Britain*. Oxford: Blackwell. pp. 203–21.

Patten, T.H. (1968) 'The authority and responsibilities of supervisors in a multi-plant', *Journal of Management Studies*, 5: 61–82.

Phelps-Brown, E.H. (1959) *The Growth of British Industrial Relations*. London: Macmillan.

Pollard, S. (1968) *The Genesis of Modern Management*. Harmondsworth: Penguin.

Poole, M. (1990) 'Editorial: HRM in an international perspective', *International Journal of Human Resource Management Journal*, 1 (1): 1–15.

Roethlisberger, F.J. (1945) 'The foreman: master and victim of double talk', *Harvard Business Review*, 23: 283–98.

Rose, D., Marshall, G., Newby, H. and Vogler, C. (1987) 'Goodbye to supervisors', *Work, Employment, and Society*, 1 (1): 7–24.

Schloss, D.F. (1892) *Methods of Industrial Remuneration*. London: Williams & Norgate.

Skinner, W. (1981) 'Big hat, no cattle: managing human resources', *Harvard Business Review*, 59 (5): 106–14.

Sisson, K. (1990) 'Introducing the *Human Resource Management Journal*', *Human Resource Management Journal*, 1 (1): 1–11.

Steedman, H. and Wagner, K. (1987) 'A second look at productivity, machinery, and skills in Britain and Germany', *National Institute Economic Review*, November.

Storey, J. (1987) 'Locating the "line"', Paper presented to Industrial Relations Research Unit seminar, University of Warwick.

Thurley, K.E. and Wirdenius, H. (1973) *Supervision: A Reappraisal*. London: Heinemann.

Torrington, D. and Hall, L. (1987) *Personnel Management: A New Approach*. London: Prentice Hall.

Townley, B. (1989) 'Selection and appraisal: reconstituting social relations', in J. Storey (ed.), *New Perspectives on Human Resource Management*. London: Routledge. pp. 92–108.

Tressell, R. (1917/1955) *The Ragged Trousered Philanthropist*. London: Paladin.

TUC (1910) *Premium Bonus Payment Report*. London: Trades Union Congress.

Tyson, S. (1987) 'Management of the personnel function', *Journal of Management Studies*, 24 (5): 523–32.

Walton, R.E. (1985) 'From control to commitment in the workplace', *Harvard Business Review*, 64 (3): 76–84.

Webb, S. (1917) *The Works Manager Today*. London: Longman.

Weiner, M.J. (1981) *English Culture and the Decline of the Industrial Spirit, 1850–1980*. Cambridge: Cambridge University Press.

Weir, D. and Mills, S. (1973) 'The supervisor as a change catalyst', *Industrial Relations Journal*, 4 (4): 61–9.

White, M. and Trevor, M. (1983) *Under Japanese Management*, London: Heinemann.

Wickens, P. (1987) *The Road to Nissan*. London: Macmillan.

Wickens, P. (1991) 'Front line leaders and the new workforce', Paper presented at 'Recession or Opportunity? – Human Resource Strategies to Meet the Challenge', ACAS Wales Conference, Swansea.

Wilkinson, A., Allen, P. and Snape, E. (1991) 'TQM and the management of labour', *Employee Relations*, 13 (1): 24–31.

Williams, A. (1915) *Life in a Railway Factory*. London: Duckworth.

Wray, D.E. (1949) 'Marginal men of industry: the foremen', *American Journal of Sociology*, 54 (4): 298–301.

10 REWARD MANAGEMENT AND HRM

Ian Smith

The notion of human resource management has been tied into the 'Enterprise Culture' (see Keenoy and Anthony, Chapter 14, this volume) and the 'Enterprise Culture' in turn has been seen as the context and driving force for organizations to move away from traditional wage and salary administration to something called 'Reward Management'. The provision of rewards, usually in the form of incentive payments for all categories of manpower, is deemed to underpin a more purposeful and 'objective achieving' strategy for managing the human resource. This chapter will assess whether the management of pay in general, and incentives in particular, has been transformed in this period of Reward Management from the traditional 'muddling through' approach to a long-term strategy which is an integral part of human resource management (HRM), underpinning the ongoing achievement of corporate objectives and improvement. The degree of consistency and alignment between HRM and Reward Management will also be examined, for example to see if the move to merit and discretionary pay destroys cohesiveness and mutual understanding on objectives for performance.

The last point is important to the debate about the role of Reward Management within a human resource management strategy. The application of Reward Management has emphasized the individual, thus creating a degree of competitiveness which conflicts with the teamwork required to ensure the organization-wide qualitative and quantitative improvements in the performance of human resources pursued by HRM. The linking of pay to individual performance is as yet unexplained and unrelated to the objective of organization performance based on the integration of human resource contributions. This objective tends to be central to the application of HRM policies. The uncomfortable 'fit' of Reward Management within HRM signals a possible contradiction within any assessment of current developments in the management of remuneration.

Performance, Pay and Management

Considerable debate has centred around the issue of the management of pay in UK organizations for the past three decades. Wilfrid Brown (1963), the National Incomes Commission (1963 and 1964) and the National Board for Prices and Incomes (between 1965 and 1970) provided much of the hard 'prime-mover' evidence which laid bare the weaknesses and chaos in the management of wages and salaries. The conclusion to be drawn from this early evidence was that pay was badly managed in a multitude of British organizations across all sectors of the economy; this situation persisted despite the growth of personnel management as a specialist and significant element of the management task between the 1950s and 1970s. It is often claimed that the results of this persistent weakness have ranged from micro-level problems with attraction, retention and motivation of manpower to the macro-level issues of skill shortages, inflation and the strength of the pound. But while these problems have often been blamed on the inadequate management of pay, there is a singular lack of authoritative evidence or reference to other issues and influences.

Nevertheless, in the case of and as a result of this situation, successive post-war Conservative and Labour governments have felt obliged to intervene in the various processes of wage and salary determination from Sir Stafford Cripps's policies for restraint in the late 1940s, through official and unofficial incomes policies in the 1960s, 1970s and 1980s culminating in Profit-related Pay introduced in the 1987 Budget and revamped in the 1991 Budget. And this 'saga' continues: government feels compelled to intervene in the determination of remuneration at the micro level in the hope of some 'pay-off' in the state of the national economy. At the heart of these interventions has been the stimulation of incentive payments in the hope that labour productivity at a simplistic level and corporate perform- ance at a more complex level will be enhanced (Smith, 1991).

Post-war government policy, as far as it has influenced remuneration in Britain, has tended to be identified with performance: in the immediate post-war years to restore the economy to some strength following the ravages of war time; during the 1960s and 1970s to contain inflation, maintain a balance of payments surplus and support the international value of the pound; and in the 1980s, to underpin a 'return' to enterprise and the development of a 'reward culture'. Thus, successive government policies aimed at micro-level issues in pursuit of macro-level outputs have been the evidence of government intentions, if not achievements, to influence economic performance through the reward dimension.

The position of trade unions in the relatively 'secure' full employment years of the 1950s and 1960s helped them achieve, by the beginning of the 1970s, the annual bargaining round. The outcome, according to some accounts, was an inflationary spiral within which managerial control of remuneration structures and their power to attract, retain and motivate employees was substantially weakened. To re-establish managerial con- trol, incentive schemes were redesigned (piecework giving way to Measured Daywork, for example), and pay was enhanced to maintain the relative attractiveness of remuneration structures in the face of leap- frogging wage and salary settlements. The Conservative government elected in 1979 came to office determined to stop this spiral and the associated industrial disputes. Since 1980 the greater role accorded to performance as an underlying influence on remuneration has become the government's stated policy to underpin labour force effectiveness, company effectiveness, and to reward achievement. In other words, a process of Reward Management.

A British Phenomenon

The term 'Reward Management' and its practice are unique to the United Kingdom. Despite the American origins of human resource management there is nothing comparable to Reward Management on the other side of the Atlantic. The basic characteristic of Reward Management in Britain is either the provision of a performance related addition to basic remuneration or, less popularly, the determination of total remuneration on the basis of performance. Thus some form of 'global' sum is the reward. Very rarely has the reward taken the form of an improvement in benefit or perquisite provision. Additions to pay linked to performance hark back to the earliest days of piecework and in a very real sense indicate how the practice of Reward Management is unlikely to merit such descriptions as 'progressive' or 'sophisticated'. American academics and managers have at times been fascinated with the British approach to linking at least an element of pay to performance. For example, at the beginning of the 1970s, McKersie and Hunter (1973) published a major work on productivity bargaining and incentives in the United Kingdom with the following aim: 'the book tries to assess the future role of productivity bargaining and the extent to which some of the lessons learned in the experience of the 1960s may be applied in future in the United States' (McKersie and Hunter, 1973: 15). These 'lessons' were not applied in America where remuneration policies and practices tend to concentrate on remuneration as a whole. Pay is for the job and the performance expected of the employee is not generally linked to any specific isolated element which might be termed reward, as we know it in Britain.

American organizations, and indeed the American literature, have moved the debate about reward to the level of 'reward systems' integrated with human resource management. The emphasis here is not on some crude link between pay and performance outputs but rather on a much wider set of motivational issues including attraction, retention, expectancy, skill development, culture and reinforcement of organization structure. This lifts the debate about rewards to a much higher plane that has been the case in the United Kingdom. In Britain rewards have been linked to individual or group performance criteria. In America rewards have been linked to business strategy and other related features of the organization, with the ultimate goal being: 'an integrated human resource management strategy that is consistent in the way it encourages people to behave, attracts the kind of people that can support the business strategy' (Lawler 1987: 271). Reward Management in this context is not limited to the UK aim 'of spelling out what people are expected to achieve and what they will get for doing so' (Armstrong and Murliss, 1988: 12). Instead it is an integral element of human resource management: not 'supported' by it or 'related' to it but a natural part of it, underpinning the business strategy.

Nor has the debate in the American literature been convinced of financial rewards in any form impacting on performance. The analyses of such approaches provides a detailed and far-reaching debate for different employee groupings. Failures in linking reward to performance have been exposed (Hamner, 1973; Perham, 1971; Redling, 1981) with a major argument being the marginal influence of financial incentives on worker performance when compared with issues such as labour market demand, pay compression, demands for pay comparability and inflation. Much of the argument has concluded that organizations are successful because of cooperation among members of the labour force rather than because of any discrete relationship between pay and performance (Pearce, 1987). The reader is reminded of how Reward Management was identified as potentially in conflict with the aims of teamwork and the issue will be returned to later.

The American approach to remuneration has tended to concentrate on organization context issues much more than has been the case in the UK, where individual effort has been a prime concern. But methods of delivery have also been very different, particularly during the past ten to fifteen years. In Britain, the provision of reward has been characterized by some form of lump sum payment; but in America there has been a noticeable shift to tailor-made remuneration packages for the individual, with an emphasis on reconciling the approach with the business strategy (IDS, 1988a). Section 125 of the US Tax Code allows employees to participate in the process of determining how earnings are to be allocated among cash and benefits. Fifty of these 'cafeteria systems' were in operation in 1983 but the number had grown to 800 companies in 1988 and is continuing to rise rapidly (Hewitt Associates, 1991; IDS, 1988a). These schemes are spread across manufacturing, finance and health care organizations and the level of application in America is in stark contrast to the situation in the United Kingdom and Europe. Furthermore, by meeting different employee needs with one cost-effective strategy, the American approach has considerably streamlined pay administration, which again is in stark contrast to the situation in Britain where incentive schemes have rendered pay administration an overly complicated exercise (Smith, 1983). Thus, the differences between the US and Britain in terms of pay administration reveal why the management of pay in the US is more effective, in particular the way it integrates with human resource and business strategies. Reward management has (at least until recently) tended to lie outside such strategies in the UK and remains a subject deemed worthy of separate consideration.

Reward Management

Despite its uniqueness to these shores there is no doubt that the term 'Reward Management' has become the means to describe the administration of pay in the late 1980s and early 1990s. Nowhere has this concept received clearer definition than in Armstrong and Murliss (1988: 10):

> The emphasis has moved from relatively inflexible salary structures to the increasing use of performance-related reward systems . . . the remuneration strategies of an organisation should not only be appropriate to the corporate culture but can as necessary be used to change that culture to one which encourages innovation, enterprise and the entrepreneurial spirit.

These are heady words but underline the key role of pay administration (now transformed into Reward Management) in the 'Enterprise Spirit' or 'Culture'. Government itself has openly supported the role of reward in boosting economic performance; the following quotes are taken from Chancellor Nigel Lawson's Budget speech of March 1987.

> Pay is now deemed to be a reward and as such is a key part of the so-called Enterprise Culture . . . Payments to Employees should be designed and used to encourage their very real interest in the quality of the management of the enterprise . . . Adequate rewards are the means to improving the quality of manpower and the performance of the enterprise.

In these terms reward is seen as the means to achieving more than performance. Attitudes to corporate well-being could now be changed. In 1986 Mrs Thatcher herself argued that, '[the employee] should be wanting to satisfy himself that management is efficient and that profits are as good as they should be'. Some of this change was to be achieved as a result of the 1987 Finance Act by the introduction of the government's own 'brain child', 'Profit-related Pay'.

The outcome of government policies with regard to 'Reward Management' has been anticipated by Kanter (1987: 60) as follows:

> Pay has reflected where jobs rank in the corporate hierarchy – not what comes out of them. Today this system is under attack. More and more senior executives are trying to turn their employees into entrepreneurs – people who earn a direct return on the value they help create . . . The shift towards contribution-based pay makes sense on grounds of equity, cost, productivity and enterprise.

There is no doubt that in a significant number of British organizations there has indeed been a trend towards reducing the fixed portion of pay and increasing the variable performance-related part. This is even the case in universities where the employers' 1991 pay offer of 6 per cent contained a 2 per cent discretionary or performance-related element, the third such offer in two years.

The emphasis on adding risk-related money to basic wages and salaries in order to enhance employee motivation and contribution characterizes more than two-thirds of UK employing organizations (Armstrong and

Murliss, 1988). This risk-related element is normally, but not always, some form of cash bonus which can be calculated in many ways for the various employee groupings as described below.

1. *Blue-collar rewards*: cash bonuses related to outputs, inputs or value added.
2. *Sales staff*: cash bonuses in the form of commission on sales and/or bonus for achieving sales targets.
3. *White-collar staffs, management and technical staffs*: bonus based on appraisal, salary progression based on appraisal and salary progression based on length of service.
4. *Executives*: thirteenth month bonuses, target-related bonuses.

The above list omits non-cash rewards including 'incentives in kind' popular with sales and executive groupings in some sectors (retailing, finance and leisure) and the claimed growth in profit-sharing more noticeable in government intentions than micro-level applications (Poole and Jenkins, 1988). But the main thrust of Reward Management since the late 1970s has been a substantial increase in the provision of cash rewards, particularly in the areas of technical and white-collar staffs and executives (Fowler, 1988; Hewitt Associates, 1991; IDS, 1988b; Vernon-Harcourt, 1987). Therefore Reward Management in practice has been characterized by a growth in performance-related cash payments even though the theory may have searched for higher order characteristics particularly within the context of HRM.

Whatever the detailed developments, however, the foregoing illustrates the general impression that the techniques of wage and salary administration have given way to Reward Management with the primary emphasis on performance and the success of the organization, a system of rewards linked to hands-on responsibility for creating innovation (Kanter, 1987). Contribution-based pay is now the key issue in the remuneration debate; rewarding contribution is the most significant element of Reward Management fostered by the Conservative governments of the 1980s. As Reward Management has developed in popularity so has the 'switch' from personnel management to human resource management.

Reward Management and HRM

The link between human resource management and Reward Management within organizations is usually forged through the medium of change to a 'performance culture'. A 1988 survey of HRM strategies in private and public sector organizations found that 'attempts to create a performance-oriented cultural change were characteristic of both the public and private sector employers' (Hendry et al., 1988: 38). The researchers found that such change was managed in several areas including 'rewards management'. Sisson (1989: 32) has pointed out how a switch from traditional personnel management to HRM has been accompanied by 'a departure from a long established practice of the rate for the job . . . the introduction of merit pay based on systematic performance or appraisal'. Likewise, in developing a skeleton theory of HRM Guest (1989) has identified Reward Management as one of six essential policies which should underpin the application of HRM even though positive outcomes for the organization may prove difficult to achieve.

There is little doubt that much of the literature and research on HRM includes a key integrated role for what has become known as Reward Management. Yet the subject is lacking the sharpness in definition and role which characterizes the US debate on rewards and strategy. It is not at all clear how Reward Management helps to achieve HRM outcomes. Furthermore, it is difficult to determine what is unique about the approach to make it different from what has gone before. That this situation contrasts with the debate about the role of pay administration within human resource and business strategies in the United States stems directly from the British tradition of fixing and managing rewards without reference to wider organizational issues and values and without regard to medium and long-term outcomes of reward provision.

Muddling Through v. Strategy

At the beginning of this chapter, reference was made to the traditionally weak and at times chaotic management of pay systems in UK organizations. The lack of any medium- to long-term thinking in the management of remuneration means that the art of 'muddling through' has taken precedence over strategy. In recent years the 'received wisdom' has suggested that a policy of wages and salaries cannot be designed unless it is based on a personnel policy, and in turn a personnel policy cannot be designed (or indeed successfully implemented) unless it is based on a company-wide approach to objective setting and achievement such as is represented by corporate policy and plans. An integral element of corporate planning is a strategy which represents a translation of a general framework of intent into aims and operational terminology and methodologies. Such a strategic approach to the management of remuneration has been seen as appropriate and achievable in the right context (Cooke and Armstrong, 1990; Smith, 1989). That 'right context' is suggested in Figure 10. 1 below.

The decisions made about remuneration issues, along the lines suggested in Figure 10.1, are strategic to the achievement of the personnel or human resource policy. In this way some degree of purpose and perhaps rationality can be injected into the design and management of remuneration structures and elements in pursuance of human resource policy.

Strategic planning can help managements to improve organizational performance, as suggested in numerous publications based on substantial

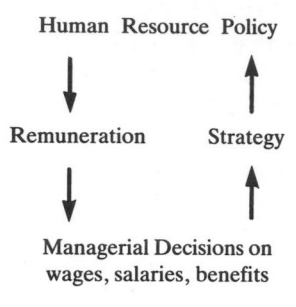

Figure 10.1   *Policy, strategy and remuneration*

research (Charam, 1982; Tregoe and Zimmerman, 1979). By extension, Reward Management ought to replace the traditional 'muddling through' of pay administration with a strategic approach. Such an approach should be conducive to the formulation of remuneration methods and structures, could be related to performance issues and could be given purpose, direction and measures for effectiveness by an embracing company policy for HRM. This strategy for remuneration might be concerned with the achievement of the following usual objectives for pay administration:

1. the attraction of effective employees who can directly or indirectly, immediately or remotely contribute to organizational well-being;
2. the retention of these effective employees;
3. the stimulation (or motivation) of these employees to work in the interests of organizational well-being;
4. the maintenance of equity in support of satisfactory levels of attraction, retention and motivation.

These four objectives represent the type of contribution which the management of remuneration could make to the work and outcomes of the organization. Thus what we have is Reward Management identified as nothing more or less than effective pay management, hopefully elevating the quality of managerial decisions on pay away from mere muddling through.

HRM, Reward Management and Strategy

A potential link between HRM and Reward Management has been identified in this chapter but the question remains whether HRM can provide a theoretical stimulus to a strategic approach to Reward Management. Certainly this 'stimulus' is claimed in much of the literature on HRM in America as well as the UK. At this juncture, however, it should also be admitted that HRM in the UK can mean different things to different people ranging from an attempt to raise the status of the personnel function to the introduction of a strategic approach to the function of personnel management (see Guest, 1989; Miller, 1989). In the latter strategic approach a key characteristic is claimed to be the supplanting of specialist managers in personnel by line management, who assume responsibility for personnel management within the business planning process. The management of people becomes a key, if not *the* key element in the strategic planning of the business, and attempts are made to integrate policies both with one another and with business planning more generally. By implication, a different time span is involved; whereas personnel management might be said to deal with the short term, human resource management is concerned with the long term (Sisson, 1989: 31). This statement sums up much of the hopes and claims made for HRM. All the key elements are there – the strategic approach, the involvement of the line managers in human resource decisions and last but not least the idea of employee commitment. Pay is now for performance within HRM and, in theory at least, Reward Management and strategic management go hand in hand.

Research has indeed revealed how the competitive business environment of the 1980s has caused some firms to adopt a strategic response in the area of managing the human resource. Hendry, Pettigrew and Sparrow (1988) have shown that within these firms a strategic HRM approach has been developed through seven different types of response to competitive pressure – competitive restructuring, decentralization, internationalization, acquisition and merger, quality improvement, technological change, and new concepts of service provision and distribution. Thus a strategic element to HRM may be dictated by the types of business changes which are made in response to competitive and economic pressure experienced by the enterprise. Interestingly, Hendry et al. (1988) found that all firms facing such pressures moved to a 'performance based culture' within their HRM strategy.

Organization responses to change and pressure in the business environment are not the only elements which can bring about a strategic approach to HRM. The example and influence of the line managers may be necessary for the introduction of strategic HRM (see Lowe, Chapter 9, this volume). In the words of Guest (1989: 51):

> Perhaps it is unfair to expect personnel departments to take a lead in the introduction of HRM or in strategic thinking about personnel policy. If HRM is to be taken seriously, personnel managers must give it away. Indeed, there is already some evidence to indicate that personnel issues are taken more seriously when managed by a headquarters committee of line managers.

Therefore a strategic approach to HRM may be a function of business conditions and line management involvement. Corporate policies and strategies, including remuneration, rely on line management effectiveness for achievement. Therefore we can conclude that the evidence so far indicates that Reward Management does find a useful role within a human resource strategy. In this the British literature parallels the American literature (see Lawler, 1987; Steers and Porter, 1991).

The Reality of Reward Management in the 1990s

We have so far viewed strategic Reward Management as somehow encased in a strategic model of HRM. The assumptions behind this are that reward is a primary element of pay systems, the management of the human resource, and the process of improving the performance of the employing organization. To some degree, it is the last of these improvements which provides the most important role and justification for Reward Management as an integral part of HRM. As such this represents a move away from the traditional view of rewards as incentives aimed at generating short-term improvements in employee performance, and towards rewards or total pay systems aimed at improving organization performance. But can employing organizations view and manage the human resource and the reward system in this manner, and do they?

Unfortunately there is little evidence so far to prove that the reality of Reward Management in UK organizations extends any further than the innovations which have taken place during the 1980s in cash and non-cash white-collar and executive incentive schemes, coupled with some refinements in the methods of measurement. The 'climate' in which these developments have taken place has of course been much more glamorous. Government policies aimed at generating the Enterprise Culture, the encouragement of employee shareholding, profit-related pay and the growth of appraisal linked pay in the public sector in general, and in the civil service and National Health Service in particular, have been major milestones in the hoped for journey to Reward Management. Thus, many issues in the area of remuneration have remained neglected in the so-called era of HRM (Smith, 1991). New problems have arisen which have been brought about by the sacrifice of equity in the provision of pay supplements and key player packages, in order to recruit and retain key staff. These developments in particular have been introduced at considerable cost to organizations in the finance, leisure and public sectors (Bevan and Thompson, 1991; Brindle, 1987; Smith, 1991).

This is a bleak background against which to discuss Reward Management and its integration with HRM. But the conclusion must be that serious doubts remain about whether government policy, a changing economic climate and lower taxation have caused reward schemes to push up company productivity or profitability, any more than was the case before the 1980s. Government strategy in the 1980s was to promote the means of linking pay to profit in particular, in the hope that employees would work towards corporate objectives and pressurize management to ensure the achievement of such objectives. Yet it is doubtful that reward schemes can work to the benefit of company performance in this manner

(Fowler, 1988; Murliss, 1987; Wright, 1986). Therefore it is easy to be over-optimistic about the implementation of strategic Reward Management to realize objectives in the 1990s which have proved so elusive in past decades.

Reward Strategy and Low Rewards

It is notable that the era of Reward Management in the 1980s has been accompanied by a massive growth in incentive scheme applications for white-collar, professional and managerial groups and also by the development of the government's own approach, Profit-related Pay. One notable characteristic of many of these schemes is the low amount of reward actually paid out (see Armstrong and Murliss, 1988; IDS, 1987; Smith, 1989, 1991). The government in particular based their approach to Profit-related Pay on the assumption that tax changes, which saw marginal rates reduced to 40 per cent and the standard rate reduced to 25 per cent, coupled with declining inflation during the 1980s, would make such rewards more attractive to employees. In connection with Profit-related Pay the Inland Revenue have forecasted that average payouts from schemes will equate to some 7 per cent of basic pay of employees who are included in these schemes. What is notable here is the difference between the payout levels for these new approaches to Reward Management in the 1980s and those levels which obtained during the 1960s and 1970s which ranged between 10 per cent and 35 per cent of basic pay (Smith, 1974).

The original aim of incentive schemes for blue-collar workers, for example, was always to provide one-third of basic pay for a one-third improvement in performance (see Smith, 1983). It is now quite normal for performance-related pay schemes to pay out very little more than 10 per cent of basic salary, whether this is for blue-collar or white-collar employees. When these kinds of figures are coupled with the large-scale redundancy programmes that have taken place across many British organizations in manufacturing and service sectors then it can be seen that HRM and Reward Management have been linked more directly to low rewards in a 'lean and mean' environment than they have to the provision of largesse in a purposive, performance-based environment. Given these developments and the kind of figures that obtain in many of the new strategies for Reward Management it is perhaps reasonable to ask whether or not Reward Management and indeed current government policy is aimed at minimizing labour costs in British organizations rather than increasing labour productivity (Nolan, 1989). In this sense it may well be that Reward Management is seen as a means of keeping British organizations competitive in the international marketplace, and that this competitiveness has to be built upon a low-wage policy. Indeed, the British economy has remained internationally competitive during the 1980s only by depressing wages *relative to* other economies.

This scenario may lead the observer to conclude that HRM and Reward Management have been developed during the past twelve years or so in pursuit of the objective of low (unit labour) costs in industry rather than in pursuit of improving the value of rewards to employees. In this connection it is also worth asking to what extent these reward strategies have actually improved the motivation of the British labour force? Certainly the history of incentive provision in Britain has never produced hard evidence to suggest that the motivation of employees is increased and/or that the productivity of organizations is increased (see Poole and Jenkins, 1988; Smith, 1974). More recent evidence suggests a similar failure for Reward Management.

It is therefore doubtful whether human resource management, and the Reward Management strategies within it, are taking British organizations any further than the 'muddling through' of the 1960s and 1970s. Certainly there are very serious questions to be raised about the impact of these strategies on the performance of British manpower and the organizations for which they work. Motivation may well have taken a back seat, and low costs the front seat or indeed the driving seat, as far as HRM and Reward Management are concerned. More generally, Reward Management and HRM are potentially incompatible in that while the former lays emphasis on rewarding the performance of the *individual*, the latter emphasizes in addition the importance of the *team* and of integrating different position-holders to improve coordination of activities. This problem is just one manifestation of the contradiction in HRM between individualism and teamwork (Legge, 1989: 35) and is taken up in the following section.

Reward Management – An Improvement in Practice?

In summary the debate about Reward Management and its role within HRM has now led to two disappointing conclusions. First, there is no evidence to prove that the Reward Management approaches of the 1980s and early 1990s are actually improving the performance of British organizations. Such failure has been well documented in the 1960s and 1970s in connection with manual schemes (Brown, 1963; Smith, 1974), but in recent years problems in connection with white-collar and executive schemes have come to light. In the words of Bevan and Thompson (1991: 39) performance-related pay for managers 'could reinforce this predisposition to short-termism and set back organizational effectiveness in the long term'. Similar concerns have been expressed by Murliss (1988), in connection with merit payment systems, and by Poole and Jenkins (1988) in connection with profit-sharing and employee shareholding. But amid all this is the lack of evidence to prove that Reward Management impacts positively on performance. Fowler (1988: 34) has commented on this situation regarding performance pay as follows: 'What is missing . . . is any effective research into its impact on performance. This however, seems unlikely to stem the tide.' Despite a lack of evidence, or the presence of evidence which raises question marks about the effectiveness of Reward Management in raising organizational performance, personnel managers have remained undeterred, expanding the application of performance-related pay.

Second, the rewards offered by the new Reward Management approaches may not be enough to provide for motivation. Particularly in the area of white-collar pay, bonuses worth no more than 5 per cent of basic salary are quite common (Armstrong and Murliss, 1988; Smith, 1989) and have proved unattractive to the recipients. This issue has been particularly well-documented in the public sector by Brindle (1987) and Murliss (1987). These latter authors have also revealed the threat of performance-related pay to traditional methods of work and organization resulting in de-motivation among 'team-members'. Much of the new initiatives which have been ascribed to Reward Management usually revolve around such elements as 'upfront' bonuses, abandoning the idea of a going rate for the job, and paying what the market demands. It is notable that in these new rules, equity and motivation are nowhere in the forefront of consideration, while 'muddling through' continues with what are little more than short-term reactions to immediate problems with attraction and retention.

Reward and Improved Performance

Even if Reward Management could introduce changes to the management of remuneration in the United Kingdom those changes may not offer any substantial improvement over what went before. It also remains doubtful whether Reward Management can help achieve HRM objectives in practice. In order to throw light on this, attention now turns to the experience of one particular organization, Sheerness Steel, during the 1980s. This private sector example of a broad Reward Management strategy raises very serious questions about the readiness with which reward systems within an HRM strategy can effectively contribute to effective HRM. The approach adopted by Sheerness Steel is a 'Performance Improvement Plan' (PIP) in which all employees are appraised by their supervisors on the following variables:

1. attendance
2. job performance
3. safety
4. behaviour
5. willingness to study for vocational qualifications

Points earned for each of the above five variables at the end of the year entitles each employee to an appropriate financial reward. With the PIP scheme, the company established special training courses which give employees bonus points if they choose to join. The commitment to training is significant. In the first instance it has been funded as part of a Business Growth Training Programme to the extent of 50 per cent of a £166,000 company investment in training courses for the PIP programme. Such courses have ranged from New Technology for secretaries to Open University management courses and language training. This ambitious training programme has dominated the Performance Improvement Plan which has led to more efficient working to the point where man hours per ton of steel produced have fallen by 31 per cent in the period 1985 to 1989 inclusive. But this efficiency is put down to increased skill acquired in the training programme rather than greater effort generated by financial rewards. Indeed the financial incentive at Sheerness Steel has proved irrelevant and pointless. The company management intend to revamp the reward payments to make them more influential within the PIP. For the present, however, it is interesting to note that this particular attempt at Reward Management, apparently integrated with HRM and linked to corporate objectives, has so far reinforced the strategic importance of training and *not* a strategic role for rewards.

Conclusion

In theory at least, Reward Management can be an integral element of HRM, if it is seen as a strategic exercise with the objective of improved company performance. In this way HRM's influence can actually cause Reward Management to be more strategic. Such a development can be claimed to be a substantial improvement to the traditional approaches adopted for wage and salary administration in UK companies. At least this is the theory. The real world application of Reward Management is more problematical. Evidence on strategic applications and any positive results is depressingly thin, and what there is raises doubts along the following lines.

1.   Euphoria about Reward Management and government 'hype' has resulted in the 'grasp' of expectation far exceeding the 'reach' of realization.
2.   Performance and motivation have not been enhanced and may have been damaged by Reward Management strategies.
3.   Case study evidence, such as Sheerness Steel's use of a Performance Improvement Plan, illustrates that any strategy for reward does indeed need to be part of a wider human resource development strategy. Yet there are clear indications that reward in itself is not enough to promote human resource contributions to corporate improvement and may well be secondary to other non-pecuniary elements.
4.   The main benefit of a Reward Management strategy may be the improvement in the quality of management decision-making in connection with the development and the utilization of the human

resource. But this may only happen as part of a broader 'front' of improvements within HRM.

5. Reward Management in the 1980s has been characterized by *ad hoc* responses to current issues at the expense of long-term outcomes.

HRM-based Reward Management strategies may in practice be grouped under two headings: direct short-term strategies to drive down labour costs; and more indirect long-term strategies to achieve qualitative improvements in support of training and development. Short-term strategies have been built around low rewards and are probably more commonplace. The longer-term strategies have been concerned with linking Reward Management to a wider approach to the management of people at work, involving improvements in such areas as training and development. These long-term strategies are probably rare but are more likely to provide a positive impact on the process of managing people at work in the pursuit of improved company performance. The rarity of these longer-term approaches underlines the depressing conclusion that moves forward from 'muddling through' have been less notable in the management of rewards than appears to be the case in other aspects of HRM such as recruitment, training and development. Even if such an approach is developed, Reward Management has yet to come to terms with the contradiction between individual rewards and team performance.

References

Armstrong, M. and Murliss, H. (1988) *Reward Management: A Handbook of Salary Administration*. London: Kogan Page.

Bevan, S. and Thompson, M. (1991) 'Performance Management at the crossroads', *Personnel Management*, November: 36–39.

Brindle, D. (1987) 'Will performance pay work in Whitehall', *Personnel Management*, August: 36–9.

Brown, W. (1963) *Piecework Abandoned: The Effect of Wage Incentive Schemes on Managerial Authority*. London: Heinemann.

Charam, R. (1982) 'How to strengthen your strategy review process', *Journal of Business Strategy*, 3 (1): 16–24.

Cooke, R. and Armstrong, M. (1990) 'The search for strategic HRM', *Personnel Management*, December: 30–3.

Fowler, A. (1988) 'New directions in performance pay', *Personnel Management*, November: 30–6.

Guest, D. (1989) 'Personnel and HRM – can you tell the difference?' *Personnel Management*, January: 48–51.

Hamner, W.C. (1973) 'How to ruin motivation with pay', *Compensation Review*, 7 (3): 17–27.

Hendry, C., Pettigrew, A. and Sparrow, P. (1988) 'Changing patterns of human resource management', *Personnel Management*, November: 37–41.

Hewitt Associates (1991) *Total Compensation Management: Reward Management Strategies for the 1990s*. Oxford: Blackwell.

IDS (1987) *PRP and Profit Sharing*, Study 397. London: Income Data Services.

IDS (1988a) *European Report No 311*. London: Income Data Services.

IDS (1988b) *Computer Staff Pay*, Study 404. London: Income Data Services.

Kanter, R.M. (1987) 'The attack on pay', *Harvard Business Review*, March–April: 111–17.

Lawler, E.E. (1987) 'The design of effective reward systems', in J.W. Lorsch (ed.), *Handbook of Organisational Behaviour*. Englewood Cliffs, N.J.: Prentice Hall. pp. 255–71.

Legge, K. (1989) 'Human resource management: a critical analysis', in J. Storey (ed.), *New Perspectives on Human Resource Management*. London: Routledge. pp. 19–40.

McKersie, R.B. and Hunter, L.C. (1973) *Pay, Productivity and Collective Bargaining*. London: Macmillan.

Miller, P. (1989) 'Strategic HRM: what it is and what it isn't', *Personnel Management*, February: 46–51.

Murliss, H. (1987) 'Performance related pay in the public sector', *Public Money*, March: 11–15.

Murliss, H. (1988) 'Merit payment systems: the lessons so far,' *Manpower Policy and Practice*, Spring.

Nolan, P. (1989) 'Walking on water? Performance and industrial relations under Thatcher', *Industrial Relations Journal*, 20 (2): 81–92.

Pearce, J.L. (1987) 'Why merit pay doesn't work: implications from organisation theory', in A.B. Balkin, L.R. Comez-Meiza (eds), *New Perspectives on Compensation*. Englewood Cliffs, NJ: Prentice Hall. pp. 169–78.

Perham, J. (1971) 'What's wrong with bonuses?' *Dunns Review and Modern Industry*, 98: 40–4.

Poole, M. and Jenkins, G. (1988) 'How employees respond to profit sharing', *Personnel Management*, July: 30–4.

Redling, E.T. (1981) '"Myth vs. reality". The relationship between top executive pay and corporate performance', *Compensation Review*, 13 (4): 16–24.

Sisson, K. (ed.) (1989) *Personnel Management in Britain*. Oxford: Blackwell.

Smith, I. (1974) *The Measurement of Productivity*. Aldershot: Gower Press.

Smith, I. (1983) *The Management of Remuneration*. London: Institute of Personnel Management.

Smith, I. (1989) *Incentive Schemes: People and Profits*, 1st edn. London: Croner Publications.

Smith, I. (1991) *Incentive Schemes: People and Profits*, 2nd edn. London: Croner Publications.

Steers, R.M. and Porter, L.W. (eds) (1991) *Motivation and Work Behaviour*, 5th edn. Hightstown, NJ: McGraw-Hill.

Tregoe, B.B. and Zimmerman, J.W. (1979) 'Strategic thinking: key to corporate survival', *Management Review*, February: 623–9.

Vernon-Harcourt, A. (1987) *Performance Related Bonuses for Senior Managers*. London: Monks Publications.

Wright, V. (1986) 'Does profit sharing improve performance?' *Personnel Management*, November: 46–50.

11 NEW TECHNOLOGY AND HUMAN RESOURCE MANAGEMENT

Caroline Lloyd and Mike Rawlinson

Whether Human Resource Management is equally applicable in all organizations and industrial sectors has received little attention. The debate around HRM and Human Resource Development (HRD) has tended to focus on employees with scarce skills. Similarly, the few studies undertaken of firms where HRM-type practices operate have tended to concentrate on large organizations, ones which employ a significant number of 'technical experts' (Jones and Causer, 1990; Rose and Mole, 1990), or ones in which the researchers have considered only segments of the workforce (mainly managers and supervisors). If, as Ursell (1989) argues, an HRM strategy is about securing cooperation and employees identifying with the company's goals it should presumably concern all the organization's workforce. Indeed, if HRM represents a general approach to the management of people at work, then it should be applicable across the whole profile of work contexts. However, it has been suggested that HRM policies are only important where workers have skills which are difficult to replace and where job effectiveness requires them to be committed in some form to the company (Guest, 1989b; Legge, 1989). Ursell (1989: 5), for example, argues that HRM is only applied where 'the technical contribution of particular workers cannot, without incurring unacceptable penalties, be substituted or dispensed with'. It is this issue which will be explored in the present chapter: that the ability and/or willingness of an organization to implement an HRM-type strategy will depend partly on the nature of the production process involved and the relationship of employees to that production process.

To date, the advocates of HRM have paid scant attention to one core area of business where skills are often in extremely short supply: the shopfloor, in particular skilled or craft workers. We will contend that it is the (technical) abilities of such skilled workers that enables many manufacturing organizations to become more flexible and responsive to customer demands, a facet of business practice that is seen as one of the fundamental goals for HRM policies (Guest, 1989a). In this chapter we also argue that one of the key determinants of the make-up of the workforce required, and their particular abilities, is the changing nature of production and, in particular, production technology. The nature of the production process is constantly evolving and often undergoing radical change. In the past, the personnel manager's role was seen as passive, responding to change by, for example, selecting and organizing staff to train on newly purchased machinery. In contrast, the role of HRM managers is seen as proactive (Legge, 1989), which would imply that they should be more 'involved', not only in selecting staff for training and recruiting staff prior to the introduction of new technology, but also in considering the overall composition and skill levels of the workforce, as part of a long-term strategic planning policy for the business. Such an approach would necessitate a far greater level of understanding by HRM managers of the precise nature and requirements of new and emerging production machinery, and its relationship to the labour force. In other words the traditional focus on labour needs to be widened from industrial relations and short-term training issues, to incorporate the totality of the production process and the interplay of factors of production.

This chapter examines the nature of the relationship between labour and technology within the context of current understanding of HRM. First, it identifies the ways in which flexible production is central to an HRM strategy. The role of technology within current HRM thinking is critically assessed, it terms of its strategic importance and the role of computerization in changing management thinking. The ability of firms to introduce HRM is then linked to the production process and information technology. The case of the clothing industry is used to illustrate some of the current contradictions and implications of the 'management of human resources', with the introduction and use of newer computerized technologies.

Flexibility, New Technology and HRM

At the core of HRM is the need for firms to be more responsive to market demands. For more flexible production it is asserted that employees must also be more flexible and consequently need to be more skilled, or possess a greater range of skills, and have a greater commitment to the organization. The role of a flexible, skilled and committed workforce is seen as crucial, not only for individual companies but also for national economic development. Porter (1990), for example, stresses the need for firms and governments to understand that the most important factor for national competitiveness is skilled human resources. Furthermore, Krulis Randa claims that 'The employees of the business firms, with their skills and attitudes, build the competitive advantage and are the factors of strategy' (1990: 134). Proponents of HRM insist that labour should be seen as a valuable resource, rather than as a cost that should be minimized. The corporate environment should therefore be suitably modified in order to achieve maximum return on this resource. It has been described in economic terms as labour being regarded as a fixed rather than a variable cost.

HRM has therefore been proposed as *the* answer to British economic problems and as a generic solution for firms. Krulis Randa (1990) claims that firms will have to adopt 'strategic HRM' if they are to survive, although he admits that in Europe there has been little adoption of HRM, be it technique or theory. Legge outlines one approach, for example Austin Rover's Working with Pride, which suggests that HRM can be applied to a large number of companies, including mass producers:

> Given the levels of cost effectiveness achieved in the early 1980s, competitive advantage can now best be achieved by enhancing the quality of the product or service. Hence commitment must be generated in employees directly manufacturing the product or at the customer interface – whether through participative structures and policies of employee involvement or through training and development. (Legge, 1989: 34)

The need for HRM is therefore seen as a means of increasing or maintaining market position by improvements in the quality of the product or by speeding up response times.

It is often recognized that new technology is integral to an HRM strategy, both in its use in advocating a strategic approach to the use of labour and in the link between computerization and more flexible production. For example, Poole states that, in relation to work systems, 'a particular interest of human resource management is in new technology and its integration into various social systems at task level' (1990: 7). To regard labour as the prime resource within a company then, its relationship with technology must also be of major importance. Therefore, in introducing new technology within an HRM strategy, technological agreements and participation should be integral. However, Lansbury and Bamber (1989) have suggested that during the 1980s British trade unions, as their influence diminished, had little impact on or input into technological change. Managers are reluctant to involve employees in technological decisions, as these are considered to be part of management prerogative, and where new technology agreements do exist they are far more likely to be among white-collar workers than production workers. New technology, Poole (1990) suggests, is also introduced as a result of strategic policy choices in relation to changing markets and competitive pressures and as such is linked to the strategic nature of HRM. However, there has been little attempt by Poole or other commentators to investigate either the nature of these links, or whether there is any evidence on how they might work in practice.

The main focus theoretically within HRM points to new technology as being one of the causes of the change in management thinking. One main reason for this is that computer technology has been put forward as one of the elements of the 'transformation of society' that makes HRM necessary. Krulis Randa argues that: 'societal transformation is the outcome of global competition, individualization, sensitiveness towards ecology and it is the response to the impact of new computer technology' (1990: 134). Whilst Krulis Randa says nothing about the impact of new technology on the production process, Torrington (1988: 3) suggests that new technology can enhance the goals of management: 'computerization and the use of numerically controlled machines have all tended to make individual jobs more self-contained, more skilled and more varied, reducing the need for supervision and increasing the degree of workers' control over their own activities'. Unfortunately, due to the focus on information technology and changes in HRM in large corporations, it seems widely accepted that the use of computers invariably leads to an improved work environment. These assertions lie perilously close to technological determinism and have a tendency to amalgamate computer-based technology into a homogenous mass. Yet there is considerable evidence, particularly within the labour process debates, which suggests that the application of computers to the work process can have a variety of implications for workforces. This depends on a wide range of factors, including the peculiarities of the individual company and industrial sector and the external demand and supply conditions.

Work Organization

At present there is a lack of empirical evidence specifically concerning the role HRM plays in introducing or organizing work tasks around new production technology. The role of technology must be seen as a major element in understanding job definitions, redesign, problems of flexibility and the movement of workers from one job to another, as well as in determining which workers are central to the production process. Firms may choose an HRM strategy depending on the type of production process they use and its associated technology, or they may choose a type of worker to be part of this strategy based on the worker's relation to technology.

Perhaps one of the reasons for the lack of attention given to technology is that HRM is following in the tradition of personnel management. Indeed, critics of the widespread application of HRM consider that in a large number of cases, personnel departments and personnel management textbooks have simply been re-titled (Legge, 1989). Personnel management has traditionally had only a partial knowledge of the shopfloor production process. When issues concerning the introduction of new technology have arisen, the role of the personnel manager has tended to be that of mediator for its introduction, for example by arranging training courses or negotiating disputes in new working practices. At present human resource management, despite the notion of 'strategic' HRM, similarly appears to lack a coherent strategic planning approach in its consideration of the incorporation of new production technology. Latching on to personnel management in this way means that it has only a limited history of understanding of the role of technology within an organization.

Personnel management has been used, as Legge (1989: 38) points out, as a means of separating 'the sale of labour power and the performance of the labour process, thereby obscuring the commodity status of labour'. In this sense we can see that the key to personnel management is not to focus closely on the precise functioning of the production process and therefore new use and application of technology. HRM in its 'soft' version advocates labour as a fixed cost and there is therefore no 'need to separate the sale of labour power from its application in production into different management activities' (1989: 38). It would therefore be reasonable to expect a greater level of involvement in integrating newer technology by the personnel function within HRM. However, Legge suggests that the HRM approach is trying to obscure the commodity relation through a greater emphasis on workers' skills, flexibility, commitment and self-motivation.

In the 'hard' version of HRM there is an understanding that not all labour has to be seen as a resource. This borrows heavily from Atkinson's flexible firm model (Atkinson and Gregory, 1986), where the core workforce receive training and involvement in the firm and the peripheral workers receive poorer conditions and less stability. With this type of labour management strategy it would be very difficult to develop an all-encompassing approach to the 'human resources' within a company. By its very nature the implementation of this type of management would result in HRM for one group of workers and old style personnel for others. As the goal of achieving total quality is considered one of the key foundations of HRM, the introduction of divisive policies in the treatment of workers is not particularly conducive to building up commitment and quality of work from the whole workforce. Furthermore, it may also mitigate against achieving a flexible organization, as peripheral workers with less training are unable to perform the wide range of tasks demanded of core workers. The flexible firm thesis also raises the question about which sector of the workforce is going to be part of the core. This, we would argue, is likely to be linked to the worker's relation to technology and/or the production process.

Within the different variants of HRM it would appear, despite arguments to the contrary, that HRM can only be applied to workers who have jobs that are or could be redesigned to engender commitment, individual initiative and so on. The question as to how widespread HRM, whatever its version, can be applied and to whom, is therefore intimately linked to the role of technology and the production process. As Legge argues:

> patterns of demand and cost structures may argue that at least at the level of non-managerial employees flexibility is more effectively achieved through Taylorist work organisation, treating labour as a variable input, and exploiting the secondary labour market rather than through enhancing the skills and quality of the workforce. (1989: 32)

That is, HRM policies may be in conflict with a business strategy which demands the minimization of labour costs, for example in mass production where cost minimization has been a main strategy.

Guest (1989b) argues that for a strategy of HRM to be followed, a number of pre-conditions are necessary. These are corporate leadership, strategic vision, employee/industrial relations feasibility, the ability to get HRM in place and (finally) technological and production feasibility. This last factor would seem to be important but has been rarely mentioned by the proponents of HRM. Yet as Guest himself admits: 'HRM is much more difficult to introduce when a large number of employees are engaged on short-cycle repetitive production-line tasks. The heavy capital invest-ment in the production line means that job redesign is seldom feasible' (1989b: 51). This suggests that in many industries and among particular segments of the workforce, HRM will have little relevance.

In accepting that HRM cannot be applicable to all production processes we must therefore see HRM as one strategy that a firm may pursue among many. HRM 'is just one among a variety of forms of personnel management and for some companies it may not be the most viable model' (Guest, 1989b: 50).

Information Technology

The role of information technology has been linked both to management changes within HRM and to quality issues. Within the HRM strategy, performance and delivery has to become a central part of the organization of the business. The main element has been a devolution of personnel management responsibilities down the hierarchy, so that they are integrated into line management (Brewster and Smith, 1990). This has led to a widening of responsibilities of lower levels of management as a result of increased autonomy or new tasks, and responsibility for such things as discipline and absenteeism (Kinnie, 1989; Storey, 1989). However, with the development of the management function and wider use of profit/cost centres, line managers are more accountable to higher management for shopfloor performance. The delegation of managerial tasks further down the line and the associated increase in duties and responsibilities have been made much more visible by the use of computers.

In many cases the introduction of computers, linked to production machinery, has made it even easier to measure individual performance (Nobel, 1979; Sewell and Wilkinson, Chapter 6, this volume). This is especially the case where the pace of the machine determines the pace of the worker. Similarly, the introduction of computers to schedule, monitor and control the production process has made it possible to obtain an almost instantaneous measure of productivity as well as of inventories of work in progress. Information technology can thus allow a much greater degree of control by managers and supervisors of individual workers and also allows a greater degree of control of managers by senior managers. This is particularly the case if the computer operating the control systems of the machinery being used is linked to the one controlling the overall manufacturing and service functions of the company.

One of the main strands within HRM is the role given to gaining the commitment of the workforce, as a means to improve quality. Although these developments in information technology clearly allow greater monitoring of individual and group performance, HRM tends to assume that the only way quality can be improved is by gaining the commitment of the workforce. But quality of products may be achieved through other means, such as greater supervision or penalizing workers for poor quality. The role of information technology therefore raises a major problem for HRM theory. On the one hand it is argued that workers will have more control and autonomy and will therefore want to be more committed to the company and its goals, and yet the technology which is being introduced as part of that HRM strategy allows workers to be controlled and monitored much more closely.

The UK Clothing Industry – A Case Study

The following section examines empirical evidence on the incorporation and use of computer-based technologies in the clothing industry, in relation to HRM strategy. This is based on evidence from over fifty manufacturing plants that were surveyed or where interviews were carried out during 1989 and 1990. Each of the following sections will discuss the different types of production technology available to the industry, that is, computer-controlled production machines, 'desk top'-based computer technology and information technology, and assess their relevance to an HRM strategy. This will be related to the first section of this chapter, in particular focusing on the extent to which technology in the clothing industry has been introduced as part of an HRM strategy, and whether computerization is leading to a change in management strategy, or a redesign of jobs more appropriate to the implementation of HRM.

The clothing industry was chosen as a case study because it is comprised of a wide variety of company sizes from large to very small, and there has been a recent introduction of computer-based technology at a variety of levels within the production process. However, to date it has not been possible to automate and apply computer technology to several areas of the manufacturing operations of these companies. This requires companies to rely on skilled workers in order to be extremely responsive to rapidly changing customer demands, not only in terms of quantities but also in product mixes.

First and foremost, the relevance of HRM to the clothing industry needs to be questioned. At one level it may appear to be important, in that over recent years the industry has had to respond to both consumer demands and competitive pressures by becoming more flexible. This has been a result of increased demands by retailers during the 1980s for improved product quality and delivery, shorter runs and more varied styles, at little or no extra cost (Rainnie, 1984: Totterdill et al., 1989). This flexibility has become a prerequisite for an increasing number of firms, not only for profitability but also for survival. This flexibility is not new to the industry, however, as historically a segment of the market has always behaved in this way (Wray, 1957). This has generally been the remit of the small firm, yet HRM would suggest that larger firms can also play this role, partly as a result of technological developments. There are a number of larger companies which might be in a position to implement an HRM strategy within their clothing manufacturing sectors, for example, Tootals, Coates Viyella and Courtaulds. Among the companies where interviews were carried out, however, there was no wholesale adoption of HRM strategies, although some elements could be identified. The following sections will look at those elements of HRM which relate to the production process and new technology and asks whether it would be feasible to adopt such a strategy within an industry such as clothing.

Assembly and New Technology

The clothing industry has traditionally tended to rely upon a combination of Taylorist methods of work, sweated labour and skilled craft workers. Machining, which accounts for 80 per cent of labour costs, is overwhelmingly dominated by women working on piece rates. There are two basic ways of organizing the assembly of a garment, although in practice there is not such a strict divide. Make-through production usually involves three operators assembling a whole garment and therefore relies heavily on their skills. This method tends to be more effective in plants which produce short runs, with a large number of changing styles, although traditionally it has been associated with the problem of excessive work-in-progress. Section work is similar to an assembly line process, where the garment is divided among about twenty different operators, all undertaking operations lasting a couple of minutes. Section work tends to be more cost effective where a firm makes long runs of particular styles. Changing styles involves a large amount of work study and reorganization of operators before a relatively smooth flow of garments through the production line can be achieved. It needs less skilled workers, but suffers more from the effects of absenteeism and turnover, as machinists have to be replaced quickly in order to avoid disrupting the production line. These work systems have existed side by side since the interwar years, and are organized on the basis of different levels of sub-division of the work process.

In recent years there have been a number of developments in computerization within the clothing industry, but the vast majority of operations are still performed by the basic sewing machine. Apart from a number of adaptations, this has changed very little over a hundred years.

These are very flexible machines and can do a variety of operations, but productivity is restrained by the time spent in handling the garment, established to be around 80 per cent of the operator's total working time. Dedicated machines have been used quite widely throughout this century but have been limited to repetitive, short-cycle operations, like button-holing. Since the 1970s dedicated microprocessors and numerical control units have been introduced, which can carry out these operations with greater speed and accuracy. They are relatively expensive, however, and are most suited, according to Hoffman and Rush (1988), to firms with long production runs. More flexible machines have been introduced, the most advanced being the operator programmable sewing machines, which can perform a variety of operations and be reprogrammed by the operator. These machines undertake small part stitching, however, and are therefore only suitable for a minimal part of the assembly process.

The variety and complexity of operations involved in producing a garment, the amount of handling involved and the variety of styles, sizes and so on, means that applications of microelectronics to sewing machines are not flexible enough and are too costly for the main part of garment assembly. Flexibility of production is achieved instead through the skills of the operator, using the traditional lockstitch and chainstitch machines. One plant manager reflected the views of a number of firms: 'We've got machines with computers on which give you stitch length and configuration of stitch. But quite honestly we don't use them much. We are generally still at the mercy of the skill of these operators.'

Computerization of machining has been based on improving productivity and accuracy for a minority of routine operations, based on the deskilling of the operator's role, especially to cut costs rather than to allow a greater variety of styles to be produced. The advertisement for the automatic bottom hemmer for trousers, for example, stated 'The design of the machine has taken into consideration ease of operation, thereby greatly contributing to reduced labour costs and the realisation of work requiring no skill' (Juki Corporation, 1990: 73).

The production process has never been fully automated in the clothing industry. In an industry dominated by intense competition, there has been little scope for R&D and large-scale capital investment. Given the relatively cheap cost of labour and the weak union strength of operators to resist intensification, it is not surprising that automated production has not been extensively developed. In a similar way, we can see that, as argued by Legge (1989), there is no *need* to introduce an HRM strategy. It is more cost effective, while the labour supply exists, to use the incentives of money, through piece rates, as a means of increasing productivity, than to consider the redesign of jobs.

Using labour in this way has created a number of related problems. These include high levels of turnover and absenteeism, which is costly both in terms of lost productivity and increased costs of training. In response, one innovation new to the industry had been introduced in one of the plants studied and a number of similar schemes were being considered in other larger companies. Faced with a particular absenteeism problem this plant had introduced substantial extra weekly payments to those operators not absent during each week. The aim was both to improve productivity by reducing the numbers absent and also to attract or retain workers in the plant by offering higher wages than competitors in the local area. A number of the managers in larger companies were also discussing the introduction of teamwork and abolition of piece rates. As one manager said 'piecework is demoralising and divisive'.

The main impetus for this 'change' in management thinking was that, in certain parts of Britain, firms were facing great difficulties in recruiting operators. The boom in consumer spending in the late 1980s had led to the expansion of many firms. Yet many of these companies were faced with a tight labour market for full-time women, both within the industry and in particular local economies. This situation was aggravated by growth in the service sector, which absorbed an increasing number of school leavers and women workers, and demographic changes which have reduced the number of young women seeking employment. This meant that high levels of turnover were becoming increasingly costly and disruptive, particularly when new demands were being made by retailers for fast and reliable delivery. With the 1990–91 recession, these firms are again likely to be finding ample supplies of cheap labour, which may mean that reorganization of production and job redesign will become a costly irrelevance.

Pre-assembly Technology

In pre-assembly work, the graders, marker and pattern makers and cutters have traditionally been the most skilled workers in the industry. They earned relatively high wages, based on hours rather than productivity, and had a significant degree of control over their work. They were mainly men, although as Cockburn (1985) argues, as their craft occupations were being broken down, more women were entering into these jobs, although at the lowest levels.

Computerized grading, marking and cutting is gradually being introduced into the pre-assembly stage. In the plants surveyed, eight had installed computer-aided grading and marking systems of whom four had also introduced computer-aided cutting. All the systems were in plants which had over one hundred employees and which were part of a larger company. This computerization involves a high level of investment, but improves productivity, quality and, it has been argued, increases flexibility (Whitaker et al., 1989). The grading and marker systems allow styles to be changed quickly, therefore enabling the firm to respond more quickly and with greater flexibility, suggesting that larger firms may have the ability to act in a similar way to small firms. This, though, does not necessarily mean that computerization is in some way inherently more flexible than the technology which was previously used. HRM theorists would suggest that these jobs would, as a result of computerization, become more self-contained and skilled. But as was found by other research (Cockburn, 1985), there has been a considerable amount of deskilling involved. These systems are replacing some of the most highly skilled workers within the industry, using traditional manual tools. The new jobs of computer operators have either been given to those highly skilled workers, with some retraining, or increasingly to women workers with no previous clothing manufacturing experience. These new jobs were described, for example, by one technical manager as 'up-market typewriter operators'. He 'regretted that people are trained on the system and not trained manually. The basic skills of grading manually are being lost.' This suggests that the implicit knowledge and flexibility inherent in the skills and work experience of these workers would, in a few years, no longer be available.

Computerized cutting is being implemented more slowly than computerized lay planning and grading, because of the greater capital outlay involved and the large volumes of garments which are needed to make the system cost effective. The cutters' job has become that of watching the knife to make sure that it follows the paper marker and that there are no overlaps. The result of this for one firm was that they were considering introducing piece rates for 'cutters'. Thus, computerization is effectively replacing a group of highly skilled and well-organized workers with lower paid, largely female, computer operators. As Mitter argues, 'The main benefit of the system lies in the potential increase in managerial control by reducing the industry's reliance on the moodiness of skilled workers' (1986: 46).

In both cases of pre-assembly and assembly, then, computer technology has been introduced to speed up production and improve productivity and to gain greater control over the work process. The evidence suggests that there is no link to a wider HRM strategy and there was no evidence of union involvement in technological change, except in relation to redeployment of displaced workers.

Information Technology

In terms of the applicability of HRM to the industry, information technology perhaps offers the greatest opportunities. This can allow all individuals to be monitored instantly: their speeds, faults and waiting times (that is, when they are not working). Total Quality Management (TQM) notions were being considered and introduced in a number of firms, along with team briefings and steering groups as a means of problem-solving. All these initiatives were based on maintaining the quality demanded of the product, a basic tenet of HRM. However, there was only one company that appeared to be seriously attempting to gain commitment from the workforce to the product and the company. The plant manager explained how he tried to run the factory based on teamwork. The workers were 'treated as human beings . . . There's a closer bond with the team and the company.' He felt the workforce were committed and that this was due, in part, to the company's 'family firm' image. However, how this commitment registered for the operators was perhaps highlighted by one, who when asked about teamworking, said 'I work for myself . . . but I'll work for the company.' This is perhaps not an expected response from someone working on piece rates in what was one of the best payers in the area and within the company.

It was also clear that this 'team' approach was seen as a means of encouraging workers to stay at the company, while other methods were still being used to improve individual performance, such as piece rates and closer monitoring of quality standards. The firm had installed an automated handling equipment system and moved from make-through production to section work. This in itself would seem to go against what has been described as the general trend towards batch production and flexibility often associated with an HRM strategy. The introduction of the new work process was followed by an immense turnover problem as the majority of the old operators left, finding the work too boring and monotonous. After two years the plant manager felt they had finally made the system work effectively with the existing workforce. However, any notion of 'teamworking' established around the new technology was soon destroyed when it was announced the plant was closing and the technology was to be moved elsewhere. The development of human resources, which this manager had attempted, was not taken on board by higher levels of management, nor were the difficulties involved in moving the equipment and installing it elsewhere, despite the previous problems. This also raises the question of how effective an HRM strategy can be where firms are subject to intense competition or where redundancies are made during an economic downturn.

Within the clothing industry, to what extent is quality gained through intensive monitoring rather than through workforce commitment to company goals? Information technology allows all faults to be quickly assigned to the offending worker and in almost all cases they were penalized in terms of their piece rates. In a number of firms the quality standards were based on the number of faults. In one case, operators were 'red-pencilled' and it seemed common for firms to interview and 'counsel' workers if they fell below a certain standard. One firm had introduced a bonus payment, which was given to those workers who remained below a certain level of defects. Financial penalties or rewards were therefore given in order to maintain quality standards.

Linked to the quality issues and increased monitoring, supervisors (line managers) were, in some plants, being delegated more of the personnel function, such as discipline and the control of absenteeism. With the use of information technology they were having to set hourly and daily production targets. This allowed greater monitoring and control of individual operators and of increased responsibility and performance evaluation of supervisors.

Conclusions

Within clothing, the production technology would appear to have little in common with HRM. The effects of the introduction of new technology have been largely deskilling or the removal of a section of the workforce. Computerization in this sector has not brought a change of management attitude or a need for the introduction of HRM policies. Despite the view often found in HRM texts that computerization will lead to more skilled and varied work, there is little evidence for this. This is in sharp contrast to the conclusions reached by Kassalow who argues that managers often find the need 'for greater input and initiative from employees if the technology is to work well. (There is also a realization, perhaps, that the Taylorist methods were never truly the best way to utilise human resources in production)' (1989: 47). The only case where this may be true in the clothing industry is the increased role of supervisors produced by the added information available from information technology. This has, though, been accompanied by greater pressure to get results and to be responsible for discipline, absenteeism and production output. In addition, information technology also enables greater levels of surveillance and more accurate means of monitoring individual performance.

To date there would seem to have been limited application of HRM policies in the UK clothing industry. Like many other industries, this sector is still characterized by low pay, piecework, low profit margins and frequent poaching of workers. Consequently, the nature of the industry, its reliance on low-cost labour and the high levels of competition, would suggest that scope for an HRM strategy to be successfully implemented is limited. The evidence would seem to suggest that in order for a firm to be flexible and responsive, it does not need a committed and highly skilled workforce, with high levels of personal responsibility. In areas where opportunities do exist for jobs to be redesigned, such as pre-assembly, the strategy of firms has been to deskill. Computer technology can therefore be used as a means to replace highly skilled workers, yet retain or increase its external flexibility. This would suggest that firms can choose from a variety of strategies in order to achieve competitiveness within a flexible environment, and that job redesign on the basis of reskilling is not the only alternative.

The reality of work and employee management in industries such as clothing thus remains far removed from the HRM model. At best, HRM should be seen as just *one* managerial approach among many, and whether it will be introduced, and in what form, will depend on conditions specific to the individual organization. New technology and the nature of the production process can play an important role in managerial decision-making and structure the conditions under which an HRM strategy might be implemented. Conceptually, however, HRM has yet to progress beyond a uni-dimensional characterization of technology and work organization, while at the level of application there is limited evidence of technology being integrated explicitly within an HRM strategy. Given the 'low tech' character of many industries, the nature of the jobs involved, and the availability of labour, this may continue to be the case for the foreseeable future.

References

Atkinson, J. and Gregory, D. (1986) 'A flexible future – Britain's dual labour force', *Marxism Today*, April: 12–17.

Brewster, C. and Smith, C. (1990) 'Corporate strategy: a no-go area for personnel?' *Personnel Management*, July: 36–40.

Cockburn, C. (1985) *Machinery of Dominance: Women, Men and Technical Know-how*. London: Pluto Press.

Guest, D. (1989a) 'Human resource management: its implications for industrial relations and trade unions', in J. Storey (ed.), *New Perspectives on Human Resource Management*. London: Routledge. pp. 41–55.

Guest, D. (1989b) 'Personnel and HRM: can you tell the difference?' *Personnel Management*, January: 48–51.

Hoffman, K. and Rush, H. (1988) *Microelectronics and Clothing: The Impact of Technical Change on a Global Industry*. Geneva: Praeger.

Jones, C. and Causer, G. (1990) 'Human resource management policies and the retention of technical specialists in the electronics industry', Paper presented at the Employment Research Unit Annual Conference, Cardiff Business School.

Juki Corporation (1990) *Juki Global Linkage*. Tokyo: Juki.

Kassalow, E.M. (1989) 'Technological change: American unions and employers in a new era', in G.J. Bamber and R.D. Lansbury (eds), *New Technology: International Perspectives on Human Resources and Industrial Relations*. London: Unwin Hyman. pp. 41–59.

Kinnie, N. (1989) 'Human resource management and changes in management control systems', in J. Storey (ed.), *New Perspectives on Human Resource Management*. London: Routledge. pp. 137–53.

Krulis Randa, J.S. (1990) 'Strategic human resource management (SHRM) in Europe after 1992', *International Journal of Human Resource Management*, 1 (2): 131–9.

Lansbury, R.D. and Bamber, G.J. (1989) 'Technological change, industrial relations and human resource management', G.J. Bamber and R.D. Lansbury (eds), *New Technology: International Perspectives on Human Resources and Industrial Relations*. London: Unwin Hyman. pp. 3–37.

Legge, K. (1989) 'Human resource management: a critical analysis', in J. Storey (ed.), *New Perspectives on Human Resource Management*. London: Routledge. pp. 19–40.

Mitter, S. (1986) 'Industrial restructuring and manufacturing homework: immigrant women in the UK clothing industry', *Capital and Class*, (27): 37–80.

Nobel, D.F. (1979) 'Social choice in machine design: the case of automatically controlled machine tools', in A. Zimbalist (ed.), *Case Studies on the Labour Process*. London: Monthly Review Press. pp. 18–50.

Poole, M. (1990) 'Editorial: human resource management in an international perspective', *International Journal of Human Resource Management*, 1 (1): 1–15.

Porter, M.E. (1990) *The Competitive Advantage of Nations*. London: Collier-Macmillan.

Rainnie, A. (1984) 'Combined and uneven development in the clothing industry: the effects of competition on accumulation', *Capital and Class*, 22: 141–56.

Rose, H. and Mole, V. (1990) 'The changing character of managerial and technical role in the information technology based enterprise', Paper presented at the Employment Research Unit Annual Conference, Cardiff Business School.

Storey, J. (1989) 'Introduction: from personnel management to human resource management', in J. Storey (ed.), *New Perspectives on Human Resource Management*. London: Routledge. pp. 1–18.

Torrington, D. (1988) 'How does human resources management change the personnel function', *Personnel Review*, 17 (6): 3–9.

Totterdill, P., Farrands, C., Gawith, M. and Gillingwater, D. (1989) 'Industrial policy and the regeneration of British manufacturing industry: the case of clothing', *Local Economic Policy Review*, 1, Loughborough University.

Ursell, G. (1989) 'Human resource management and labour flexibility: reflections based on cross-national and sectoral studies in Canada and the United Kingdom', Paper presented at the Employment Research Unit Annual Conference, Cardiff Business School.

Whitaker, M., Rush, H. and Haywood, B. (1989) 'Technical change in the British clothing industry', *Occasional Paper 6*, Centre for Business Research, Brighton Polytechnic.

Wray, M. (1957) *The Women's Outerwear Industry*. London: Duckworth.

PART THREE: MANAGEMENT, UNIONS AND HRM

12 MANAGERS' ATTITUDES TO HUMAN RESOURCE MANAGEMENT: RHETORIC AND REALITY

Michael Poole and Roger Mansfield

On a global scale, interest in human resource management (HRM) expanded very rapidly in the 1980s and early 1990s. In a series of studies, these international developments in HRM have been charted (Brewster and Tyson, 1991; Dowling and Schuler, 1990; Pieper, 1990). There have also been seminal investigations of the links between HRM and corporate strategy (Hendry and Pettigrew, 1986, 1990), while the argument has been increasingly advanced that strategic human resource management is central to the competitive advantage of both corporations and nations (Krulis-Randa, 1990). However, at an empirical level, considerable doubts remain on the extent and depth of the so-called transformation to HRM within the actual enterprise. This applies not least to the generality of companies rather than to a few isolated 'exemplar' cases. Above all, relatively little is known about the extent to which managers endorse human resource management. This is particularly important because, as Legge (1989: 27) points out, one of the distinguishing features of HRM is its focus on the development of the 'management team'. In short 'it is experienced by managers, as the most valued company resource to be managed, it concerns them in the achievement of business goals and it expresses senior management's preferred organizational values' (1989: 28)

Essentially, our aim in this chapter is therefore to examine some of the main areas of focus of human resource management in relation to the attitudes and behaviour of managers in Britain. Following a general assessment of the key elements of human resource management, data will be presented from two surveys of British Institute of Management members conducted in 1980 and 1990. Three main areas of human resource management are selected for special focus: (1) employee participation and involvement; (2) approaches to trade unionism; and (3) training and management development.

Human Resource Management

One version of the idea of human resource management is that it is in many respects distinct from personnel management. On this view, it has a strategic focus and it is aligned with the overall business policies of the firm. It involves all managerial personnel (and especially general managers). It regards people as the most important single asset of the firm. It incorporates the view that managers should be proactive in relation to people. And it has a variety of objectives including enhancing company performance, satisfying employee 'needs' and advancing societal well-being (Beer et al., 1984).

Nonetheless there are distinctive approaches. The Michigan perspective (Fombrun, Tichy and Devanna, 1984) has focused particularly on strategy; whereas the Harvard perspective linked with the work of Beer and his colleagues (1984) has a more pronounced 'human relations' emphasis (see Hendry and Pettigrew, 1990). The Harvard definition, too, is particularly broad, since it conceived HRM in terms of 'all management decisions that affect the nature of the relationship between the organization and employees – its human resources' (Beer et al., 1984: 1). However, it was specific in its location of the main policy choices noting four main foci: (1) employee influence, (2) human resource flow, (3) reward systems and (4) work systems.

In the debates which have followed the publication of these seminal works, a key issue is the extent to which there has been a radical transformation in practices within firms or whether, rather, the movement has been more of a superficial re-labelling of ongoing activities which have proved to be largely impervious to change (Guest, 1987; Keenoy, 1990; Storey, 1989). Our objective in this contribution is not to enter into these debates in any detail but rather to isolate a number of areas of HRM and to analyse the extent to which managers broadly endorse or reject specific practices.

The British Institute of Management Surveys

The data reported in this chapter are part of a much wider study which involved tracing constancies and patterns of change in managerial attitudes and behaviour between 1980 and 1990. Random samples of members and fellows of the British Institute of Management were taken in both cases, with questionnaires being posted to 2000 different groups of managers at each point in time. In 1980, 1058 responses were received representing nearly 53 per cent of the sample (for details see Mansfield et al., 1981; and Poole et al., 1981). In 1990, 827 replies were received comprising just over 41 per cent of the sample. The reasonably good response rates in each case provide valuable data to discuss various themes in HRM, although they are not designed explicitly to test propositions about the so-called transformation to HRM within the firm itself.

Employee Participation and Involvement

International interest in organizational democracy grew appreciably in the 1980s (Stern and McCarthy, 1986; Wilpert and Sorge, 1984). According to Beer et al. (1984: 8), one of the central policy areas of HRM is to enhance employee influence:

> This policy area has to do with a key question that all managers must ask: How much responsibility, authority, and power should the organization voluntarily delegate and to whom? If required by government legislation to bargain with unions or consult with worker councils, how should management enter into these institutional relationships? Will they seek to minimize the power and influence of these legislated mechanisms? Or will they share influence and work to create greater congruence of interest between management and the employee groups represented through these mechanisms? The managerial task here is to develop the organization's policy regarding the amount of influence employee stakeholders have with respect to such diverse matters as business goals, pay, working conditions, career progression, employment security, or the task itself; and to attempt to implement these policies. Inevitably, decisions about employee influence affect traditional management prerogatives and can reshape the very purpose of the firm. Employee influence decisions are therefore critical general management decisions whether they are made explicitly or, as is often the case, implicitly.

The first issue addressed is thus how far has the transformation to HRM encompassed an extension of employee influence and an endorsement by managers of a variety of practices for employee participation and involvement? Moreover, given that HRM is supposedly the responsibility of *all* managers, similarities and differences between personnel managers and the rest of the managers in our 1990 sample are also traced. Our central argument is that although views on employee participation remain broadly favourable, an important factor affecting attitudes has almost certainly been a decline in the power of trade unions. This is also arguably one of the most significant changes leading to the rise of HRM in any case, and it is often argued that some firms may have used HRM precisely to undermine trade union influence (see Martinez Lucio and Weston, Chapter 13, this volume). One particular form of participation associated with HRM is financial participation (see Schuller, 1989). Managers in the 1990 survey are broadly supportive of most forms of profit-sharing and employee shareholding, and personnel managers' attitudes are especially favourable towards these developments (although for the most part their views are not *significantly* different from other managers in a statistical sense). Broadly our thesis is that managers appear to support most employee involvement practices so long as these do not radically affect their control function within the firm. In other words, they tend to prefer a unitary rather than pluralist approach to employee participation in decision-making.

So far as employee participation is concerned, it appears that managers in the UK support individualistic 'human resource management-type' practices as opposed to collectivist trade union based participation. The relevant findings are presented in Table 12. 1 where it will be seen that, in both 1980 and 1990, managers not only considered that their own views ought to be represented on any participation machinery (1980: 81.1 per cent; 1990: 60.5 per cent) but also *endorsed* the ideas of regular meetings between supervisors and work groups (1980: 66.5 per cent; 1990: 57.9 per cent), the provision of information to employees (1980: 53.7 per cent; 1990: 50.7 per cent) and joint consultation committees (1980: 48.5 per cent; 1990: 38.4 per cent). Moreover, they remained broadly *opposed* to board level and/or trade union-type participation channels such as two-tier boards (1980: 51.6 per cent; 1990: 42.2 per cent), extending collective bargaining (1980: 47.7 per cent; 1990: 43.4 per cent) and worker directors elected through trade unions (1980: 72.9 per cent; 1990: 52.8 per cent).

Table 12.1 *Managers' views on employee participation*[1]

		% Respondents				
		Definitely agree 1	2	3	4	Definitely disagree 5
Managers' views ought to be represented in any scheme for employee participation as are the views of the workers	1980	48.9	32.2	13.4	3.6	1.8
	1990	21.3	39.2	17.9	13.9	7.7
Regular meetings between work groups and their supervisors are an appropriate form of employee participation	1980	25.9	40.6	21.4	8.8	3.3
	1990	17.3	40.6	21.3	15.3	5.5
There is a need for the provision of more information to employees	1980	22.0	31.7	24.6	15.0	6.8
	1990	15.9	34.8	27.2	16.5	5.6
Joint consultation committees are an appropriate form of employee participation	1980	13.3	35.2	31.3	15.3	4.9
	1990	9.2	29.2	36.5	19.7	5.4
There is a need for greater employee participation in my organization	1980	12.2	19.5	31.3	22.0	14.9
	1990	13.2	26.6	34.3	17.5	8.4

Table 12.1 (*cont.*)

		% Respondents				
		Definitely agree 1	2	3	4	Definitely disagree 5
Employee participation diminishes the role of middle and junior managers	1980	10.8	19.6	18.5	22.9	21.2
	1990	12.3	16.2	22.7	33.0	15.8
Two-tier boards (management and supervisory) are an appropriate form of employee participation	1980	3.7	16.1	28.6	24.3	27.3
	1990	10.1	17.5	30.2	25.0	17.2
Extending collective bargaining is an appropriate form of participation	1980	4.5	14.5	33.3	32.0	15.7
	1990	8.5	13.8	34.2	28.2	15.2
Worker directors elected through trade unions are an appropriate form of employee participation	1980	2.7	8.2	16.2	26.6	46.3
	1990	12.5	13.9	20.8	27.7	25.1
Worker directors elected through employees are an appropriate form of participation	1990	13.1	21.7	23.6	23.0	18.6

[1] Total sample, 1980 n = 1058; 1990, n = 827.

Nonetheless, it will be seen that there have been a number of interesting changes over time which are best explained by a reduction in the pressure for board-level practices by government and by a decline in the power of trade unions. In particular, the absence of Bullock-style industrial democracy initiatives in the 1980s may well account for the lower levels of opposition to (a) two-tier boards and (b) worker directors elected through trade unions. Moreover, the loss of power of trade unions probably occasioned less antipathy to extending collective bargaining in 1990 compared with a decade earlier. It is also worth mentioning that the views of personnel managers are not markedly different from other managers in the 1990 sample. Indeed, on only two items were views significantly different, with personnel managers being more prone to favour extensions in the provision of more information to employees ($X^2 = 21.3$, $p < 0.001$)

and joint consultation committees ($X^2 = 13.7$, $p < 0.01$). Overall, then, even if their enthusiasm is less pronounced, managers tend to support forms of employee involvement which are integrative in purpose, which do not radically undermine their freedom to manage and in which the role of trade unions is circumscribed. These findings are clearly consistent with the notion of managerial endorsement of unitaristic modes of employee influence and involvement rather than pluralistic methods based on the extension of trade union activities.

One development which is arguably central to HRM is profit-sharing and employee shareholding, although Schuller (1989: 136) argues that, in practice, its 'links with actual human resource development in the sense of a strategy to make better use of the labour force's skills and potential are far from clear'. It is true that many of these schemes have emerged as tax efficient forms of remuneration for employees. Nevertheless, taking the central policy choice areas of the Harvard framework (Beer et al., 1984), employee influence *and* HRM reward systems are both, *in principle*, enhanced by profit-sharing. Moreover, to obtain commitment from a workforce and to encourage employee loyalty, profit-sharing and employee shareholding schemes are potentially valuable inducements. It is to the examination of these forms of employee involvement that our attention now turns.

Although we do not have comparative data for 1980 and 1990, it is of interest to note the strong endorsement by managers in the more recent survey of profit-sharing and related schemes. As is seen in Table 12.2, 81.6 per cent of managers support profit-sharing with cash awards, 82.3 per cent endorse profit-sharing through shares in the company, 70.7 per cent concur with Save-As-You-Earn (SAYE) share ownership schemes and 60 per cent agree with Executive Share schemes. The pronounced support for

Table 12.2 *Managers' views on profit-sharing and employee shareholding schemes*[1]

	% Respondents				
	Strongly agree	Agree	Indifferent	Disagree	Strongly disagree
Profit-sharing (with cash awards)	33.0	48.6	11.7	4.9	1.7
Profit-sharing (through shares in the company)	38.2	44.1	12.0	3.5	2.2
Save-As-You-Earn share ownership schemes	28.3	42.4	23.3	3.6	2.5
Executive Share schemes	27.4	38.6	22.8	7.8	3.5

[1] Total sample, n = 827.

all-employee share-based schemes (which are arguably especially close to the core of HRM) is particularly interesting. Moreover, to reinforce the idea of a general endorsement by managers of these practices, it should be stressed that personnel managers' views are not significantly different from those of other managerial colleagues. In short, the overwhelming support for profit-sharing schemes is indicative of the firm commitment by modern managers to at least one aspect of HRM.

Trade Unionism and Collective Bargaining

One of the most controversial of the potential and, indeed, the actual consequences of the implementation of HRM policies is of course the effect on trade unions (see Martinez Lucio and Weston, Chapter 13, this volume). It should be stressed that trade unionism and collective bargaining *can* be accommodated within an HRM strategy. Indeed, the Harvard approach (Beer et al., 1984) is avowedly pluralistic in its compass. Moreover, in the USA, writers such as Heckscher (1988) have sought to conceptualize new roles for trade unionism in the evolving corporation. Nonetheless, the focus on high commitment to the employing organization and to higher congruence (whereby the firm shapes the work system, reward systems and flow policies so that there is a greater consistency of interests among management, shareholders and workers) tends to run counter to traditional unionism and collective bargaining. And of course, the so-called new realism in trade unions encompassing single union agreements and no strike clauses fits HRM strategy very well indeed.

The attitudes of managers to trade unions and their experience of actual collective bargaining are thus of particular interest to the debates on HRM and its impact within the firm. Turning to our actual survey data, it is clear

Table 12.3 *Experience of collective bargaining*

	% Respondents					
	Total sample		Private sector managers		Public sector managers	
	1980 (n = 1058)	1990 (n = 827)	1980 (n = 731)	1990 (n = 497)	1980 (n = 320)	1990 (n = 169)
Formal collective bargaining	20.0	17.4	23.3	17.8	17.0	16.1
Informal meetings with union representatives	48.5	31.3	42.0	31.9	62.4	27.8
Handling individual grievances brought by union representatives	42.2	38.2	38.8	32.2	49.7	61.4

first of all that managers' experience of collective bargaining did indeed decline in the 1980s. The relevant data are set out in Table 12.3 where it will be noted that there was a particularly marked reduction in managers reporting experience of informal collective bargaining (48.5 per cent in 1980 compared with 31.3 per cent in 1990) indicating that this was no longer a particularly common method of dealing with the workforce. It will also be noted that this decline was especially apparent in the public sector (62.4 per cent in 1980; 27.8 per cent in 1990).

Moreover, the view that personnel management (as opposed to HRM) is particularly linked with traditional union practices received some support from our survey. Hence, there were highly significant differences between the experience of personnel managers of formal collective bargaining compared with the rest of their management colleagues (X^2: 21.4, p < 0.0001). And the same applied for informal collective bargaining (X^2 = 6.7, p < 0.01). Of course, we cannot directly comment on whether firms

Table 12.4 *Trade unions: managers' attitudes*[1]

		% Respondents				
		Strongly agree 1	Agree 2	Indifferent 3	Disagree 4	Strongly disagree 5
Trade union membership should be purely voluntary	1980	51.8	37.2	5.0	5.1	0.8
	1990	51.2	42.4	3.7	1.4	1.4
Trade unions are not acting in the country's economic interests	1980	40.4	46.2	7.2	5.4	0.8
	1990	11.4	48.8	19.5	19.0	1.2
Trade unions today have too much power	1980	37.6	44.5	7.0	9.2	1.7
	1990	4.7	27.0	28.1	37.1	3.1
All in all trade unions have more power than management	1980	11.2	41.7	10.5	31.2	5.4
	1990	2.0	12.1	13.8	61.9	10.2
Unions should be solely concerned with pay and conditions	1980	17.8	26.9	9.6	38.4	7.3
	1990	10.1	32.5	9.5	40.7	7.3
A trade union should be prepared if necessary to use any form of industrial action which may be effective	1980	1.9	13.8	5.6	38.8	39.7
	1990	3.1	11.3	7.3	39.2	39.1

[1] Total sample, 1980 n = 1058; 1990 n = 827.

with declining unionism are particularly likely to replace traditional personnel management with strategic HRM, but our data are at least consistent with such an interpretation of recent trends and tendencies.

But what about attitudes of managers to trade unions more generally? This issue has assumed increasing importance given the changes in trade unions in the 1980s (Kelly, 1990). We have argued first of all that a decline in trade union power, while not a *sine qua non*, was undoubtedly coterminous with the rise of HRM. And certainly managers are prepared to acknowledge that a reduction in union power occurred quite markedly during the course of the 1980s. The relevant data are set out in Table 12.4 which sets out the attitudes of our British Institute of Management samples to various aspects of trade unionism. It is particularly noteworthy that while in 1980 a majority of managers (52.9 per cent) agreed with the view that all in all trade unions had more power than management, by 1990 only 14.1 per cent of the sample felt that this situation still obtained. Moreover, by 1990 only just over 30 per cent of managers felt that trade unions had too much power compared with over 80 per cent of their colleagues in 1980. The relatively 'pro union' attitude of personnel managers was also evident in our findings. Indeed, in 1990, personnel managers were particularly likely to reject the view that trade unions have too much power ($X^2 = 20.0$, $p < 0.0005$).

So far as HRM is concerned, then, it is clear from our findings that the 'challenge from below' which had been experienced by management as a consequence of the growth in power and influence of trade unions (Flanders, 1975) was significantly less of a problem in 1990 than had been the case a decade earlier. And this certainly provided the potential for introducing different approaches to the management of people in the firm and to the assertion of management's 'freedom to manage'.

Training and Management Development

The focus of our analysis now alters to encompass the very different themes in HRM of training and management development. It is of course basic to the premises of HRM that 'the firm's most important single asset is its people'; and hence the training and development of all employees (including the managers themselves) is of far reaching consequence. Indeed, an acid test of any general endorsement of HRM in actual practice is the extent to which managers foster a variety of forms of training and development rather than continue to rely on the external labour market.

Furthermore, training and development have the added significance of being (1) interlinked with other aspects of HRM and (2) the focal point of issues of current concern in Britain and overseas (see Holden, 1991; Locke, 1989; Silver, 1991). To begin with, then, training and development are connected with enhancing satisfaction and commitment, the growth of competences, motivation to work and higher congruence between personal and corporate 'needs'. They are a means of articulating a company's culture, adapting to rapid technological change and ensuring that a core workforce remains loyal and committed to the enterprise. In particular, as Beer et al. (1984: 228–9) have argued:

> The developmental approach may increase the competence of employees as well as change the relationship between the organization and the employee. Employees who believe they are receiving an opportunity for development often feel a greater sense of commitment to the organization.

As for managers, the concern over training and development has been further enhanced by the arguments in various studies which have indicated that managers in the UK still receive less training than their contemporaries in competitive nations (Constable and McCormick, 1987; Handy et al., 1987; Silver, 1991). As Handy (1991: 44) has observed:

> There can be little doubt that, by comparison with the other countries . . . Britain has neglected her managerial stock. With some notable exceptions her companies have asked too little from their would-be managers and given them too little in terms of education, training and development. Quantity does not guarantee quality, but in crude statistical terms we should probably need to be doing nearly ten times as much as we now are as a nation.

It has been against this background that the Council for Management Education and Development (CMED) and the Management Charter Initiative emerged. Moreover, the 'crediting competences' scheme which has developed will ensure that job experience will substitute for part of the course work in conventional schemes.

How extensive, then, is the commitment of managers to training and development, and to what extent do they enthusiastically support this central aspect of HRM? Although we do not have any longitudinal data, using categories which were in part derived from a Deloitte, Haskins and Sells (1988) report we asked respondents a series of general questions about the training and development of managers. The replies are set out in Table 12.5 and it is apparent that there is substantial support for management training and development. Thus, 98.4 per cent of respondents agreed that management development should be a highly important objective of the company or organization. It will also be noted that 97.7 per cent of respondents considered that corporate support should be provided for management development in both time and resources. A further 93.3 per cent felt that there should be provision of a coherent framework for planned management development through personal target setting, performance appraisals and performance-related advancement. Other aspects of HRM received strong support. For example, 93 per cent of respondents considered that managers should have a responsibility for the development of their colleagues; 98.6 per cent agreed that there should be encouragement for continuous self-development; and 92 per cent felt that there should be encouragement to obtain recognized qualifications.

Table 12.5 *Managers' views on management training and development*[1]

	% Respondents				
	Strongly agree	Agree	Indifferent	Disagree	Strongly disagree
Management development should be a highly important objective of the company or organization	65.6	32.8	1.2	0.4	0
Corporate support should be provided for management development in both time and resources	57.4	40.3	2.1	0.2	0
There should be provision of a coherent framework for planned management development through personal target setting, performance appraisals and performance-related advancement	51.2	42.1	4.7	2.0	0
Managers should have a responsibility for the development of colleagues	48.8	44.2	4.7	2.0	0.4
There should be encouragement for continuous self-development	54.9	43.7	1.5	0	0
There should be encouragement to obtain recognized qualifications	48.0	44.0	7.4	0.6	0

[1] Total sample, all managers, n = 827.

So far as their own specific work is concerned, managers also strongly supported the growth of training and development programmes. Thus, 87.8 per cent felt that management development and training was important to helping them personally to do their jobs well, 76.4 per cent rejected the view that training is *not* a good way of keeping up to date with recent developments in management, and 86.3 per cent considered training to be important in helping them to develop as a manager (see Table 12.6). Nonetheless, they were more sceptical about some of the more in-strumental advantages of management training and development even though, for the most part, their views were positive in these respects as well. Thus, as is again shown in Table 12.6, 54.9 per cent disagreed with the statement that a managerial qualification would *not* help them to change jobs, and there was a balance of positive scores (35 per cent) over negative scores (30 per cent) on the advantages of a management qualification for promotion. There was also a balance of positive scores (43.1 per cent compared with 20.9 per cent) on whether a management qualification was likely to increase respondents' personal interest in undertaking further training. However, 75.1 per cent of respondents agreed with the view that a 'management qualification does *not* show that I am a good manager'.

Table 12.6 *Managers' views on further aspects of training and development*[1]

	% Respondents				
	Strongly agree	Agree	Neither agree nor disagree	Disagree	Strongly disagree
Management development and training is important to help me do my job well	39.0	48.8	10.1	1.8	0.2
Training is *not* a good way of keeping up to date with recent developments in management	1.4	5.8	16.9	56.4	19.6
Training is important in helping me to develop as a manager	22.7	63.6	10.7	2.7	0.2
A management qualification would *not* help me to change jobs	5.4	19.4	20.3	39.5	15.4
A management qualification does *not* show that I am a good manager	20.2	54.9	11.8	9.8	3.3
A management qualification will help me to be promoted to a more senior management role	6.7	28.3	34.9	25.2	4.8
Receiving a management qualification would increase my interest in undertaking further training	7.1	36.0	36.0	17.2	3.7

[1] Total sample, all managers, n = 827.

In the more recent survey, managers received, on average, off-the-job training in their own time of 3.3 days and for 5.3 days in their employer's time. If the on-the-job training is added (2.2 days on average), managers in our sample averaged approximately eleven days of training per year. This suggests a significant increase in management training as foreshadowed by Storey (1989: 7) and Keep (1989: 118–19), although whether this applies to training for *all* employees is debatable.

Among management grades, then, it appears that this particular aspect of HRM has enthusiastic support, and it should be stressed that personnel managers in particular are convinced of the importance of these developments. Thus they are more likely than their colleagues as a whole to agree with the views that management development should be a highly important objective of the company or organization ($X^2 = 19.3$, p < 0.001); that corporate support should be provided for management development ($X^2 = 20.8$, p < 0.0001); that managers should have responsibility for the development their colleagues ($X^2 = 18.2$, p < 0.001); and that there should be encouragement for continued self-development ($X^2 = 13.1$, p < 0.001). Given the broad endorsement of these objectives by managers generally, it is clear that this aspect of HRM has been incorporated into managers' attitudes and recent behaviour.

Conclusions – Rhetoric or Reality?

Human resource management, as we have seen, is a multidimensional phenomenon encompassing employee influence (involvement), human resource flow policies, reward systems and work systems. In the compass of a single chapter we have only been able to comment on a small part of this development. But the original data which we have been able to present does highlight aspects of the reality rather than the rhetoric of change relating to managerial attitudes and behaviour in the firm.

Our central conclusions may be summarized as follows. Employee involvement is certainly favoured by managers but there remains a preference for schemes which are integrative and which do not directly challenge the managerial controlling function. There is also strong support for most forms of employee shareholding and profit-sharing, and these are in turn consistent both with extending employee (financial) involvement and with HRM-style reward systems.

With respect to trade unions, collective bargaining has been declining, though it remains an important part of the personnel manager's role. The decline in trade union power has also helped to enhance managerial 'freedom to manage' and to occasion a more proactive managerial approach to a variety of human resource issues. Finally, training and development are strongly supported by managers and this is indicative of a high degree of internalization of one main area within HRM.

So far as the basic issue of rhetoric or reality is concerned, the data presented in this chapter indicate a pattern which is consistent with the adoption of HRM in many British firms, at least along several dimensions. But what, it may be reasonably asked, is the situation with respect to other aspects of HRM? On one view, the links with strategy and with general management are vital components of the 'new' HRM. Moreover, the tendency to view people as the key asset of the firm, to be proactive with regard to people and to encourage individual and societal well-being alongside organizational effectiveness are integral to recent departures. In most respects our data only permit very general impressions about these further aspects of HRM. The pronounced support for training and management development undoubtedly suggests some degree of long-term thinking with regard to the management of people and it certainly indicates a concern for the development of the human (management) assets of the firm. But this is some way from the HRM objective of focusing the strategy of the company on the people employed by the firm in question. And the so-called transformation of personnel management to HRM is not unequivocally supported by data of this type in any case. Again it is likely that wider economic conditions will continue to impact on training in the firm and that the ideals of individual and societal well-being will be generally subordinated to the more pressing concern for organizational effectiveness. On the other hand, there does seem to be a greater degree of 'proactivity' with regard to people than might have been anticipated in British industry a decade or so earlier.

Hence our conclusion must be that, notwithstanding considerable variations in the implementation of HRM practices, there are undoubtedly indications that management attitudes are consistent with many of the core elements of HRM. Of course, this arises not least because managers are currently in a uniquely favourable position to ensure that these policies actually come to fruition in the decision-making processes in the firm; a situation which is likely to remain in force so long as state intervention remains muted and the power of trade unions continues to be circumscribed.

References

Beer, M., Spector, B., Lawrence, P.R., Mills, D.Q. and Walton, R.E. (1984) *Managing Human Assets*. New York: Free Press.

Brewster, C. and Tyson, S. (eds) (1991) *International Comparisons in Human Resource Management*. London: Pitman.

Constable, J. and McCormick, R. (1987) *The Making of British Managers*. London: British Institute of Management and Confederation of British Industry.

Deloitte, Haskins and Sells (1988) *A Final Report of a Study into a Charter for Managers*. London: Deloitte, Haskins and Sells.

Dowling, P.S. and Schuler, R.S. (1990) *International Dimensions of Human Resource Management*. Boston: PWS Kent.

Flanders, A. (1975) *Management and Unions*. London: Faber & Faber.

Fombrun, C., Tichy, N.M. and Devanna, M.A. (1984) *Strategic Human Resource Management*. New York: Wiley.

Guest, D.E. (1987) 'Human resource management and industrial relations', *Journal of Management Studies*, 24 (5): 503–21.

Handy, C. (1991) 'How to compare with other countries', in M. Silver (ed.), *Competent to Manage*. London: Routledge. pp. 32–47.

Handy, C., Gow, I., Gordon, C., Randlesome, C. and Moloney, M. (1987) *The Making of Managers*. London: National Economic Development Office.

Heckscher, C.C. (1988) *The New Unionism*. New York: Basic Books.

Hendry, C. and Pettigrew, A. (1986) 'The practice of strategic human resource management', *Personnel Review*, 15 (3): 3–8.

Hendry, C. and Pettigrew, A. (1990) 'Human resource management: an agenda for the 1990s', *International Journal of Human Resource Management*, 1 (1): 17–44.

Holden, L. (1991) 'European trends in training and development', *International Journal of Human Resource Management*, 2 (2): 113–32.

Keep, E. (1989) 'Corporate training strategies: the vital component?' in J. Storey (ed.), *New Perspectives on Human Resource Management*. London: Routledge. pp. 109–25.

Keenoy, T. (1990) 'Human resource management: rhetoric, reality and contradiction', *International Journal of Human Resource Management*, 1 (3): 363–84.

Kelly, J. (1990) 'British trade unionism 1979–89: change, continuity and contradictions', *Work, Employment and Society*, Special Issue, 4, May: 29–65.

Krulis-Randa, J.A. (1990) 'Strategic human resource management (SHRM) in Europe after 1992', *International Journal of Human Resource Management*, 1 (2): 131–9.

Legge, K. (1989) 'Human resource management: a critical analysis', in J. Storey (ed.), *New Perspectives on Human Resource Management*. London: Routledge. pp. 19–40.

Locke, R.R. (1989) *Management and Higher Education Since 1940*. Cambridge: Cambridge University Press.

Mansfield, R., Poole, M.J.F., Blyton, P. and Frost, P.E. (1981) *The British Manager in Profile*. London: British Institute of Management.

Pieper, R. (ed.) (1990) *Human Resource Management: An International Comparison*. Berlin: de Gruyter.

Poole, M.J.F., Mansfield, R., Blyton, P.R. and Frost, P.E. (1981) *Managers in Focus*. Aldershot: Gower.

Schuller, T. (1989) 'Financial participation', in J. Storey (ed.), *New Perspectives on Human Resource Management*. London: Routledge. pp. 126–36.

Silver, M. (ed.) (1991) *Competent to Manage*. London: Routledge.

Storey, J. (ed.) (1989) *New Perspectives on Human Resource Management*. London: Routledge.

Stern, R.N. and McCarthy, S. (1986) *International Yearbook of Organizational Democracy*. Chichester: Wiley.

Wilpert, B. and Sorge, A. (eds) (1984) *International Yearbook of Organizational Democracy*, Vol. 2. Chichester: Wiley.

13 HUMAN RESOURCE MANAGEMENT AND TRADE UNION RESPONSES: BRINGING THE POLITICS OF THE WORKPLACE BACK INTO THE DEBATE

Miguel Martinez Lucio and Syd Weston

The impact of management strategies commonly placed under the heading of human resource management (HRM) have become the subject of considerable interest within academic and practitioner circles alike. One particularly significant issue to emerge is the impact that 'strong' HRM strategies may have upon traditional industrial relations systems (Guest, 1989a; Horowitz, 1991). More specifically, in recent years HRM strategies have become a main concern of many trade unions, as commented on by the General Secretary of Britain's largest general union:

> a new era of crafty Rambo managers has come into existence which seek to ignore or deliberately disrupt union organisation and collective bargaining procedures, by bringing in their own schemes based on fake committees and centred on the individual worker, not the organised worker, with the aim of undermining established working practices and bargaining methods. (T&GWU, 1989: 4)

What this statement clearly indicates is that HRM strategies are being taken very seriously by trade unions, and that such practices may pose a threat to the established industrial relations institutions and the roles that trade unions have adopted within them. In other words, the traditional functions of workplace trade unionism over worker representation and rights are being perceived in trade union circles as increasingly being captured by management. If such fears have legitimacy then it must follow that worker representation and rights need to be viewed not as the sole domain for trade unions to occupy, but arenas where competing projects (such as HRM) attempt to locate themselves. The current concerns of trade unions surrounding these issues are not, however, in themselves new. For example, British trade unions had previously expressed great concern over very similar issues to McCarthy when he was compiling evidence for the Donovan Commission (McCarthy, 1967). The question remains as to whether or not there is justification for the concerns now being expressed by trade unions over HRM type practices. Is there something unique within HRM practices that may legitimize their fears? To address such a question, an understanding of why such practices are being introduced is essential, together with the initial responses that trade unions have developed towards them.

Unfortunately, many contemporary approaches addressing HRM practices and contemporary innovations in the world of work have naively presented management as being the innovator and strategist, unilaterally determining the structure and restructuring of employee relations. Such approaches have, in the main, divorced employment and work from any wider political and ideological environment. Furthermore, uniformity and a reactive nature are assumed for trade union responses, the political climate and the development of debate around key issues pertinent to the structure of the employment relationship (for example, worker rights on representation and the meaning of quality as a production concept). Where opposition to management strategy is addressed it is assumed to be of a reactive nature, rather than part of any broad strategy in trade union thinking.

What will be argued in this chapter is the following. First, if HRM type strategies are to be understood as an attempt to redefine the realm of worker representation and rights around managerial objectives and company-led agendas then it needs to be recognized from the outset that they are not easily manipulable features of the employment relation. Secondly, that trade unions themselves are varied and complex organizations which react to change in a variety of ways according to their organizational identities, structures and characteristics of their workplace. Thirdly, that trade union responses occur along various lines which then in turn contribute to a macro-level debate on specific issues which will be central to the success or failure of HRM strategies. Indeed, the link between HRM strategies and the political projects of the 1980s, with specific definitions of 'the market' and 'employee involvement', have been key ingredients of the development of HRM (Legge, 1989). The counter-debates which have developed within trade union circles as a result of these projects have contributed both directly and indirectly to the responses of local groups of workers and to the points of reference they seek beyond their immediate workplace. It is these local responses and interactions which will in turn determine the eventual outcomes and varieties of HRM practices. To this end, there can be no uniformity or inevitable outcome of HRM.

To explore these issues, an outline of the form and content of HRM strategies will be presented. Following this, the debates and responses of the trade unions will be explored by using three examples:

1. a conciliatory/concessionary approach (equated with 'market unionism');

2. a formalistic and procedural approach classified as 'institutional strategies' (with the emphasis towards wider collective bargaining and worker rights);
3. an isolated local workplace response classified here as 'independent strategies' (from both formal union policies and management proposals).

Finally, an assessment will be made as to the compatibility (or incompatibility) of such union responses to HRM practices. This ultimately depends on the perspective and values of individual unions in the first instance, as well as broader political dimensions.

The Nature and Form of Human Resource Management

Several commentators have correctly warned that the use of management strategy has to be carefully dissected before its impact can be measured. For example, Marchington and Parker (1990) have emphasized that management strategy varies in its implementation and that the structure of a company's product market and its competitive status can exert a significant influence (see also Whipp, Chapter 3, this volume). It is the competitive element which forces managers to rethink their production process which in turn can lead to a need for change within personnel management and industrial relations. This argument has been central to the writings of various post-Fordist analysts who have seen fragmentation in the consumption environment as a precursor to changes in the realm of production itself (Aglietta, 1979; Piore and Sabel, 1984). New competitive pressures from other producers and the nature of new markets are seen to destabilize the Fordist relation between mass consumption and mass production which had been crystallized in the production methods of Taylorism and traditional industrial relations systems. According to this line of argument, there is now a need for management to represent the changes and uncertainties in the product market within the workplace itself by alerting their employees to this more 'hostile' market environment.

In addition to these developments in the product market, management have also had to respond to changes in the internal environment, most notably in the area of industrial relations. Historically this reflects the changing expectations and struggles of workers themselves. During the 1970s, for example, an evolving corpus of employee rights was derived both externally via legislation and internally by trade union activity, in particular demands for worker participation (Martinez Lucio and Weston, 1991). The development of 'civil rights' in industry via collective bargaining processes (Slichter, 1941) was, under existing and traditional management practices, unable to contain the emerging issues concerning employment such as health and safety, equal opportunities, worker participation and others which culminated in the events of the 1970s. These new employment issues, however, developed in an uneven manner and, to a significant extent, became detached from the core collective labour activities which continued to reflect the narrow areas of pay and conditions. While developments in health and safety issues, equal opportunities and participation may have been key trade union issues they have nevertheless rarely been core items on the collective bargaining agenda. As the trade unions neglected to tie the new issues back into collective bargaining, the legislative framework surrounding these issues left management the task of unifying this broadening of issues and rights within the employment relation. Hence the call for a new managerial design in employee relations irrespective of its external environment. Therefore, management has not only had to respond to exogenous factors such as a more hostile market environment, but also to endogenous factors within the employment relation, a factor overlooked in the current literature on HRM.

The aims and policies of these new approaches had to be a part of a more coherent and managerial led project to incorporate these endogenous and exogenous factors. In this sense, elements had to be tied together and brought closer to general corporate strategies (Guest, 1989b; Purcell, 1989). Within such strategies the previously autonomous status of trade unions, and their role surrounding worker representation and rights in the form of collective bargaining, are not the inevitable and easily acquired allies of such new management practices. Hence, one of the evolving management strategies in replacing or developing a new industrial relations framework has been the integration of workers into a managerial led agenda that is closer to the 'needs' of the product market. In many cases this has involved an attempt to redesign worker representation with or without the collaboration of the trade unions. It is the manner in which this integration takes place, coupled with the 'approximation' of the workplace to the market, that will be a central point of engagement between management, unions and workforce. The complexities of this engagement have been, as yet, rarely addressed. However, it has been suggested that the implementation of HRM practices will not displace the traditional role that trade unions currently occupy within industrial relations institutions and that coexistence between traditional industrial relations institutions and HRM practices is possible (Storey, 1987). Nevertheless, when one thinks of HRM encompassing and redefining, in a concerted manner, worker representation, rights and worker identity, traditional industrial relations institutions could become totally redefined or circumvented. To this end HRM may be perceived as undermining any degree of effective and relatively autonomous worker control. However, these industrial relations changes and implications can only become significant if HRM-type strategies are left unchallenged by trade unions and workers alike; as examined below, the evidence indicates that this is not the case.

Concessionary and Conciliatory Union Responses to HRM

Much of the debate and material on HRM in Britain has centred on new work environments classified as greenfield sites. The emerging industries have been seen to indicate a change of direction towards lighter and more flexible high-tech industries. With this would come a new industrial relations system that had as its objectives higher efficiency and productivity via formal arrangements between management and workers, supposedly burying the world of overmanning, inflexible practices and industrial conflict (Bassett, 1987). HRM became seen as the basis of restructuring this problematic heritage. A more hostile political and legislative framework towards trade unions in Britain ran parallel with these developments and gave rise to a conciliatory and concessionary trade union approach, with a specific strategy of embracing much of these managerially led developments, and realizing long term possibilities in locating unionism within such emerging sectors of the economy. This meant negotiating agreements such as single union deals and no-strike agreements (often with pendulum arbitration) which conceded much of the autonomy of trade union influence with respect to worker representation *vis-à-vis* management.

Such developments were not, however, specific to Britain, but have also been reflected in some of the policies and strategies within US trade unionism since the late 1970s, such as concession bargaining in more traditional sectors. For example, the 1979 two-year collective agreement at the crisis ridden Chrysler car company included a pay freeze along with other concessions in the area of vacations. A pattern established itself on the back of such experiences during the 1980s in the USA that signified a set of reversals in substantive rights and gains at work, which was considered by some as the only solution to the growing ills of American capitalism (Slaughter, 1983). Adversarial industrial relations were considered antiquated compared to this new climate of compromise and concession: the concessions by workers and their respective trade unions on economic issues were seen as contributing to a new labour–management relation that could facilitate even broader and more deep-seated changes in employment and work itself (Moody, 1988).

In the British context, there was also a macro-level reflection of these responses to assertive management and HRM-type practices – albeit with a chequered history – in the form of the New Realism that was debated during most of the 1980s (McIlroy, 1988: 54–6). This represented a desire to move beyond 'traditional' and 'antiquated' forms of trade union activity of a conflict oriented nature. Compromise and partnership with employers was considered by the 'new realists' to be the best response to increasingly assertive managerial styles as well as a hostile Conservative government (McIlroy, 1988: 55). Ranged against this position, however, was that of the more cynical trade unions, characterized by the National Union of Mineworkers during the 1984–85 miners' strike. Strike action, alongside broader political activity, was perceived by some unions as the best response to the Conservative government and assertive management. It was perceived as the best mechanism for maintaining the established system of collective bargaining and worker representation. While collective bargaining was perceived by this group of unions as being limited in extending union influence on managerial decisions, it was nevertheless seen as preserving the autonomy of worker representation *vis-à-vis* management. For these unions, the adoption of the New Realism approach would undermine worker autonomy in the long term.

Within the 'new realist' approach, the Electrical, Electronic, Telecommunication and Plumbing Union (EETPU) best exemplifies the most consistent adoption of new industrial relations practices with its desire to tie the union much closer to the strategic considerations of companies and management. HRM-type practices and the new political framework were perceived by the EETPU as being incompatible with traditional industrial relations and even presaging non-unionism. To overcome this dilemma the Union adopted specific policies which were to complement this new managerially led initiative. First, the EETPU adopted a policy of approaching employers rather than employees to gain a presence within the new workplace environment. This assisted employers to recognize and allow only a single union within certain companies, especially on greenfield sites, and on the specific condition that the union presence be complementary and not adversarial to HRM-type practices. These developments conditioned and led other employers to adopt similar strategies and, in turn, conditioned various other unions to adopt not dissimilar practices. Hence the often termed 'beauty contest' of trade unions competing with each other for selection by employers. Secondly, within this concessionary framework, the role of conflict was to be superseded or minimized by either a 'no-strike' agreement and/or pendulum arbitration. Thirdly, a supportive trade union attitude was developed towards new forms of worker involvement at company level (for example, advisory and company councils) and workplace level (for example, teamworking, quality circles) and in this sense the union was no longer considered to be the sole representative of worker interests. Nevertheless, it was perceived by the union(s) adopting this approach that concessions concerning worker representation would be counteracted by 'encroachment' in certain managerial functions. For example, the EETPU developed a range of educational and training services for the purpose of retraining members as part of the requirements of multi-skilling central to the flexible approach integral to HRM practices. These services extended to areas such as job evaluation and work study (Bassett, 1987: 67).

These union initiatives can be classified as market unionism, with their emphasis on providing a wide range of services to their members, supposedly making the union more relevant to the needs of workers, and hopefully also making it more central to the concerns and needs of management. The relevant point here is that the adoption of managerial functions by the union does not necessarily imply any qualitative development in these roles, such as a rethinking of the form and content of job evaluation along union lines, and may indeed further erode the degree of autonomy a union has in representing the various interests of its members. In this sense, whilst there is a perceived continuation of collective bargaining under these new developments it has been paralleled by major shifts in the form and content of a company's industrial relations system.

For many observers this has not just been the most dominant trade union response but the actual basis of a new system of representation of interests at work. A combination of a much sought for consensus in industry through claims of a common interest between managers and workers, coupled with the miraculous impact of new technology, was envisaged in the greenfield and 'fresher' areas of industry. Underpinning these developments was a symbolism providing the basis for a break with the 'inefficient and conflict-ridden' past which captured the imagination of a range of apparently diverse observers on both the left and right of the political spectrum (Dunn, 1990).

Institutional Strategies and the Extension of Collective Bargaining

Regardless of the apparent 'reactive' nature of trade unionism it would be premature to consider new management strategies as having led to very little response or simply the type of response illustrated by market unionism. Other responses are also evident in the UK, which are partly in accord with individual trade union traditions. The General, Municipal and Boilermakers' Union (GMB), for example, provides a different illustration of the problems and possibilities of trade union influence over the outcomes of HRM-type practice. Although this trade union's response has encompassed single union 'beauty contest' deals and the signing of agreements that are not dissimilar from the EETPU's (Yeandle and Clark, 1989), the GMB in 1991 launched with the Union of Communication Workers (UCW) an initiative which illustrates the way change in industrial relations is visualized. The starting point for the union's strategy was the realization that it was becoming 'irrelevant' to an increasing array of issues now constituting a large part of the employment relationship. According to this New Agenda (GMB and UCW, 1991) the developments in sophisticated management techniques along with the changing expectations of workers themselves were challenging the relevance and effectiveness of traditional forms of joint regulation at work such as collective bargaining.

This initiative was defined by various observers as an attempt to resurrect the social contract politics of the 1970s via the notion of synchronized pay bargaining. But the New Agenda is meant to be more than that. Pay is perceived as becoming but one feature of a highly differentiated employment package for an increasingly diversified workforce. At the heart of the New Agenda is the intention of extending the scope of collective bargaining into such areas as training, careers and recruitment issues. Whilst there is nothing new about extending collective bargaining into new issues, the attempt to formalize bargaining at company level is the lost ark of British industrial relations (as was the case in the 1970s). Leaders within the British Trades Union Congress (TUC) also began to see developments such as HRM offering the possible basis for a broader, formal involvement by trade unions through collective bargaining structures, since HRM developments were seen as broadening the understanding and role of employees and their needs (IRRR, 1991).

Furthermore, the GMB's approach envisages bargaining and the union's role being extended into areas such as the quality of production – 'talking to Britain's employers about how to achieve quality performance, cost and price competitiveness and a fairer society' – and the company's preparation for the Single European Market – 'to ensure that their company is prepared for what lies ahead' (GMB and UCW, 1991; GMB, 1989). The implications for the workplace are that the established and extended joint regulation would tie it closer into the broader concerns of the enterprise – apparently 'socialized' by the union's new role. So while being a formalistic and moderate union, the GMB's approach ultimately differs from that of market unionism through its emphasis on the social objectives of trade unionism, manifested in the approach to, and use of, collective bargaining. That the GMB's policies are distinct from the EETPU's is also partly a reflection of the broader characteristics of the GMB's membership and the centre-left political make up of its leadership.

The Keiper Recaro plant in the Midlands is a good example of the New Agenda – 'a bit of Germany in Britain' – where the GMB has signed an agreement which exchanges flexible production measures for a union presence and access to company information via a company council with GMB members on the management board (Parry, 1990). What the GMB leadership has clearly identified is that the European dimension of industrial relations, especially that of the German model with its constitutional works council system, can be an effective method to maintain union influence under HRM-type practices. In the Keiper case it was envisaged that the strong constitutionalist and permanent character of worker representation at company level would guarantee a broad union role within the enterprise. As a result, this form of worker representation cannot be easily circumvented.

Any evaluation of the success of such a union strategy towards developments in HRM practices must nevertheless take account of two vital factors. First, the implementation of such a strategy represents a qualitative change in the existing industrial relations framework, with its traditional institutions of joint regulation covering a broader range of strategic, long-term issues. As HRM strategies seek to integrate workers into a managerial led agenda that is closer to the needs of the market, then the approach of the GMB would seem to be at odds with HRM, given the Union's demands for a 'socialization' of the employment agenda. The accommodation of wider social and economic dimensions is not central to HRM as it stands and therefore if such a policy as that of the New Agenda is pursued it would require compromise on the part of management in pursuing their goals. Secondly, the New Agenda was the product of the Union's leadership (and its research units), which have had to contend with diverse interests and strong officer traditions within the Union's own organization. In recognition of this, the leadership has developed a coherent training programme for its officers as a means of securing the adoption and implementation of this strategy. It is necessary, therefore, to take into account these organizational issues if trade union responses to HRM practices are to be fully appreciated.

Active Workplace Responses to HRM: A Case Study

The trade union responses to HRM practices discussed thus far have been predominantly leadership driven, rather than reflecting autonomous initiatives taken at the workplace level. This is due, in the main, to the organizational and political cultures of these unions. In contrast, the following case is an example of a relatively independent workplace response, which was facilitated by the decentralized structure of the principal union involved. The case is a British plant owned by a multinational vehicle producer. It typifies many of the experiences that workplace trade unionism is confronted by when HRM practices are being introduced into a typical manufacturing plant with a long history of a multi-union presence and influence. The study highlights how the local and national trade unions responded to management demands, why they were unable to resist the implementation of new management practices, and their fears of what it means for traditional industrial relations. It further demonstrates the relationship between competing forms of worker representation and why unions may be justified in their fears that HRM practices can act to undermine trade union influence at the workplace.

The workforce size at the plant had reduced dramatically from a strength of 11,000 in the early 1980s to just under 5000 in 1991. Over 50 per cent of employees within the plant are represented by the Transport and General Workers' Union (T&GWU), 30 per cent by the Amalgamated Engineering Union (AEU), with the remainder being represented by the EETPU and the Manufacturing, Science and Finance Union (MSF). Traditionally the T&GWU was the major influence on the industrial relations system within the plant due to its numerical advantage *vis-à-vis* the other unions. In this sense the case study serves as an example of inter-union divisions and rivalry which is common in much of the British manufacturing sector.

Pay and conditions for employees at all the company's plants in the UK had traditionally been set at the national level through a Joint National Council (JNC), supplemented by local level collective bargaining structures. During the past eight years pay and conditions set at the national level had shifted from the traditional annual to a biennial round. No signficant industrial action had been taken during this period but more recently there had been one day per week strikes in pursuance of a shorter working week (this dispute was undermined and eventually collapsed due to a lack of support from the craft unions). Time off for trade union duties, and the numbers of trade union representatives recognized in the plant, had never been a cause of concern for management, in line with previous findings on these issues (Millward and Stevens, 1986). Although management had sought improvements in productivity and greater flexibility within the plant throughout the 1980s, no real effort had been made to implement any radical changes in working practices. In this respect, the traditional lines of demarcation and multi-union recognition had been adhered to and trade union influence had been maintained despite the sharp decrease in production and workforce size.

Throughout the 1980s the trade unions in the plant, particularly the T&GWU, had become more than aware of new management practices and the 'Japanization' of British manufacturing industry (Oliver and Wilkinson, 1988), although national trade union policy and interest towards these issues was not extensive. Quality circles, teamworking, team briefings and company councils had become familiar language to the unions within the plant and, as an individual branch of the union, they had vigorously monitored their development. Nevertheless, the wider policy of the T&GWU in the late 1980s towards this new management agenda was to resist such practices at all cost, in the belief that they could undermine trade union representation and influence at the workplace. However, such practices had either been forced through or negotiated at many plants where the same union had recognition rights and where resistance to them at plant level was perceived as a 'no-win situation' due to management's approach. For example, at the Nordsk Hydro Immingham plant in 1985 the local union representatives were unable to adhere to national union policy and were forced to accept a single union deal and totally new working practices compatible with HRM (Heaton, 1986). Similar developments had occurred throughout key sectors of British industry along the lines referred to above, involving in particular the EETPU. The acknowledgement of these developments – a contradiction between national union policy and local level reality – led the shop stewards within the plant to the conclusion that it was not a question of whether or not management would attempt to implement the new concepts, but when.

Through their own initiative, the shop stewards invited a leading US researcher on current managerial practices such as quality circles to run a week-long workshop as a means to assess the issues more fully and to determine the most appropriate trade union response. The workshop led the local union to believe that new management concepts such as quality circles, teamworking, team briefings and company councils would impinge on the existing role the union played and may, over time, undermine worker representation and influence. In this respect, HRM practices were perceived as undermining the strength of the collective bargaining process by encouraging employees to think of themselves as an 'individual' member of a 'company team' and not as part of the union organization. They clearly identified that such managerial concepts were aimed at diverting traditional loyalties away from the union and towards the company. The plant stewards further discovered through their own education and research initiatives that whilst there were many so-called 'experts' on HRM issues, none knew how to respond to them successfully from a trade union perspective.

In 1989 the long expected moment of qualitative change to the existing industrial relations framework within the plant arrived. This began by the company informing the unions that a new engine plant was to be built in Europe but that its location had not yet been decided upon. They were also told that within the multinational, plant management and unions in Germany had been working closely together in compiling a case as to why the new investment should be attracted to Germany. Management informed the British trade unionists that it was possible that the investment could be attracted to their own plant on the condition of major changes being implemented. The managing director bluntly stated 'Tell us to shove it and we'll forget it', and the engine plant would be located in Germany. In return for new investment the company sought a new plant agreement which had to be competitive, innovative and required a 'quantum leap' in trade union–management relations. The approach by senior management shows great similarity with other cases where the inward investor has demanded major concessions from the unions in terms of the internal industrial relations structures. The case of Ford at Dundee is a prime example of how investment was located elsewhere when management failed to secure the deal they sought (Oliver and Wilkinson, 1990). Such cases were, of course, prominent in trade union minds and give a clear indication how competitive processes can serve to modify the institutions of industrial relations by bringing the market logic much closer to inter-plant relations. Whilst such management tactics are not in themselves new, what is new is the conscious packaging of these threats within an HRM strategy that brings internal market relations to every level of the company.

National, regional and local union officials, together with governmental bodies, were informed of the planned investment and the conditions necessary to attract it. They in turn advised the plant shop stewards that, given new technology and market demand predictions, major vehicle plant closures within Europe in the mid-1990s would be forthcoming and that it would be suicide if the plant did not attract the investment. In this respect, the national union agenda was determined by quantitative issues rather than qualitative ones. The official union body appeared to have no reservations in advising the shop stewards to negotiate the new agreement that management sought, although at that time it was at odds with union policy. However, in doing so, the local officers were to attempt to adhere to three main principles:

1. to maintain JNC wage rates and stay within this collective bargaining arena;
2. to maintain the shop steward organization within the plant and;
3. to maintain union influence within the workplace.

A strategy of resistance or counter-intelligence gathering via other European plants and unions, to assess the validity of management's plans, was not considered. A parochial self-interest to maintain the plant's viability was the principal guiding light for both plant level union representatives and union officials alike. The shop stewards further highlighted why this had to be the case with one steward stating, 'If we had chosen not to negotiate a new deal to attract the investment we would have been voted out and a new body would have been voted in who would negotiate a new deal – we had no alternative but to negotiate.'

The unions were informed that a single union agreement was not being pursued, though management still spoke in terms of viewing the plant as a greenfield site and wanting a 'Toyota' style agreement (Titherington, 1991). Negotiating the new agreement took six months and was overwhelmingly accepted by the workforce. The main points of the new agreement were as follows:

1. The establishment of a new Joint Plant Committee comprising fourteen members, six appointed by the company (including chairman and secretary) and eight appointed by the unions. The purpose of this committee was essentially to promote communication and harmonious relationships and to discuss matters concerning the business of the company such as quality, production volume, productivity, market share, profitability and investment.
2. The use of temporary workers as the need arose.
3. A new grievance procedure with the option of arbitration (not compulsory, although management had initially insisted on compulsory arbitration).
4. A new pay structure giving new occupational classifications which allowed for movement through the range in recognition of employee efforts and contributions with pay and conditions still being negotiated through the JNC.
5. The introduction of team working and team leaders, which is emphasized in the agreement as forming 'a critical part of the new system'. The main ingredient of this is that employees 'have an opportunity to impact on the success of the business through their own decision making, pride in their work and co-operative efforts among each other'. This meant a change from a traditional section composed of sixty employees, to teamworking consisting of between ten to fifteen employees. The agreement also stated that 'the full benefits of teamworking will accrue over time and after the concept has been fully developed; and will involve ongoing training'. This statement in the agreement is an admission by management that such concepts are both

fragile and open to intervention which may undermine their development; an issue which the T&GWU has already recognized.

Since implementation of the new agreement, trade union representation and structures have been maintained. Due to their belief that their role and influence may be undermined over time by these new management concepts, the shop stewards expressed their concern by communicating directly with the membership through such media as notice board displays and newsletters. Information on company matters had traditionally been passed to shop stewards by management but under the new communication practices of management they were now being directly passed onto the workforce or through other (management) channels. For example, the team leader's role encompassed the role of communicator in respect of company matters, which further undermined the role of the shop steward as the previously key proprietor of such information. In response to this, the union implemented a random surveillance system on team briefings and checked team leaders to monitor whether they overstepped their lines of authority and encroached on the shop steward's role. This has required the drawing of boundaries between the role of the team leader and the union representative in the T&GWU organized sector of the plant. It was further established that union representatives were to be present at team briefings. Such observations support the view that issues traditionally dealt with via collective bargaining may become removed from the collective bargaining arena due to the introduction of team working (*International Labour Reports*, April 1983). A different approach, however, was taken by the other unions operating in the plant where the idea of teamworking and team leaders was not opposed but totally embraced, which is a reflection of the more conciliatory approaches of these unions and their leadership. Thus, due to multi-unionism, there have been diverse responses to the new management initiatives even within the same plant. These initial developments and responses by local trade unionists show many parallels with those taken by other local union representatives in similar situations, albeit in an uncoordinated manner (Heaton and Linn, 1989).

In addition to the use of competition to create inter-plant tendering to attract investment, another development in the plant since implementation of the new agreement has been management's policy to consider contracting-out certain work on grounds of the costs incurred in maintaining the work in-house. The teams working in the most affected section devised alternative working methods to make the system more viable and acceptable to management to maintain the work in-house. Nevertheless, for the workforce this meant reduced employment levels. Whilst this was perceived as a partial success by the unions they clearly recognized that the approach to maintaining the work in-house had shifted as the logic of the market was drawn directly into the workplace. Previously it would have been union policy to hold on to the work rather than compete on cost and quality. This example parallels the wider development of sub-contracting within industry generally, and in particular in the public sector since the introduction of compulsory competitive tendering, which has inserted market-style relations within the production process itself.

To date, no direct threat has been posed to the traditional role of the union(s) within the plant. Co-existence with HRM, as explained by Guest (1989a), appears to be the situation in the short term. However, the new practices have affected the way in which the unions view their position; a new language of efficiency, quality and participation have become evident. The initial and ongoing responses of the plant unions to the new management initiatives clearly indicates the unions' insecurity in maintaining their present role and function in the area of worker representation. What the case study clearly demonstrates is how HRM-type practices, similar if not the same as those introduced unilaterally by management on greenfield sites, can emerge. It also illustrates how the traditional role of the unions operating in well-organized brownfield plants can be redefined, without being displaced, through a coherent system of market oriented communication, participation and representation. In this particular case, many of the developments appear to be still conditioned by the traditional modes of representation for the time being whilst the consequences of the new system take effect. The longer-term consequences of the managerial initiatives are, as yet, unclear.

The response of both regional and national union officials of the T&GWU further demonstrated how they accepted the 'logic of the situation' with membership and national union interests coming clearly to the fore. A more coherent and overall strategy to the new management practices by the official union, however, had been undermined due to the union's prior policy towards these issues. Through such experiences, the T&GWU had begun to recognize that HRM practices had not been given the attention they deserved by either their own union or the TUC. To this end the union have begun to give new management practices a higher priority in terms of research and education. A strategy of monitoring the changes being implemented throughout the UK where the union has a presence is being pursued, with closer attention being given to the most appropriate response. Pamphlets and videos describing the new practices, how they have been implemented, and local responses have been compiled for educational purposes for both official and lay union representatives. The Union has also recognized that its structure and the shift to decentralized collective bargaining at company and plant level (occasionally viewed as an advantage in the past) is making the implementation of new management practices (via inter-plant competition) much simpler. The Union has therefore begun to take the new management initiatives very seriously and in their 1991 Biannual Delegate Conference subsequently changed their policy to accommodate a wider variety of responses to HRM on the condition that union independence within the workplace is maintained.

It is evident from the case study that the attempted transformation by management, and responses by unions, occurred along two critical dimensions. First, the 'needs' of the market were represented by management at various levels of the company and at various levels of change. This was done in order to shift the nature of oppositional tactics between the two sides into a common opposition against competitors. Secondly, the introduction of a more direct and coherent system of communication and representation by management attempts to relocate the role and position of the union. Whether or not this is achieved will of course be dependent on the ongoing responses and the nature of the struggle over worker representation and rights at workplace level between autonomous union representatives and HRM practices. Unlike the two earlier examples of trade union response, the very identification of the importance of autonomous representation as the core theme in the T&GWU debate conditioned the nature of the interaction between management and workers and hence the nature of the outcomes. What this case study indicates is the continued importance of the interaction between management and workers, and the potential for both management and union to modify their approach in the light of pre-existing industrial relations arrangements.

Conclusion

What is apparent from the responses outlined in this chapter is the ongoing and changing positions of trade unions to HRM policies. The question remains, however, as to whether or not HRM practices will inevitably lead to a permanent transformation and/or decline of trade union influence within the employment relation and, indeed, society as a whole.

In the case of market unionism the approach would seem to facilitate and complement the adoption and philosophy of HRM type practices and exclude any alternative trade union response which is incompatible with such policies. This is a result of the concessions made by the unions' approach over core principles such as autonomous worker representation and rights at work. In this respect market unionism accommodates HRM practices and attempts to maintain a presence and influence in the employment relation. However, the rationale of market unionism rests upon a narrow economic view of trade unionism (that is, rates of pay, training and other individual incentives) and excludes any broad political or social aspirations of a solidaristic nature. Furthermore, it accepts and recognizes the continual pressures on management to adopt HRM policies to survive within the market place. This leaves unions no alternative but to adopt policies that make them more compatible with HRM, since the perceived alternative is quite simply non-unionism. Hence, in its own terms, market unionism may be viewed as being relatively judicious for unions since it provides a viable option for management to accommodate within their HRM policies. However, the possible success of market unionism must be assessed against an understanding of what is actually meant by 'trade unionism'. If trade unionism is to have a political and social dimension then clearly market unionism cannot guarantee the long-term viability of trade unionism; and indeed may contribute to the demise of trade union*ism* while keeping trade unions alive.

Our second example highlighted what we term the institutional approach to HRM. This approach clearly maintained a social and, to an extent, political dimension to HRM. Its position towards new management initiatives was a recognition of the likely deterioration of traditional industrial relations institutions and issues covered by collective bargaining between management and unions. Compatibility between this approach and HRM practices, however, would not seem possible. Given that the rationale of HRM policies is to enrol workers on an individual basis and tie them closer to the needs of the company, the policy of 'socializing' the employment relationship through extended collective bargaining does not fit easily. To accommodate this approach management would need to compromise and dilute the ultimate aims and objectives of HRM. Under the present political and economic circumstances such a compromise seems unlikely to be acceptable to management (though management may consider the possibility of a short-term accommodation of such a traditional union policy for purely strategic reasons, while implementing HRM policies). Inevitably, the coexistence of a strong HRM approach and a typical industrial relations system, as foreseen in the institutional policy, is an uneasy fit and therefore of questionable viability in the longer term.

The issues of compatibility and a vibrant trade union role showed themselves clearly in our third example of trade union response to HRM practices. The example of the T&GWU addressed the question of to what extent trade unions could continue to represent the independent interests of workers (in an independent manner) given the nature of HRM strategies. It further illustrated that in any formal exchange the nature of established structures and procedures, at the workplace, are not simple negotiable items. This was due to the very clear identification by the union branch of the importance of autonomous and independent worker representation. This was also the core theme in the T&GWU's internal debate and in this respect separates it clearly from the previous two responses where such an internal debate was absent. It therefore makes a valid contribution to a different meaning of unionism as far as responding to HRM practices is concerned. The clear aims and objectives of this trade union position was how best to respond to HRM policies so as to maintain the traditional understanding of the role and function of trade unionism in a market economy. In this sense it is again incompatible, like the institutional approach, with HRM unless the latter is compromised and diluted *vis-à-vis* a traditional industrial relations framework.

Any analysis of the effectiveness of trade union responses to HRM practices must therefore account for whether or not they are incompatible with HRM. Without compromise independent trade unionism and strong

HRM policies cannot be reconciled as each attempts to monopolize worker representation. But ultimately, strong HRM policies are dependent in the first instance upon management pursuing such a strategy consistently and coherently. Current evidence indicates that the establishment of a strong HRM policy is by no means unproblematic and inevitable (Hill, 1991), which in itself provides the opportunity for trade unions to respond in different ways according to their organizational traditions. This is the reality of the current situation and thus the interaction and interface between management and unions will be a continuing process. Therefore steadfast conclusions cannot be made as so much will depend upon this ongoing interaction between the parties. Some unions will have both the organization and traditions which will contribute more to these ongoing responses compared to the market unionism approach. Moreover, it has been argued that trade union responses to HRM will change from a 'reactive' approach to a 'proactive' approach (Beaumont, 1991; Horowitz, 1991), and this indeed may be the case as these developments unfold (Martinez Lucio and Weston, 1992). There is, and will continue to be, an exchange of information within the labour movement concerning new management practices which will, in turn, contribute to the responses of trade unions, both at the macro and micro level. Furthermore, the political and ideological context within which these exchanges and responses take place may indeed develop in ways which facilitate a more proactive approach from trade unions.

References

Aglietta, M. (1979) *A Theory of Capitalist Regulation*. London: New Left Books.

Bassett, P. (1987) *Strike Free: New Industrial Relations in Britain*. London: Macmillan.

Beaumont, P.B. (1991) 'Trade unions and HRM', *Industrial Relations Journal*, 22 (4): 300–8.

Dunn, S. (1990) 'Root metaphor and the old and new industrial relations', *British Journal of Industrial Relations*, 28 (1): 1–27.

GMB (1989) *New Frontiers: Companies, Unions and 1992*. London.

GMB (1991) *The New Agenda* (with the UCW). London.

Guest, D. (1989a) 'Human resource management: its implications for industrial relations and trade unions', in J. Storey (ed.), *New Perspectives on Human Resource Management*. London: Routledge. pp. 41–55.

Guest, D. (1989b) 'Personnel and HRM: can you tell the difference?' *Personnel Management*, January: 48–51

Heaton, N. (1986) *Single Union Deals*. Northern College in association with the T&GWU Region 10.

Heaton, N. and Linn, I. (1989) *Fighting Back*. Northern College in association with T&GWU Region 10.

Hill, S. (1991) 'Why quality circles failed but total quality management might succeed', *British Journal of Industrial Relations*, 29 (4): 541–68.

Horowitz, F.M. (1991) 'HRM: an ideological perspective', *International Journal of Manpower*, 12 (6): 4–9.

IRRR (1991) 'Trade Unionism in the 1990s', *Industrial Relations Review and Report*, 492: 7–15.

Legge, K. (1989) 'Human resource management: a critical analysis', in J. Storey (ed.), *New Perspectives on Human Resource Management*. London: Routledge. pp. 19–40.

Marchington, M. and Parker, P. (1990) *Changing Patterns of Employee Relations*. Hemel Hempstead: Harvester Wheatsheaf.

Martinez Lucio, M. and Weston, S. (1991) 'Worker representation and worker rights in the context of new management strategies', Paper presented at the British Universities Industrial Relations Associations Annual Conference, University of Manchester, July.

Martinez Lucio, M. and Weston, S. (1992) 'The politics and complexity of trade union responses to new management practices', *Human Resource Management Journal* (forthcoming).

McCarthy, W.E.J. (1967) *The Role of the Shop Steward in British Industrial Relations*. Royal Commission on Trade Unions and Employers Associations, Research Paper 1, London: HMSO.

McIlroy, J. (1988) *Trade Unions in Britain Today*. Manchester: Manchester University Press.

Millward, N. and Stevens, M. (1986) *British Workplace Industrial Relations 1980–1984*. Aldershot: Gower.

Moody, K. (1988) *An Injury to All: The Decline of American Unionism*. London: Verso.

Oliver, N. and Wilkinson, B. (1988) *The Japanization of British Industry*. Oxford: Blackwell.

Oliver, N. and Wilkinson, B. (1990) 'Obstacles to Japanization: the case of Ford UK', *Employee Relations*, 12 (1): 17–21.

Parry, J. (1990) 'The struggle for European unions?' *International Management*, December: 70–5.

Piore, M. and Sabel, C. (1984) *The Second Industrial Divide*. New York: Basic Books.

Purcell, J. (1989) 'The impact of corporate strategy on human resource management', in J. Storey (ed.), *New Perspectives on Human Resource Management*. London: Routledge. pp. 67–91.

Slaughter, J. (1983) *Concessions and How to Beat Them*. Detroit: Labour Notes.

Slichter, S.H. (1941) *Union Policies and Industrial Management*. Washington: The Brookings Institution.

Storey, J. (1987) 'Developments in the management of human resources: an interim report', *Warwick Papers in Industrial Relations*, no. 17, Coventry: University of Warwick.

Titherington, P. (1991) 'Teamworking – rethinking our strategies', *Trade Union News*, May.

T&GWU (1989) *Employee Involvement and Quality Circles*. London: T&GWU Policy Booklet.

Yeandle, D. and Clark, J. (1989) 'Growing a compatible IR set-up', *Personnel Management*, July: 36–9.

PART FOUR: A NEW FORM OF MANAGEMENT PRACTICE?

14 HRM: METAPHOR, MEANING AND MORALITY

Tom Keenoy and Peter Anthony

In Mrs Thatcher's populist rhetoric, the cultural transformation of British society pursued in the 1980s is captured in a speech she made in 1984:

> I came to office with one deliberate intent: to change Britain from a dependent to a self-reliant society – from a give-it-to-me to a do-it-yourself nation; to a get-up-and-go instead of a sit-back-and-wait-for-it Britain. (*Economist*, 24 November 1990)

The implicit agenda of her policies was vividly reflected in popular culture. In the early 1980s, one cultural image encapsulated the socio-economic trauma which assaulted our moral conception of how the employment relationship ought to be conducted: that of Yozzer in *The Boys from the Black Stuff*. His manic march, pasty face and unkempt children bedraggled in his wake symbolized the passing of collectivism. At the same time, his defiant but somehow rhetorical demand, 'Giz a job!', reflected a collective bewilderment that so much we had thought secure had been overturned with hardly a public protest, far less a general strike.

By the late 1980s, the compassion evoked by Yozzer's *cri de coeur* had been supplanted by an alternative cultural image: Harry Enfield's Loadsamoney, the archetypal stereotype of success in the enterprise culture – he could have been a market maker, an estate agent, a porn king or the eponymous 'entrepreneur' instead of a plasterer. Class, education, the work ethic, professionalism and vocation were all vanquished under his fistful of 'twentipandnotes'. The aggressive contempt for those without means and his singular script – 'loadsamoney!, loadsamoney!' – echoed what had become enshrined as the singular value to be pursued in the new times: individual self-interest. Lockwood's (1966) hypothetical 'pecuniary society' seemed to have been realized.

It is entirely appropriate that we start our analysis of HRM with metaphor, for much that has passed for organizational change in recent years has reflected attempts to fundamentally reconstruct our images of 'reality'. In the context of a putative monetarism, the undermining of the collectivist norms of trade unionism and the welfare state, and the 'deregulation' of economic activity, we have experienced a seemingly wide and contradictory variety of regenerative initiatives. Following a brief and overblown foray into 'macho-management', we have seen, among other things, quality circles, communication cascades, team briefings, total quality management, just-in-time production, customer care programmes, appraisal schemes, performance-related pay, core and periphery work-forces, single union no-strike agreements, status harmonization, pendulum arbitration, decentralized and single-table bargaining. All have enjoyed Warhol's fifteen minutes of fame and all have been force-fed to a battered, bewildered and defensive workforce and a newly confident management. As we were repeatedly informed, 'There is no alternative.'

These initiatives have been driven by the need to regain 'the competitive edge' (Hendry and Pettigrew, 1986), prospered on the desire for mutual economic survival (Edwards, 1987) and ostensibly legitimized through the moral imperatives of Thatcherism which seemed to reduce all social interaction to economic exchange. At the level of rhetoric, these initiatives can be accommodated within the rubric of charismatic leaders creating new enterprise oriented organizational cultures while, in terms of management practice, they are encompassed within human resource management.

Cultural Constructions

The central thrust of our argument is that to understand the HRM phenomenon in Britain it is necessary to treat it as a cultural construction comprised of a series of metaphors which constitute a 'new reality'. HRM reflects an attempt to redefine both the meaning of work and the way individual employees relate to their employers. As such, it is both a reflection and a constitutive element of the historical project known as the 'enterprise culture' which, as du Gay (1991: 45) observes, 'involved not only an economic revival but also a moral crusade'. The institutional form and ideological character of the 'enterprise culture' which were to evolve during the 1980s (Gamble, 1988; Keat and Abercrombie, 1991) was succinctly summarized by Mrs Thatcher in 1981:

> What's irritated me about the whole direction of politics in the last thirty years is that it's always been towards the collectivist society. People have forgotten about the personal society. And they say, 'Do I count, do I matter?' To which the short answer is, yes. And, therefore, it isn't that I set out on economic policies; it's that I set out to really change the approach. If you change the approach, you really are after the heart and soul of the nation. Economics are the method; the object is to change the heart and soul. (*Sunday Times*, 3 May 1981, quoted in Saad, 1990)

While objectives are one thing and outcomes another, it was this philosophy which informed the political direction of recent times and, in particular, informed the attempt to reconstruct employment relations in the 1980s. But changing hearts and souls is no mean task. At the level of meaning, the problem was how to square the ideological conviction that social justice is best ensured through 'the market' with the empirical consequences of 'deregulation' for our taken-for-granted assumptions as to how the employment relationship ought to be managed. A fundamental requirement of the policies was a sharpened exposure of both organizations and individuals to the 'competitive edge'. This inevitably promoted an increase in socio-economic struggle: competition, despite its ideological desirability, is, of course, a synonym for conflict. Hence, one function of the ideological script of HRM is to provide an occlusion between the imagery of the 'enterprise culture' and the experienced reality of increased competition. It is for this reason we suggest that HRM is a meta-narrative locating, informing and legitimizing managerial practice in a time of rapid economic restructuring: the 'messages' carried by HRM are far more important than the specific devices employed.

Of course, the 'real' processes of change (and continuity) which have characterized recent times are far more complex, convoluted and contradictory than this implies (Beardwell, 1990; Beaumont, 1987; Keenoy, 1990a; Kelly, 1990; Lash and Urry, 1987; MacInnes, 1987; Marginson et al., 1988; Oliver and Wilkinson, 1988; Storey, 1989; Wickens, 1987). However, it is part of our argument that empirical refutation of the claims of HRM is of marginal relevance to the cultural impact of HRM (Keenoy, 1990b) for, as we will illustrate throughout what follows, much of the real debate about HRM and the reconstruction of the employment relationship has been conducted through rhetoric and metaphor (Armstrong, 1988; Dunn, 1990; Guest, 1990; Keenoy, 1991; Legge, 1989). In other words, the 'empirical reality' that must be penetrated before we can come to a properly informed understanding of the nature of HRM is what might be called the internal logic of the histrionics of HRM. In order to analyse the implications of this we wish to explore – or, perhaps more accurately, flirt with – the postmodernist heuristic.

Hence, we suggest, the litany of innovative HRM social practices noted above should be regarded as cultural constructions fabricated through government policy and corporate administrative fiat. They are self-conscious attempts not merely to change social behaviour but to transform the norms and values guiding social behaviour. As such, in the majority of cases, their introduction and implementation has been based on a fairly simplistic set of psychologistic behavioural assumptions: the structural context of social interaction is changed while, at the same time, attempts are made to engineer change in the interpretive frameworks of social action. We have seen the techniques of advertising, marketing and proselytizing enlisted to propagate new images of organizational 'reality' (Berg, 1986). The imposition of this new social order has been mediated by the 'market' and massaged with management exhortation to induce not merely the acceptance of a negotiated order but, ultimately, individual normative commitment (Etzioni, 1961) to the 'facticity' of the new 'realities'. In this respect, we suggest, the 1980s must also be seen as a period of moral regeneration. The HRM 'movement', a self-seeking cultural product, has been installed to manufacture, mediate and administer cultural transformation in an environment softened up by recession and unemployment. Fear is a great catalyst; but what is being constructed to replace it?

The New 'Reality'

With respect to the seemingly endless task of legitimizing managerial authority, we can refer to a history of meta-narratives concerned to explain the nature of employment and to overcome our difficulties in the experience of its realities (Anthony, 1986). Myths, metaphors and ideologies are central ingredients of cultures and have long served to obscure or explain the irksome problem of reality that confuses our understanding of the world and our place in it. However, the aspirations of contemporary attempts to reconstruct and manage organizational cultures begin to suggest that these terms no longer represent a kindly escape from the 'real' world but that they *are* the real world.

This proposition takes two forms. The first form, based on the philosophical assumption that there is no materiality independent of sense perception, is the subjectivist argument that the world is and can only be what we make of it: 'reality' – it cannot be spoken of without inverted commas – is what we think it. As Zukav (1980: 328) concludes:

> 'Reality' is what we take to be true. What we take to be true is what we believe. What we believe is based upon our perceptions. What we perceive depends upon what we look for. What we look for depends upon what we think. What we think depends upon what we perceive. What we perceive determines what we believe. What we believe determines what we take to be true. What we take to be true is our reality.

The second more contingent form is that the postmodern world is increasingly occupied with the production and exchange of images rather than goods or things. This position takes a weaker and a stronger form.

The weaker form is familiar to us in the advertisements for a brand of instant coffee which identify it with a lifestyle of supersensual romance conducted by transatlantic Concorde. Product differentiation in markets where reliability, performance and price are almost indistinguishable, is achieved by image, not of the product but of the people that use it. This domination of the image over 'reality' is associated, we are told, with the evolution of capitalism to the domination of consumption over production. Abercrombie (1991: 173) gives an account of this change which is significantly associated with the postmodernist movement:

> Producers, and regimes of production, are associated with the forces of rationalization and order; the activities of production cannot be conducted without high levels of organization. Consumption, on the other hand, especially

modern (or post-modern) consumption, is associated with undisciplined play and disorder; it does not require organization and may, indeed, actively deny it.

But we have called this, in no pejorative sense, the weaker form of the argument. The stronger or more extreme form is advanced by Jameson: multinational, consumer capitalism, the most advanced form of capitalism, has evolved to a point where symbols and representations are subject to the process of commodification. Thus capitalism is now concerned with the production and exchange of cultural forms: 'images, styles and representation are not the promotional accessories to economic products, they are the products themselves' (quoted in Connor, 1989: 46). Hence the material product is merely a vehicle for the real product. The latter may incorporate not only the material product but also the consumer 'itself': mundane objects like jeans, track-suits and tennis shoes, with the addition of a designer label (and a considerable increase in price), have become adornments which, in our pecuniary society, provide a powerful basis of social differentiation. By purchasing the product, the consumer acquires access to the image of the product. In donning the product, the consumer enters and becomes the advertisement: hence the consumer *becomes* the image. What has been purchased is a manufactured 'reality'. Everything is 'cultural' and 'we are within the culture of postmodernism to the point where its facile repudiation is as impossible as any equally facile celebration of it is complacent and corrupt' (Connor, 1989: 50).

In principle, cultural constructions, such as HRM policies and practices, can be seen to embody this most advanced form of commodification process. The culture (a product) is employed to create the images (products) which in turn are used to reconstruct the culture (a product). The inherent potential of such circularity, du Gay and Salaman (1990: 12) suggest, is such that employee identities can 'be built around cultural change programmes, can be chosen, in an analogous way to the consumer's choice of life-style'. There is, it would seem, nothing more to be said.

The Construction of HRM

Even if we regard HRM as an archetypal and unredeemable Jamesonian postmodernist cultural product (and, in this respect, academic journals of HRM and books about HRM should be regarded as cultural artifacts propagating and sustaining this cultural commodity), such pessimism is undue and, perhaps, unnecessary. First, this perspective helps us to come to terms with the conceptual ambiguity of HRM; secondly, it directs attention to the functioning of HRM as a medium for manufacturing meaning in the process of culture management; and, thirdly, as we will argue in the final section of this chapter, it forces us to examine the moral implications of promoting HRM.

One singular advantage of the postmodernist idiom is that we do not need to agonize over the conceptual clarity of HRM. Most commentaries on the literature start with bewilderment and end in frustration, for HRM is characterized by obscure origins,[1] seemingly endless internal contradictions (Legge, 1989), the absence of significant empirical support (Guest, 1987, 1990, 1991; Storey, 1989) and a constant process of conceptual elision. Elsewhere, commenting on this, it was argued that this 'brilliant ambiguity' is not merely a case of academics catching up with 'reality' or of slipshod attention to definitional niceties, but integral to the historical project of HRM (Keenoy, 1990b). A conventional interpretation would be that HRM is merely the latest in a long line of managerial legitimatory meta-narratives; and, as was ever the case with such devices, managerial practice treats employees as a cost while the espoused rhetoric insists they are valued human assets capable of commitment, loyalty and responsible autonomy. Such a conclusion is hardly novel. It also misses the point.

In common with Sorellian social myths (Sorel, 1961), once we seek to explain HRM, to subject it to any analysis or criticism, it ceases to function as intended. Its purpose is to transform, to inspire, to motivate and, above all, to create a new 'reality' which is freely available to those who choose or are persuaded to believe. To explain it is to destroy it. In this respect, there is nothing mundane about HRM. Proponents insist it transcends the pedestrian activities of personnel management in the design and maintenance of simple matters like wage and salary structures, negotiation, selection and training. HRM goes beyond humdrum administration and bureaucratic control to the creation of the organization's view of itself, to the formulation of the image of its taken-for-granted values and beliefs and the kind of employer it is. A precise, coherent and internally consistent definition would be dysfunctional: HRM does not start with a set of policy objectives but with a mission statement.

This brings us to the second point. Cultural transformation or, at the very least, the rhetoric of such change, is central to the mission of HRM. 'Most HRM models emphasize the organization's culture as the central activity for senior management' (Legge, 1989: 26) and it seems reasonable to suppose, in such cases, that HRM becomes the primary agent of change.

Cultural change is portrayed as fundamental to organizational survival and success (see Ogbonna, Chapter 5, this volume). Of course, 'real' change in institutionalized practices has long been regarded as among the most difficult of managerial tasks. There should be little wonder in the conclusion that there are parts of the organization that personnel management cannot reach, because its engagement in practical control makes it impossible to avoid the contradictions between apparent and espoused values that aspirations to cultural change reveal. HRM is not so disadvantaged. It is concerned with the management of beliefs, with the manufacture of acquiescence in corporate values, with the production of images. The attempt at cultural change rests upon ideological foundations, upon an ideological construction of the organization. As such, it is immune from a logical critique which reveals the contradictions between it and reality, 'for ideology does not "work" in a logical, intellectual fashion. It does not collapse as the result of a logical contradiction . . . ideology does not obey the logic of rational discourse' (du Gay and Salaman, 1990: 24).

Thus, ontologically, the 'discourse' of cultural construction shifts us from descriptive and systematic accounts of the organization to the unassailably metaphysical. One of the functions of metaphor and myth 'is that they place explanation beyond doubt and argumentation' (Pondy, 1983: 163) and they do it by comprehending and transcending contradiction, by rhetorical influence over the frame of reference of the audience.

If this is the case, if the symbolic rather than the social construction of 'reality' *is* the central concern of strategic HRM, then the separation of powers between personnel and human resource management is necessary: shamans cannot be expected to do the chores. Consequently, it is no good carping about the differences between image and reality if it is the business of HRM to shift perceptions of reality: criticism at this level might, in fact, be welcome as negative feedback which simply requires corrective attention by way of a better script. To sneer at HRM for its detachment from the practical is equally mistaken. There are several reasons for suggesting that HRM has succeeded in placing itself at a new frontier of control, at that pinnacle of organizational influence which always eluded the personnel managers. While personnel management was not short of imperialist ambition for organizational control, the means to achieve it were both tentative and contested and rested, in any case, upon an anxious pursuit of status. The proposed application of social science always suffered from a worrying ambiguity: its intentions seemed to be kindly and ambivalent with respect to the pursuit of profit. There are no such doubts now. Human resources are for management, indeed for managers, to dispose of behind the scenes while, out front, HRM takes the applause for giving meaning back to work (du Gay, 1991; Peters and Waterman, 1982). And the offer this time is the ultimate in control, the management of meaning. Once it was deemed sufficient to redesign the organization so as to make it fit human capacity and understanding: now it is better to redesign human understanding to fit the organization's purpose. It is clearly time to take HRM very seriously indeed.

Manufacturing Meaning

One reason for doing so is the potential that exists for the progressive exclusion of critical discourse from the literature of management and management education. For the irony is that, despite the inherently unreflexive and frequently vacuous character of the images and messages, the cultural construction of HRM is now centre-stage in the description and management – if not the analysis – of contemporary employment relations. We seem to be constructing images of images to explain 'reality'.

In this respect, HRM must be viewed as the keystone of the panoply of symbols, images and metaphors which are central to the so-called 'excellence movement' (Goldsmith and Clutterbuck, 1985; Peters and Waterman, 1982; Wood, 1989). The concern with 'quality', 'commitment', 'integration', 'flexibility', 'transformation', 'charisma' and the eponymous 'excellence' itself are embedded in the 'culture of change' essential to meet and overcome the perils of the wave after wave of 'competitive challenge' unleashed to ensure our economy becomes lean, healthy and strong again.

Initially, these messianic histrionics were met with scholarly disdain by observers schooled in autonomic salary progression and the differential realities of pluralism. Mission statements? Quality crusades? Customer care? Images; nothing but images: it was all too transparent, evangelical and, above all, too theatrical to be embraced by hard-bitten, pragmatic British management. But we were mistaken. The ease with which the post-war consensus was swept aside by the combined effect of Thatcherite policies and the global economic crisis (Lash and Urry, 1987) of the early 1980s created not only fear (Metcalf, 1989) but also the conviction that nothing could be the same again. The historical context provided, so to speak, a window of opportunity for the construction of a new 'reality'. While Mrs Thatcher espoused liberal individualism, the TUC, that carthorse of foresight, advocated a 'new realism' and companies braced themselves to set out on the marketing edge.

The metaphorical wallpaper appears to function on at least two analytically significant levels. First, it operates generically as a meta-narrative: an image intensifier which presents us with a set of idealized action imperatives. All 'good' companies should have a mission, a charismatic leader with vision, pursue excellence and crusade for quality. The imagery embodies total conviction: it is uncompromising, exemplary and endows economic activity with a higher, virtually religious purpose. All bow down before the almighty dollar and, on the other side of the Atlantic, the nation-state has become UK plc. The narrative portrays a pristine, almost naive, populist solution to the problem of business survival and prosperity – but then the bottom line is a quite singular criterion.

The fundamental message is one designed to construct certainty in a context where none exists. Action at the leading edge is perilous. We are forever on the brink of chaos for perpetual transformation is the norm: the 'market' is quixotic, merciless and, but say this quietly, non-rational. As Jackall's (1988) managers were only too aware, you can do all the right things and still get it wrong. Hence neither vision nor vigilance is enough: a committed, loyal, flexible and hard-working unified team is essential to overcome the permanent threat of, usually, foreign competition.

Such a script echoes the timeless exhortations of all ideological tyrannies from Orwell's *1984* to the Stakanhovite movement in the USSR (Siegelbaum, 1988). As the Director-General of the Institute of Directors observed, 'We are all soldiers in a global economic war' (*Financial Times*, 2 March 1990). We are embattled; the quest does indeed involve a perilous journey in a hostile environment (Dunn, 1990) and should we trip and fall, we have no one to blame but ourselves. Once employees are persuaded the script reflects reality, their subordination and control becomes immeasurably easier. In addition, the circumstances legitimize harsh action. Sinners – and coming second is a sin – can expect no less. Bankruptcy and unemployment are quite singular punishments.

Secondly, our script provides the interpretive framework within which specific managerial policies are laundered: it structures the social meanings of managerial practice. Given the millennial character of the 'reality' we face, the end always justifies the means and this goes some way to explaining why HRM initiatives can range from the unilateral proposal to terminate the contracts of all employees at Rolls-Royce (*Financial Times*, 14 May 1991) to a leading British car manufacturer sending their assembly-line supervisors on outward bound courses (Lowe, 1991). Indeed, in contrast to the relatively closed models of HRM which have been erected by Beer et al. (1984, 1985), Fombrun et al. (1984), Guest (1987) and Poole (1990), the sheer diversity of HRM practice (Guest, 1991; Storey, 1989) will ensure continued academic perplexity and empirical elusiveness. We cannot see the angels on the head of the pin, far less count them.

Thus, the management of meaning inherent in HRM practices can take a wide variety of forms. However, all seem to involve two inter-related processes: the mystification of prosaic 'realities' in the day-to-day regulation of the employment relationship and the distancing of management from responsibility for the character and consequences of managerial action.

Mystification of the Prosaic

Predictably, since language structures meaning, it occupies a central role in the mystification of the prosaic. This is exemplified by the litany of new 'concepts' designed to obfuscate sacking employees. The term 'getting the sack' was once a description of the literal consequence of becoming unemployed and, like the American equivalent, 'getting fired' or 'getting the bullet', provides an easily read metaphor of the effect of losing one's livelihood. In Britain in the 1960s it was sanitized to being 'made redundant' and cushioned by the Redundancy Payments Act (1965) which not only provided temporary recompense but, by supporting the unemployed out of communal funds, went some way to recognizing redundancy as a collective responsibility and not merely an individual misfortune. From the 1970s onwards the notion has been subject to increasing ambiguity.

Organizational change and development is frequently referred to as 'rationalization' or 'restructuring': processes which, freely translated, invariably mean *mass* redundancies. But it is the 1980s which provides the greatest euphemistic innovation. 'Early retirement' begat 'premature early retirement' which in turn begat 'pre-retirement'; 'golden handshakes' and 'parachutes' were matched by the exponentially more common 'severance' and 'short-time payments'. The most remarkable solution to job-loss is 'job-sharing'. This cultural artifact is little short of miraculous for one lost job produces two new ones. 'Technological redundancy', 'outplacing' and 'downsizing' – the favoured term in American HRM textbooks – have been accompanied by 'manpower transfer' and 'headcount reduction'; both of which may result in 'workforce re-profiling'. These are all evident euphemisms, but whence came 'retrenchment'?

Such 'rationalization' or 'downsizing' of the experience of loss of livelihood serves a number of purposes. At one level it protects those high profile images enterprises have striven so hard to construct. At times the reality of job loss seems to be banished altogether from our linguistic experience of the enterprise culture; a mere footnote in the voluminous 'strategy' documents. British Telecom, in their 1990 report to shareholders, noted: 'Our profit figure includes an exceptional charge of £390 million relating to our restructuring – particularly manpower release costs – and associated provisions for refocusing our operations' (BT, 1990: 2). The planned sacking of some 19,000 employees (7.7 per cent of the total workforce) becomes a minor distraction between the 'profit figure' and the projected developments which were doubtless designed to have beneficial consequences for next year's 'profit figure'. But the reality of redundancy is not only marginalized: it is portrayed as a positive managerial act. The following year, at one point, the workforce reduction is attributed to 'good cost control and to the effects of our capital investment programme' while elsewhere it is reported that 'BT's workforce was reduced by 18,000 during the year, *by simplifying the management structure and improving productivity*. Operating profit . . . increased by 10 per cent' (BT, 1991: 2, 14, emphasis added). It would seem that the aesthetic of the 'bottom line' rules all value judgment (Earl, 1983).

But it is not merely the image of the company which is protected. Such elisions also function politically at the macro level to sterilize the reality of 'free' market forces. It is no accident that the proliferation of disembodied ersatz euphemisms for redundancy coincides with the promotion of the socially beneficent effects of 'the market'. As the dominant icon informing political values and public policy, the market must enjoy unquestioned legitimacy. Unbounded economic activity is supposed to produce unbounded economic opportunity and wealth not destroy people's livelihoods. Hence such mystification operates not merely to cushion the *experience* of unemployment as a normal feature of market relations but also to obfuscate the *fact* that unemployment is a normal and necessary social cost of 'efficient' market relations.

A perhaps more 'concrete' example of the mystification of the prosaic is unreflectively reported in Hendry and Pettigrew's (1987) account of how a major British bank, the Trustee Savings Bank (TSB), is transforming the organization through the use of strategic HRM. One element of constructing 'an achievement-oriented culture' involves relating TSB branch managers' rewards to branch performance. Conceptually, this sounds remarkably like introducing an old-fashioned payment-by-results system. The car-assembly workers of the 1960s would be amused by the suggestion that they enjoyed the self-actualizing experience of an 'achievement-oriented work culture'. More generally, Hendry and Petti-grew also reported that:

> the personnel function is playing a key role in managing the evolution of the culture by balancing training and development with recruitment, through a philosophy of 'blending' and in managing the careers of old and new staff to serve both the requirements of 'key' branches and individual careers and job satisfaction; and through the use of the reward and disciplinary systems, through appraisal and targetting, to achieve the change in strategic focus towards lending [from saving] and towards being profit-oriented. (1987: 32)

Apart from the casual reference to 'discipline', the researchers present us with an idyllic vision of HRM as the thoughtful, reflective humanistic cultivator of resourceful human beings. The account is also remarkable in that it presents us with an image of a highly sophisticated and, doubtless, highly flexible bureaucatic personnel department finely tuning human resources to business strategy. We are not told what the employees thought – the research design did not include talking to them. But what we do know is that, not long after the study was completed, TSB announced that 5000 staff were to be made redundant (*Financial Times*, 21 November 1989). Is this what was meant by 'managing the evolution of the culture by balancing training and development with recruitment'?

At the level of social practice it would be easy to impute a manipulative or malign intent to this HRM strategy. However, our concern here is with the construction of images and the management of meaning. Analytically, the account of TSB's HRM policy and practice illustrates two critical operational aspects of managing meaning. First, there is the all-embracing character of the policy which appears to integrate the different elements of HR practice – selection, recruitment, training, deployment, career-planning, rewards, discipline, appraisal and replacement – in such a fashion that the organization appears to have the rational capacity to allocate units of human resource to appropriate locations within the organization. And, secondly, it displays the potential to confine individual employee behaviour to a highly restricted preordained set of acceptable organizational behaviours. Individual 'success' depends on adopting – if not internalizing – the approved 'mind-set': in this case, the 'achievement-oriented culture'. As a cultural filter, HRM embraces the uncertainties of employee existence, imposes order and meaning on them and provides the employee with a predictable, secure and carefully projected and rewarded understanding of organizational life.

However, organizational life, for most people, is not their sole source of symbolic or cultural meaning and, in any case, long before HRM strategies, 'success' in the organization depended on 'playing the game', telling superiors what they wanted to hear, fulfilling assumed expectations and trading on tacit knowledge of those organizational values which attract reward. What some HRM practices attempt is to refine such informal understandings of 'how to succeed in large organizations', parcel them up in a formal policy controlled by management, and try to induce *all* employees to adopt such behaviours. Such practices may be underpinned by trying to expunge all evidence of sub- or counter-cultures from the universe of available meanings or – a more radical solution – establishing the organization on an 'uncontaminated' greenfield site (Wickens, 1987). In minimizing the range of alternative meanings, the payoff lies in an increase in managerial control. Logic dictates that the net result can only be more effective and efficient exploitation of human resources. Or so it would seem.

The Limits of Responsibility

This brings us to the second critical aspect highlighted by the TSB case. It concerns the apparent ease with which the carefully modulated constructed 'realities' of HRM can be undermined by the indiscriminate deconstructive impact of 'free' market forces – which offer no discount for good intentions. This suggests that constructing 'realities' might be a futile or even counter-productive process.

However, it is precisely this kind of contradiction that the 'discourse' of HRM is designed to accommodate. The generic promise to treat human resources as a valuable and valued asset is conditioned and conditional on the vicissitudes of the all-conquering 'market'. As Barley (1990: 14) observes of contradictory myths: 'Truth, however, is largely irrelevant to them since they merely organize data without external comparisions.' The legitimatory rationale has been constructed through an historical process in which, ideologically, economic criteria have come to dominate all other moral values (Dumont, 1977) while, empirically, the traditional liberal restraint of organized capitalism has finally succumbed to the disintegrative forces of 'economic freedom' (Lash and Urry, 1987). As noted above, the meta-narrative portrays the 'market' as the volatile mistress of the contemporary business environment. By definition, it is uncontrollable and management, despite their best efforts, can only reflect this stark and uncompromising 'reality'. Against the political backcloth of the 'enterprise culture' – which sought to construct markets even where they did not previously exist – the markets in virtually every industrial sector have been highly unstable in the 1980s and early 1990s. This reality finds reflection in the literature which has consistently emphasized the contingent nature of strategic HRM policy and practice (Hendry et al., 1988; Miller, 1987, 1989; Schuler, 1989). The central (and sobering) emphasis in this strain of HRM thinking has been the fundamental vulnerability of HRM practice to market forces.

The 'demands' of product, labour and capital markets have become the source of both explanation and legitimation for whatever HR policy or practice management are 'forced' to pursue. Managerial responsibility is divorced from both managerial action and sentiment and located in the natural hurricane of the 'free market'. Thus is it possible for the humanistic promise of HRM to promote the increased commodification of labour (Keenoy, 1990b). More specifically, this distancing of managerial responsibility from the outcomes of HR policies is also reflected in the particular practices which have come to be associated with HRM. In general what they seek to do is to incorporate responsibility for outcomes into the performance of the individual employee.

The agenda has been extensive. The inculcation of Total Quality Management (TQM) or Just-in-Time (JIT) into the consciousness of subordinates gives them managerial responsibility (and managerial vulnerability) without its rewards (Delbridge and Turnbull; Sewell and Wilkinson, Chapters 4, 6, this volume; Wilkinson et al., 1991). Discretionary judgement, once the measure of reward in time span theory (Jaques, 1961), becomes almost an inverted objective. Risk taking, once a matter left to entrepreneurs, is universally encouraged and recompensed by individual contracts of employment and performance bonuses (Kanter, 1986; Schuler, 1989). Responsibility, in all directions, to colleagues, the company, the culture and the ubiquitous customer, is pressed downwards and measured by individual accountability, performance appraisal and budgetary controls. We all have to 'own' the problems. Bureaucracies have to be flattened, hierarchies dismantled and values espoused while the pursuit of these intentions is monitored and enforced by improved mechanisms of control.

All of which underlines the *praxical* importance of the much remarked shift from collectivism to individualism in employment relations. Mrs Thatcher's quest for hearts and souls marks not merely the decline of trade union influence and the re-legitimization of managerial prerogative but, much more significantly, the *apparent* derogation of managerial control within the labour process. This appears to be particularly the case with respect to responsibility for individual performance which, through the cultural constructions of HRM – in both symbolic and empirical terms – has produced a blurring of managerial and employee accountability. It would seem that responsible autonomy (Friedman, 1977) or, given the additional demand that everything has to be simultaneously 'loose' and 'tight', the narrative of responsible autonomy, has become the rule rather than the exception. The final *apparent* paradox is that the managers charged with bringing about such 'cultural' change are likely to have been ordered to do so and held accountable for its achievement.

Analytically, these trends are indicative of the attempt to incorporate manufactured organizational 'realities' within the production process itself. Labour, once merely commodified in the external labour market, is now being 're-commodified' within the regime of production to ensure 'autonomic' concern with quality and customer satisfaction. The 'customer' within the narrative, having been invested with influence of mythic proportion, is invoked to induce the producer within the labour process to identify with the perceived and projected needs of the customer. As the customer mirrors the advert, so the producer must mirror the customer.[2] All it requires, it seems, is employee endorsement of the metaphysic of the 'market' and persistent immersion in the cultural constructions of HRM. We would not want to imply that such cultural closure is easily achieved; but it is by no means impossible (Dickson et al., 1988; Peach, 1983).

Manufacturing Critique

If, as we began by suggesting, the production of goods and services has given way to the production of images which are themselves marketable, valuable and profitable (because the product is entirely value-added), then there is at least a certain symmetry in the producer 'itself' turning into an image. HRM appears to offer the prospect of the total control of meaning with respect to both the nature of the external environment and the internal character of the organization. An intrinsic by-product of this process is to secure the organization and, in particular, the 'reality' constructed within the organization, from the 'facticity' of alternative 'discourses'.

How can we possibly enter any critical discussion of HRM if, with extraordinary cunning, it embodies techniques designed 'to place explanation beyond doubt and argumentation'? Such techniques are designed to achieve the management of meaning and, if they work, what more can be said? Indeed, managers might well ask whether anything more needs to be said; if HRM has discovered the grail of cultural control, why should they enquire further? If managers, for their own purposes, can order inchoate experience through the organizing functions of narrative, image and mataphor, then they have surely harnessed a powerful human capacity for their own ends. *If* this can be done then HRM is a potent acquisition in the battery of organizational controls and no manager can afford to be without it.

There are a variety of possible responses to such questions. Our theoretical conundrum lies in what there is to say about a circuitously closed ideological system designed to encapsulate meaning itself and protected from comparison with 'reality' because it defines 'reality'. A reply couched in terms of conventional empirical evaluation might suggest, quite simply, that HRM does not exist (Guest, 1990) and is unlikely to work (Kelly, 1990; MacInnes, 1987; Ogbonna and Wilkinson, 1990) except under very particular conditions (Foulkes, 1980; Trevor, 1988; Wickens, 1987). Such studies are essential (and deeply comforting) but, since they attack the issue from the confines of an alien epistemology, may be brushed aside by managers as academic irrelevances. Carefully modulated empirical scepticism is no competition for passionate conviction.

However archaic it may sound, political action, as ever, is another possible response. An appropriate programme is beyond the scope (and the wit) of this chapter, but the present experience and direction of real living socialism provides no basis for optimism. Despite this, at the level of ideology, a Marxist critique of HRM as representing the intensification of commodity fetishism and a deepening of societal alienation might indicate, against all the contemporary historical trends, that Mrs Thatcher's efforts have done nothing but dig a few more feet of the capitalist grave. However, this is not a redoubt from which we would choose to fight.

The postmodernist response seems limited to resigned analytic observation. For example, du Gay (1991: 56–7), while recognizing that Guest (1990) has performed a singular service in identifying the cultural construction of the HRM–Excellence syndrome as a contemporary incarnation of the American Dream, questions his conclusion that 'the evidence suggests that in most cases [HRM] is no more than a fantasy, a dream'. The problem, for du Gay, lies with the ontological significance of the term 'evidence', for this reintroduces the 'reality/representation dichotomy' which, within the postmodernist heuristic, is simply a retreat to an alternative fantasy for *all* perception is ideologically structured:

> What does it mean to say that ideological fantasy structures reality itself? It suggests, first, that a certain misrecognition characterizes the human condition. In Lacanian terms, this misrecognition occurs because all attempts to capture the Real symbolically ultimately fail. There is always a leftover, a surplus separating the Real from its symbolization . . . Rather than viewing ideology as a false or illusory representation of reality, it is reality itself which should already be conceived of as ideological. *Ideology is a social reality whose very existence implies the non-knowledge of its participants as to its essence.* Ideology is a fantasy-construct that serves as a support for our 'reality' itself. (1991: 56, emphasis in original)

It is at this point that we part company with the postmodernist heuristic for we have reached the epistemological quicksands. In the circumstances, our reasoning is necessarily brief and assertive.

First, while HRM, as we have argued, represents an attempt to construct cultural closure, du Gay's argument seems to indicate intellectual closure. It is protected by precisely the same constitutive 'logic': it defines 'reality' and, in so doing, excludes all possible alternative 'realities'. Ideology is reality and reality is ideology. While tautology may be a useful figurative device it explains nothing. In this case we are left with a conclusion which suggests that all 'reality' or 'realities' comprise impenetrable and unremovable cataracts. We are not only back where we started but can never arrive anywhere else. The postmodernist heuristic seems to reduce itself to little more than a laconic intellectual and moral nihilism.

Secondly, however, there does appear to be a significant fracture in his argument: the use of the term 'Real' to 'represent' the 'essence' which can never be grasped. The 'Real', according to du Gay, constitutes the 'real kernel' of that 'objective reality' for which we constantly strive but, *because of our human condition*, constantly fail to reach. (In skirting this problem, we would point out that to require the epistemological apparatus of social science to transcend the human condition seems over-optimistic.) However, the important point, in our view, is that there seems to be something other than or outside the grasp of the black hole of the 'ideological'.

Thirdly, we are all, it would seem, subject to 'passionate convictions'. This is because whatever particular 'symbolization' we *choose* to represent reality, it reflects not merely mundane social constructions such as interests, power and socialization but also our particular, albeit stylized and perhaps only barely conscious, conception of the 'Real' society and the criteria by which we evaluate movement towards it. The 'Real' is a condition we can envisage (or fantasize) as impossible to reach, while at the same time it represents an absolute abstraction which, through our actions, we aim to approach. The pursuit of such 'Reals' – perhaps reflecting our intuitive recognition of that inherent human frailty – seems to characterize all cultures: in an older discourse, it used to be referred to as the 'Sacred'.

Hence it would seem that the 'Real' – and here we are stretching du Gay's characterization – can only refer to a transcendental 'objective reality' or, in more secular terms, an ultimate end. 'For new wave management, as for Thatcherism', du Gay (1991: 57) concludes, 'economic and moral revival involves the construction of an appropriate culture of Enterprise: Enterprise is their ideological fantasy.' In a more detailed account of this fantasy, Morris (1991) elaborates how the Thatcherite vision, in search of transcendental legitimacy, came to insist that the essential morality of the market is derived from Christian values. Hence the 'market' is protected from its own tendencies to greed and exploitation by the self-same Christian values which enclose it. Our fantasies, it would seem, are tested and, we want to suggest, testable in terms of what, for the moment, must be called the moral discourse of the 'Real'.

Clearly, the practice and study of management has never been confined to an evaluation of the effectiveness of techniques. With the arrival of HRM we have moved on to an ultimate control of performance in the management of meaning. But it is also an inherently moral project. If, in its various forms, management is to sustain itself as an academic activity, it must be able to submit this world view to reflective analysis. Since the subject matter of this analysis is cultural construction, we must find a platform for a cultural critique. One of the defining characteristics of a culture is the presence of moral codes and values. Without them, social interaction is impossible (Anthony, 1986; MacIntyre, 1981; Weber, 1949).

Culture and Morality

The first step is to observe that the ideological project of HRM is still in the process of fabrication. No one proposes that the system of values it espouses is already shared by organizations, their employees or even their managers; no one claims to have uncovered it residing in the organizational undergrowth. As noted above, the reverse is the case: HRM is the medium for the nurturing of a new 'reality':

> Organizational change consists in part of a series of emerging constructions of reality, including revision of the past, to correspond to the requisites of new players and new demands. Organizational history *does* need to be rewritten to permit events to move on. (Kanter, 1986: 287)

However innocent the intent, rewriting history awakens ominous echoes. But the suggestion alerts us not merely to the ambitions of HRM but also the fact that it bears some resemblance to a 'total ideology': an 'all inclusive system of comprehensive reality, it is a set of beliefs, infused with passion, and seeks to transform the whole of a way of life' (Bell, quoted in Geuss, 1981: 11). Unlike more familiar total ideologies which have sought the 'Real' perfect society in universal socialism, Aryan supremacy or religious salvation, HRM pursues a safer but more risible objective: the excellent pretzel. HRM is less dramatically dangerous but, insofar as it mystifies the prosaic and deflects human responsibility to the hidden hand of the market in the justification of means for ultimate ends, it remains subject to the same moral scrutiny.

Indeed, the public rhetoric of HRM invites such scrutiny. In accepting the claims of HRM's ideological project at face value, as a postmodernist enterprise in which the fantasy is the reality, then it must be the nature of the image that is the subject of critical review. Imagery and narrative must be examined in themselves. Cultural products are unassailable other than by reference to the measures against which they seek legitimation.

The proponents of HRM claim that effective performance is related to the creation of an organizational community sustained by leadership and nurtured through appropriate cultural values. Each of these terms is essentially moral. Communities are commonly held to be bound together by moral reciprocity (Gouldner, 1960), reinforced by traditions (MacIntyre, 1981) which are associated with common values enshrined in their culture (Schein, 1985). That much has been established in studies ranging from the Trobriand Islands to the G.E. Hawthorne plant, Chicago street gangs to IBM. Coercion has been replaced by transformational leadership and the authority conferred through the legitimation of subordinates. Legitimation cannot be explained without reference to the moral character of organizational relationships. The practice of effective management is increasingly being seen to be dependent upon the maintenance of community bonds of a more substantial and more coherently moral nature than can be bought in from consultants.

This, we suggest, provides us with three self-evident foci for the moral scrutiny of HRM: the moral ends of the product, the image or narrative; the degree of moral commitment deemed necessary to achieve these ends; and the morality of the methods employed. In addition, since we propose to briefly illustrate the value of such an approach with reference to the impact of HRM on management education, there is a fourth focus: the moral conscience of its teachers.

Management and its Teaching

With respect to contingencies of management 'practice' (Reed, 1985, 1989), there is an argument, which received considerable support from the ethics of the 'enterprise culture', for accepting that managers are entitled to pursue their objectives by any effective means within the law and subject to the occasional revulsion of public opinion. Whatever techniques or nostrums they use are their business and should be evaluated by business criteria. Such a view is encapsulated in its extreme form in the portrayal of the moral codes governing the business practices of rival mobsters in Mafia movies. Just as he is about to kill his adversary, the murderer says: 'Nothing personal, Julio, it's just business.' This subordination of all other values to 'natural' economic morality is echoed in the more conventional business context – as is vividly demonstrated by Jackall's (1988) analysis of the ethical 'imperatives' governing senior management behaviour in American corporations. The master narrative of the 'market', which has been projected as the most elegaic measure of efficiency and an impartial arbiter of not only economic justice but also social and personal ethics, has increasingly come to be employed as the all-pervading touchstone for organizational decision-making about 'human resources'. While fully recognizing the inevitably contingent character of managerial practice, the central problem with this position is that it eliminates all but a financial morality from the discussion of organizational life. Unsurprisingly, a central theme in the literature – but not the rhetoric – of HRM is the subordination of HR policies to the cultural constructions of management accountancy (Armstrong, 1987, 1989a, b; Earl, 1983).

This, of course, raises the much more fundamental moral issue which has always been central to the rhetoric if not always the substance of management theory: the problem of how to balance the pursuit of economic goals with the provision of socio-economic 'goods'. Concern with the social purposes and consequences of economic activity is at the heart of the argument that managers are such influential actors in society that their behaviour must be subjected to analytic and moral scrutiny (Anthony, 1986; Fox, 1974; Jackall 1988; MacIntyre, 1981). In this context it is significant that in the debate about pluralism (Clegg, 1975; Fox, 1973), the central issue concerned the appropriateness of pluralistic methods to the achievement of social justice. While Fox argued that pluralism merely cements pre-existing social inequalities in the work–employment relationship, Clegg insisted pluralism be regarded as an 'incomplete moral doctrine'. Pluralism, he argued, addresses the morality of the processes of regulation not the outcomes of such processes. The latter, he suggested, reflect other moral criteria such as those of socialism or capitalism. Thus, pluralism can only provide the necessary participative framework, the pre-conditions for the achievement of social justice.

In these new times, such an argument seems archaic and barely relevant but it highlights our difficulty with the historical project of HRM. In seeking to control meaning, HRM dispenses with such issues for cultural closure also involves moral closure. The 'market' has become the incarnation of the philosopher-king. There *is* no more to be said.

This leaves management education in a somewhat parlous position. If we are to 'teach' the essentials of HRM, if we are to follow Kanter's injunction, it implies that the role of management educators is to provide the catechism of myth-creation and cultural construction. Rather than dissect the perceived 'reality' of organizational experience, our function will be to generate visionary images of that reality. If students are to enter the world of management suitably pre-socialized, their obedience to the icons must be unqualified: myths only function for believers. Business schools must become the seminaries of the bottom line.

Such a prospect may seem histrionic. However, in the realm of management training and consultancy, it is already commonplace. An examination of the curricula of management staff college educational programmes suggested that 'management education programmes have a life of their own . . . they are insulated from the real world because they exist to protect managerial shibboleths from damage . . . Much of management education is irrelevant and some of the rest is naive' (Anthony, 1986: 138–9, 141). The analysis by Graham (1988), which suggested that the practice of JIT is best regarded as an exercise in myth-making, has been reinforced by Oliver's (1990) account of one of Eli Goldratt's one-day seminars on the transformative effects of Goldratt's version of JIT. Oliver examined the pedagogical technique employed and suggests that it had more in common with an evangelical crusade than a pragmatic analysis of technique. His view is supported by the suggestion from Storey and Sisson (1989: 168) that corporate viewings of Tom Peters's video 'are not so much an ideational exercise as an emboldening one'.

The danger in such a 'missionary' approach should be self-evident. Leaving aside the intellectual and moral trimming consequent on becoming what Baritz (1960) called the servants of power, it has already been argued (Anthony, 1990) that one consequence of cultural construction may be to enclose managers in a therapeutic carapace, isolated not merely from criticism but also from any possibility of regaining contact with the 'real' world. Students reared in a similar carapace would be singularly ill-equipped to survive, far less prosper, if their primary analytical equipment comprises no more than pedagogic marketing techniques, a conviction of their own 'empowerment' and a manual on the transformative impact of corporate videos. The more serious point is that such an 'educational' programme is antithetical to the 'production' of effective managers. While fully recognizing the contingent socially constructed nature of organizational reality, all the available evidence suggests that 'real' management involves a sensitivity to the political structuring of organizational life, an awareness of the multiple 'realities' pursued by organizational actors and a capacity to engineer social processes which generate appropriate cooperative behaviour (Kotter, 1982; Mintzberg, 1973; Pettigrew, 1985; Reed and Anthony, 1990; Stewart, 1982, 1986; Whitley, 1989).

If management education is a serious business – in any sense of the word – we cannot confine ourselves to an unreflective account of what managers do in the context of a series of 'emboldening' case-studies. The educational process is necessarily analytical, critical and judgmental. If we are to take management practice as our subject matter, we are surely obliged to submit it to critical attention? What this means, we suggest, is that the only way to teach HRM 'effectively' is recognize that it represents a fantasy of the 'Real'. The only sure route to an informed understanding of the mission of HRM is through apostasy.

Notes

The authors would like to thank Barbara Adam and Michael Reed for their valuable comments on earlier versions of this chapter. The inconsistencies that remain are our own.

1. Springer and Springer (1990: 41) insist that the 1990s 'marks the centenary of HRM in the United States'. They claim HRM dates from the establishment of a separate personnel office by the NCR Corporation in the 1890s. Similarly, Lawrence (1985) employs HRM as a generic concept to chart the distinctive historical patterns of employee relations management in the United States. Hendry and Pettigrew (1990) link the contemporary concern with strategic HRM to the emergence of human capital theory in the 1960s while for those working in the personnel and industrial relations arenas in Britain, HRM appeared, seemingly fully-formed, in the mid-1980s.

2. The extent to which this process is being realized is reflected in Fuller and Smith's (1991) study of 'customer-initiated-management' in the control of 'interactive service employees'. They vividly demonstrate not only the apparent distancing of management from monitoring performance but also the attempt to merge employee behaviour with customer expectation. 'Quality service requires that workers rely on inner arsenals of affective and interpersonal skills'; employees are induced to exercise 'workers' control over their own labour'; in some instances, customers are directly involved in disciplinary proceedings. One customer relations manager commented: 'We want every employee to internalise responsibility for customer service. My unit's job is to disseminate this philosophy to every individual. Once we've done that we [the unit] disappear' (Fuller and Smith, 1991: 3,4,8,14).

References

Abercrombie, N. (1991) 'The privilege of the producer', in R. Keat and N. Abercrombie (eds), *Enterprise Culture*. London: Routledge. pp. 171–85.

Anthony, P.D. (1986) *The Foundation of Management*. London and New York: Tavistock.

Anthony, P.D. (1990) 'The paradox of the management of culture or "He who leads is lost"', *Personnel Review*, 19 (4): 3–8.

Armstrong, M. (1988) *A Handbook of Human Resource Management*. London: Kogan Page.

Armstrong, P. (1987) 'The rise of accounting controls in British capitalist enterprises', *Accounting, Organisations and Society*, 12 (5): 415–36.

Armstrong, P. (1989a) 'Limits and possibilities for HRM in an age of management accountancy', in J. Storey (ed.), *New Perspectives on Human Resource Management*. London: Routledge. pp. 154–66.

Armstrong, P. (1989b) 'Management, labour process and agency', *Work, Employment and Society*, 3 (3): 307–22.

Baritz, L. (1960) *The Servants of Power*. Middletown, CT: Wesleyan University Press.

Barley, N. (1990) *Native Land*. London: Penguin Books.

Beardwell, I. (1990) 'Annual review article 1989', *British Journal of Industrial Relations*, 28 (1): 113–28.

Beaumont, P. (1987) *The Decline of Trade Union Organisation*. London: Croom Helm.

Beer, M., Spector, B., Lawrence, P., Quinn-Mills, D. and Walton, R. (1984) *Managing Human Assets*. New York: Free Press.

Beer, M., Spector, B., Lawrence, P., Quinn-Mills, D. and Walton, R. (1985) *HRM: A General Manager's Perspective*. New York: Free Press.

Berg, Per-Olaf (1986) 'Symbolic management of human resources', *Human Resource Management*, 25 (4): 557–79.

BT (1990) *Annual Review 1990*. London: British Telecommunications.

BT (1991) *Annual Review 1991*. London: British Telecommunications.

Clegg, H.A. (1975) 'Pluralism in industrial relations', *British Journal of Industrial Relations*, 13 (3): 309–16.

Connor, S. (1989) *Post-modernist Culture: An Introduction to Theories of the Contemporary*. Oxford: Blackwell.

Dickson, T., McLachlan, P., Prior, P. and Swales, K. (1988) 'Big Blue and the unions: IBM, individualism and trade union strategy', *Work, Employment and Society*, 2 (4): 506–20.

du Gay, P. (1991) 'Enterprise culture and the ideology of excellence', *New Formations*, Spring, 13: 45–61.

du Gay, P. and Salaman, G. (1990) 'Enterprise culture and the search for "Excellence"', Paper presented at the Employment Research Unit Annual Conference, Cardiff Business School, Cardiff.

Dumont, L. (1977) *From Mandeville to Marx: The Genesis and Triumphs of Economic Ideology*. Chicago: University of Chicago Press.

Dunn, S. (1990) 'Root metaphor in the old and the new industrial relations', *British Journal of Industrial Relations*, 28 (1): 1–31.

Earl, M. J. (1983) 'Accounting in management', in M.J. Earl (ed.), *Perspectives in Management*. Oxford: Oxford University Press.

Edwards, P.K. (1987) *Managing the Factory*. Oxford: Blackwell.

Etzioni, A. (1961) *The Comparative Analysis of Complex Organisations*. Glencoe, Ill: Free Press.

Fombrun, C., Tichy, N.M. and Devanna, M.A. (1984) *Strategic Human Resource Management*. New York: John Wiley.

Foulkes, F. (1980) *Personnel Policies in Large Non-Union Companies*. Englewood Cliffs, N J: Prentice-Hall.

Fox, A. (1973) 'Industrial relations: a social critique of pluralist ideology', in J. Child (ed.), *Man and Organisation: The Search for Explanation and Social Relevance*. London: Allen & Unwin, pp. 185–233.

Fox, A. (1974) *Beyond Contract: Work, Power and Trust Relations*. London: Faber.

Friedman, A.L. (1977) *Industry and Labour*. London: Macmillan.

Fuller, L. and Smith, V. (1991) 'Consumers' reports: management by customers in a changing economy', *Work, Employment and Society*, 5 (1): 1–16.

Gamble, A. (1988) *The Free Economy and the Strong State*. London: Macmillan.

Geuss, R. (1981) *The Idea of a Critical Theory: Habermas and the Frankfurt School*. Cambridge: Cambridge University Press.

Goldsmith, W. and Clutterbuck, D. (1985) *The Winning Streak*. London: Penguin Books.

Gouldner, A. W. (1960) 'The norm of reciprocity: a preliminary statement', *American Sociological Review*, 25 (2): 161–78.

Graham, I.R. (1988) 'Japanization as mythology', *Industrial Relations Journal*, 29 (1): 69–75.

Guest, D.E. (1987) 'Human resource management and industrial relations', *Journal of Management Studies*, 24 (5): 503–21.

Guest, D.E. (1990) 'Human resource management and the American Dream', *Journal of Management Studies*, 27 (4): 377–97.

Guest, D.E. (1991) 'Personnel management: the end of orthodoxy', *British Journal of Industrial Relations*, 29 (2): 149–75.

Hendry, C. and Pettigrew, A. (1986) 'The practice of strategic human resource management', *Personnel Review*, 15 (5): 3–8.

Hendry, C. and Pettigrew, A. (1987) 'Banking on HRM to respond to change', *Personnel Management*, 19 (11): 29–32.

Hendry, C. and Pettigrew, A. (1990) 'Human resource management: an agenda for the 1990s', *International Journal of Human Resource Management*, 1 (1): 17–44.

Hendry, C., Pettigrew, A. and Sparrow, P. (1988) 'Changing patterns of human resource management', *Personnel Management*, 20 (11): 37–41.

Jackall, R. (1988) *Moral Mazes: The World of Corporate Managers*. New York and Oxford: Oxford University Press.

Jaques, E. (1961) *Equitable Payment*. London: Heinemann.

Kanter, R.M. (1984) *The Change Masters*. New York: Simon and Schuster.

Kanter, R.M. (1986) 'The new workforce meets the changing workplace: strains, dilemmas, and contradictions in attempts to implement participative and entrepreneurial management', *Human Resource Management*, 25 (4): 515–37.

Keat, R. and Abercrombie, N. (eds) (1991) *Enterprise Culture*. London: Routledge.

Keenoy, T. (1990a) 'HRM: a case of the wolf in sheep's clothing?' *Personnel Review*, 19 (2): 3–9.

Keenoy, T. (1990b) 'HRM: rhetoric, reality and contradiction', *International Journal of Human Resource Management*, 1 (3): 363–84.

Keenoy, T. (1991) 'The roots of metaphor in the old and the new industrial relations', *British Journal of Industrial Relations*, 29 (2): 313–28.

Kelly, J. (1990) 'British trade unionism: change, continuity and contradictions', *Work, Employment and Society*, 4, Special Issue, May: 29–65.

Kotter, J.P. (1982) *The General Managers*. New York: Free Press.

Lash, S. and Urry, J. (1987) *The End of Organised Capitalism*. Oxford: Polity Press.

Lawrence, P.R. (1985) 'The history of human resource management in American industry', in R.E. Walton and P.R. Lawrence (eds), *Human Resource Management: Trends and Challenges*. Boston, MA: Harvard Business School Press. pp. 15–34.

Legge, K. (1989) 'HRM: A critical analysis', in J. Storey (ed.), *New Perspectives on Human Resource Management*. London: Routledge. pp.19–55.

Lockwood, D. (1966) 'Sources of variation in working-class images of society', *Sociological Review*, 14 (3): 249–67.

Lowe, J. (1991) 'Teambuilding via outdoor training: experiences from a U.K. automotive plant', *Human Resource Management Journal*, 2 (1): 42–59.

MacInnes, J. (1987) *Thatcherism at Work*. Milton Keynes: Open University Press.

MacIntyre, D. (1981) *After Virtue: A Study in Moral Theory*. London: Duckworth.

Marginson, P., Edwards, P.K., Martin, R., Purcell, J. and Sisson, K. (1988) *Beyond the Workplace*. Oxford: Blackwell.

Metcalf, D. (1989) 'Water notes dry up: the impact of the Donovan proposals and Thatcherism at work on labour productivity in British manufacturing industry', *British Journal of Industrial Relations*, 27 (1): 1–28.

Miller, P. (1987) 'Strategic industrial relations and HRM: distinction, definition and recognition', *Journal of Management Studies*, 24 (4): 347–61.

Miller, P. (1989) 'Strategic HRM: what it is and what it isn't', *Personnel Management*, 21 (2): 46–51.

Mintzberg, H. (1973) *The Nature of Managerial Work*. New York: Harper & Row.

Morris, P. (1991) 'Freeing the spirit of enterprise: the genesis and development of the concept of enterprise culture', in R. Keat and N. Abercrombie (eds), *Enterprise Culture*. London: Routledge. pp. 21–37.

Ogbonna, E. and Wilkinson, B. (1990) 'Corporate strategy and corporate culture: the view from the checkout', *Personnel Review*, 19 (4): 9–15.

Oliver, N. (1990) 'Just-in-time: the new religion of Western manufacturing', British Academy of Management Conference Proceedings.

Oliver, N. and Wilkinson, B. (1988) *The Japanization of British Industry*. Oxford: Blackwell.

Peach, L.H. (1983) 'Employee relations at IBM', *Employee Relations*, 5 (3): 17–20

Peters, T. and Waterman, R. (1982) *In Search of Excellence*. New York: Harper & Row.

Pettigrew, A. (1985) *The Awakening Giant: Continuity and Change at ICI*. Oxford: Blackwell.

Pondy, L.R. (1983) 'The role of metaphors and myths in organisation', in L.R. Pondy, P.J. Frost, G. Morgan and T.C. Dandridge (eds), *Organisational Symbolism*. Greenwich, CT: JAI Press. pp. 157–66.

Poole, M. (1990) 'Editorial: HRM in an international perspective', *International Journal of Human Resource Management*, 1 (1): 1–15.

Reed, M. (1985) *Redirections in Organisational Analysis*. London: Tavistock.

Reed, M. (1989) *The Sociology of Management*. London: Harvester Wheatsheaf.

Reed, M. and Anthony, P.D. (1990) 'Professionalising management and managing professionalisation: British management in the 1980s', Paper presented at the Employment Research Unit Annual Conference, Cardiff Business School, Cardiff.

Saad, H. (1990) 'Ideology, work and employment'. PhD Dissertation, University of Wales.

Schein, E. (1985) *Organizational Culture and Leadership*. San Francisco: Jossey-Bass.

Schuler, R.S. (1986) 'Fostering and facilitating entrepreneurship in organisations: implications for organisation structure and HRM practices', *Human Resource Management*, 25 (4): 607–29.

Schuler, R.S. (1989) 'Strategic HRM and industrial relations', *Human Relations*, 42 (2): 157–84.

Siegelbaum, L.H. (1988) *Stakhanovism and the Politics of Productivity in the USSR 1935–1941*. Cambridge: Cambridge University Press.

Sorel, G. (1961) *Reflections on Violence*. New York: Collier Books.

Springer, B. and Springer, S. (1990) 'HRM in the US – celebration of its centenary', in R. Pieper (ed.), *HRM: An International Comparison*. Berlin and New York: de Gruyter. pp. 41–60.

Stewart, R. (1982) *Choices for the Manager: A Guide to Managerial Work and Behaviour*. Maidenhead: McGraw-Hill.

Stewart, R. (1986) *The Reality of Management*. London: Heinemann.

Storey, J. (ed.) (1989) *New Perspectives on Human Resource Management*. London: Routledge.

Storey, J. and Sisson, K. (1989) 'Looking to the future', in J. Storey (ed.), *New Perspectives on Human Resource Management*. London: Routledge. pp. 167–83.

Trevor, M. (1988) *Toshiba's New British Company: Competitiveness through Innovation in Industry*. London: Policy Studies Institute.

Weber, M. (1949) *The Methodology of the Social Sciences*. New York: Free Press.

Whitley, R. (1989) 'On the nature of managerial tasks and skills: their distinguishing characteristics and organisation', *Journal of Management Studies*, 27 (3): 209–24.

Wickens, P. (1987) *The Road to Nissan*. London: MacMillan.

Wilkinson, A., Allen, P. and Snape, E. (1991) 'TQM and the management of labour', *Employee Relations*, 13 (1): 24–31.

Wood, S. (1989) 'New wave management?' *Work, Employment and Society*, 3 (3): 379–402.

Zukav, G. (1980) *The Dancing Wu Li Masters*. London: Fontana.

15 AFTERWORD

Paul Blyton and Peter Turnbull

One of the central concerns informing this collection has been that of HRM being raised to the status of a new *lingua franca* among those practising and teaching in the areas of personnel management, industrial relations and organizational behaviour, without its conceptual and empirical validity being sufficiently tested. The conceptual weaknesses and dearth of empirical support for the practice of HRM have been evidenced throughout the book. Conceptually, it has been demonstrated that HRM is a 'map' rather than a theory of management, and as such could provide organizations with guiding principles and signposts for the management of employees. In this respect, HRM could conceivably be put forward as a new management 'style'. Purcell (1987: 544) identifies management style as: 'an extra dimension linked to wider business policy and, at the least, related to guiding principles which infuse management behaviour in dealing with employees'. Since a supposed defining characteristic of HRM is its linkage with wider business policies, it would appear that HRM satisfies at least part of this definition. The 'guiding principles' of HRM are clearly the ideas (or ideals) of labour as the most valuable of all organizational assets, representing an investment rather than a cost, and ultimately a key source of competitive advantage. But does this constitute a new 'style'? At a minimum, if a style is a set of guiding principles, this presupposes that managers will hold attitudes commensurate with those principles. This may indeed be the case with HRM in Britain, but attitudes do not necessarily translate into behaviour. In other words, management attitudes consistent with HRM are a necessary but not in themselves *sufficient* condition for human resource management to develop. As has been demonstrated in many of the foregoing chapters, managerial behaviour in practice falls well short of the 'ideals' of HRM.

The principal reasons for this are that first, HRM is invariably *subordinate to* and not integrated with, wider business policy. 'Commercial' considerations predominate over 'human' considerations. Secondly, HRM does *not* represent a coherent or consistent approach to the management of employees. Indeed, as has been demonstrated at many points throughout the book, many of the shortcomings of HRM are related to this issue of coherency: both its external coherency *vis-à-vis* its relationship to broader business strategies, and its internal coherency among its constituent elements. It is evident that HRM does not provide a consistent set of policies and procedures which together could constitute a guiding set of principles. At the most elementary level, the inconsistency is reflected in the distinction between 'hard' and 'soft' forms of HRM, which together offer management two sharply contrasting alternatives within a supposedly single approach. Thus both conceptually and empirically, HRM fails to constitute a clear or distinctive management style.

At best, therefore, HRM should be viewed as a series of practices which rose to prominence in management circles in the later 1980s. In the early part of the decade, 'macho management' appeared to be an increasingly prominent management approach, characterized by a 'new breed of tough managers, almost contemptuous of unions and negotiating procedures' (Purcell, 1982: 3). Management's approach was now one of 'firmness and determination' in their dealings with labour, 'even if it means direct confrontations' (1982: 3). In the public sector in particular, 'management through confrontation' appeared to be the norm for much of the 1980s (Ferner, 1989). The problem with this approach, however, as many organizations soon realized, was that 'coerced compliance' was no substitute for 'co-operative commitment'. Moreover, when the boot was on the other foot the workforce, through the trade unions, were likely to kick back just as hard. Accordingly, management began to stress not so much their 'right to' as their 'need to' manage, emphasizing the 'business realities' of an 'ever more competitive world'. In this approach, which Edwards (1987: 149–50) described as 'enlightened managerialism', organizations 'try to take workers along with them, and indeed must do so if they are to retain the flexibility that is increasingly necessary in new competitive conditions'. As with macho management, however, Edwards (1987: 150–1) questioned the extent and effectiveness of this new approach, largely because it was regarded as a product of recession and not of long-term planning, but equally because managerial power is not total:

> It would be a mistake, for managers and analysts alike, to suppose that absolute managerial power has been instituted or that long-established ways of doing things, in particular the practice of negotiating the terms on which workers will work directly at the point of production, have been totally destroyed. (Edwards, 1987: 151).

Although enlightened managerialism was associated with greater flexibility, teamworking, quality circles and the like, it was its rhetoric as much as its practice which distinguished it from macho management. This rhetoric has continued, and some would argue has been refined, with the emergence of HRM. In fact, the evidence presented in this volume suggests that it is the rhetoric rather than the practice of HRM which accounts for its rise during the latter half of the past decade. The socio-economic, political and legal conditions of the 1980s were highly conducive to a fundamental refashioning of the vocabulary of labour management and labour control. The time was ripe for the emergence of the new rhetoric of HRM: a union movement weakened by membership losses and legislative restraint, and as a result less able to defend established patterns of labour relations; a competitive environment instilling the search for change; a general climate of 'enterprise' in which managers were 'emboldened' to extend their prerogatives; and a government willing to buttress managerial power and reduce employee protection. And yet, on the evidence to date, HRM may prove as ephemeral and ethereal as macho management and enlightened managerialism before it. There are two main reasons for this. First and foremost, it is well-established that most British firms adopt a reactive, *ad hoc* and largely pragmatic approach towards the management of employees; as such, this cannot therefore be classified as a 'style' of management (Purcell, 1987; Purcell and Sisson, 1983).

Management attitudes and their approach towards labour thus tend to 'wax and wane' with the prevailing climate: for example, the Donovan approach of 'regaining control by sharing it' with labour giving way to a more aggressive approach which reasserted managerial prerogatives; the 'right' to manage giving way to the less abrasive 'need' to manage. This in turn gave way to labour suddenly being 'discovered' as the most valuable of all company resources in an attempt to win the 'hearts and minds' of the workforce. Given that most organizations operate without any clearly defined or consistent style, past experience suggests that as the prevailing climate changes, so too will the approach to managing labour.

Equally important is the reaction of the workforce and the trade union movement to new management initiatives. The loss of union membership in the 1980s has clearly weakened the trade unions, but just as workers' control at the point of production has not been eradicated, neither can union power be discounted. The decline of trade unionism is believed by many to reflect long-term structural shifts in the economy which have transformed the composition of the working class. As the union 'heartland' of full-time male, manual workers employed in manufacturing has gradually receded, employment has grown in sectors where unions have found it more difficult to recruit. It is argued that a 'new industrial relations' is associated with these new areas of industry and commerce, marking the beginning of the end for the union movement. But as Kelly (1990: 34) maintains, this argument is 'a perfect example of a plausible but specious correlation'. Noting that manufacturing has been in decline since the mid-1960s, and that union membership increased rapidly during the 1970s when the proportion of women and white-collar employees in the economy was expanding, Kelly (1990: 35–42) argues that cyclical effects and the lack of union resources devoted to recruitment are more convincing explanations for the decline of union membership. The latter has been addressed with some urgency in recent years by the Trades Union Congress and a number of individual unions, marking a change of approach from the ideas of 'new realism' in the mid-1980s (1983–87) and political mobilization and opposition prior to that (1980–83). These phases of union activity appear to broadly coincide with macho management, enlightened managerialism and HRM.

Cyclical effects appear to be particularly important because they affect the incentives and opportunities for workers to unionize, and likewise the incentives and opportunities for employees to resist unionism (Kelly, 1990: 38–9). High levels of unemployment, for example, limit the opportunities for union growth, just as falling inflation and rising real wages (for those in employment) could make workers less inclined to join a trade union. On the other hand, employers have been in a position to more effectively resist unionism as a result of these conditions, while successive Thatcher governments provided ample incentive and opportunity for them to do so. But again, if conditions change, so too will the fortunes of management and labour, especially given that HRM has failed to take firm root in the 1980s and early 1990s. The prospects for the development of HRM in the current decade are therefore highly uncertain, as much will depend on a range of economic and political variables. What does appear to be the case, however, is that in several important respects, the conditions of the 1990s are unlikely to mirror those of the previous decade.

If nothing else, greater European integration could see at least some elements of continental industrial relations patterns gaining influence in Britain: not least the greater acceptance of trade unions as members of the national body-politic and as 'social partners' within the enterprise. Economic success in Germany and elsewhere, and the lack of similar success in Britain in recent years, could act to stimulate a deeper questioning of the relative merits of UK approaches to labour management, compared with certain European ones. Economic gains have been achieved in these countries partly *because of*, not *in spite of*, the greater influence afforded to trade unions and other forms of worker representation. Hence, if the 1980s in Britain were characterized by the adoption of an HRM vocabulary based on US and Japanese experience, the 1990s may see a greater influence being exerted by successful European systems. The upshot could be a reassertion of a management approach re-emphasizing the positive values of collectivism and constitutional relations with unions, but probably in less adversarial ways than characterized the past.

Part of the research agenda for the 1990s should therefore be to consider the impact of changing economic, social and political conditions on management–worker relations, and it is crucial that a concerted return is made to the fundamental issues of labour management in contemporary capitalism. For while the pursuit of HRM may have yielded some fresh insights for researchers in particular areas, it has also acted to obscure many of the core issues surrounding the question of control. The vocabulary and practice of HRM may conceivably be viewed as an attempt to relegitimate managerial authority, redefine worker rights and redraw the frontier of control. Under conditions of intensifying competition, the nature of the relationship between capital and labour becomes ever more stark. HRM serves to render the defining character of those relations opaque, through a language of individualism, reciprocity and shared commitment. What it must not be allowed to do is extend this obfuscation over the core managerial problems which define their relationship with the workforce: how is control exercised, power exerted, authority legitimated, compliance achieved, consent maintained? In the contemporary interpretation of these issues, human resource management has a particular significance, but that significance can only be appreciated as one attempt to resolve or manage these central problems. It cannot replace or remove them.

References

Edwards, P.K. (1987) *Managing the Factory*. Oxford: Blackwell.

Ferner, A. (1989) 'Ten years of Thatcherism: changing industrial relations in British public enterprises', *Warwick Papers in Industrial Relations 27*, IRRU, University of Warwick.

Kelly, J. (1990) 'British trade unionism 1979–89: change, continuity and contradictions', *Work, Employment and Society*, 4 (Special Issue): 29–65.

Purcell, J. (1982) 'Macho managers and the new industrial relations', *Employee Relations*, 4 (1): 3–5.

Purcell, J. (1987) 'Mapping management styles in employee relations', *Journal of Management Studies*, 24 (5): 533–48.

Purcell, J. and Sisson, K. (1983) 'Strategies and practice in the management of industrial relations', in G.S. Bain (ed.), *Industrial Relations in Britain*. Oxford: Blackwell, pp. 95–120.

SUBJECT INDEX

AUTHOR INDEX